Advance Praise for Keren Blankfeld's
LOVERS IN AUSCHWITZ

"In *Lovers in Auschwitz,* Keren Blankfeld offers a vivid portrait of the brutality of daily life at Auschwitz, alongside formidable tales of people who risked their lives to save others—even strangers—through sabotage, sympathy, and love. Mesmerizing and inspirational."

—Judy Batalion, *New York Times* bestselling author of *The Light of Days: The Untold Story of Women Resistance Fighters in Hitler's Ghettos*

"A story of hope in one of humanity's most hopeless places, *Lovers in Auschwitz* honors those who were lost while producing fresh insights into the nature of survival, the resilience of memory, the unseen debts we all owe one another, and, yes, the transformative power of love."

—Robert Kolker, *New York Times* bestselling author of *Hidden Valley Road: Inside the Mind of an American Family* and *Lost Girls: An Unsolved American Mystery*

"A tale so incredible, so improbable, that it could only be true; a story so moving, so poignant, that it could only be inspired by love. Your Holocaust library is incomplete without this book."

—Larry Loftis, *New York Times* bestselling author of *The Watchmaker's Daughter: The True Story of World War II Heroine Corrie ten Boom*

"What could be a greater act of defiance than two young, Jewish inmates finding love in a Nazi concentration camp? With skill and painstaking research, Blankfeld introduces her readers to the extraordinary women and men who worked to undermine the Nazis while interned at Auschwitz, risking what little hope of life they had left to help save each other. Anyone meeting these individuals on Blankfeld's pages will not forget them."

—Rebecca Frankel, *New York Times* bestselling author of *Into the Forest*

"What will a woman do for the man she loves? *Lovers in Auschwitz* is a reminder of how we desperately need love to survive. Keren Blankfeld's research and scholarly attention to detail is exquisite; her narrative covers decades, inside and outside of the camps, from the prewar era to liberation and old age. A powerful reminder that love can conquer all."

—Heather Dune Macadam, author of *999: The Extraordinary Young Women of the First Official Jewish Transport to Auschwitz* and *Star Crossed: A Romeo and Juliet Story in Hitler's Paris*

"Moving and tragic…A true tale of love amid unimaginable suffering." —*Kirkus Reviews*

"Alternately heart-warming, thrilling, and achingly poignant, Keren Blankfeld's *Lovers in Auschwitz* is the true story of Zippi and David, young Jews who against all odds found love in the living hell that was Birkenau. Deeply researched and brilliantly told, it is a tale that will remain with readers long after they've turned the final page. Very highly recommended."

—Stephen Harding, *New York Times* bestselling author of *The Last Battle*

"Most of what we know about the life of prisoners in Auschwitz comes from testimonies by men. In *Lovers in Auschwitz,* we see it through the eyes of the indomitable Zippi, who uses her grit and ingenuity to protect herself and others. Demonstrating both copious research and narrative flair, Keren Blankfeld offers an intimate and surprising story of Auschwitz from the inside, remarkable for both its insights into the workings of the camp and its heart."

—Ruth Franklin, National Book Critics Circle Award–winning author of *Shirley Jackson: A Rather Haunted Life* and *A Thousand Darknesses: Lies and Truth in Holocaust Fiction*

"A love story like no other, this profoundly moving book teaches us how the human spirit can never be entirely extinguished—even in the hell of Auschwitz."

—Julia Boyd, *Sunday Times* bestselling author of *Travellers in the Third Reich: The Rise of Fascism through the Eyes of Everyday People* and *A Village in the Third Reich: How Ordinary Lives Were Transformed by the Rise of Fascism*

"A journey of discovery into one of the darkest moments in modern history, *Lovers in Auschwitz* is a haunting and nuanced account of two Auschwitz prisoners who risked the unimaginable to find moments of love and humanity in each other, against a backdrop of evil. With extraordinary research and effortless prose, Keren Blankfeld guides us through war, heartache, and resilience."

—Alexis Clark, author of *Enemies in Love: A German POW, A Black Nurse, and An Unlikely Romance*

LOVERS
IN
AUSCHWITZ

A True Story

KEREN BLANKFELD

Little, Brown and Company
New York   Boston   London

Little, Brown and Company
Hachette Book Group
1290 Avenue of the Americas, New York, NY 10104
littlebrown.com

First Edition: January 2024

Little, Brown and Company is a division of Hachette Book Group, Inc. The Little, Brown name and logo are trademarks of Hachette Book Group, Inc.

The publisher is not responsible for websites (or their content) that are not owned by the publisher.

The Hachette Speakers Bureau provides a wide range of authors for speaking events. To find out more, go to hachettespeakersbureau.com or email HachetteSpeakers@hbgusa.com.

Photography credits appear on p.381.

ISBN 978-0-316-56477-9

LCCN is available at the Library of Congress

Printing 1, 2023

LSC-C

Printed in the United States of America

In memory of my grandmothers, Helena and Zipora
and my grandfather Eliezer

For my parents, Desirée and Max

CONTENTS

CONTENTS

Part IV: Interlude

Part V: Cadenza

AUTHOR'S NOTE

This is a work of nonfiction based on extensive interviews, oral testimonies, documents, and published and unpublished memoirs. As part of that research, I had the opportunity to interview David Wisnia several times beginning in 2018 and up until shortly before his death in 2021. Unfortunately, by the time I discovered her story, Helen "Zippi" Tichauer had already passed away. She left behind dozens of testimonies and one recently discovered manuscript of a memoir (see Notes on Sources). In these formal interviews and in her writings, Zippi never acknowledged her relationship with David, although she did speak about it with confidants on occasion. For this reason, most of the descriptions of Zippi and David's interactions within these pages are based primarily on my conversations with David. The endnotes will provide context about sourcing. Wherever they appear, words between quotation marks are direct quotations.

*T*hey first saw each other at the Sauna, surrounded by piles of cloth-ing. The air was thick and hot; they were in one of the few places that provided warmth during the unforgiving Polish winter. Here, workers submerged garments in steam kettles and watched smoke rise outside a window. Here, surrounded by worn, soiled rags, a boy and a girl met.

He was seventeen, with a clean-shaven head and a round face. Despite it all, he was relatively well fed. His striped uniform was neat and tailored—clean. Perhaps this was part of his allure: he stood out. In a world of stripes, you weren't supposed to stand out. You had to live by the rules, blend like shadows on the verge of disappearing.

Sometimes at night he was summoned out of his wooden bunk to sing. His tenor was beautiful, operatic. It had once earned him an audience in his hometown. Here, he remained a soloist, still a star of sorts.

When she showed up, he could almost forget where he was. The sight of her gave him something to look forward to. At four feet and eleven inches, she was petite but sturdy, her legs muscular, her face wide and angled, framed by thick chestnut hair that was still growing in. From a distance, she seemed unassuming, easy to ignore. Up close, she was anything but. Her deep-set eyes — brown, like his — were sharp and alert, but she had an easy smile. She moved with a self-assurance that was rare in their milieu.

His eyes on her, he felt a flutter.

A girl was looking at him.

Her glance lingered. He was sure of it.

In here, it was easy to forget that his old world still existed, a world of possibilities, promises — of desire.

When he saw her, he remembered.

★　　★　　★

She wasn't supposed to be there, in the all-male part of the grounds. Yet she'd made a habit of getting herself into places where she shouldn't be.

She was twenty-five years old and she knew what she wanted. She'd been like this as a young girl and hadn't changed in all the years since. If anything, her tenacity had only grown.

It wasn't that she believed in taking unnecessary risks. In a world of chaos, she craved structure and order, logic and reason. But this place had a way of making you do what you least expected. It had a way of making life-threatening risks seem reasonable. Perhaps because here, nothing was reasonable.

She had her escape— her art— and yet she was alone. The boy across the room had a pleasant face. He seemed sweet, eager. Something about him made her want to come back, made her reckless.

It was wintertime in Birkenau, the largest and deadliest camp in Auschwitz.

PART I

OVERTURE

CHAPTER ONE

"Small Stuff"

Rosa Spitzer was due to give birth in the throes of a revolution. It was early October of 1918, and the normally quiet streets outside her Pressburg apartment were electric: throngs of Slovakian soldiers were returning home from war. Bitter winds tousled the city's oak trees and weeping birches, the frigid fall air foreboding a harsh winter ahead.

Dark-haired Rosa had little choice but to stay inside, and not just because of the weather. As the Great War came to an end, the Austro-Hungarian Empire was coming undone, and some Slovak soldiers who'd long resented life under the Hungarian thumb streamed back into Pressburg with a wrath that had been pent up for generations. At the cobblestoned city center, they looted shops and restaurants. Rioters accused the Austro-Hungarian Empire of tyranny and oppression, and they stormed into military prisons to free inmates, mostly common criminals, to join in their fight for the city.

Rosa's twenty-first birthday came and went, her due date imminent. Outside her window, tensions mounted. Slovak nationalists were not the only ones interested in an independent state. Ethnic Germans, who'd long been a minority in the region, were already dreaming of a "national rebirth."

Across Europe, antisemites blamed their misfortunes on the Jews, longtime scapegoats for losses and suffering. Some Slovak veterans chanted "Down with the Jews!" and accused their Jewish neighbors of being agents provocateurs, spies and agitators for the Magyars, ethnic Hungarians. They set fire to Jewish shops and businesses across town. Meanwhile, many Magyars blamed Jews for military defeat and still others accused Jews of wartime profiteering. Rosa, her husband, Vojtech, and their unborn child were among those whose deaths were being called for out in the streets.

On November 10, Rosa finally gave birth to a daughter, Helen Zipora. Her family would call her Hilanka, but in time she came to prefer an abbreviation of Zipora, which translates to "bird" in Hebrew. Zippi, pronounced "tsippi," evoked motion—a name well-suiting for a world whose contours were beginning to blur.

When Zippi was three months old, Czechoslovak troops, volunteer forces who'd fought in the Great War and were determined to form a united state, arrived in Pressburg armed with machine guns and bayonets. They took aim at a crowd made up of German and Magyar social democrats who opposed the new nation. Seven rioters died.

Then came the reprieve.

By Zippi's first birthday, Pressburg no longer existed. The city was now called Bratislava, part of a new, independent state known as Czechoslovakia. The Germans and Magyars remained minorities, each nationalist aspiration an ember that smoldered just beneath the city's surface. The Slovak People's Party, yearning for Slovak autonomy, remained influential. For now, the Jews of Bratislava lived in peace.

Among the most significant ramifications of the new constitution was that Czech became the official language of the land. Before, residents had spoken Slovak and German. Zippi continued speaking German, her mother tongue, at home, but was also fluent in Hungarian and Slovak, and studied French and Hebrew in school.

To Zippi, childhood was idyllic. On sultry summer days she basked in the sun on the banks of the Danube and learned to swim in the waters of a hundred-foot-long river pool by a natural gravel beach. In cooler months, she hiked along the trails of the Low Tatras Mountains and enjoyed boat rides beneath the Bratislava Castle.

Zippi's middle-class family was small compared to their neighbors', many of whose broods grew to five or six children. Besides her parents, Zippi only had her brother, Sam. Almost four years younger, he was born feisty, with his father's widow's peak and wide, curious eyes.

Their family might've grown, but when Zippi was six years old and Sam was three, Rosa fell ill. The Spitzers went on holiday to a resort town two hours north of Bratislava where natural springs were believed to treat rheumatic afflictions—a broad category that, at this point, Rosa's sickness seemed to fall into. Wearing a bathing suit, her dark hair pulled into two tight buns on the sides of her head, Zippi sat on a sand bank and squinted at a camera. She was slight and delicate, her smile tentative—almost a grimace, as though she had an inkling of tragedies to come.

When tuberculosis hits, initial symptoms may be subtle. Victims may suffer from chills and exhaustion. Sometimes they experience body aches. It is only once they spit up blood that their ailment becomes all too clear. Often, they're confined to bed, unable to perform the smallest of tasks, taxed by the effort of taking a few steps across a small room.

The Spitzers had few options at their disposal. Antibiotics weren't yet viable. Sanitariums, however, had been popping up in the remote lands of Eastern Europe, fashionable hubs to institutionalize the sick and ease their pain.

So it was that twenty-eight-year-old Rosa went to a specialized sanitarium tucked in a pocket of the picturesque High Tatras mountain range. There, Rosa would enjoy crisp air and a nutritious diet. But more importantly, this environment would keep her illness from spreading any further before it consumed its host.

Rosa's illness sent her family into a tailspin. Vojtech was too bereft to take care of himself, much less his two children. Sam was too young to understand the repercussions of his mother's departure. Still, it was impossible for him not to feel that something monumental had been taken from him, that his life would be forever changed. Zippi, now a precocious six-year-old, was alone in what must have been a bewildering, frightening moment. Not only was her mother gone, but her father was struggling.

This being Czechoslovakia in the 1920s, however, it was common for sprawling extended families to live nearby and to help pick up the pieces when disaster struck. So it was that Zippi's nuclear family splintered: Zippi moved in with her maternal grandparents, down the hall from her father's apartment. Three-year-old Sam was sent to live with his paternal grandparents in another building. And just like that, Zippi and Sam's little family was scattered, like ashes across the face of a river.

In 1927, after more than a year away from home, Rosa succumbed to tuberculosis. Zippi's grandmother, Julia Nichtburger, tried to fill the void as best she could. Small and unassuming, Julia was a hard worker with thin lips and hollowed-out cheeks. She decided, while still mourning the death of her eldest daughter, that she would now dedicate herself to the care of her granddaughter. Julia's husband, Zippi's grandfather Lipot Nichtburger, a stern-eyed, unsmiling local antiques dealer, left the child-rearing to Julia. The couple was used to having their hands and home full, but by the time Rosa died, seven of their children had gone off to start families of their own, leaving behind a near-empty nest.

One son remained, Julia and Lipot's youngest, Leo. Nearly ten years Zippi's senior, her uncle would play the role of her charming surrogate brother. At eighteen, Leo had a wide network of friends and hobbies. Yet he also had plans for the future, plans that kept him busy and that would eventually take him far away from Bratislava and his young, half-orphaned niece—who by the age of eight was learning to get used to loneliness.

At thirty-five, Zippi's father, Vojtech, was a widower—and this would not do. Within a year of Rosa's death, Julia Nichtburger had a talk with her grieving son-in-law. It was time to move on with his life, she said, time to find a nice woman and remarry. He wasn't getting any younger, and he certainly wasn't doing himself or his children any favors by being alone. Julia had lived long enough to know the importance of being practical.

Vojtech took his mother-in-law's words to heart. A high-end tailor with protruding ears, he wore his hair slicked back and his dark mustache carefully trimmed. Within two years of Rosa's death, Vojtech had remarried. By 1929, the couple welcomed a son; four years later they would welcome another.

The family shuffled once more. Sam, now almost seven years old, joined his father's new family. The adults agreed that ten-year-old Zippi would remain with Julia and Lipot. Zippi, her father, and Sam were under the same roof again but now in apartments down the hall from each other. Their relationship would never be the same. While Sam felt like the odd one out with his two baby half-brothers, Zippi endured the pain of abandonment in private.

The best remedy, the siblings came to find, was to keep themselves busy.

Each week, the Nichtburgers gathered in Julia's living room to enjoy private concerts, through *Hausmusik,* a tradition of German origin that was popular among western European intellectual families. A string quartet performed operettas, one uncle played the mandola, another played a mandolin, and a neighbor played the guitar. The compositions they performed ranged from the work of Austro-Hungarian Franz Léhar to that of the Hungarian maestro Emmerich Kálmán.

Zippi wanted to join them. She played the piano, but it was the mandolin that dazzled her. Uncle Leo suggested she take it up. From the moment she stroked its strings, Zippi was enamored. The mandolin was compact and perfect for a petite player's fingers to strum, easy to lug around, and it produced an elegant, sweet sound with surprising power. Uncle Leo introduced Zippi to his Italian tutor, and Zippi, ever the perfectionist, threw herself into practice. Within months, her tutor had invited Zippi to join his mandolin orchestra as the lone child among adults. The popular overture to *Orpheus in the Underworld,* by Jacques Offenbach, a composition of sophisticated arrangements and subtle solos that build up to the playful, galloping cancan, was a favorite. The ensemble was featured on the local radio station, performing around town and in nearby cities.

In the wintertime, the temperature dipped to 30 degrees Fahrenheit and a white swarm descended from dark skies, blanketing the city in snow. As the Jewish community paraded the streets in masquerades to celebrate Purim, Uncle Leo and Zippi stepped out with their mandolins, on a mission. They knocked on friends' doors and played Jewish songs — music that the mandolin orchestra would never play. They brought along a blue box, a familiar sight among Zionist Jews, to collect donations for purchasing land in Palestine. By the time they returned home, the box was full.

This is not to say that Zippi or her family were particularly devout Jews. They had grown up on Zámocká Street, near Bratislava's main square, and not far from the Danube River. Had they wanted to worship, the Zámocká Street Synagogue, a Moorish temple from the nineteenth century, was only a few steps down the road. But neither Sam nor Zippi cared to attend services if they could help it. Zippi dropped in once a year to say the kaddish, the mourner's prayer, for her mother; Sam opted to spend his weekends playing soccer.

While the family wasn't observant, they were Zionists. Uncle Leo was a devoted member of Hashomer Hatzair, "Young Watchman," a Zionist organization with some seventy thousand members in Europe, North and South America, and Palestine. The group had taken root in Poland in the wake of World War I, when many young, secular Jews ran into professional, educational, and social barriers while attempting to assimilate to Polish life. It rose to prominence following a wave of more than a thousand pogroms— violent massacres targeted at specific racial or religious groups— during the Ukrainian-Polish civil war of 1918 and 1919, which killed over one hundred thousand Jews and created six hundred thousand Jewish refugees.

Uncle Leo introduced Zippi and Sam to the group, whose mission had evolved to prepare its members to go to Palestine. But neither sibling cared for the dogmatic lectures; neither aspired to become a Zionist leader. Zippi and Sam were in it for the wildlife excursions, for the fun: members hiked, played sports, and communed in nature.

To Zippi, life was good. While she missed her mother and often felt like a child among adults, she saw no conflict, felt no hostility, and knew no restrictions. For the time being, she was safe and free.

As a teenager, Zippi dreamed of being a botanist. She loved nature and had an analytical mind. Julia impressed on Zippi that she could do anything that she wanted. Under its constitution, the new Czechoslovakia gave women more political, social, and cultural equality. Importantly, this included better access to education. Julia hoped Zippi would benefit from freedoms that the older generation never had.

The best place to study botany was Moravia, where some three million Sudeten Germans — ethnic Germans who lived in the region along the border of northern Czechoslovakia — made up the majority of the population. They had long dreamed of a nationalist state and when Hitler became chancellor, in 1933, when Zippi was fourteen years old, these Sudeten Germans eagerly embraced National Socialism and the antisemitic tropes that the party evangelized. Hitler's radical far-right Nazi Party platform made German citizenship and involvement with the press off-limits to Jews; Jewish shops in Germany were to be boycotted nationally, and Jews were excluded from German universities.

So studying botany in Moravia was a nonstarter for Zippi, and all the talk of new freedoms was not so realistic after all. Instead, Julia prepared her granddaughter for marriage. Zippi gamely mastered how to sew a button, how to cook, how to clean. But she never was one to stop at the basics. She also taught herself detailed embroidery, drawing, and painting.

Then one day it hit her: her calling. Zippi was walking by the storefront window of an atelier when she saw a woman designing advertising signs. Intrigued, Zippi stopped, went inside, and asked for the owner. She wanted to know more about what the woman was doing. The atelier, she learned, produced ads for movie theaters, banks, exhibitions, and commercial fairs. Its employees made glass letterings and designed signs. Now *this* was exciting. Zippi was good with her hands and enjoyed the arts. She'd found her career.

Not one to waste time, Zippi informed the owner that she would become his apprentice. She would work hard — she'd study the tools, the color combinations, the intricacies of design and pattern, and she'd ace the required exams. He had nothing to lose. But the man declined. Graphic design wasn't for women, he said. The woman at the front window was his wife; he had no other female employees.

Zippi wasn't interested in employee demographics; she wanted to learn graphic design. She pushed.

Worn down, the shop owner told Zippi that if she passed her exams, he'd take her on as his apprentice.

And so, at fourteen, Zippi gave up the mandolin orchestra. Instead, she focused on her studies and took on a variety of apprenticeships, working with a woman's tailor and for the local fashion atelier, where she painted ads and posters. As a Jewish woman, she had two strikes against her, but Zippi knew her worth. She demanded—and apparently was paid—wages equal to those of her male colleagues. With her paycheck, Zippi indulged herself in a shoe collection and tailored coats. She understood the power of presentation and dressed herself well. She was determined to succeed in her newfound career.

Bratislava, one of Czechoslovakia's largest cities, was brimming with possibilities. Families in nearby smaller agrarian villages sent their children to Bratislava to embark on careers ranging from barbers to kindergarten teachers to doctors. On Friday nights, Zippi anticipated dinners with out-of-town students who'd join in the family meal. She craved the engaging discussions, particularly with medical students from abroad. While most Bratislava Jews earned their living from business and finance, Zippi was drawn to the intellectuals and artists.

Zippi herself, after spending three years at a public high school for girls, continued her studies in an advanced class of a coeducational institution, and went on to become the only female student in Bratislava's sole graphic arts school. She learned intricate lettering for signs and how to create art with glass. She studied the nuances of using design to convey messages. She committed herself to learning her craft and went on to graduate at the top of her class.

Between her studies, her professional work, and Hashomer Hatzair's increasingly busy calendar, Zippi had little downtime. Zippi didn't care for Hashomer Hatzair's organized lectures on the revolutionaries Lenin and Marx, and while she appreciated lessons on the practical aspects of being scouts—from how to live in communal environments to how to cultivate land in a semi-arid, desert environment—the group's increasingly fervent socialist agenda didn't sit well with her. Ultimately, its goal was to send members to Palestine, to work in a kibbutz and harvest land. And indeed, in 1933, Uncle Leo took off for Palestine to work on an orange plantation. Neither Zippi nor Sam had any intention of joining him. Their home, they thought, was in Czechoslovakia.

Hashomer Hatzair's lecture schedule required attendance on weeknights and Sundays. But Sam dreamed of one day playing soccer for the local league, and his Sunday practice was not negotiable. In addition, he was studying interior design and apprenticing at another uncle's carpet warehouse. He was proud of his work. With his uncle, he outfitted some of the city's most renowned architectural institutions, including the Hall of Mirrors, the most famous chamber in the Primate's Palace. He gave up his membership in Hashomer Hatzair without much thought.

Zippi remained a member, but with a caveat: if they asked her to give up her studies and go off to Palestine, she would quit, too. She saw no reason to leave Bratislava. Not to mention, Zippi didn't intend to ruin her hands with agricultural work. Her hands were her livelihood. And she loved her livelihood.

Before long, though, she'd come to wonder if she'd made the right decision.

Beyond their small world, all was not well. In Bratislava, reports of the Nazis' rise to power had become an ominous part of the daily radio broadcast. In Breslau, then a German city, Jewish lawyers were not allowed inside courthouses. Soon after, Jewish judges were dismissed from their posts. Meanwhile, a Nazi-incited boycott against Jewish products and businesses took off throughout Germany. Red posters appeared outside German shops: "Recognized German–Christian Enterprise." Other placards advised:

"Whoever buys from the Jew supports the foreign boycott and destroys the German economy."

Not content with inciting economic terror, some Nazi Germans turned to violence. A respected rabbi in Munich was dragged out of his bed and home at night and taunted by rifle-bearing civilians. Even Jewish American tourists in Berlin became targets: one such man was forced to drink castor oil until he fainted.

Most Bratislava Jews were incredulous that Germany, a civilized nation, was capable of such vitriol and violence. But the warning signs grew steadily brighter. The Nuremberg Race Laws, enacted in 1935, proclaimed that Jews belonged to a disparate race and could be legally persecuted. Following this declaration, Bratislava became a gateway for Polish and German Jewish refugees on their way out of an increasingly inhospitable Europe. Zippi's grandparents took in refugees for dinner and listened, flabbergasted, to their stories of terror. Many joined Hashomer Hatzair, which helped them cross borders in the hope of reaching the relative safety of Hungary with the goal of reaching Palestine. For the most part, they were well received in Germany's neighboring countries, but as their numbers grew their welcome wore off. Many chartered steamers to Palestine, where they aspired to create a safe place, a Jewish home state. Zippi's expertise in graphic arts would have made her an ideal candidate to forge documents for refugees such as these—but if she contributed to their escape in this way, she left no record of it.

Violent flare-ups were getting closer to home; ethnic tensions that had stewed since the creation of Czechoslovakia now bubbled up to the surface. Soon after Hitler's rise to power, the Slovak People's Party, a nationalist political movement, gained momentum. The party, run by Catholic priest Andrej Hlinka, had resisted the new nation of Czechoslovakia from the outset. It spurned the thought of allowing Slovak history and language to be eclipsed by Czech culture. Its population, made up primarily of Catholics, resented the immigration of Hungarian and Czech intellectuals, many of them Jews. They saw Czechoslovakia's multi-ethnicity as a threat, its anti-religious and socialist leanings as abhorrent. They yearned for an autonomous Slovak territory with its own traditions, its own values.

With the rise of Hitler, the Slovak People's Party shifted from a silent majority to an aggressive one. Anti-Jewish rhetoric and violence that had been confined to small eastern villages now awakened in Bratislava. In 1936, students broke out in violent antisemitic demonstrations during the showing of the Jewish folklore film *Le Golem*. Protesters armed with firecrackers and stink bombs smashed windows of Jewish homes and paralyzed Bratislava for days in a chilling manifestation of what was to come.

With this new reality dawning, Sam gravitated toward leftist politics and got involved in resistance work—what he called "small stuff" at first. He distributed leaflets with information about subversive activities around town. Known for his adventurous streak and for being an enfant terrible with the best intentions, he helped out friends from Hashomer Hatzair and colleagues from the trade union at his uncle's carpet warehouse. He never asked questions, knowing that the less he knew, the better off he'd be—and the less likely he'd be tortured into giving up secrets if he were caught.

It was likely around then that Zippi began dating Tibor Justh, a Jew from Nitra, a city with a longstanding Jewish community, some sixty miles east of Bratislava. Tibor was three years older and, unlike Zippi, was engaged in the politics of the region. Zippi introduced Tibor to her brother. The two young men, both headstrong idealists, found common ground.

One evening, Tibor asked Sam if he could tour the carpet warehouse where Sam worked. It was a large, easily accessible space, and Tibor wanted to know if a few men could spend the night inside the underground storage room on occasion. Sam didn't hesitate.

From then on, each night around 10 p.m., a cluster of young men trickled in from the dark streets into the warehouse. They were gone by dawn.

Meanwhile, Zippi kept her head down and worked. A 1938 snapshot captures her smiling at the camera in a skirt and heels as she stands on a step stool on the sidewalk. Her sleeves are rolled up as she paints lettering on the window of the Luxor Palace in Bratislava.

Zippi painting letters at the premises of Luxor Palace in Bratislava, 1938.

Each day, she practiced her skill set, honed her techniques. She amassed knowledge of her craft, which she recorded in a notebook. She expected that this expertise would lead her to a fulfilling career—a working life in which she'd break ground as a woman, and as a Jew. In a sense, she was right.

CHAPTER TWO

The End of an Era

When David Wisnia was a little boy, he began a lifelong love affair with the opera. By age nine, wearing his very own tuxedo, he would walk to the bus station near his family's home, along with his parents and two brothers, heading to the big city to visit the Grand Theatre of Warsaw. A confident child, his dark chestnut hair buzzed short, he was accustomed to dressing well, to having eyes on him.

Warsaw was not far from their small Polish town of Sochaczew—the bus ride lasted less than an hour—but it might as well have been a different world. At first, the dark skies outside the bus window enveloped quiet cities similar to their own. Vast green fields dotted with the occasional roaming cows surrounded the small villages. Ragged dirt roads connected small wooden houses. Just beyond lay thick forests of pine and birch.

But as the bus lurched farther east and then pivoted slightly northward, the scenery changed. The sky brightened with the glow of streetlamps. Buildings became taller than those in Sochaczew, and yet elegant. Made of brick and stone, their architecture was intricate, sophisticated. In Warsaw, the roads and the cobblestone streets were well tended. Town squares were garnished with water fountains and flower banks. In October of 1935, the freshly paved Washington Boulevard had just become the city's largest traffic artery, making headlines around the world. Blood-red trams, horse-drawn carriages, and polished Cadillacs shared the roads.

Warsaw was Poland's cultural center, the self-purported "Paris of the North." Stylized theaters and intimate playhouses hid within its nooks and crannies; street musicians scattered about, strumming guitars and playing the harmonica; smiling women in rumpled dresses, faded kerchiefs over their hair, sold bouquets of fragrant flowers.

Here, housed in a majestic neoclassical building at the center of town, was the Grand Theatre, home to one of the largest stages in the world. The opera had been revitalized in 1933 under the direction of Janina Korolewicz-Waydowa, a former singer who felt strongly that dropping prices was the best way to save the theater. The experiment worked; attendance shot up. When the Wisnias visited, David's trained ears tuned in to the performers, the pitch of the altos and sopranos, the rich vibrato undulating throughout the room. Most singers were local Poles. They were good enough— but, David thought, not great.

And David wanted to be great. His father, Eliahu, was an opera aficionado. He and his wife, Machla, had encouraged David to appreciate music from a young age, and by the time he was ten he was eagerly memorizing melodies, reading librettos, and singing. Of the three boys in the family, David was the middle child, and also the golden child—and he knew it. Sometimes he worried that his parents' doting made his brothers jealous.

By age seven, David had mastered the piano and could accompany himself singing. Opera was a second language. In his youth, David had memorized "E lucevan le stelle," an emotionally charged aria from Giacomo Puccini's romantic tragedy *Tosca*. He dreamed of becoming a famous opera singer in the United States. His conviction only grew when, at around age eight, he performed at the biggest arena of his young career. On stage at Kinomeva, one of Sochaczew's largest movie theaters, David and his school friend Sara Lewin sang the Hebrew song "Shnei Michtavim" ("The Two Letters"), an operatic poem. It narrated a letter exchange between a Polish mother and her son, who'd moved to Jerusalem. Sara, seven years older than David, played the part of his mother. In a haunting refrain, mother and son grappled with the pains of separation—a mother in the Diaspora and the son who has embraced his new home and is determined to make a life in Jerusalem. His eyes shining, his voice strong, David seized the moment, elated. This, he felt, was where he belonged.

It was 1934, about a year after Nazi Germany had begun to pass its antisemitic laws and spread its propaganda, and Poland and Germany had just signed a nonaggression agreement. The two countries promised to cooperate with each other toward a guarantee of a "lasting peace." The poem "Shnei Michtavim," put to music by Russian composer Joel Engel a decade earlier, reflected the Zionist spirit coursing through the Jewish youth of Poland.

When the performance ended, the audience leapt to its feet and cheered. David and Sara glowed. They had no way of knowing that nine years later they would revive the song—this time off-stage, and in a very different venue.

Life up until this point had been good in Sochaczew, at least for those with the means to enjoy it. Together with David's maternal grandparents, the Wisnias lived in a three-story building on the town's main strip. David and his two brothers, Moshe and Dov, shared a bedroom; their grandparents occupied the ground floor. Their home was among the few in town with its own telephone, making it a popular stop for friends and neighbors.

Eliahu worked hard to afford the best for his family. Each Sunday, he hopped on a bus to Warsaw, where he owned an upholstery shop. Meanwhile, Machla and her sister Helen took care of the home and the children. On occasion David accompanied his grand-father, a casket maker, to work. He listened as his patriarch ban-tered with his employees, a handful of men who'd become close friends over the years. David looked up to his grandfather, a gen-tleman, ever elegant with his trademark goatee, always with a brush in hand to whip his hair into shape.

On Fridays, Eliahu returned home to a fragrant feast of chicken soup with homemade noodles and matzah balls. Each week David observed as his aunt Helen lovingly made the dish and cut up the chicken. In addition to helping take care of the children, Aunt Helen also doubled as the family cook. After their traditional Sab-bath dinner, David sang in the choir of the town's only synagogue. On Saturday mornings he'd sing again. David, the choir's youngest member, had become a soloist by the age of seven.

But even as David and his family enjoyed a good life in Sochaczew, they were forced to continuously look over their shoulders. To be Jewish in 1930s Poland was to be in a perpetual state of unease.

In this sense, Sochaczew was all too typical of small Polish towns. Villagers taunted Jews with the derogatory slur *Jid*. A local policeman beat up Jewish kids at a monthly fair where local farm-ers sold horses and cows. Signs greeted shoppers at the market: "If you buy from a Jew, you're a dog." The taunts and the assaults had occurred off and on for centuries, occasionally exploding into murderous violence — the infamous pogroms that, practically over-night, could leave material devastation and many Jewish Poles dead. Sochaczew was once predominantly Jewish and had a Hasidic center, but its Sochaczew's Jewish population had dwin-dled as many residents emigrated to Warsaw or left Poland alto-gether, often to Palestine. By the 1930s, Sochaczew's population of 13,500 was only about a quarter Jewish.

David's first antisemitic experience had come at the start of public school, when he was four. He'd refused to kneel during school prayers. At recess, his classmates beat him up. His father yanked David from the school that same week and moved him to a prestigious private day school, Yavneh, where subjects were taught in Hebrew and Polish. So it was that David joined an insular world within the Jewish community—a protected sphere that would nurture his self-confidence and his desire to perform.

For the Wisnias, a move from their small Polish town to the United States wasn't far-fetched. One of Machla's sisters, Aunt Rose, had moved to Brooklyn with her husband and children years ago. This, to David, meant possibility. And his beloved Aunt Helen, who was helping raise David, was making plans of her own to join her older sister in New York City. Why shouldn't they all go?

David's father was the main obstacle. Eliahu didn't care for America, a land where children didn't respect their elders, he scoffed, and where money was god. In Warsaw, he had a solid busi-ness, a house. They were comfortable. Only peasants left Poland, Eliahu told his son—those who had nothing worth staying for.

Still, David pleaded. He felt danger lurking, even at the age of ten. Jews had been economically and politically ostracized in Poland for decades, he knew, but the animosity toward them was clearly reaching a fever pitch, and there were other warnings signs as well. In 1936, Warsaw University students staged hunger strikes, demand-ing that Jews be segregated, a precedent that had already been set by other nearby campuses. David pointed to circulating rumors, to the radio broadcasts that warned of a looming war. Even in War-saw, preparations were underway. At night, officials tested the city's readiness with sirens and drumrolls. They turned off streetlights, leaving the town in darkness to "test the discipline of the popula-tion," newspapers reported.

But David's arguments with his father went nowhere. Instead, in 1937, when David was eleven years old, Eliahu Wisnia moved his family to Warsaw, ending his weekly commute. The Wisnias made a new home in a large and elegant fourth-floor apartment at

Krochmalna Street, close to Eliahu's upholstery shop. They were a few steps away from an impoverished Jewish enclave primarily made up of traditional Yiddish-speaking Jews, merchants and cobblers. The Wisnias, however, avoided speaking Yiddish, a vernacular language that wealthy Jews considered a vulgar form of German. Now the Wisnias spoke Polish almost exclusively. At his private Zionist Jewish school, the Tarbut, David studied both Hebrew and Polish.

Through it all, David's singing career remained a priority. At first, he performed at the Nożyk synagogue, among the five biggest congregations in town, which seated some six hundred congregants. But Eliahu wanted a wider exposure for his son. The

Warsaw's Great Synagogue, where David Wisnia performed as a boy.

Great Synagogue on Tłomackie Street was a premier synagogue of Europe. The cantor, Moshe Koussevitzky, was a gifted tenor with a following. David joined his tutelage in 1938.

While his training as a singer progressed, David's hope of going to the United States became less viable. American quotas for new immigrants had reached record lows. For decades, nativists had lobbied Congress to guard against a "foreign invasion." As early as 1924, a national-origins quota limited immigrants from Southern and Eastern Europe as well as those from Africa and Asia. By the 1930s, nativists focused on a new slogan: "America's children are America's problem! Refugee children in Europe are Europe's problem!" Americans were still reeling from the Great War and the country was battling a depression. A 1939 Gallup poll found that a majority of Americans didn't want new immigrants, particularly those from Europe. That same year, a North Carolina senator introduced a bill that called for halting all immigration into the United States for ten years.

The door to the United States was about to slam shut. But before it did, David's aunt Helen made it to New York, joining her sister Rose just in time. Helen was off to live the dream, just feet away from the Harlem River in the South Bronx, at 750 Grand Concourse. David memorized her new address. His doting aunt — the woman who'd cared for him since birth, who'd spent her Fridays teaching him how to make her special broth and noodles — was gone. But David held out hope. He repeated the address to himself. He'd join her yet.

On Thursday, August 31, 1939, David celebrated his bar mitzvah. He was thirteen years old: by Jewish tradition, officially a man. He led services at his synagogue and enjoyed a small celebration in the building's back room. The usual festive refreshments were passed around to the adults — whiskey and wine — and everyone enjoyed the cake, challah bread, and herring.

Later, the celebration continued at the Wisnias' home. David looked around the crowded family living room and felt the presence of hundreds of guests, all attending the occasion in his honor. The entire Jewish community, David marveled, was there to toast him. He savored the orange marmalade, reserved for special occasions, and the candy, the cakes, the chocolates. The day was filled with sweetness. Aunt Helen's boyfriend—who had stayed behind when she left for New York—gave David his first watch. David was thrilled. He was embarking on a new phase of his life.

David Wisnia at his bar mitzvah on August 31, 1939.

The atmosphere was festive inside the apartment on Krochmalna Street—but below, in the streets of Warsaw, the summer air felt exceptionally thick. Many Poles tried to shrug it off. Who in their right mind would imagine that Germany would attack Poland? In any case, the English and French would protect their Polish allies—or so hoped many in Warsaw.

Notices of a "general mobilization" had been posted around town, and on this day—the day of David's bar mitzvah—Poland finally took the dramatic step of mobilizing its troops in preparation for war. It was undeniable: the Nazi threat was getting closer to home. Polish men between the ages of twenty-one and forty were called in for military service. Poland's future was under threat.

At that moment, though, none of it mattered. David had spent months studying in anticipation of his bar mitzvah. He'd memorized his Torah portion, he'd practiced his readings and performed them beautifully. As it turned out, he and his family were ringing in the end of an era.

The celebration, the feeling of elation and pride that he'd felt the night before, were still fresh when David woke up the following morning. His stomach ached; perhaps he'd eaten too much candy, he thought. Outside his window, he heard the crescendo of what sounded like a swarm of angry bees. David got up to try to see where the bizarre buzz was coming from. His brothers were still asleep.

Outside, David saw squadrons of silver airplanes whisk through the crisp morning sky in tight formation. He rushed to his parents' bedroom and shook his father awake.

Eliahu was not yet fully conscious when David told him what he'd seen. These were not Polish airplanes, David stressed to his father. He knew what Polish airplanes looked like.

Eliahu lay dewy-eyed in his bed. It was still dawn, sunlight just beginning to creep inside the window. Inside, the world remained quiet, at peace.

David tried to convey the significance of what he'd seen mere moments ago, so close by. Poland didn't have these kinds of airplanes, he repeated, animated. The airplanes he'd seen were much too sophisticated. They were foreign.

But Eliahu didn't budge. *Go back to sleep,* he said. These are just maneuvers, the air force training.

True, Polish pilots had been training in recent days. But David knew what those planes looked like—and he knew that they were not what he'd seen just now.

He was right. A few hours earlier, German troops dressed in Polish army uniforms had attacked a German broadcast station in Gleiwitz, then a German border town along the southern edge of Poland. The BBC broadcast the so-called Polish attack within hours. The ruse was used to justify Germany's invasion of Poland.

At 5:11 that morning, Hitler had made a proclamation that reverberated around the world. He accused the Polish people of persecuting Germans. He warned that the German nation would "meet force with force."

Soon after Eliahu told his son to return to bed, air raid sirens blasted across Warsaw. For a brief moment, the city went gray. Overhanging mist and clouds protected the city from the sudden air raids. A new reality was upon them—the Wisnias, the rest of Warsaw's 1.3 million residents, and the wider world.

CHAPTER THREE

"He Was Bluffing"

I t was supposed to be a joyous time.

Zippi and Tibor were engaged to be married. It was 1938, the world was falling apart, reality losing its shape—and yet the two dared to plan a future together.

Then Zippi's grandmother, Julia, died. It was a peaceful, uncomplicated death at the age of seventy-two. Still, Julia had been Zippi's rock, her most fervent supporter and role model. She'd taught her so much. And now she was gone.

When Zippi's mother had died, eleven years earlier, Julia had shown Zippi that life didn't stop to accommodate grief, and neither should she. Julia, ever lively and curious, an insatiable consumer of books and newspapers, always game to learn more, always eager to fold new faces into her life, had bestowed all these passions on her granddaughter. Zippi would honor her. She'd go on with her life. At least Julia wouldn't have to watch as Bratislava's promising future was painfully dismantled.

Hitler's rise posed an existential threat to Czechoslovakia. Germany had been eyeing the Sudetenland, the territory in northern Czechoslovakia that was occupied by some 2.8 million Sudeten

Germans. Now it had become a pretext for Germany to slink across Czechoslovakia's borders.

Unlike most Eastern European countries, which had fallen to fascism with hardly a fight, the Czechoslovak government wouldn't budge. When Hitler had tried strong-arming Czechoslovakia into ceding control of the Sudetenland, the government had responded with a resounding no. Instead, it took Germany by surprise by mobilizing its men up to the age of forty. Germany's army stood down. That August, *Fortune* magazine marveled that the "little country of Czechoslovakia, a democratic enclave in the heart of autocratic Central Europe, [had] stood up to Hitler and discovered he was bluffing." In September, Czechoslovak prime minister Jan Syrový, a four-star general, swore that the army, considered among Europe's strongest forces, would "defend our liberties to the very end."

But the bulwark wouldn't hold. For all its might, the Czechoslovak army couldn't win against Hitler's war machine without Western support. Not only were they met with silence, they were also, in effect, undermined: on September 30, 1938, Germany, Italy, Great Britain, and France signed the Munich Agreement, placing the Sudetenland under German control.

General Syrový again addressed his nation, this time with a broken heart. He had no choice, he said. Czechoslovakia was, after all, a "little country" and there was only so much it could do on its own. The Czechoslovak government surrendered to the conditions of the Munich Agreement: the Sudetenland would be incorporated into Germany.

Emboldened, Hitler began to pave the way for an "independent" Slovak state. Already the unified nation was beginning to fall apart; Czechoslovak president Edvard Beneš resigned and fled to Paris, leaving General Syrový as the country's de facto leader. A flurry of Czech and Slovak soldiers fled to other Eastern European countries and still others escaped to Great Britain.

The ominous cloud of Nazism loomed nearer, casting its shadow. One by one, the freedoms and opportunities that had sprouted during Julia's lifetime would be plucked away. In November 1938, Bratislava University dismissed five hundred Jewish students with the excuse that they were "Communists." Zippi had earned her degrees in the nick of time. Certified as a licensed graphic designer, she was poised to become the first woman in Bratislava at work in this field.

So many Jews had refused to believe that the horrifying actions of thriving Nazism reported in Eastern Europe would reach them. But the undercurrents of antisemitism that had permeated the region for centuries only intensified. The persecution of Jews had once been largely confined to smaller villages, but now acts of terror and propaganda were spreading to cultured and educated metropolises.

Antisemitic sentiment spread among the Slovaks, many of whom eagerly joined the ranks of the Hlinka Guards, the militia wing of the Slovak People's Party, a force named after the party's founder, Catholic priest Andrej Hlinka. *The Slovak,* a newspaper dedicated to the Slovak People's Party, justified its actions: "We had and have even today reasons to look upon the Jews not only with reserve and distaste but we can also rightly blame them for failures and disasters brought on our nation."

The streets of Bratislava took on the menacing feel of World War I–era Europe. Jewish shops were vandalized. Women were terrified to be outside unaccompanied during evening hours. Hlinka guardsmen multiplied around town, hoodlums resembling a comic-opera version of Italian fascist militiamen who roamed the streets in their black uniforms, tall dark boots, and boat-shaped hats with gold trim and a tassel. One night, a friend of Zippi's came home from a Hashomer Hatzair meeting with a bloody nose, after encountering hecklers on the way. Jewish and Czech life in Bratislava was becoming unbearable.

Zippi and Tibor Justh snapped photographs of each other as part of her graphics and photography training.

Zippi was the only woman and the only Jew to work at her prestigious, twelve-person German firm. But the job was short-lived. Because she was a Jew, the firm was forced to let her go.

Zippi strung together a series of odd jobs: she taught practical graphic design skills to Jews, and she painted license plates, notices, posters, advertisements, and street signs. While Jews were ostracized from society, trained graphic designers were rare and in demand. Still, no matter how hard she worked or how good she was at her job, there was no escaping her identity as a Jew and what that meant in this new world.

In March of 1939, Slovakia formally declared its independence from Czechoslovakia. The new nation established a puppet government supported by the Third Reich and ostensibly headed by Jozef Tiso, the Catholic priest who'd become leader of the Hlinka Party after Andrej Hlinka's death in 1938. Czechoslovakia was no more. Beneš tried to form a Czechoslovak government in exile in Paris, but the French government refused to recognize his provisional government—supporting instead the Czechoslovak ambassador to France, Štefan Osuský, who'd already established a Czechoslovak army in Paris. Although both men wanted a reunified Czechsolovakia, Osuský had more of a Slovak platform than Beneš. In July, after France's fall, Beneš reestablished the Czechoslovak government in exile in London, where it was recognized by the Allies, with Osuský as a minister.

Almost immediately after Czechoslovakia's dismemberment, the Spitzers lost their home. The Hlinka Guard ordered Jews to the old Jewish Quarter. The Spitzers left behind their apartment and furniture and moved into a shared room in a dilapidated building.

All the while, Sam took on greater roles within his resistance work. He helped the Jewish volunteers in the International Brigades, who'd traveled from Palestine to fight fascism in Spain in 1936 and had been unable to return home. Most had become political prisoners in internment camps near the Pyrenees mountains. Sam hid refugees within crevices of the Little Carpathians, near Bratislava, and distributed food and pamphlets with updates from the underground.

With the surge in antisemitic policies and violence, Palestine had become enticing. On a whim, Sam bought a racing bike and a forged ID card, planning to ride through Hungary, somehow get to Turkey, and finally to Palestine, but his bike broke down before he crossed a single border. He shrugged it off, the idea aborted as quickly as it had come. Instead, he deepened his underground work, joining the *Obrana národa,* a Czech resistance organization that detonated dynamite on roads to stall German soldiers trying to enter Slovakia.

The "small stuff" he'd been involved with was growing.

Zippi's fiancé, Tibor, was also doing his part. Having been a driver for the anti-aircraft regiment of the Czechoslovak army, he now redoubled his efforts with the underground movement. He worked with both Czechoslovak soldiers and Jewish youth groups to resist fascism. He joined a secret network known as a Czech Mission. Overseen by the Czechoslovak government in exile, the operation was rooted inside the French consulate in Budapest and worked with a Polish refugee organization in Hungary. It provided refugees and Czechoslovak fighters with forged documents and transport across borders to join the Allies. In addition, Tibor worked with members of Hashomer Hatzair and with non-Jewish Czechoslovaks. He had two goals: to rid his country of fascism and to help refugees flee to Palestine.

While Zippi wasn't actively involved in resistance work, she understood what was at stake. She was twenty-one years old, she had time. Their wedding would wait.

CHAPTER FOUR

"No One's Going to Beat Them"

Many of Warsaw's residents packed up to leave town following the German invasion of Poland. The lucky ones, who owned carts and horses, carried drawers full of clothes. Most just grabbed whatever they could lug on their backs. Others left with nothing. They wanted to go eastward, where they hoped the German forces hadn't yet arrived—but the majority didn't make it far. Railway tracks had been destroyed; trains, bridges, and cars had become targets. The entire region had spiraled into chaos. Inside their apartment, the Wisnias listened to the endless artillery fire.

A week earlier, Nazi Germany and the Soviet Union had unexpectedly announced the passage of the Molotov-Ribbentrop Pact, a promise of nonaggression between the two forces. With this pact, however, the two countries' leaders had also secretly agreed to partition Poland and each would establish its own sphere of influence.

While Hitler had never intended to uphold his promise of nonaggression, he did have one goal in common with Stalin: to get rid of Judaism. The Soviets' enemies were subjected to the Gulag, a network of forced labor camps first put into place in 1918 by Russia's Bolshevik leader, Vladimir Lenin, to terrorize opponents of the Russian Revolution. It expanded exponentially under Stalin with the pretext of speeding up the Soviet Union's industrialization. In remote regions, far from their families, ethnic and political prisoners toiled on infrastructure projects in freezing cold weather, with little food. Many didn't last long. Some Jews believed that the German methods couldn't be much worse than the Soviets'.

The radio had long been a fixture at the Wisnia household. During the first week of September 1939, it broadcast a steady stream of air-raid warnings. Meanwhile, hundreds of German airplanes dotted the sky and German soldiers blockaded city gates. A church was struck during a Sunday morning mass. That afternoon, dozens of bereft parishioners knelt over wrecked pews, their hands covering their faces. The altar was split before them, surrounded by ashes and embers, no roof over their heads.

Warsaw was under siege.

In the streets, Polish volunteers built barricades in an attempt to fortify their city, to prepare for some sort of resistance against the surrounding Germans. Outside the Wisnia household, children wore makeshift cotton and gauze masks stitched up by mothers desperate to protect them from smoke and dust inhalation. Bombs landed on a Jewish hospital. Rabbis carried children to air-raid trenches that had been dug by hospital patients. "You could set the watch by the raids," a British photographer told a reporter. But the Poles' anti-aircraft guns and their attempts at resistance were no match for German artillery.

In September, the Jewish Quarter was bombarded, just when Jews would have celebrated Rosh Hashanah, the Jewish New Year. Gutted buildings and stray body parts lay twisted beneath the debris. Columns of dense gray smoke lingered in the air, obstructing the view of the carnage. Blocks of buildings were razed; those who'd spent a lifetime in the city could no longer find their way home.

A third of Warsaw was destroyed.

★   ★   ★

That first month under siege, David and his family stayed inside during the daylight hours, when most of the bombing took place. Sometimes they hid in the basement or at a nearby shelter. The earth beneath them shook and the building next door was leveled but somehow the Wisnias' apartment remained undisturbed. *If we can survive a bit longer,* they told themselves, *maybe, just maybe, the British and the French will come to our rescue.*

By night, David and his family joined the scavenge for food. Famished men, women, and children roamed from shelter to shelter, forming breadlines outside bakeries. David would wait in line for sugar with his heart pounding; air raids and shellings did not seem to dissipate. Prices for basic goods had tripled or quadrupled, and food supplies dwindled; while Eliahu had hoarded some rice and sugar, it would soon run out. Sweet rice became the family's new staple.

On September 28, 1939, Warsaw surrendered. Some five hundred fires burned around the city. More than three thousand people died during the final twenty-four hours of the siege. The once glistening city lay in ashes.

A few days after the defeat, Eliahu took David and his older brother, Moshe, out in the early morning to watch Germany's victory parade. David observed men marching to the sound of drums, machine guns resting on their shoulders; their legs shot up in unison, right, then left, leather boots kicking up dust. Soldiers in hard hats rode tall, well-fed horses, saluting their Führer, whose stoic gaze did not waver as he watched, pleased with his forces. Waves of armored vehicles, tanks, and artillery passed by in formation as airplanes hovered above. The Poles watched from the sidelines.

No one's going to beat them, David said.

What are you talking about? Eliahu said. *England is powerful.*

Only time would tell.

In the meantime, shrapnel, shards of glass, and busted buildings would be swept aside. The most obvious violence would end. And a new phase of terror would begin.

For those who hadn't lost anyone, who hadn't stumbled over bodies on the ground beneath them, whose homes hadn't been crushed to the ground, life fell into a new routine that almost resembled normalcy. Public schools were off-limits to Jews, but David returned to his private courses. His father returned to work.

David noticed placards in German and Polish, addressed to Jews: *We will treat you as all the other Poles if you will stop cheating your neighbors, stop lying and stop spreading lice or typhoid.* David was confused. He didn't know anyone with lice, or know anything about cheating neighbors. As vitriol against Jews escalated, David didn't leave his apartment unless he had to.

But even inside one's apartment, a Jew was no longer safe. SS officers appeared at rich Jews' doorsteps to remove the furniture from inside. They conducted random night raids in Jewish homes. At gunpoint, they ordered that money and jewelry be handed over. Posters materialized on street poles and storefronts: JEWS, LICE, TYPHUS. Their message was clear: Jews were a threat to public health. City sections became restricted. Various parks, stores, and roads were all of a sudden off-limits. By the end of September, certain streetcars were designated FOR JEWS ONLY.

On October 12, 1940, newly installed loudspeakers on street poles throughout town blasted to life with an announcement: Warsaw was to be divided into three quarters, German, Polish, and Jewish. All residents, except Germans, had until the end of the month to move to their designated quarters. Anything they could not carry with them, they would have to leave behind.

It had been thirteen months since David's bar mitzvah. The Grand Theatre, where he and his family had sat enraptured by music a decade earlier, now lay in rubble. His dreams of singing opera in America were beginning to seem like a fairy tale, a wish gone by.

Warsaw was a city on the brink. Poles and Jews crowded the cobblestone streets. Breathless, they pushed handcarts and wagons down the streets, carrying with them what they could. "Home" was a moving target. At any moment, boundaries would shift, apartments would be requisitioned, a new order of expulsion would demand a hasty exit. Ready to move, they only held on to the essentials. The rest of it, left behind, was loot for the Germans. Tables, chairs and beds, linens, and sometimes photo albums became abandoned relics of past lives.

In October of 1940, over a span of two weeks, eighty thousand Christian Poles were forced out of their homes to make room for the hundred and forty thousand Jews ordered to move in. This became Warsaw's newly appointed quarantine zone, the Jewish Quarter. The area took up about a hundred acres, although it would fluctuate in size and eventually take up as many as 375 acres of residential space. Jagged strands of barbed wire topped ten-foot-high walls that bounded the ghetto.

David and his family didn't have to move—they already lived within the ghetto's boundaries. Their household of seven, however, now doubled its occupancy. They took in an aunt, an uncle, two babies, plus another family.

By then Warsaw, once a glittering city of music and beauty, had morphed into a collection of barricaded slums. Each day new walls were erected. Residents wondered whether the ghetto gates would remain open. Would they be able to leave and visit other quarters, tend to their jobs outside the zone? Or would they be sealed off, isolated? No one knew. David continued to attend class within the ghetto, but singing in the choir at the Great Synagogue was no longer an option: the temple had been shut down and the building had become a repository for looted furniture.

David's father, Eliahu, clung to the reins of his business for as long as he could, but inevitably the Germans took over, Aryanizing his business and leaving him out of a job. Desperate for work, Eliahu scoured for extra food he could bring home to his three growing boys, his wife, and his in-laws.

But Eliahu was resourceful. Some German officers, he learned, were not as hell-bent as others on killing Jews. Eliahu ingratiated himself with one of these less menacing Germans. As a young man, he'd learned carpentry from his father, and now he told a *Luftwaffe* sergeant that he was a carpenter, happy to offer his services. The *Luftwaffe* was the air force of the *Wehrmacht,* Germany's armed forces. While Hitler was its supreme commander, soldiers of the *Wehrmacht* were not necessarily members of the Nazi Party (officially the National Socialist German Workers' Party).

The sergeant gave Eliahu a job at Warsaw-Okęcie Airport, an airfield for the German army. From then on, a German truck hauled Eliahu back and forth to and from work three times a week. In exchange, he brought home extra bread and potatoes. For a time, this would save his family's lives.

David, who by 1940 was a tall, light-haired fourteen-year-old, did his best to pitch in. When he wasn't in school, he volunteered for odd jobs, making the rounds with a broom, sweeping away ghetto grit; other days, he mopped. With this, he could bring home more scraps of food. And in keeping busy, he managed to avoid the Nazis' elite corps, known as the *Schutzstaffel* (Protection Squad), the SS.

Hitler had established the SS in 1925—a select group of Nazis who'd sworn an oath of loyalty to the Führer himself. Members trailed Hitler and high-ranking members of the Nazi Party to rallies and served as personal bodyguards. Members' responsibilities grew, in campaigning and gathering intelligence, and they became more entertwined with the Nazi Party itself. A hierarchical system was formed and Heinrich Himmler, a slight, bespectacled chicken farmer, worked his way up through propaganda and intelligence-gathering roles. In 1929, he was promoted to national leader of the SS. In his hands, the SS grew into a multipronged beast. By 1940, it controlled the Nazis' main vehicles of terror, including the Gestapo, the secret police that terrorized so-called enemies of the Reich, as well as concentration and extermination camps. The SS also had its own military arm: the *Waffen-SS,* which worked in parallel to the *Wehrmacht.*

Himmler also created the SS Race and Settlement Main Office, whose functions included ideological training for SS members, vetting of recruits, and filtering of SS officers' spouses based on racial criteria. The swarms of applicants were evaluated based on physical characteristics, including eye color and body measurements, and whether they fit the Nordic bloodline requirement. SS members became, in essence, guardians of the German race, empowered to tyrannize—and ultimately eliminate—the impure, sub-human other. Most relished the duty.

For the most part, the SS and the Gestapo ruled over the Warsaw Ghetto. But it did so in conjunction with both *Wehrmacht* and SS officers, and German civil administration. For organization, the SS appointed a *Judenrat,* or Jewish Council, which would essentially serve as middlemen between the SS and the Jews. The *Judenräte* were responsible for executing SS directives—often discriminatory and cruel decrees aimed at their own community. The *Judenräte* also organized ghetto maintenance, policed Jews, and mobilized Jewish labor.

Still, German soldiers and SS stayed on-site, tormenting Jews. Sometimes Jews were chosen at random to perform backbreaking manual labor. Some had to load gravel onto trucks or build walls. Instead of getting food, they were beaten with rubber truncheons.

Streets became more crowded. With each day that passed, carts filled with families arrived from near and far: a hundred and fifty Jews from Berlin, a handful from neighboring provinces. Newcomers squeezed into already packed apartments. Lines snaked down streets outside the few stores that still sold bread. Men, women, and children bartered for food.

On November 16, 1940, a day of Sabbath, the ghetto was officially sealed. Panic and unrest ensued. Guards were installed on every ghetto street corner demanding identification, deciding who could pass through the gates. German guards seized the opportunity to torment pedestrians. On his way to school, David might have seen newly posted SS guards cackle as they ordered elderly Jews to do pushups and gymnastics, or to sing and dance for their entertainment. The SS had pistols and batons and were eager to use them; Jews had nothing left but their hunger and thirst. They did as they were told.

Within a day, shops in the Jewish Quarter ran out of bread and produce. Food supplies from other quarters were cut off. Charitable Christians crossed over to smuggle bread for Jewish friends. One who dared to throw a sack of bread over a wall was murdered on the spot. The Wisnias, like all Warsaw Ghetto residents, relied on rations—typically around eight hundred daily calories per person, made up of potatoes and bread. Bodies became smaller, weaker, until the life within them disappeared.

A year earlier, a regulation had passed that Jews ages ten and older had to wear a white armband with the Star of David on their right sleeve. The star had to be at least ten centimeters wide, visible from a distance. Those who ignored these rules would be imprisoned. Those who wore dirty or wrinkled armbands were fined. Kiosks down the street from the Wisnias' apartment sold the required armbands.

David wore his with pride, defiant.

By January 1941, the ghetto covered 2.4 percent of Warsaw and held within it 30 percent of the city's population. Conditions in the congested space led to gestures of despair, the affectations of a madhouse. Running out of options, families with emaciated children pleaded for sustenance outside the courthouses. One man

Street vendors and ghetto residents at the Warsaw Ghetto, 1941.

muttered jokes and witty sayings in exchange for food or money. Another sang while his wife pushed a stroller down narrow streets and collected donations. Ghetto dwellers became professional food smugglers. Intrepid children in ragged scraps, disaffected youth with nothing left to lose, learned how to distract German and Polish guards so they could sneak in and out of the gates.

The ghetto was becoming a death trap, and not just because of the gunshots that snuffed out many lives at random. Starvation was a major killer. Typhus, at first a fabricated excuse to ostracize the Jews from the rest of the city, became a reality, thanks to overcrowded, unsanitary conditions. Streets reeked of human disease and waste. A lice outbreak arrived with refugees who'd been transported into Warsaw from outside provinces. A particularly harsh winter topped off the nightmare that life had become.

Random probes became common. The sight of a black limousine at any time of day or night was bad news. Often, a Gestapo officer loaded up the limo with human targets to shoot in the center of town. Families would wake up to loud pounding on their apartment doors followed by figures waving rifles and nightsticks. The freshly woken prey, dazed and disoriented, was dragged out to the street and executed. Gunshots were part of the city backdrop.

David woke up one morning to find that his oldest brother, Moshe, had fled without warning, wanting to leave his family with one less mouth to feed. Moshe had gone to Otwock, a small town about fifteen miles southeast of Warsaw, where an uncle lived. In normal times the family had enjoyed summertime vacations in Otwock. Now, they could only hope that Moshe had fled undetected. Failed escape attempts meant a bullet on the spot.

CHAPTER FIVE

The Jewish Codex

It was futile for Zippi to try to keep tabs on Tibor's whereabouts. He now had a nom de guerre: Jusek. He'd crossed the border from Slovakia to Hungary, and had made it to the French consulate in Budapest. He was working with Czech agents to facilitate clandestine border crossings from Slovakia to Hungary, but he was also helping men join the Czech Legion or escape to Yugoslavia. Not only that, he also ran a smuggling ring that transported Czech Jews to Palestine.

And so Zippi had no way of knowing where he was until she got word: Tibor had been arrested.

The Hungarian police made the arrest in July of 1940 at Stuhlweissenburg, a major railway junction in central Hungary. They accused him of organizing forty refugee transports and accompanying twenty-five of them—each containing anywhere from three to twelve refugees.

His work had been fruitful but had come to a resounding halt. By November the Hungarian police would turn Tibor over to the Germans.

News from the underground traveled fast. It likely didn't take long before Zippi learned of his arrest, but there was nothing she could do for her fiancé. He was beyond her reach. It was the third time in her short life that she'd experienced the loss of someone she loved. Still, she'd likely held on to every hope that he'd return to her, that they'd marry, that life would get back on track. What more could she do?

In 1941, Slovakia established what came to be known as the Jewish Codex, modeled after the Nuremberg Race Laws that Germany had originated and spread to its occupied territories. These ever-evolving laws spelled out what it meant to be a Jew. At that point, a Jew was defined as someone of the Jewish faith—in Slovakia they were not yet considered a race.

Jewish-owned businesses across Bratislava were Aryanized—taken over by Slovaks and Germans. Sam kept his job at the carpet warehouse, training new workers, but his salary was reduced by nearly 90 percent. At least he *had* a salary, he thought; Sam's uncle, the Jewish owner, had been replaced by a Slovak member of the Hlinka Party and was out of a job.

For months, Sam worked without incident.

Then, on a January afternoon in 1942, the loud trot of black boots and the kick of the door brought everyone at the warehouse to attention. Hlinka guardsmen swept inside, pistols and batons primed in their hands. They grabbed a number of workers—including Sam.

The men whom Sam had let sleep inside the warehouse at Tibor's request, it turned out, were former Czechoslovak officers routed to London, or sometimes to Palestine. Most hoped to organize and become part of the Czechoslovak resistance against the fascist Germans and Slovaks. Sam may not have known this—but it's likely that the Hlinka did. Or had they grabbed him because of his pamphleteering, or his work with refugees, or any of the rest of it? Official documents of the new regime's secret services indicated he was arrested for being active in illegal communist activities.

The guardsmen wanted names. At the police headquarters they spat out questions: *Who are the other resisters? Who was Sam working with?* Each time Sam said "I don't know," they struck him.

Still, Sam kept his mouth shut. After hours of beatings they gave up and threw him into a cell. He was designated a political prisoner.

That day, the Hlinka Guard had organized a great sweep across the entire town. Hundreds of other resistance members were arrested alongside Sam. In his mug shot, Sam is wearing a ruffled dark jacket and a collared shirt. The thin twenty-year-old appears tormented, defeated.

Sam Spitzer's mug shot following his arrest by Hlinka guardsmen for resistance activities, 1942.

Word got to Zippi. Now both her fiancé and her brother were gone. Sam, at least, hadn't been locked up by the Germans. He was still in town—still in Bratislava, by the courthouse, behind bars.

Sam was relatively lucky: as a political prisoner he was, unlike most Jews, protected from transports to concentration or labor camps. Sam's prison job was to glue together ice-cream cone paper. For a job well done, he earned two extra slices of bread. Charming and charismatic, Sam easily befriended prisoners and guards, some of whom were even persuaded to spread the latest news broadcast on their radios. In this way, intelligence from the resistance traveled even faster inside prison.

The news was never good. The Slovaks wanted to get rid of their Jews, and the Germans wanted laborers, so the two nations came up with a mutually satisfying solution: Slovakia would organize a mass deportation to German-run labor camps. It would pay Germany to take its unwanted Jews. The sum was explained as a "colonization fee."

Sam, of course, heard the news in prison. He was sure that the political prisoners would be among the first to go. He was wrong.

Bratislava was just recovering from a blizzard and February 1942 was drawing to a close when placards materialized in kiosks around town. The signs were large, with writing in bold letters: All unmarried Jewish girls and women in Bratislava under the age of forty-five were ordered to go to a designated spot with no more than 110 pounds of luggage. They were to present themselves within four weeks, on March 21. If the women didn't volunteer, their parents would be taken instead.

Rumors filled in the gaps; families compared notes. When Zippi heard what was behind the order, she was stunned: her government had made a deal to sell them to the Germans like cattle. The realization that her country saw her as merchandise hit her hard.

At twenty-three, Zippi was losing everything and everyone she loved. All she had left was her work — and her father and his new family. Zippi decided that she'd make this sacrifice for them. She would leave her work behind, her city, her whole life. She would turn herself in.

Maybe leaving Bratislava wouldn't be so bad, the women told

themselves. They were informed that they would work in the fields of Northern Slovakia. The work would only last a couple of months.

The excuse seemed plausible. Or at least Zippi wanted to believe it.

A few days before she had to present herself for deportation, Zippi learned she could potentially avoid transport without putting her father's family in jeopardy. Churches of various orders — from Protestant to Catholic to Greek Orthodox — were offering mass conversions to Jews, often at a cost. It wouldn't really mean anything, Zippi reasoned — it wouldn't be a big deal. She knew who she was. The conversion would be a transaction.

The process usually simply involved participation in a large-scale baptism. The practice was so prevalent that the Slovak Nazi newspaper, *Der Grenzbote,* reported that pastors and priests who continued to baptize Jews would be strongly disciplined. Anyway, it wouldn't help: according to the Nuremberg Race Laws, anyone who had three or four Jewish grandparents was considered a Jew. "A Jew remains a Jew even if he is baptized by a hundred bishops," Slovak's president, Jozef Tiso, a Roman Catholic priest, was reported to have said.

In the eleventh hour, Zippi tried still another tactic. Her new employer, a German, prepared an official letter requesting an exemption that would excuse Zippi from the transport. But ultimately bureaucracy prevailed: Zippi was told to pick up the letter on Monday at nine o'clock in the morning — an hour after she had to appear at the gathering point. Those sixty minutes made all the difference. She couldn't risk being late.

Her time had run out.

She thought of what the Slovakian government had told them, that this would be a temporary situation. Three months, they'd said. The women would fulfill their patriotic duty, then return to their regular life. Zippi made herself believe that this was true.

She was to go to Patrónka, a junction named after a defunct bullet-producing factory—a sinister omen of what lay ahead.

Zippi arrived at Patrónka with a swarm of women and girls clad in skirts and tailored coats, each carrying suitcases weighing up to 110 pounds with their most crucial valuables. Zippi had dressed strategically. She wore her cherished Austrian-made Goiserer mountain boots: sturdy and practical. She'd picked out a tailored wool winter coat and a pair of warm gloves; a dark-green knitted angora turban covered her hair. She'd also slipped on a skirt and a pullover. First impressions mattered.

At twenty-three, Zippi was among the oldest in the crowd, but its age range was narrow; hardly anyone was under sixteen. They stood around by a building that resembled a soldier's dormitory, surrounded by Hlinka guards, who ordered them not to speak to each other. Many of the women had arrived in their best clothing, hair freshly permed, clearly expecting only a brief inconvenience. But at the building's entrance, guards grabbed handbags, identification cards, cash, and jewelry. One woman's reading glasses were yanked from the bridge of her nose.

Zippi clutched her most prized possession: a textbook of sorts. It was the notebook she'd filled up with lecture notes on color combinations, formulas, and methods of mixing colors for various effects. Her meticulous writing explained how to mount art, how to drill, and how to select hardware. This was her bible—knowledge amassed during years of diligent study, its pages thumbed daily.

The Hlinka guards grabbed it, along with her other books, money, and ID cards. What good would her notes, her books do the guard? It didn't matter; they were gone. She'd have to rely on her memory.

Slovakian peasant women waited their turn with the Jewish women. They'd been instructed to probe for contraband. When

Zippi's turn came, they wasted no time. Skirt pushed to the side, Zippi felt thick bare hands inside her vagina, inside her anus.

The Jewish women would have to get used to it, this casual violence, these offhand violations, the utter lack of provisions. There was no hint of water or food to come. Already their terror was palpable. Some of them recognized each other from youth groups and school, from swims in the Danube, hikes on mountains—mirages of a prior life. They didn't dare speak to each other.

After the women were searched, they were herded into narrow, bare rooms that each held about forty bodies. Some were led upstairs to rooms with a single window and bags of hay covering the ground. Others shuffled to a basement, where they'd sleep on a cold stone floor. Doors were shut, windows and gates locked, leaving no way out.

Zippi had begun to settle on the dirty straw when the wailing began. A lone woman: her hiccups echoing, her sobs reminding Zippi of an irrational baby. How could someone lose control like that? This woman could be putting them all at risk. Zippi walked over to the bawling blonde and sat next to her. *Stop crying,* she urged the woman. *We are all in the same boat. You have no right to scream and cry—it will not help.*

But the woman was inconsolable. She wasn't Jewish, she said, she didn't deserve this. Her family wasn't religious and she was a Christian, the woman cried. She rarely spent time with Jews, she added between sobs, this was a mistake. Zippi urged her to be quiet, for her own sake. After some time, the woman calmed down.

Her name was Katya Singer, she said. Katya was tall and thin, with a beautiful porcelain face. She was in her twenties—among the "old" ones, too. Zippi didn't dare leave her side and risk another meltdown that might draw the Hlinka guardsmen's attention.

One night followed the next and they stayed put in the old factory hall, under the gaze of guards who came in and out at random. Each day new bodies materialized, small-town girls who'd been snatched out of their homes without warning. The space around them tightened. The fruit, bread, cheese, and water that they'd brought dwindled to crumbs and drops. They were famished and parched.

Zippi and Katya shared their food and slept next to each other on the straw that covered the ground. They whispered, without drawing attention. Despite Zippi's initial impression of Katya, she liked her.

They would leave soon, the Hlinka warned. They passed around postcards and ordered the women to write home, to let their families know they were well. The women wrote clipped messages, uncertain that their words would get anywhere, knowing that everything they jotted down would be censored.

Zippi wrote a coded message to Sam, using his pet name, Schani.

Dear Schani,

I am writing a few lines to you today because it is not possible that we will come to see you this time. We are all in good health here at home. The children enjoy going to school and I am working. If you feel like it and it is possible for you, please send a few lines. Do you need anything? Maybe shoes or a suit to trade? I hope we will see each other again in a few days. Feel kissed by our parents and the children.

Your sister Honka

Zippi knew that when Sam read the words "our parents," he'd know that she was not well—that in fact, something was very wrong. This was her warning to him: avoid transports—they are a trap.

On a Saturday morning, the guards shouted commands: *Head outside! Line up in rows of five! March to the railroad station!*

By then, they'd been in Patrónka for almost a week.

Zippi and Katya remained together as 798 women (a few hundred short of the original 1,000—some had likely fled) stumbled inside cattle cars. Anywhere between forty and eighty women squeezed inside each boxlike car. Some sat, others stood. The wooden doors slammed behind them. Zippi sat in the dark in the windowless compartment, grateful for the thin slivers of light that seeped in from a crack in the roof.

She thought of summers she'd set out to camp with friends from her youth group. Back when they'd gone on adventures throughout the country, slept underneath the stars, traveled in trains and buses, hiked mountains. Now they passed around buckets and crouched to relieve themselves. The cattle car reeked of urine and feces.

Zippi climbed on a girl's shoulders and tried to see railroad signs from an opening in the roof of the cattle car. When the names began to look foreign, they realized they were near Poland. In the faint light of dawn a girl caught a glimpse of bearded Jews with black top hats, sleeves with yellow stars. These men appeared to walk freely. This was a good sign, the women thought.

One woman distributed postcards and a pen she'd somehow smuggled out with her. A few girls wrote the truth of what they'd seen. They slipped the cards out through a slat on the cattle car. As the train moved, cards fluttered into the snow and disappeared. Perhaps a card or two would find its way to their families. Most likely, the postcards would become soggy scraps, ink smudged beneath sheets of snow.

The train rumbled on, while haze and rain kept pace. Inside the cattle car, it was sweltering. It was becoming hard to breathe.

On Saturday, March 28, 1942, one day after they'd left Patrónka, the train finally slowed to a crawl. Zippi heard voices outside. Some could see out through the strips of wood. The sign at the train station read OŚWIĘCIM.

Bangs and squeals erupted as the train came to a halt. The women in Zippi's car could hear the doors to the other cars roar open. At first, she saw nothing but the women in the compartments ahead of them being pushed outside. She listened to barking dogs and gruff, muffled German voices.

From between the slats of her overcrowded train car, Zippi negotiated a better look. The train had arrived on a frigid afternoon, the day already dark and gusty by five o'clock, the landscape veiled in fog. From watchtowers, the Gestapo had a clear view of the new arrivals, along with all the movement inside the camp. Zippi could not see this, but she did catch a glimpse of half-finished stone buildings surrounded by barbed wire. Through the cracks Zippi strained to make out figures dressed in stripes. They looked like skeletons — except they were walking.

Then the door to Zippi's own compartment slid open, revealing an alien world.

CHAPTER SIX

"You Go"

For months, Eliahu had been going to his job at the airfield three times each week without interruption. So it was unusual when, one particular summer morning in 1941, he told David that he was so unwell that he could not report for work. He needed someone to cover for him.

You want to go out today? Eliahu asked David. Perhaps he had an inkling of what was to come, or perhaps this was a moment of pure coincidence. David would never know.

You go and report to the truck, his father said. And that is what David did.

David hadn't stepped outside the ghetto walls since they'd been erected. Everyone knew that an attempt to escape was punishable by death. If his brother Moshe were alive, it would be a miracle. David was eager to see what the world looked like outside his quarters, to see whether there was anything left of the Warsaw that he remembered.

He walked the three blocks from his home over to Grzybowska Street, by the Jewish Community Center. Scrawny children sat on the pavement, toes poking out of tattered shoes, matchstick legs stretching on the dirty ground. Men crowded around a vendor's cart, thumbing through the pages of old Hebrew books. From a distance, a song crackled from a gramophone that a man wheeled on an old baby carriage as he begged for money. The streets were as busy as ever, a cacophony of music, wailing, and gunshots. David didn't stray. Anyone could be stopped by German and Polish guards at random. Anything could happen.

David joined dozens of others waiting for the truck. When it arrived, he climbed onto the wide wooden bed of the open-wheeled truck. Other workers who'd been picked up before, also destined for the airport, made room.

They rode out through the ghetto gates, bouncing at each bump. The pungent smell — of feces and urine, of disease, odors that had penetrated every pore of his body and every fiber of his clothing for months — dissolved. The air here was relatively fresh. The street corners weren't heaped with trash. This world seemed foreign: a distant memory, a dream.

Some of the airport had been destroyed during the siege of 1939 and the remainder had been converted into an air base and a rest point for troops. Upon arrival, David swept the barracks and stacked boxes and barrels that were filled with war supplies. Everything was neat, down to the tidy beds in the barracks. David thought about the bed he once had, before he'd been relegated to the floor with his family. At least they could still share in each other's warmth.

David worked in silence. For lunch, each worker got a slice of bread. They spoke to each other quietly, comparing notes on how they'd managed to survive. When they were sure no guard could hear them, they fantasized about escaping the ghetto. A few months ago, all that David had wanted was a life in America. Now he would make do with life outside those walls.

Finally the guards decided to call it a day. The same open truck they'd arrived in was waiting to take them back. Within moments they would bounce their way into the ghetto, and the stench of their reality would return.

The ride back home was brief. At the entrance to the ghetto a sign read, EPIDEMIC QUARANTINE AREA: ONLY THROUGH TRAFFIC IS PERMITTED. They drove in, the streetside mounds of garbage welcoming them home. Now David knew how his father spent his days.

As the truck rolled through the gates, nothing seemed out of the ordinary.

Then a guard approached. He gestured. Something was wrong.

The truck swerved, turned around, and stopped. Perhaps this was normal, this abrupt change of direction. It was David's first time on the job; he couldn't know for sure. He jumped off and headed toward his street, through the habitual chaos.

But David's street was cordoned off. He took a better look. A small section of the ghetto appeared to have been sealed. The Jewish police, which had been organized by the Nazis to help keep order in the ghetto, said there'd been some shootings. This wasn't surprising. David tried to get closer. He wanted to see which house had been targeted.

He snuck toward his building's courtyard. SS guards waved their machine guns at him. A warning: stay away. David pivoted. He had to find his family.

David knew these alleyways better than most. He snuck around to the back of the building and walked quickly toward the courtyard.

Then he saw a pile a few feet away from him — and he couldn't look away.

A stack. A stack of corpses. A heap of human bodies. Like fresh cut wood, ready to build a fire, except these were humans whose chests had once heaved up and down. The breath in them was gone.

David stared.

He was close enough to see the shape of his mother. A flap of her brown coat. Then, stiff, sticking out: his father's hand. He knew his father's hand. How could he not? Then he saw his little brother, Dov. And his grandfather.

David flung himself onto the pile.

★　　★　　★

How long did he lie there? Seconds? Minutes? He couldn't remember. No one stopped him or said a word. Did he even fall onto the pile at all? Could it have been a hallucination?

Somehow, David pulled himself together. He didn't have the luxury of time.

He had to get out of there. Despite it all, David wanted to live.

He ran to the end of the street. He couldn't risk going inside their apartment. He took nothing with him; no mementos could offset the awful memories of what he'd just seen.

David ripped off the armband he'd been wearing like a badge of honor for so long. He tossed it behind him and ran. While most of the ghetto was surrounded by tall brick walls, David knew of a small portion cordoned off with barbed wire. He climbed through.

David was fifteen years old, and he was on his own.

The world around David had ruptured. Outside of the ghetto, the landscape had been ravaged by war, just as in the ghetto. It was the summer of 1941 and Warsaw had hardly recovered from the siege of 1939. Railroads and bridges came to abrupt ends, blown up into crevices inside the scorched earth. Across Poland, the Nazis had been working to "germanize" as much of the country as they could. Those in the resistance aimed to make the Nazis' reach as difficult as possible.

David went to a station and waited. Some trolleys were still running. He tried to look normal, even though he didn't know what normal was anymore. He checked his clothes. He had no blood on him: The massacre must have happened earlier in the day. His parents' blood had dried up under the summer sun by the time he threw himself on top of them.

When the trolley arrived, he climbed on. He would go to Praga, a Warsaw district where his friend Wanda waitressed. The ride took twenty minutes. He saw Wanda through the restaurant window and tapped on the glass. They met in the small garden outside the restaurant.

How did David explain to his friend what he had just seen? How could anyone convey that mere hours before, their family had been alive and they'd all been together, and now they were gone?

I have to get out of here, he said. *Can you help me? I want to go to Sochaczew.*

His childhood home was the first place that came to David's mind. It had been safe, once. He'd known his neighbors. At the very least, it would surely be a more predictable environment than the madness of Warsaw. But he would need Wanda—a blond-haired, blue-eyed Christian Pole—to buy him a train ticket. Plus, he didn't want to be alone.

I'll take you to the train station, Wanda said.

He waited outside at the garden until she finished her shift.

He tried to look inconspicuous. He tried not to fall apart.

By the time she was done it was dusk. They took a trolley to the train station. On the platform, she reached for his hand and squeezed it as they walked through a crowd.

Let me buy the ticket, she told David as she went to the sales window.

He waited while she made the purchase, then let her lead him down to the tracks. Wanda hugged him, wishing him luck, tears streaming down her cheeks. David tried to remain stoic. He couldn't lose his composure; not here, not now.

The ride to Sochaczew lasted about an hour. Outside the windows, fields were cratered by bombs, farmhouse windows shattered by bullets.

When the train halted, passengers scattered out to their horse-drawn carriages. By instinct, David walked toward his old home, his eyes adjusting to the pitch-black night. But it had been four years since David moved away from Sochaczew, and the town had changed. Especially in one crucial way: David had forgotten that, months earlier, the Jews of Sochaczew had been sent off to the Warsaw Ghetto.

His once-familiar town had been the battleground of one of the bloodiest fights of the Polish resistance against the Germans, the Battle of the Bzura River. By mid-September of 1940, most surviving Poles had fled. Just as in Warsaw, the Germans had marched into town, confiscated Jewish businesses, shut down Jewish schools, forced the Jews to wear armbands, and herded them into the Sochaczew ghetto, which was created alongside the Bzura River in January 1941. David's old friend and singing partner, Sara, along with her sisters, had been instructed to pack only what they could carry to resettle in the ghetto. But within a month, the Nazis had decided to make the town *Judenrein*—free of Jews. Once more, Jews had to pack whatever they could carry with them, this time relocating to the Warsaw Ghetto by way of a daylong horse-and-buggy ride.

By the summer of 1941, when David arrived in Sochaczew, the Nazis had succeeded in their mission: no Jews were left. Not much of the town was left, either. The house that his father and grandfather had built decades earlier was now just a charred skeleton. Most of his neighbors' homes were ashes.

The only doors he could knock on, David realized, belonged to Christian friends who hadn't fled. But he had no choice: he knocked.

Get out of here, an old neighbor bristled, panicking at the sight of David.

There are some Germans over here, another whispered. *I can't do anything for you.*

He found the home of the woman who'd once ironed his family's clothes.

Mrs. Smigielska, it's David, he said. *I escaped from Warsaw. Please let me in.*

Davidek, she said, using his nickname. *I'm scared. Please find somewhere else, because there are Germans living here.*

The fourth door he knocked on was close to a soccer field where he'd once played. The house belonged to the family of a former soccer buddy. His friend's mother asked David where his family was.

Come, she said then. *You'll eat something.* Before he could make himself comfortable, she told David that Germans lived in the building.

Look, she said. *I can't keep you here, because if they catch you, they'll kill us, too.*

David finished his food and she showed him out. Before he left, she advised David to find a man who had once worked for his grandfather. The man, a Christian, lived around the corner, she said; he would probably help him.

It was one o'clock in the morning, and the night's silence was absolute. David rushed to the man's home and knocked on the door. He was running out of options. The old man lived alone; maybe he'd be too scared to answer. Or he wouldn't hear his knock.

Within moments, the door swung open. The man's eyes widened as he recognized David. He quickly ushered him in. Again, David explained what happened: his parents, his younger brother, all dead. The pile of corpses was still fresh in his mind, the image so clear he could practically touch it. As far as he knew, his brother Moshe was dead, too. Had it really been less than twenty-four hours?

His grandfather's former employee watched David struggle through these memories — just a young, skinny boy, alone in the world. As David spoke, the man wept.

They had to be practical. The man gave David his bed — a wooden shelf with a straw mattress on top. That night the man would take the floor.

Get a good night's sleep, he urged David.

There was nothing left for David in Sochaczew. In the morning they would cross the bridge that spanned the Bzura River. The man would help David toward the border to Czerwińsk nad Wisłą, a small village twenty miles to the north, where there was a Jewish ghetto just a fraction of the size of Warsaw's.

I know you have a cousin there, Fayge Leah, the man said. *You go to the ghetto and at least you'll be able to live with family.*

In the morning, the man put a large hat on David's head and they walked together, pretending to be father and son, all the way to the Polish–German border.

You'll have to cross by yourself, the man said.

He hugged David and kissed him, weeping. This time, David didn't hold back his tears.

Czerwińsk was even smaller than Sochaczew, a tiny shtetl made up of a handful of cobblestone and dirt roads. The ghetto, surrounded by a wooden fence near a Catholic cemetery, took up the majority of the town. Before long, David found Fayge Leah, his mother's cousin, sharing tight, decrepit quarters with her two children and her father.

David arrived with a tragic story that was becoming all too familiar. His cousin and her family embraced the boy and told him that they wanted to take him in, but there was a problem: David had no identification card. He could not get food or rations, and already they were going hungry. His sudden appearance meant another mouth to feed.

He stayed with them for a couple of days, but the arrangement was unsustainable. Fayge Leah appealed to the *Judenrat,* the Jewish Council, to help David get a ration card. But no help came, and David quickly realized that they each had to fend for themselves.

David had no professional training and few useful skills. He was a kid; a gifted student, yes, but the last thing the camp needed was another academic type. They needed laborers. Most able-bodied Jews were already working for the occupiers, clearing the roads of trash and repairing the streets. Others worked the fields. At night, prisoners were rounded up and sent to labor camps. The Nazis would not hand out rations to those who served no purpose to them.

The one thing David could do well, he thought, was sing. That had to count for something. So each morning, he woke up from his corner on the floor, took to the streets of the Czerwińsk ghetto, and sang in English, in Yiddish, and in German. He performed for the police, for families that walked by and for whomever would listen. In exchange, he gathered scraps of food. All the while, familiar faces disappeared at random and new ones multiplied in their place. Jews from neighboring towns arrived in droves.

A typhus epidemic was inevitable as the already tight space became overcrowded. The Gestapo decided to transfer all survivors to a ghetto at Nowy Dwór Mazowiecki, a slightly larger city by the Vistula River. And so, in October 1942, David and some 2,600 Jews crowded into wagons to Nowy Dwór, roughly a hundred and fifty miles to the south of Czerwińsk and only twenty-five miles away from Warsaw. They found themselves in yet another overrun space where five or six families shared a single room. The typhus outbreak followed them.

Within weeks, the Gestapo had surrounded the ghetto. In November they ordered the elderly, those who were ill, and those unable to work to assemble in the town square. David's great uncle went on that first transport. The next transport, two weeks later, included families with more than two children, widows, and orphans. Fayge Leah asked David to join her and her family. She'd been a widow for a long time and hoped that David would help take care of them. David considered it: he had no family left. But he decided to wait.

On Saturday, December 12, at seven in the morning, the SS arrived, brandishing rifles and handguns and spraying bullets into the air. All remaining ghetto residents were ordered to go to the central square.

David joined a row of five. With some fifteen hundred others, he was corralled into sealed cattle cars.

He sat on the floor, unable to move in the crush of bodies. They traveled with no food, no water. When they had to relieve themselves, they shared a bucket. Using it required previously unthinkable contortions.

David hadn't had a sip of water in at least two days. He had seen so many ways in which one might die, and here was another.

But if he didn't die, would that be worse?

Back when David had lived in the Warsaw Ghetto, he'd heard of a man who'd managed to escape from a concentration camp in Treblinka. The man had told tales that seemed like nightmarish hallucinations, stories that simply couldn't be real. He'd spoken of a place where humans electrocuted and tortured each other, where the chaos of the ghetto was replaced with something worse: a vast system in which human lives were worth less than those of animals. A place of misery and death.

These stories sounded fantastical, unimaginable—impossible, really.

David heard that the man had been committed to an insane asylum inside the ghetto. Because, well, how could anyone believe him?

*L*ater, when they were encircled by fire, the boy and the girl would imagine themselves in a living hell.

The girl would wonder about love and hate. Could the two exist side by side? Can beauty still exist in an inferno?

She would wonder about self-sacrifice, too, and how it could coexist with the need to survive.

Just how much of themselves were they willing to sacrifice for love?

PART II

ARIA

CHAPTER SEVEN

An Ordinary Affair

As daylight spilled into the cattle car, Zippi and the women around her jostled for room. For days their bodies had been squeezed together, knees bent, joints stiff, bottoms sore. The year was 1942. But was it still March? They couldn't be sure. In fact, only one night and one day had gone by since they'd left Patrónka. It was after five o'clock and the sun was just beginning to set.

A voice from outside commanded them to *get up!* and *get in line!*—*Los, los heraus und einreihen!*

Germans dressed in dark-green uniforms, half-calf jackboots, and tunics had replaced the Hlinka guardsmen. Zippi's eyes fell on the *Totenkopf,* a metal insignia of a skull that topped the Nazis' visor caps: these were SS officers. It was the first time she'd ever encountered the SS. They chased the women out of the railway cars using batons, the heels of their boots, and hungry German shepherds. The women had to move fast. Faster than fast.

Sleep-deprived and hungry, Zippi and her travel mates stumbled into an open field just beyond the railway station. They walked through muddy roads, trying to follow a constant chorus of orders: *Line up in rows of five! March! Fast! Faster!*

As they marched across town, unnerved and hyperalert, Zippi saw what looked to be corpses lifting massive stones. Soon, she'd learn that they were building her new home—and that these corpses were the camp's inmates. Soon she'd be among them, a silhouette of the living, hauling stones.

Mud sucked at her boots; spring's thaw was setting in. Lombardy poplar trees were scattered at random, their leaves dried out, twigs like arthritic fingers pointing to the darkening sky.

They marched toward a massive steel gate. A Gothic-lettered sign inscribed with tall letters gave her pause: ARBEIT MACHT FREI— work will set you free.

Barbed wire sprouted from the gates, prickly shrubs of metal. The women entered the encircled field.

Zippi glanced to her left, looking for a sign to ground her. Her eyes focused on a small white placard. In thick black print on an eight-by-eleven piece of paper, it read: *Konzentrationslager*— concentration camp.

At last, she understood. This was not a labor camp. She'd arrived at one of the Nazis' concentration camps. The fantasy that this would be a brief stint of field work evaporated. This, Zippi realized, was something much more sinister.

Before Oświęcim became the notorious Auschwitz, it had been an unremarkable city in the backwoods of Poland. Its moist climate created a perpetual fog, skies cloaked in a near-year-round mist.

Oświęcim had a history of floods and fires. In the space of three centuries, the Oświęcim Castle, a medieval castle on a hill, burned down at least three times, usually as a casualty of whatever war was ravaging the region. The surviving residents rebuilt their city from its ashes time after time, but the fortifications around the Gothic castle were eventually abandoned.

When the Nazis occupied Poland in 1939 and made their way to Oświęcim, they rechristened it with its German name, Auschwitz.

Upon arrival, they made plans to depopulate the area of its twelve thousand Polish residents to make room for SS officers. Best known for being a central railway hub that connected Silesia, Czechoslovakia, and Austria, Auschwitz was also the former setting of Polish artillery barracks near the intersection of the Soła and Vistula rivers. The combination of Auschwitz's robust transportation facilities and its isolated barracks made it especially enticing for the Nazis, who had in mind an entirely new purpose for the timeworn town.

The Nazis first used the area as a transit camp for arrested Poles, who were shipped off elsewhere for slave labor. In 1940, Heinrich Himmler, the commander and highest-ranking member of the SS, selected the site for the Auschwitz concentration camp. At the same time, IG Farben, a distinguished German chemical conglomerate, had been eyeing Auschwitz as the home of a new plant for synthetic rubber and liquid fuels. The setting could be mutually beneficial: IG Farben would pay the SS for incoming prisoners' cheap labor.

Himmler appointed Rudolf Höss, a stocky family man who'd proven himself a loyal Nazi, as Auschwitz's commander. Raised in a devout Catholic household, Höss was taught from a young age to follow orders. When it came to family expectations, he did this selectively, but as a Nazi he obeyed commands with unwavering fanaticism and without question.

In 1934, Himmler asked Höss to join the SS. Höss couldn't resist. He became a drill instructor at Dachau, Germany's prototype for the system of concentration camps that would soon spring up throughout occupied Europe. From that point on, Höss focused his compulsive work ethic on whatever role the SS assigned him as he climbed its ranks. By the time he arrived in Oświęcim, Höss had learned the best practices of running concentration camps as an assistant officer at the Sachsenhausen concentration camp in Germany.

When he first came to Oświęcim, in April of 1940, Höss was disappointed with what he saw. The twenty brick barracks that made up the nerve center of the camp were dilapidated and filthy, teeming with vermin. Höss planned for a new delousing station, clothing deposits, showers, a canteen, and administrative offices. In a self-described obsessive haze, Höss set to work, creating the kind of concentration camp he could be proud of. He expected those around him to work with the same fervor.

Polish civilian laborers, from electricians to construction workers, strove to create a suitable space in which Polish prisoners could quarantine while in transit to German concentration camps. Höss also ordered an assortment of German political and common criminals to be transferred to Auschwitz and work under the SS. Various roles were devised for these prisoner functionaries. Some would supervise future inmates as *Kapos*; others would be *Blockälteste*, block supervisors responsible for a given block. Still others would work in administrative positions higher up in the camp's hierarchy.

The first group of Polish inmates arrived in Auschwitz in June of 1940. These were mostly healthy young men, underground resistance organizers and fighters who'd been caught attempting to cross the border in southern Poland. They were greeted into the camp with beatings and torture, the beginning of a camp tradition. They went on to build new barracks—or "blocks"—and renovate existing ones.

Before long, the Polish civilian workers and the Polish prisoners had become friendly. The civilians, learning of the depraved beatings and horrid conditions the prisoners endured, snuck over food from home. Within a month of working together, they helped organize one prisoner's escape.

Tadeusz Wiejowski's plan was simple: all it took was civilian clothes, some money, an armband identifying him as a civilian worker, a ride out of Auschwitz in a cargo train—and the help of the workers.

The SS realized a man was missing during the camp's regular 6 p.m. roll call. Furious, they began a special roll call that lasted for twenty hours—from 6 p.m. on July 6 to 2 p.m. on July 7. Demanding a confession, SS guards beat, kicked, and flogged prisoners with dense wooden batons. They deprived them of water and food for days. At the end of the roll call, a Jewish man died of his injuries, becoming the first prisoner to perish in Auschwitz.

The SS spent months interrogating and torturing a group of workers they suspected of helping Wiejowski escape. At least eleven suspects were killed.

Then, more than a year after his escape, Wiejowski was discovered hiding out in his old hometown. He was arrested, thrown in prison, and shot. His body was left to rot inside an abandoned oil well.

The ordeal made it less likely for outsiders to help inmates flee. But it didn't stop prisoners from trying—or resisting in other ways.

Soon after Wiejowski's escape, Auschwitz prisoners were encouraged to send letters and postcards home to their families. In return, their families were allowed to send prisoners money to spend at the camp canteen. The arrangement was meant to prevent civilian workers from supplying inmates with contraband like food and tobacco. So prisoners dictated letters, sometimes using coded language to describe life at camp as best they could within their fifteen-line limit. This became another Auschwitz convention and part of its camouflage: prisoners could send and receive two letters a month—but only after they had passed through the camp's censorship administration.

Himmler visited Auschwitz in March of 1941, with the intention of impressing IG Farben officials with the land's potential. During this visit, he ordered an expansion to include a subcamp at the neighboring village of Birkenau, known as Brzezinka prior to German occupation. This new camp, which came to be known as

Auschwitz II–Birkenau, would hold more than a hundred thousand slaves—Russian prisoners of war—who would work for IG Farben. The original camp, known as Auschwitz I, was the main camp. Himmler also wanted to cultivate the surrounding area agriculturally and build facilities for armaments production.

During the summer of 1941, Himmler invited Höss to his Berlin office and shared, in confidence, that Auschwitz was to become the prime setting to carry out the Final Solution to the Jewish Question. The name was code for the elimination of all Jews. The plan was authorized by a group of fifteen Nazis during a ninety-minute meeting in a villa on the shores of Wannsee Lake in Berlin.

"The Jews are the eternal enemies of the German people and must be exterminated," Höss recalled Himmler saying to him. "All the Jews within our reach must be annihilated during this war." Auschwitz was to be the center for Jewish extermination and Höss had to make this happen immediately. The order had come from the Führer himself.

In addition to exterminating the Jews, Hitler also intended to wipe out communism and destroy the Soviet Union. Captured Soviet soldiers, having already endured hell as prisoners of war, became the first large group brought to Auschwitz. Birkenau, the new subcamp intended to house them, was still under construction, and the POWs were expected to build it with their bare hands, brick by brick, while living in rudimentary, unfinished barracks. The soldiers arrived emaciated in their tattered cotton uniforms, their only protection from the cold. They were put to work digging gravel pits, and if they didn't drop dead on their own, the SS beat them with shovels or shot them point blank. They were quickly dying off, and simultaneously Soviet POW transports stopped arriving, needed elsewhere to perform labor for Germany's war industry. When it was finally ready, Auschwitz II–Birkenau would have a new raison d'être.

In the months following his top-secret meeting with Himmler, Höss hustled to create the kind of killing machine that would fulfill the Reich's mission. Perhaps his most important assignment was to determine the most practical and cost-efficient method of mass murder. Nearly a million Jews had already been killed by the Einsatzgruppen, special Nazi forces tasked with executing mass shootings.

"Only gas was possible since killing by shooting the huge numbers expected would be absolutely impossible and would also be a tremendous strain on the SS soldiers who would have to carry out the order as far as the women and children were concerned," he would later write.

Cost and ease mattered to Höss, and showerheads seemed like the perfect instruments to deliver lethal gas. He also sought a suitable location — remote, hidden, and large enough to accommodate millions of buried bodies. Then came more questions of logistics: how to conduct arrests, where to house prisoners, how to transport them, and how to create a daily schedule.

Until March of 1941, only about 10,900 prisoners at a time could be held in the camp. If they were to reach the kind of scale required to solve the Jewish Question, various crematoria and mass graves had to be constructed — and the prisoners themselves would be the ones to build them.

By the fall of 1941, a constant stream of prisoner transports was arriving in Auschwitz as the SS tinkered with murder methods. The September before Zippi arrived, they experimented with Zyklon B gas, whose primary purpose was pest control — and which was produced by IG Farben, the same company whose synthetic-fuel factory would be powered by the enslaved labor of Auschwitz's inmates. The gas, which came in crystal form, was used initially to fumigate Polish barracks and prisoners' clothing. Inmates who operated the delousing facilities would run inside wearing nothing but a gas mask—to avoid getting lice on their clothes—and toss the crystals on the floor, then run out and latch the door shut. They'd return twenty-four hours later, again donning gas masks, to find layers of dead lice. They'd then ventilate the room for two hours.

Now the SS tried using this same chemical to kill Soviet prisoners of war. The results, Höss thought, were promising, although it took two days to clear the fumes out of the cellar of Block 11, where they conducted the first trial. He needed a more efficient system to keep up with the sheer volume of prisoners overcrowding the camp.

Birkenau was still under construction when, on March 20, 1942, it became the site of the camp's first official gas chamber. A former Polish farmhouse dubbed the Little Red House, or Bunker I, was fitted with airtight doors and walled-up windows and put into operation. The converted two-room cottage fit about eight hundred people. The SS would see to it that both rooms were filled to capacity before shutting the airtight doors and leaving the prisoners to die.

Just a few days later, the first group of twenty thousand Jews was slated to arrive in Auschwitz. The few surviving Soviet POWs were ordered to evacuate. On its completion, Birkenau would become the women's quarters. The men's quarters would be separated from the women's by an electrified fence. There was much to organize; at least seven thousand Slovakian women were expected within mere weeks, and the SS had to mobilize female guards to supervise the new arrivals.

Within days, Himmler selected a handful of SS officers who ran the exclusively female Ravensbrück concentration camp, set in an otherwise idyllic lakeside village just about an hour outside of Berlin. SS matron Johanna Langefeld had been running a smooth operation there, overseeing five thousand prisoners; she would take charge of the women's camp in Auschwitz, with the support of a cadre of SS guards—and 999 female inmates would be transferred from Ravensbrück. Most of the inmates from Ravensbrück would serve as *Kapos*, who enjoyed a variety of privileges in exchange for supervising the Jewish prisoners. The Ravensbrück *Kapos*, mostly Germans who opposed Hitler or were considered "asocials"— Romani, sex workers, lesbians, and criminals—were selected for exhibiting levels of "toughness, vileness, and depravity" far surpassing their male counterparts, according to Höss.

Plucked from the slave labor camp where they'd been tormented and tortured, the Ravensbrück prisoners now suffered the same terror in a less picturesque setting. But now they would wield power. They would have carte blanche to keep order however they saw fit. Many would be named *Blockälteste,* or block supervisors, expected to maintain order and discipline in their designated barracks.

On March 26, 1942, the same day these inmates arrived from Ravensbrück, the first trainload of Jewish women from Slovakia pulled into the station at Auschwitz. While Zippi waited in limbo with Katya at the abandoned factory in Patrónka, another trainload carrying 999 Slovakian Jewish women was waiting, about three hundred kilometers to the east. They would be known as transport no. 1.

Zippi and the other women from Patrónka arrived two days later.

The commands continued: *Strip everything off!* The women from Ravensbrück were waiting to clean the new arrivals.

Inmates who tried to cover up their private parts quickly learned their efforts were futile. Ravensbrück's roughest recruits probed inside selected women's genitals and anuses in search of hidden jewelry, an echo of their brutal welcome to Patrónka. The blast of a hose filled with disinfectant pierced every inch of their bodies. Next was their hair. Dull scissors and shearing machines carved off every strand on Zippi's skull. Blood seeped from their scalps in a warm trickle, down their foreheads and onto their cheeks, like tears. Eyebrows and pubic hair were next. The inmates stood on chairs so every inch of their body could be shaved. Then fingernails, toenails, all clipped to the quick. Cold air electrified each wound, each gash.

They were no longer human; they were cattle, being sterilized for slaughter. SS officers inspected this fresh new shipment, commanding them to spin in place, tops in the buff. They spun; they shivered.

A decade earlier, Zippi had been sunbathing in the Danube. She'd been camping, studying her craft, building a life. Now, she was forced inside a bin of grimy ice-cold water for a bath.

The women waited outside, still in the nude. Their clothing was disinfected, then stockpiled; it would never be returned. They gaped at each other, these bald, unrecognizable bulging-eyed creatures. *Who are these lunatics?* some thought, eyes darting—not realizing that they, too, looked the part.

An SS guard walked down the row of naked women and girls. He laughed. They'd arrived so elegant, so well dressed. They weren't so pretty anymore.

The women's fine clothing and jewelry were replaced with the remains of Russian POW uniforms, cotton scraps, shrunken from the disinfection process. Some of these rags were caked with the blood of their former owners. Some were perforated with bullet holes.

Ill-fitting, mismatched pairs of wooden clogs snapped to the ground when they walked. A lucky few, inexplicably, got to keep their own shoes. Zippi was among them. She supposed her feet were so small that her climbing boots wouldn't fit any of the SS officers. A small victory, but a victory nonetheless.

Each inmate got a piece of bread, and they were sent to brick barracks, single-room dormitories crowded to the brim. The women, in shock, were to lie on a layer of old straw left behind by the Soviet POWs, and try to sleep.

Jewish women who survived the selection process are marched toward their barracks after processing.

It was still dark outside when the whistles and yelling began.

Appell! Appell! Roll call.

As the women stirred, Zippi wondered if the SS were trying to make soldiers out of them. What else would roll call be used for? *Kapos* roused the women and chased them out of the block and into the yard. Zippi's eyes were still adjusting to the dark as the wind whistled. SS officers smacked the women with sticks, shoving them into rows of five.

The disorganization and disorder, and the utter ineptitude of the people who were supposed to be in charge, astonished Zippi. Indeed, Johanna Langefeld, the longtime SS member who'd been handpicked from Ravensbrück to head up the new women's camp, had never dealt with so many inmates before; she was out of her depth. *These people have no clue how to keep order among such a huge group,* Zippi thought with disdain. They were barely literate, as far as she could tell, and had no system for keeping track of their prisoners.

Inmates scurried into rows, trying to find solace among those they recognized. *Kapos* kicked and punched. German shepherds growled. Guards yelled for the women to stay still. *Keep in place!* Some women collapsed to the ground; others twirled on the spot, trying to keep their muscles active, to stay warm.

All the while, Zippi despaired at the Nazis' incompetence. The women were counted by row, but the rows kept shifting and the interminable process took at least four cold hours, thanks to Langefeld and her subordinates' blundering.

The torturous roll call would become a camp linchpin, observed before and after work and on Sunday afternoons. The process inevitably took hours to complete. The arrival of newcomers only made it worse. Those who wouldn't stand still made it more painful, and those who insisted on shuffling toward someone they knew made it impossible. As the temperature dropped, women grew numb to frostbitten toes and fingers. These would be the metrics that marked Zippi's time in Auschwitz.

Two days after her arrival in Auschwitz, Zippi's transformation was complete. Her birth name, Helen Zipora Spitzer, was struck from the record, forgotten, discarded. She was now Prisoner 2286. She sewed a piece of fabric with her number onto her sleeve. Along with her number, Zippi received a tin: her food bowl. Lost tins would not be replaced.

Weeks later, a double needle and India ink would officially brand Zippi as Prisoner 2286. The number, etched in her consciousness, was now carved on her body, visible on the pale patch of skin on her forearm just below her left elbow. It was a perpetual reminder of the person she was becoming—and the person that she'd lost.

Zippi's new home was the top floor of Block 9 in Auschwitz I, a brick living space with little insulation. Like the other blocks, it had two levels that were divided into smaller units. Usually more than twelve hundred inmates shared the twenty-two toilets on the ground floor. Zippi estimated that between four hundred and six hundred women shared her living space.

They'd been upgraded from their initial beds of hay to bunks. On average, four women shared a twin-size mattress measuring about 78 by 31 inches, although sometimes eight women had to squeeze in together. Each night, they negotiated positions like a puzzle board: sideways, head to foot, stretching and crouching. Bunks were stacked in threes. Zippi opted for the top bunk, where she'd have a sliver of air, she figured. The space between the bunk and the ceiling was less claustrophobic than being trapped in a middle bunk or at the bottom.

The ten blocks that made up the women's camp were in worse condition than the rest of the camp. The population was in a frantic state of flux; whenever chaos seemed total, another group of women would arrive.

More than once, Zippi drank contaminated water, suffered from diarrhea, became overwhelmed with thirst, and, unable to help herself, drank more infected water. The cycle perpetuated itself.

Hundreds of desperate women clawed over one other to relieve themselves in one of the few latrines available. Zippi gritted her teeth through what she came to think of as the "ugly business."

Sometimes space was so tight that they couldn't help but relieve themselves on the ground where they stood, soiling their uniforms and underpants, which were not replaced. During storms, they collected rainwater inside their tins to wash their underpants. Barracks reeked of urine and excrement. Lice and bedbugs made themselves at home on the women's skin. Parched prisoners sucked on their own frozen urine, a practice that inevitably led to more acute dehydration and sometimes kidney damage.

A rusty barrel filled with murky liquid materialized each

morning. Breakfast. Zippi couldn't quite decide whether it was supposed to be tea or coffee. She used it to wash herself. In place of a toothbrush and paste, she used it on scraps of clothes, rubbing it over her teeth. It would have to do.

Disease and rumors spread at an almost equal pace. Prisoners of war had slept on the very spot they now occupied, voices whispered at night. They'd been gassed to death at Birkenau, the new camp that was under construction practically next door to Auschwitz I. The women pointed to the evidence: the POW's clothing, stamped with their numbers, was now replaced by the women's fresh new numbers. The dead men's uniforms draped over them like an omen.

The parched women, desperate with hunger, eyed the stingy pour of tea or coffee-like substance in their tin bowls with suspicion. Who knew what it might be laced with? Anything could be tainted. Maybe the foul-smelling soup they got for dinner was spiked with bromide to stop their menstrual cycles.

One night, Zippi went to the old-timers for information, daring to approach the Ravensbrück *Kapo*s. Her fluent German got their attention. *What do you know about this place, Auschwitz?* she asked. Many were willing to talk. Some opened up to Zippi about their past in Ravensbrück. It was a vacation compared to Auschwitz, they said.

Zippi didn't discriminate among her sources. She approached political prisoners, Jehovah's Witnesses, and the "asocial" women. She'd learned to be curious as a child; she'd branched out beyond the Slovakian Jewish community, worked with Germans, befriended both Jews and gentiles. She wasn't fazed by cultural differences; on the contrary, she spoke with whomever she could. Connections, she was coming to realize, were currency.

Most women chose to unite by common tongue and common culture, but the women from Ravensbrück were different, thought Zippi. They sought companionship with other women, even striking romantic relationships with each other and courting Jewish girls.

Zippi understood the desire to couple up. Her fiancé was imprisoned somewhere in Germany. The dream of being married, of sharing a life, was dissolving. It didn't help to think about Tibor. She turned her focus to collecting new friends.

After roll call each morning, the women marched off to different *Kommando*s, or workforce units. Zippi felt part of a hunt. Guards grabbed them at random and assigned different jobs: five hundred women here, six hundred there. In the evening, *Kommando* leaders picked the women they liked best to join them again the next day.

The best jobs were indoors, never in the field, where one might freeze or get heat stroke. The lucky ones got jobs in the kitchen, sorting and mending uniforms, or cleaning up filthy barracks using the stumps of their fingernails. Some became secretaries to the SS, organizing stacks of paperwork, typing up death certificates, and handling other administrative tasks. The few who'd trained as doctors or nurses were forced into the infirmary, where most patients went to die.

But outdoor work was the real killer. Since the camp's early days, Himmler had envisioned transforming the area surrounding Auschwitz into an agricultural estate—even if it sat in a swamp region that was constantly flooding. Much of the women's jobs involved digging drainage canals in the dense earth. Each day, the swamp detail became drenched in dirty water. They dried off in the wind. In other *Kommando*s, women used their bare fingers to clean muddied bricks that had been knocked down from buildings during air raids back when the Germans had taken over the town. These bricks were recycled to build new barracks. A handful of women carried stones back and forth, for a guard's amusement. Others were assigned to work with steamrollers, heavy contraptions filled with sand that the inmates used to flatten out Auschwitz's roads of dried, rutted mud. The majority of women who worked outside didn't live beyond a month or two.

Women who worked at the orchard managed to smuggle back trophies, perhaps a tomato, in their underpants. Himmler's desire to create an agricultural territory using slave labor eventually paid off: a chicken farm was established, and fisheries, and orchards cultivating flowers and vegetables. Anyone caught bringing food back to their barracks was flogged, then killed. Although all were facing starvation, the bounty was usually intended for the sick.

The construction *Kommando* was among the worst. While these workers received a special serving of sausage and margarine, only those who gave up their ration to their supervisor got shovels; those without shovels dug with their bare hands. Rocks and heavy equipment could fall on the women without warning. Casualties were not unusual. The prisoners who'd caught Zippi's eye as she'd first entered the camp were part of a construction *Kommando*. Bone-thin and bald, they were Russian POWs charged with building the women's camp, stone by stone — apparitions of the future for many unfortunate women in Zippi's transport.

After a few weeks, Zippi, who by then had experienced a variety of *Kommando*s, volunteered to join the ranks of the wrecking *Kommando*. Here, the women broke up bombed houses that had once belonged to the local Polish population. Each day, debris dropped on a few of these workers, and the ones who couldn't make it back to the barracks on their own were left to die. Zippi wanted to see for herself why so many of the women who left to work for that *Kommando* never returned to their barracks. Once again, it was clear that disorganization and chaos were at the root of the problem. Zippi was certain she could improve the women's situation and save them from SS brutality by increasing the women's productivity.

When Zippi joined the wrecking *Kommando,* they were busily demolishing brick houses in Birkenau, finishing the job that the

Soviet POWs had started before their death. Birkenau would soon dwarf the main camp in size—and terror.

Using a battering ram, Zippi positioned herself in the front of the group, and together they pushed against a brick wall. As fragments of brick and stone crumbled to the ground, the workers jumped back. They learned to work in sync, to be efficient and move fast. The SS officers were pleased; fewer women died.

But the job was not meant to be sustainable. Zippi was lucky to survive more than a couple of months. She had volunteered her way in; now, she'd have to find her way out.

Katya Singer was outraged: she didn't belong here.

Katya had never considered herself Jewish. Her family had never been Orthodox and she'd hardly spent any time around Jews, she repeated to anyone who would listen. But Zippi was right: throwing a tantrum would only hurt her. So she kept quiet. Zippi had probably saved Katya's life in the old bullet factory in Patrónka, and they had been friends ever since. The two women were a sight: tiny Zippi squinting for clues as she scanned the scene, and tall, graceful Katya—still beautiful, even with her blond hair shorn.

Soon after arriving, Katya thought she recognized a man from her former life. Decked out in SS gear from his boots to his cap, he looked like one of her professors from the Olomouc business academy in Slovakia, where she'd studied bookkeeping. If she wasn't mistaken, he'd been her German teacher, and had seemed to like her. She decided she had nothing to lose. She walked over and addressed him in broken German.

He slapped her hard across the cheek. How dare she approach him?

Then, beneath her shaved head, with no eyebrows, he recognized Katya.

Aren't you Katarine? he asked. He inspected her pretty face, pale save for the red imprint of the palm of his hand.

She nodded.

The exchange was quick. Her former professor would soon disappear to the front, but before he did, he spoke with his fellow SS officers about Katya's bookkeeping training. The SS took a special interest in her, likely noting her Aryan looks. Her work experience helped; they desperately needed help creating order within the chaos of roll call, and although she was just twenty-two, Katya had a deep, authoritative voice and a knack for organization.

Probably, she was a godsend. Johanna Langefeld was struggling as the head matron of the women's camp. A stout brunette with a strong appreciation for order and discipline, Langefeld was a fervent Hitler supporter who had arrived from Ravensbrück at Himmler's personal request in March. But the *Kapos* she'd selected were undermining her, sneaking around with SS men, having affairs with male and female prisoners, and smuggling jewelry, extra clothing, and food for themselves. Some took special pleasure in rounding up and abusing prisoners. Margot Drechsel, the SS officer in charge of roll call, was notorious for smacking women with rubber-covered sticks. And still, the inefficient process took hours to complete. They could use someone like Katya.

Just as Zippi had suspected, the *Blockälteste* in charge of roll call was illiterate and was relieved to have the support. Before long, Katya was appointed a *Stubendienst,* a senior prisoner in charge of an upper floor of a block: from there, in almost no time, she was put in charge of half the block.

Katya asked Zippi to assist her with roll call and escape her horrid outdoor *Kommando.* Despite her situation, Zippi declined. She didn't want to be in charge of other inmates. She had no desire to scream and push people around. Zippi had seen *Kapos* in action and was afraid that this was what Katya was asking of her. Her situation was not that dire. Not yet.

Rudolf Höss had planned to pack a hundred and twenty-five thousand inmates into the new camp at Birkenau as soon as possible.

But by May of 1942, Auschwitz only held 14,624 prisoners and the second camp was hardly ready. They still had a lot of work to do.

Each day at the crack of dawn, Zippi and her *Kommando*—which, in addition to wrecking duty, also performed some construction work—marched nearly two miles from Auschwitz I to Auschwitz II–Birkenau. Guards with rifles and German shepherds followed along. Zippi and the other inmates trudged on their bare feet, their shoes dangling in their hands. Footwear was forbidden during the march to work. In addition to happily inflicting pain, the Nazis wanted to save money on the wooden clogs by using them as little as possible. Only when the prisoners began their work could they wear shoes.

Once in Birkenau, the women spent eleven hours toiling under extreme duress. With bare hands, they tore down abandoned houses and built barracks. German guards watched, often on horseback, with leather whips in hand.

Frustrated by the slow progress, Höss decided to hedge his bets, ordering 253 prefabricated wooden huts to be delivered to the camp. The huts, originally designed as horse stables, could be built in less than a day. But they wouldn't arrive for at least another three months—by then it would be summer of 1942. Meanwhile, the women continued their backbreaking work.

Bored guards found counterproductive ways to amuse themselves. They ordered inmates to climb to the top of bombed buildings and toss down bricks on each other. Some were injured. Still others died. The guards got a good laugh.

The dismal weather didn't help. In the springtime, snow thawed and wooden clogs became anchored in the mud of Birkenau's marshes. Rather than fish them out, the inmates kept working, lest they feel the burn of leather whips on their backs. Bare, callused feet became bloody, infected, frostbitten. Zippi didn't lose sight of how lucky she was to have her boots.

After a day's work, the women endured a mad dash to use the

bathroom. Some fell in the latrine hole and were stuck in the sewage. A few tumbled into ditches, dizzy with thirst and hunger, and disappeared. Their absence was registered only at roll call. Sirens sounded: the lost women, if found alive, would be disciplined.

Death became an ordinary affair. Inmates slogged to work in the mornings and didn't return to their bunk in the evenings. Gunshots no longer startled. The prisoners bolstered one another to hide signs of weakness, literally propping up the sick on their elbows during roll call and marches, trying to avoid the inevitable. The gas chambers were far from complete and already prisoners were dying by the thousands: of illness, of starvation, from gunshots and beatings.

Zippi had learned early in life that appearances mattered. Here they were paramount. To avoid death, she had to exhibit health; she had to look good, to the extent that was possible. When she could get her hands on margarine, she used it as face cream: with the worn pads of her thickened fingers, she massaged it on the thin skin below her eyes, on the quick line of her dulled lips, on the peach fuzz atop her head. She filed her fingernails with rough-edged stones. She discovered a broken comb and a cracked mirror and arranged her face the best she could. But for all her efforts, when a German *Kapo* called her *du hässlicher Jude*—"you ugly Jew"—she took the words to heart.

In so many ways, the camp was taking its toll.

One June day in 1942, just three months after arriving in Auschwitz, Zippi was demolishing a brick house. She heaved and hauled, pushed and pulled, and jumped back as bricks from a wall came crashing down. This was part of her method—only this time, as she stepped back, she slipped and fell.

Gravel rained from the sky. Then came the larger stones—and finally part of a chimney, which crashed directly onto her back as she cowered below.

The SS guard in charge saw it all happen. Zippi was a work-horse; he couldn't afford to lose her. He lifted her crumpled body in his arms and placed her on a stack of hay. Frantic, he searched his bag until he found two aspirins.

Zippi was in agony; still, she struggled to her feet, forcing the curve of her back upright, putting one foot in front of the other as the guard led her to the infirmary. The doctor, a Jewish inmate who was previously a medical student, smacked Zippi square across each cheek. This was her treatment. Zippi was sent back to her barracks.

Weeks later, all the inmates in the infirmary were gassed to death. Zippi was forever grateful that the doctor had slapped her and sent her away. But for now she only wanted a reprieve.

As Zippi left the infirmary, her back crushed, her face bruised, she knew she had to find indoor work. At roll call, guards assessed those who were too damaged to work, those who looked unhealthy, unusable—discardable. Zippi's injuries, visible and raw, did not bode well.

She'd declined a job with Katya; now she considered her other options. As she headed toward her barracks, the doctor's slaps still stinging, Zippi encountered Eva Weigl, a German political pris-oner she'd befriended. Eva worked for one of the camp's superior officers and had a hand in labor assignments.

Zippi told Eva everything. She would not march out to work again, and she didn't want to work for Katya and scream at people. She was a professional sign painter and wanted to use her skills.

This is my profession, Zippi told Eva. *Maybe you can help me.*

As it turned out, Eva's boyfriend had been a graphic designer; she knew the profession well. She would make Zippi *verfügbar*— available for an indoor position.

Stay home, Eva told Zippi. *Don't go out to work, and if the woman in charge of roll call asks why you're there, just say Eva asked me to stay home because she has some work for me.*

It was a risky proposition. If she were caught, it could be the end. But she was bone tired, her back in agony, her face a mess.

Zippi spent two days in her bunk, recuperating. Somehow she was spared punishment. She rested, regained some strength. She'd been granted a gift: her life.

On the third day, an officer approached her. He needed someone who could mix paint from dry material, he said. The order had come from the very top: Hans Aumeier, the deputy commander of the camp, Höss's right-hand man, had asked for Zippi.

Eva had come through. The SS were running out of Russian POW uniforms and had resorted to furnishing new inmates with civilian clothing. They planned to use paint to distinguish inmates from civilians, making escape less likely. Zippi was ordered to paint a thick red stripe on the back of every female prisoner's dress. The SS were firm about keeping men and women separate and wanted a woman with experience mixing dry paint and oil. It was the perfect job for Zippi.

Eva walked Zippi to the laundry room, where Aumeier was speaking with a group of newly arrived French women. The women, naked and distraught, asked Aumeier whether what they'd heard from other inmates about Auschwitz was true. Aumeier lied in French. *These women have no idea what they were getting into,* Zippi thought.

Aumeier turned to Zippi and asked what she needed to mix paint. Zippi gave him a list of brushes and drying agents and was dismissed.

The next day, a truckload of oil drums, paints, and brushes was delivered to the *Bekleidungskammer,* the women's clothing warehouse. Zippi mixed the paint and drew long stripes on the raggedy dresses that had accumulated in the warehouse. But she wasn't moving fast enough. Hordes of women arrived every day, needing the striped dresses immediately. Zippi moved to the Sauna facilities, where prisoners and clothing were disinfected, and where women got outfitted with their uniforms. The Nazis didn't have the time to wait for the stripes to dry on the dresses before the women could start working. Zippi would have to draw stripes on the dresses while the women were wearing them.

Incoming prisoners stepped up to Zippi at the receiving area. They'd been through their initiation, the indignities of disinfection. They'd given up their clothing for the ragged dresses once owned by other inmates. Now they turned their backs to Zippi. At first, she used a ruler to paint a perfect two-centimeter-thick line directly onto their clothes—from the crooks of their necks down to their legs. But her hands were steady; she didn't need the ruler for long. Once she'd painted a stripe on each prisoner, Zippi furnished them with a strip of clothing that bore their number, to be sewn onto their uniform.

Down the assembly line they went, the newly hairless creatures, stripped of their names, their backs branded blood red—a conveyer belt of numbers whose digits kept growing.

In June of 1942, just a few months after Zippi's arrival, hundreds of new prisoners were entering Auschwitz on a daily basis, with transports ranging from single prisoners to 1,004. Often men and women lurched off trains together; workhorses and expendables. Two gas chambers were now functional.

Juden raus schnell! All Jews out, fast! *Schneller! Schneller!* Faster! Faster!

Guards shouted commands, holding their dogs loosely on their leashes in one hand, and in the other gripping their weapons of choice: rifles or bayonets, canes or whips. They shoved and kicked the men, women, and children into position.

The Nazis needed inmates with strong bodies, who could perform hard labor. "Selections" were implemented as unsuspecting newcomers stumbled off the ramp at the railroad station. The selections winnowed those with potential from those who were expendable. A man in his fifties with soft hands and poor posture would likely end up on the left. A baby in her mother's arms would inevitably be yanked away, tossed at someone also headed in that direction. Those on the right side were led to Auschwitz. The ones sent to the left—the elderly, the sick, the handicapped, or pregnant women—were led to trucks. Often, these trucks bore the Red Cross insignia. They weren't told where the trucks were headed, but they could only hope to be reunited with their loved ones soon.

Zippi had survived Auschwitz for four months—enough time to make her a hardened veteran. From her front-row seat, she saw the naive eyes of the new inmates, still shining with misplaced hope, and the looks of grief that also shuffled through the registra-

New arrivals undergoing "selection" at the train platform in the center of the Auschwitz complex. The cattle cars that brought these prisoners—many of them Jews from modern-day Ukraine—are visible in the background.

A Jewish woman with three young children in tow and a baby in her arms makes her way to the gas chambers after selection.

tion area. On one occasion, she watched as a woman gripped the only photograph left of her dead children and wailed, begging an SS officer not to take it away from her. Zippi knew it was no use. She knew it was best to stay quiet, to survive hour by hour.

As Auschwitz's population grew, so did the need to conceal the camp's diabolical functions. The SS didn't want to cause panic among the prisoners or risk interference from the world. Inmates planted new trees while guards shouted orders. Lombardy poplars and birches lined the blocks. The poplars grew quickly, their branches tightly parallel to their trunks, making a good screen from any interlopers. The birches did well in the cold weather and where the soil was wet and acidic. The greenery would conceal the killing apparatus.

The camouflage worked. Outsiders didn't know what was happening within Auschwitz's fences. Most insiders weren't quite sure either. But they had their suspicions.

Thousands of Russian prisoners of war had disappeared. Zippi heard that there had been forty thousand prisoners lodged in the blocks when they'd first arrived. Now, thirty-two thousand remained. Just like that, eight thousand had vanished into the dark.

In the distance a little white house, surrounded by cherry trees, apple and pear trees — a second Polish farmhouse that had been converted into a gas chamber that summer, or Bunker II — began to operate.

Outsiders read the postcards that prisoners mailed back home, notes composed under the guards' gaze. Zippi wrote to Sam, back in his prison cell in Bratislava, at every opportunity; she heard back from him in spurts. Tibor, too, remained alive, as far as she knew, but he could have been anywhere. Perhaps he was in a labor camp, or in a prison like the one Sam was in, biding his time with other political prisoners. Possibly he'd been beaten and tortured. Or might he have escaped? It was no use to wonder. She focused on keeping the red lines straight.

By midsummer of 1942, word had gotten around among the SS that Zippi had a talent for design and impeccable attention to detail, that she was organized and reliable. They came to her with odd jobs: painting signs and numbers on cabinets, labeling SS lockers.

Each time Zippi was summoned to the administrative office, she would prostrate herself before Langefeld, the highest-ranking woman at the camp.

Prisoner 2286 requests permission to enter, Zippi would say from outside Langefeld's door. Granted entrance, Zippi would stand almost ten feet from Langefeld: prisoners had to keep that exact distance from all SS men and women at all times, in order not to infect them with whatever diseases they might carry.

After receiving her orders, Zippi would debase herself once more. *Prisoner 2286 begs permission to leave,* Zippi would call out.

Once dismissed, she would go off to perform whatever task she'd been assigned.

Now that Zippi had an indoor job, she no longer had to survive on the watered-down soup that the demolition workers received each day at noon—soup where they sometimes fished out combs and compacts, accidental ingredients. She now feasted on a slice of moldy bread and a pour of the mystery tea-coffee drink. Hunger and thirst continued to plague her, but her situation was no longer quite as dire as it had been.

She'd been strategic in creating connections, seeking out prisoners and guards who had been dragged into Auschwitz for ideological reasons. She'd gravitated toward communists, socialists, and *Mischlinge* mongrels, to use the Nazi's derogatory term for the offspring of Christians who'd partnered with Jews. She was drawn to doctors, as she had been in her youth. Now these connections were proving invaluable—particularly the medical ones.

No one could afford to be sick in Auschwitz. Yet Zippi's health hadn't been the same since the chimney had collapsed on her back. On top of that, poor hygiene and malnutrition made illness unavoidable. At one point, Zippi's mouth, tongue, and gums were so covered in pus that she couldn't swallow, likely due to dental abscesses. Thankfully, a friend, a former doctor, found her a cure. And when Zippi was suffering from a recurring bout of malaria, a German Jehovah's Witness slipped Zippi quinine pills pilfered from the pharmacy. Each time, she improved without missing a day of work.

She found ways to mask her afflictions. She used red powder from her work tools to rouge her lips and cheeks with a healthy-looking glow. She partnered with a religious Jew from Slovakia who worked at the camp office and who collected "goodies" from friends working the fields—garlic and onion. Together, she and Zippi made sandwiches out of bread, margarine, garlic, and onion.

When they got cheese and sausage, Zippi would trade her cheese for the woman's sausage.

But there was only so much she could do. Tainted water remained a constant threat. Zippi developed gastroenteritis and bloody diarrhea that sent her to the latrine endlessly.

When a prisoner in a striped dress pushed her off her seat, Zippi was incredulous.

What are you doing to me? Zippi asked.

I am a Yugoslavian and you are a Jew, the woman said as she sat down in Zippi's seat. *I have the right.*

Zippi gritted her teeth and left. She learned to relieve herself inside the empty tin that she kept by her bed at night; in the morning, she would empty it into a bucket.

She would disappear into her work.

Zippi quickly realized that morning roll call was the most important administrative task of the SS concentration camps. Inmates were convinced that the process was simply a means of torture, but Zippi knew that it was more than that. It was designed to track inmates, of course—but it was also the SS's way of accounting for clothing, shoes, food, cots, and work. It was a balance sheet of sorts, Zippi realized, one that tracked the prisoners in order to keep them minimally fed and barely clothed—all while working them to death. With the constant flux of newly registered inmates, fresh data was necessary to keep the camp appropriately supplied. The ineptitude surrounding this key process, Zippi thought, helped create the torture.

Katya wanted to change things and was acquiring the authority to do so. She now wielded real power. From time to time, Zippi would ask her to move a friend, or a friend of a friend, from a "bad assignment"—meaning a dangerous *Kommando*—into a better living situation. Some of Auschwitz's subcamps were known to be safer than others. When Zippi's friends asked for assistance, she suggested they be moved to Budy, a smaller camp within the Auschwitz complex, housed at a farm about two and a half miles from the main camp. Katya often managed to rearrange the numbers, shuffling people from one list to another, manipulating the paperwork ever so slightly.

She had to be precise. If she wasn't careful, one prisoner's salvation could be another's damnation. The best way was to substitute the number of a dead prisoner into the "bad assignment." She had to be fastidious, lest the SS notice. However high she might rise in the camp hierarchy, she was still a Jew; she could easily wind up among the fumes in the fruit trees.

Zippi was unwell. Again.

Her timing was unfortunate. It was August 1942, and Birkenau—the new camp on whose construction site Zippi had nearly died—had just been deemed operational. The women were about to move from Auschwitz I to their new quarters in Birkenau. The prefabricated horse stables had finally arrived.

That summer, a typhus and spotted fever epidemic was raging through the Auschwitz camp system. A constant stream of new arrivals brought lice and fleas. The latrines were vile from the beginning, but now they were practically unusable. Inmates scavenged for sticks, leaves, and shredded paper to use as toilet paper.

Weeks earlier, Zippi had performed the daily march to Birkenau barefoot with her *Kommando*. Now, during the hottest month of the year, it required all of her strength to drag herself along the same route to her new home. Feverish, she tried to keep her body from visibly shaking.

When she arrived at her new barracks, the misery continued. While the stables were by far the cleanest quarters in camp, Zippi's health declined. Her face grew hollower. In a sleep-deprived daze, she forced herself to rise at the sound of a gong for roll call around four o'clock each morning. She headed to work, printed numbers, and painted stripes. She tried to keep her hands from shaking. Mistakes were unacceptable. She could not, she would not, go to the infirmary.

A new rumor about a "major delousing operation" was circulating. People whispered that sick patients would be sent from the infirmary to Birkenau's farmhouses—the two little buildings, one white and one red, that had been converted into the camp's first official gas chambers. These bucolic-looking buildings had the capacity to exterminate two thousand prisoners at a time. The Gestapo's secretaries typed up four to five hundred death certificates daily.

Selections were routine upon arrival, often at random. They could also take place in the barracks, at the hospital, or at roll call. Inmates who were caught in the field unable to work went straight to the farmhouse. Camp doctors even carried out selections among their patients, picking out the sickest and killing them with phenol injections straight to the heart. Sometimes the SS cast a wider net. Desperate to contain disease, they ordered that Zyklon B be used to disinfect blocks around the camp. The camp doctor and SS superiors, terrified of being contaminated, inoculated themselves against typhus.

The rumors of a "major delousing operation" were real. On the last Saturday of August 1942, sick and recovering prisoners huddled in staircases and a hallway. As a *Blockälteste* called out their numbers, inmates lined up against a wall. Trucks waited outside. By day's end, 746 prisoners had been deposited into Birkenau's gas chambers. Zippi kept her poor health a secret as hundreds of inmates disappeared. She had to stay out of the infirmary. But she was only getting worse.

Zippi no longer needed rouge to color her cheeks: her face was perpetually flushed, streaked with sweat. At night, she shivered so violently that the *Blockälteste* noticed. Zippi was likely contagious, and no one was taking chances.

The *Blockälteste* ordered Zippi to Block 27, a block she had likely helped build. Here, in squalid conditions, inmates were sent to recover—with no medicine or treatment, no water or nourishment. Zippi joined women suffering from malaria, typhus, and a variety of other infections. Together they lay on grimy mattresses strewn across the floor, waiting for death—or a miracle.

Zippi's head throbbed; her muscles ached; her breath came short and quick. Her connections couldn't help her now. A friend of Katya's brought sardines, sausages, and sandwiches topped with caviar, all stolen from the SS canteen. An acquaintance brought Zippi polluted water. Zippi could no longer see straight. She couldn't hear. Sixteen years earlier, her mother had fallen ill with tuberculosis and was sent to the mountains, never to be seen again. She died at twenty-nine. Zippi, sick with typhus, was only twenty-three and already she was fading.

Through the infirmary's small window, Zippi could see trucks kicking up dust as they rolled away, packed with sick women. They returned bearing only old uniforms, old numbers. There was no doubting it anymore: the women were being gassed.

On September 5, another eight hundred women from the infirmary were selected.

Block 27 was surely next in line.

Before she'd fallen ill, Zippi's lifeline to the outside world had been letters from her brother, and whispers from newcomers as she'd drawn lines on their backs. Some had news of the war. Others had news from her town. Now she had no access to any information.

She had no way of knowing, as she shivered in a feverish trance, that her fiancé, Tibor Justh, was in his own hell.

On September 15, 1942, Zippi lay amid the filth on the floors of Block 27, with a high fever, losing her mind.

That same day, some five hundred miles away, in Munich, Tibor was summoned from his cell in Stadelheim Prison, one of

Germany's largest prisons. Here petty criminals served their time; even Hitler had once been imprisoned within these walls. More recently, however, it was where the Nazis had taken to carrying out executions.

In Stadelheim, a prison warden led Tibor to an enclosed, windowless chamber separate from the prison cells. If the moment was anything like others described there, he faced a black curtain. An overseer likely called out his name, to confirm Tibor's identity. A prison assistant lifted the black curtain to reveal a guillotine. Tibor's head was placed underneath the blade.

In Birkenau, inside Block 27, women ached, girls gasped, coughing up blood.

In Stadelheim, Zippi's fiancé, her future, was beheaded.

In Birkenau, Zippi clung to life.

CHAPTER EIGHT

"God Is with Us"

David Wisnia's ride in the cattle car didn't last long.

He had endured the cramped, foul misery for two, maybe three days when the wooden door slid open and David heard a storm of commands.

Raus, Juden, Schweine! Out, Jews, pigs!

Then he saw the German shepherds. Large, muscular, angry specimens, their pink tongues lolling, their eyes fixed on the new transport. It was December of 1942, the dead of winter. Snow and slush covered the earth, the trees, and the barracks. Birkenau had been operating for under half a year, but already it was a well-oiled death machine.

SS officers barked orders. Women, elderly, the sick, and children marched to the left, toward the trucks with a Red Cross insignia. The remaining men, arms limp at their sides in resignation, marched to the right. For a split second, David considered joining the group of children. He was, after all, only sixteen years old. Perhaps children would be afforded some sort of protections? More likely not.

When his turn came, there was no time to hesitate. His gaze fell on an SS officer's spotless black boots. He decided: he'd join the men, march to the right. If anyone asked, he was eighteen. There were no records proving otherwise, no proof of who he once was.

His childhood had ended anyway, with his bar mitzvah and the day that followed, when Warsaw had come under siege. Certainly the day he recognized his mother's coat in a pile of dead bodies. Either way, there was a truth to his lie. As David aged by two years, the 920 others who split off to the left were led away. Soon, an essence of their bodies would rise, reddening the sky, adding smoke to Auschwitz's aura of ash.

He marched alongside 580 other men, joining the procession to have his hair shaved off, his nails clipped. He was deloused, his clothing tossed on a pile, never to be seen again. The men shivered in the nude, pale skin covered in goosebumps.

A skinny SS officer inspected David's naked body. As the man loomed over him, David's gaze fell to the words inscribed across his brass belt buckle: *Gott ist mit uns.* "God is with us." David snickered to himself. *Impossible.* The unintended provocation gave David resolve.

With David's uniform came a new identity, tattooed on his left forearm: 83526. He stuffed his feet inside a pair of wooden clogs. He didn't receive two left or two right clogs, like some of the others, but the shoes chafed against his feet as he walked. His ankles were soon raw and bloody, and eventually callused, numb.

At David's new home, Block 15, he and four other men shared a top bunk and a blanket. At night, he arranged himself between the men's shaved heads and bare feet, the ceiling only inches above them. He thought about his two aunts, Aunt Helen and Aunt Rose, in New York, existing in a different reality, a faraway universe.

Winds howled as David mouthed his nightly prayer: *750 Grand Concourse, Bronx, New York. 723 Gates Avenue, Brooklyn, New York.*

The words, once a possibility, were becoming a fantasy.

Every morning was the same.

David awoke to the clamor of commands and shrill whistles.

The five ...eased from their wooden bunk, careful not to kick one o... the face. The easiest way for five men to share a mat-... lie down head to foot, but that arrangement was tricky ...ey all had to get up quickly, much less in the dark and after ...y sleepless night.

...Most dashed outside without pause, well-trained to line up in ...ws of five. But inevitably there were new additions who didn't yet know the rules of roll call, moving slowly through the early morning haze. Some were too sick to move at all. The ones who fell behind or drew attention to themselves, who dared to think they could slip through unnoticed to use the latrine, got a beating or were hounded by the dogs. Sometimes they were shot on the spot, satisfying a barbaric impulse for their captors. When inmates did escape, which happened nearly every week, their absence was noted during roll call. They were usually captured within days, if not hours. Upon return, they were tortured, publicly executed, and left to hang—an example for the other prisoners.

During morning roll call, the men shifted in place, standing for hours on end. They waited, watching the vapor of their breath rise and fade. Sunshine was elusive in Auschwitz during the winter; their eyes grew accustomed to the dark. They clenched their hands into fists, clogs covered in snow, holding each other up as best they could. David's skin burned in the cold, but he dared not move. All around him, people were dying. They died while standing there at roll call, bony dolls collapsing to the ground.

When his number was called, David yelled out a quick *Hier!* After the *Appell,* they'd march off with their respective *Kommandos* to spend the rest of the day toiling in the service of the German empire.

Work duties were a matter of luck, or connections. One *Kommando* would spend the day chopping down trees in the nearby forest to provide wood for the gas chambers, where bodies were burned in a furnace. Two months earlier, other prisoners had begun

to work at the subcamp Auschwitz–Monowitz, minu~
the original location. Here, prisoners worked alongside, from
at the IG Farben factory producing synthetic fuel in supp
both the German war effort and the chemical company itse,
whose Zyklon B gas had in all likelihood been recently used t~
murder these same prisoners' families. Often the civilian workers
took pity on the inmates, giving away their shares of bread and
soup and smuggling in jumpers, socks, and gloves, knowing all the
while that if they were caught, their charity would kill them.

The most unfortunate prisoners—that is, among those who
remained alive—descended into the pitch-dark pits of the earth to
crush rocks in coal mines. These men worked in a state of perpetual damp, where water covered the floor and dripped from the
ceiling. Their shoes soaked through, leaving their feet cold and
pruned. They were forced to crawl through twenty-seven-inch-
high tunnels, scraping their backs and bellies on the surrounding
rocks. Coal dust settled in their throats; they had no potable water
to alleviate the burn. Sometimes during their eight-hour shifts,
they moved into larger underground galleries where they managed
to squat or kneel. Disease mushroomed in the perpetual moisture;
life here had an early expiration date, even for Auschwitz. Some
men were buried beneath the rubble. Those who survived did so
only to endure sporadic beatings, collapsing tunnels, and lumps of
coal and stones that showered down from above without warning.

On David's first day in Auschwitz, he was sent to a vast ditch
in the middle of the campground with a work crew known as the
Leichenkommando, or corpse squad. There, in the trench of wet
earth, they'd find bodies. David's job was to gather the dead for
"proper" disposal. A few months earlier, he'd seen his mother's
coat and his father's stiff arm in a pile of corpses. Then, he ran;
now, he was surrounded by batons, guns, and dogs. Guards tracked
prisoners from watchtowers. Fleeing was not an option.

Some of the dead bodies bore bullet holes, but not all. Nearly every day, some two dozen prisoners dashed to the perimeters of the camp in an attempt to fling themselves against the electric fence. Some were shot down before they could electrocute themselves.

David's job was to grab these corpses along the perimeter of the camp, still fresh, and drag them across the snowy grounds. The bodies were lifted and tossed into a wooden wagon. Often, two inmates hauled one body. Once the grounds were cleared of corpses, David's job was done. As far as he knew, the bodies were then carted off to be buried or dumped in one of the nearby rivers. But in truth, they were burned in open pits—unwanted evidence. Another *Kommando* would toss the ashes into the Soła and Vistula rivers, which ran past the camp and were soon saturated with human ashes.

While the corpses that David cleared were displayed openly— examples of the price paid for escape and suicide attempts—the hundreds of lives that the SS snuffed out inside the gas chambers were handled with much more secrecy. Disposal of the bodies was left to a specially selected group of inmates: the *Sonderkommando,* or special unit. These men handled the final stage of the camp's factory approach to mass murder—the last witnesses to a crime so horrific that the Nazis knew they had to hide it from the world.

By the time David arrived in Auschwitz, the process was well rehearsed: SS officers escorted the victims to what they explained was a shower, innocuous enough, nothing to worry about. The key was to avoid a panic; and most prisoners wanted to believe the ruse. They walked through the pine forest, along the perimeter of Birkenau, to a clearing, where they saw a small brick farmhouse. Both it and the white farmhouse were well hidden in the forest. As they entered the farmhouse, they saw the rows of shower nozzles on the walls. Camouflage, always paramount.

The inmates received towels. They left their clothing in a

special locker room. Sometimes trained dogs were unleashed inside the room, a final touch of torment. The dogs jumped, growled, and snapped at the prisoners. Panicked inmates trampled each other inside the closed room. After their captors removed the dogs, the doors were closed—and nailed shut with boards.

When he arrived in Auschwitz a few months later, Josef Mengele, the infamous doctor who performed experiments on prisoners, would participate. He would come in the ambulance transporting cans of Zyklon B. He'd instruct his aide: *Steinmetz, mach das fertig.* Finish it.

Steinmetz would don a gas mask and use a hammer and a knife to open the cans, exposing the deadly pellets, which, on contact with oxygen, would convert to a poisonous gas. Steinmetz would quickly pour the crystals through the window and shut it tight.

After the inmates were asphyxiated and the room was cleared of poison gas, it was task of the *Sonderkommando* to remove the bodies. Some of the victims, they would inevitably discover, had died in the melee that the Germans had fomented inside the chamber before the gas was released.

A shadowy group, the *Sonderkommando* was kept separate from the other inmates. The men slept in the basement of Block 11, known as the execution block—where those who tried to escape often landed when they were caught. Later, after Auschwitz's infamous crematoria were built, the *Sonderkommando* would sleep in rooms in these buildings. Considered privileged, these prisoners wore civilian clothing and received larger portions of rations than the others. They were physically the strongest of all inmates, chosen for a special task: cleaning up the gas chambers.

Wearing gas masks, the *Sonderkommando* would remove the corpses to the yard. Then, under the SS's supervision, dentists or sometimes *Sonderkommando* members themselves would bend over the colorless faces and, using pliers, extract any gold teeth from the swollen gums of the dead. The gold was then melted and stock-piled for the SS. The *Sonderkommando* moved the bodies, stripped of their value, to pits to be burned. Later, the squad would gather the ashes—with fragments of skulls, knees, and longer bones—in a wagon and dump them in the Soła and Vistula rivers. The last step was to wash the gas chamber thoroughly, scrubbing floors and walls.

The misery of the job tended not to last: these workers knew too much. Every three to six months, members of the *Sonderkommando* were themselves "transported" to their death.

In the twisted world of Birkenau, David was fortunate in that his dealings with the dead were out in the open, at least for the moment. His job had become automatic. If he thought too much about the work he was doing, he wouldn't be able to function. And he needed to survive—another day, another hour. He repeated his mantra to himself: *750 Grand Concourse, Bronx, New York, 723 Gates Avenue, Brooklyn, New York.*

Days went by, or weeks, it was hard to say. David was getting weaker. With each moment, his survival became less certain.

One night, David collapsed, exhausted, onto his bunk. The shuffle of men negotiating bunks, the snores, the wheezes, were becoming familiar. So, too, was an aching thought: perhaps he'd wake up in the morning; perhaps he wouldn't.

Is there anyone here who sings? the *Blockälteste* called out.

The men on Wisnia's bunk pushed him down. They'd heard him sing to himself before.

We got him, they said. *Here. Here.*

Before he knew it, the spotlight was on him. The *Blockälteste,* a prisoner named Josef, waited. He motioned for David to follow him to his private room, adjacent but separate from the other prisoners.

What kinds of songs do you know? Josef asked.

I know all of them, said David, his stage confidence pure instinct.

Josef tossed him a piece of bread; David performed. He sang as though he were in a grand theater. This had to be the performance of his life. If Josef didn't like his singing, he could be shot dead.

David sang the American hit that had exploded right before the war, "Joseph! Joseph!," coincidentally the name of his *Blockälteste*. He thought of the Big Band jazz groove, voices in harmony, and sang as though a gun were pointed to his temple.

When he finished, Josef waited for the next song. David sang whatever came to mind, realizing that all that mattered was his voice—not the words, not the selection of songs, not even the language he chose. He sang in German, in Hebrew, in Yiddish, in Polish—every song that he could think of. This, he sensed, was an audition.

He was right. Throughout camp, talented performers were sometimes tapped by guards and officers to entertain them. These prisoners enjoyed perks: better treatment, more rations, and some-times protection. From that moment on, David joined their ranks: he no longer had to collect bodies. Instead, he helped clean the barracks during the day, provided he sang to Josef and his friends on demand.

David often sang at night while the others slept. The *Blockälteste* would summon him and he would crawl out of his wooden bunk, whatever the hour, to earn his keep. When he sang, his tenor was both gentle and operatic. He thought of his days singing at the Sochaczew and Warsaw altars. Now, some 170 miles from Warsaw, David performed for guards who gathered for drinks after curfew. He repeated the same verses, and the guards, too drunk to notice, didn't stop him. When they were satisfied, David returned to his cot.

Perhaps he would live a bit longer, after all.

★　　★　　★

Josef arranged for David to receive extra helpings of soup and tea. He then got David a position at the Sauna, as the prisoners called the camp's balmy disinfecting stations. These were temporary bathhouses with showers and separate rooms for sanitizing clothing. A job at the Sauna was among the most coveted positions in Auschwitz. Here, David was likelier to be protected from random selections. Here, life became bearable.

Each day, new inmates arrived at the "dirty side" of the Sauna, fresh from the cattle cars that pulled through a newly constructed ramp between Auschwitz and Birkenau. Luggage that had been carefully packed with their travelers' best clothes, jewelry, photographs, suitcases, and sometimes instruments was dumped on the ground or placed in trucks to be sorted and plundered for the Nazis. The bulk of it would be placed in the *Effektenkammern,* special warehouses that inmates called Canada, after a country that they believed represented luxury and riches.

After selection, those who survived were marched to the Sauna, where they were disrobed, shaved, and deloused. But first they would give up every personal effect they still held on to: from underwear to clothing, wallets, and jewelry. The clothing would go through a process of disinfection. Everything else was bounty for Canada. Every single prisoner who entered Auschwitz experienced this brutal rite of passage. A few might return to the Sauna, if prompted by a "delousing campaign"—the SS's attempt to halt a typhus outbreak. For many, though, this was the last time they would ever see the Sauna.

David was at the Sauna nearly every day. His new job placed him on the "clean side," disinfecting uniforms. In the morning, he'd strap on a gas mask for his own protection: Zyklon B pellets, handy for asphyxiation, also disinfected inmates' uniforms. Two 200-gram cans of Zyklon B could eliminate lice, a persistent menace, in two to six hours. The gas also killed fleas, bugs, and cockroaches.

On a typical day, two prisoners in gas masks stood alone in the middle of the room, each holding a metal can filled with the Zyklon B crystals. A third worker stood at the entrance. His job was to make sure no one accidentally poisoned themselves; the SS wanted to have complete control over where and when that happened. The two masked inmates holding the canisters of Zyklon B crystals used special chisels to crank the cans open. They poured the pellets onto the floor, then got out fast, shutting the airtight doors behind them. They would return an hour later to switch on the extractor and collect the crystals back inside their cans, to be returned to IG Farben for recycling. Once the delousing process was complete, the clothing was still worn out and dirty but now lined with dead lice. David and the others in his *Kommando* tossed the disinfected rags to the incoming prisoners awaiting their new uniforms.

When they weren't delousing, David and the other men sorted through the incoming clothing. Sometimes they discovered items that prisoners had packed with them to Auschwitz. Treasures included gold-encrusted watches, diamonds, jewelry, and fur coats. The valuable pieces were set aside for the SS. The old, worn garb would be recycled as uniforms for incoming inmates.

As he picked among these confiscated possessions, David learned to "organize," or steal—a key benefit of working at the Sauna.

You can organize, but don't get caught, a guard told them.

These organized goods were exchanged for favors, clothing, and food. David snuck himself prizes here and there. He devoured a salami slice, as valuable to him as the thousand-dollar bill he discovered inside the pocket of a pair of trousers. He swapped the bill for a clean uniform tailored by a former professional. David quickly learned that the Nazis prized good appearances. In Auschwitz, health and hygiene begot health and hygiene.

For the most part, David's Sauna *Kommando* worked in a collective silence. But sometimes, when it was safe, David would sing. This endeared him to an older prisoner, Szaja Kalfus, a Polish Jew who'd arrived in Auschwitz in 1942, shortly before David. Szaja, who worked for the Sauna *Kommando* with David, had trouble walking and sitting—months before, sick with a fever, he'd missed a roll call and the offense had earned him fifty lashes on his backside with a rubber whip. For days afterward, Szaja couldn't stand or sit, much less work. Thanks to other inmates who'd propped him up, he stood in roll call each day and then went to Canada, where he sorted and organized the variety of pilfered goods that had arrived.

David's new friend Szaja was disabled for life but was lucky to have survived and to have ended up where he did. And now he was looking after the young, earnest boy who sang. Szaja pitied the kid

Prisoners sorting confiscated goods outside of a warehouse within the Auschwitz complex called Canada.

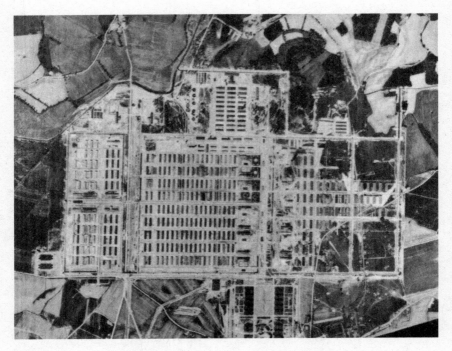

An aerial reconnaissance photo of Auschwitz II–Birkenau taken later in the war by the US Army Air Force. The new Central Sauna is the dark, T-shaped building at the upper end; the rows of warehouses facing it make up the Canada complex.

who'd lost his childhood. He slipped David some of his own rations. Thanks to his new post—and his new advocate—and despite his expectations, David was beginning to put on weight, to look healthy again.

In the weeks since David had arrived in Birkenau, he'd seen prisoners come and go. Much of the clothing he disinfected belonged to the dead. He'd been there long enough to assume that eventually his turn would come. And yet, both he and Szaja had managed to stay alive.

He'd been fortunate to work with some decent officers. Georg, his Sauna supervisor, hated his job. He wanted nothing more than to leave Auschwitz, to be sent to the front, to be anywhere else. If he could, Georg had suggested, he'd let them all out. Alas, Georg had a job to do.

David understood this. He did his work. His life settled into a rhythm. He was a cog in the Auschwitz machine—but as long as he did his job, he could at least hope to stay alive.

On the coldest days in that first winter of 1942, David tried to linger in the warmth of the Sauna for as long as possible. Sometimes he found himself alone there, hanging clothes. Sometimes, when he was done, he glanced out the window. It was hard to resist. But even a glance could spell trouble.

Not that the view changed much. There was the camp's main road separating the men's camp from the women's; the electric fence running the perimeter of the camp; the long ditch careering through the road, and the smaller ditches, choked with mud, throughout the grounds. And then there were the people: the stripes, the batons, the shaved heads, the rows of five.

One day that winter, David looked out the window and saw that the SS appeared to be celebrating—but what, he didn't know. Officers lined up some fifteen or twenty feet away, by the electric fence. They faced a ditch that ran toward the Sauna, where David watched, alone inside. Each officer held a cane and stood near a heap of sand with a group of prisoners.

They were playing a game. The prisoners opened their jackets and officers shoveled sand inside their shirts.

Schnell! the officers yelled. Run!

The inmates ran around the officers. The rule was that they couldn't spill sand. If sand leaked—*when* sand leaked—the officers would strike them with batons until the prisoners could no longer stand, until they were simply bodies, barely alive in the ditch. Then the officers shot them.

David couldn't look away. Every so often a new batch of prisoners was brought in, fresh pawns for the game. The officers laughed.

Then one officer's gaze slid past the Sauna window—and set-tled on David, an unwanted spectator.

As the man rushed toward the Sauna, David felt his chest tighten. The officer would have to go around the building to get to the door. David raced into the adjacent chamber, where clothes sat waiting to be gassed.

A voice echoed in German: *Who is there? Who is looking out?*

David squeezed behind a rack of clothes. He held his breath. No one was around to give him away.

Where are you? Where are you, man? the officer called.

David waited.

The man seemed to be gone.

After waiting for what seemed like a safe amount of time, David returned to work, hanging clothes as if nothing had happened.

He would never look out the window again. He would live by the rules. The exceptions—the careful "organizing" and bartering for extra food—were relatively minor risks. The great risks, he thought, were never worth the consequences.

CHAPTER NINE

The Number Book

Zippi spent three weeks in the infirmary before guards dragged her out. They dropped her alongside dozens of withered women sitting against the brick walls of the block, the tattered rags of their uniforms draped over their bone-thin frames. Those inmates whose eyes still had sight watched the parade of trucks drive in, drive out.

Zippi was just another body that burned with fever, but her eyes still worked, if only barely. She focused them, making out the shape of a friend: Hanni Jäger, secretary to Paul Heinrich Müller, who shared the reins of the women's camp with Johanna Langefeld. Hanni was a German political prisoner whose relationship with a Jewish man had earned her incarceration in Auschwitz.

Zippi forced her vocal cords to do their job.

Look, Hanni, I'm here, she managed.

Hanni was on her way to lunch. She recognized this frail wisp of a woman. She knew that if Zippi boarded a truck, she'd never return. She ran to her boss.

Zippi was healthy, she told Müller, and they needed her in the office. She didn't belong with the sick prisoners; the SS needed her

113

to paint, to print numbers for uniforms. Müller sent an officer to check on Zippi, to see whether she really was of any use.

What are you doing here? the officer asked Zippi.

I don't know, Zippi said, in a fever trance. *I want to go back to work.*

He took her to the barracks. *Climb up and down from the bottom bunk to the top one,* he ordered.

Zippi was weak but she was also relentless. She forced her aching body up and down. He told her to do it again. And again. Back when she'd been in Bratislava, she'd climbed ladders to paint murals. Once upon a time, she'd hiked, she'd swum, she'd been athletic. Now she gritted her teeth, mustering any reserves of strength that she had in her.

The officer ordered Zippi to jump over the wide ditches that stretched across the *Lagerstrasse,* the central camp road. Zippi forced her seventy-pound body to jump. He told her to do it again, and then again.

Finally, he took Zippi to the infirmary. A nurse took her temperature—her final test.

Zippi nearly collapsed from apprehension.

Zippi, the nurse whispered. She was a German political prisoner— an acquaintance of Zippi's. *Even if you have 109 degrees Fahrenheit of fever, I shall say nothing.*

Every few minutes, the officer returned to check on Zippi's temperature.

The nurse stalled. She pumped Zippi with valerian, an herbal medication used to sedate patients. Zippi stared outside the window at the women and girls hauled inside trucks. As soon as they left, the nurse assured the officer that Zippi didn't have a fever. She was safe, for now.

The trucks transported two thousand prisoners to the gas chambers that day. Another group went the next day, and the day after that. If the SS decided that Zippi was too ill to work, they would send her with the next transport.

A guard who'd witnessed her ordeal came to Zippi and gave her a pen and paper.

Sit down and do some work, he ordered.

By then, Zippi was so ill that she couldn't see. She tried to explain that she was "out of the world with fever," that she didn't even know what a letter looked like.

Look, said the officer. *Do whatever you want. But just work.*

She thought about the women she'd been with minutes earlier, about the shoes they left behind, now lined up against the brick wall. Zippi lifted the pen. She made herself look busy. Moments before, she'd been doing calisthenics; now gripping a pen felt like an enormous effort.

Hours passed, or seconds. Zippi looked up from the haze of her paper and found Katya staring down at her. Alongside her friend was Margot Drechsel, one of the most feared women in Birkenau. Drechsel, widely regarded as a sadist who beat women for no reason, was now the deputy head of the women's camp.

The rest of Zippi's typhus spell was a blur. She blacked out for long periods, and in between suffered stabbing pain. She could barely even recall moving into Birkenau's horse stables with the other women from Auschwitz I weeks before. She must have crawled on both legs and arms, she thought. She marveled at her luck, amazed that she'd avoided the trucks—that the SS hadn't shot her on the spot.

Zippi slowly regained her health. Each day, a Slovakian *Blockälteste* in the barracks where she recovered brought Zippi an extra helping of camp soup. Zippi forced herself to eat the slop, knowing that she needed the calories if she were to recover.

But in the aftermath of typhus, Zippi developed hepatitis. She had bloody diarrhea, her eyeballs were yellow. Another friend, a Jehovah's Witness from Ravensbrück who worked in the SS pharmacy, smuggled bouillon cubes to Zippi, which she managed to dissolve in her tea and forced herself to drink.

Eventually, Zippi recovered. She still had oozing boils underneath the skin of her legs that itched and burned. But she was alive. Thanks to an assortment of new friends, including Katya.

The day Zippi left the infirmary, Katya told her that all her paperwork was taken care of. Frail and broken, Zippi followed Katya to the unknown.

Zippi was now a part of the *Häftlingsschreibstube,* the prisoner's office. She had access to luxuries: soap, towels, toilet paper. A bra, even. Fresh underwear, socks. She no longer had to share a latrine with herds of inmates; she had her very own bucket. At her new office job, she was expected to look the part: clean and well dressed—neat.

Katya, long transformed from the girl in hysterics Zippi had first met, had proved her worth to the SS. No longer marred by shorn hair and eyebrows, or cloaked in a tattered uniform, she now wore clean dresses, expensive coats. Her golden hair was growing back. And she had confidence. When she first registered at Auschwitz, Katya was Prisoner 2098. Now she was Frau Singer, the women's camp's *Rapportschreiberin,* registration clerk. All of the women's barracks were now under Katya's jurisdiction.

While Zippi was hallucinating with fever, the women's camp's leadership was reshuffled. Johanna Langefeld had butted heads with Höss one too many times and was reassigned to Ravensbrück and replaced by Maria Mandl, a thirty-year-old Austrian guard with impeccable posture, ice-blue eyes, and hay-blond hair. Before she arrived at Auschwitz, Mandl had climbed the ranks from guard to supervisor in Lichtenburg and in Ravensbrück, cementing her role in concentration camp administration.

Fiercely loyal to the Nazi Party, Mandl was eager to scale her way up its hierarchy. She was notorious for sporadically bursting into blocks to conduct searches. She punched prisoners for minor offenses, such as wearing extra layers of clothes underneath prison uniforms. Slouching during roll call led to violent whippings that often ended in death. Mandl had a reputation for using her brute strength to knock out prisoners' teeth with a single blow. She kicked prisoners in the stomach until they were unconscious or dead. To her, the victims were subhuman. To them, she was the Beast.

Katya now reported directly to both Mandl and to Margot Drechsel, who often tortured prisoners by punching them in the face, dunking them in scalding soup, and striking them with rods.

Somehow Katya fell into their good graces. Katya knew the whereabouts and fates of each woman in Birkenau. She knew who showed up for *Appell* every morning and who didn't return from work at night. She knew who arrived at Birkenau, and when. She knew who had indoor jobs and who worked outside. This knowledge was power.

To the relief of many inmates—and to the SS—Katya was making progress in fixing the broken roll-call system. One morning, Katya took all the female inmates into the open meadow. She promised the terrified women that they need not worry; they'd be okay. She wrote down every single woman's tattooed number. The camp finally had a definitive list of everyone who was alive. At morning *Appell,* each block's *Rapportführer,* or roll-call leader, would simply confirm that the number of women in their charge matched the total from the list of women assigned to their particular block.

There was just one wrinkle. The numbers would fluctuate as new women entered the camp and as others were transferred to other camps or the infirmary, or—most likely—died. In order to keep track, Katya needed assistance. And when she told her bosses she needed something to facilitate her job, her bosses listened.

Katya's needs often involved the help of other prisoners. Now she needed Zippi.

Katya knew Zippi was astute, hardworking, and smart. She likely remembered how Zippi had soothed her when she was literally moments from stepping off a precipice, back in Patrónka. Katya told Mandl she needed help to establish a camp office and organize the place, and she wanted Zippi as her assistant.

What Katya wanted, Katya got. Her job had perks unimaginable to other inmates. She moved freely around the camp. She had her own room and her very own chambermaid, who ironed her clothes and polished her boots. Her wardrobe was furnished with gifts from prisoners who worked in the Canada warehouses. In exchange, she provided them with favors that often saved their lives.

In addition, Katya had a running list of admirers—and some time after November of 1942 she began an affair with a high-ranking SS officer. Affairs were risky in Auschwitz, especially those involving a Jew and a Nazi. If the lovers were caught, the consequences would be catastrophic for both. She kept the affair from Zippi.

Katya's lover wasn't just any SS officer; he was Gerhard Palitzsch, the quintessential Aryan German: muscular and fair, with a strong, square jaw and full lips. As *Rapportführer* responsible for inmates' discipline, he was notorious for taking special delight in performing executions. His method of choice was to line up nude prisoners, with their hands tied behind their back, against the execution wall, known as the Black Wall, which, despite its name, was often stained red with blood. Palitzsch would squeeze the barrel of his rifle or bolt gun against the back of each prisoner's skull and fire, one by one. He had a vast network of spies watching over *Kapo*s and guards and was as ruthless an overseer as he was a devoted Nazi—"the true boss with the prisoners," according to Höss, who believed that Palitzsch was better informed of the camp's goings-on than even Höss himself. Prisoners and guards alike feared Palitzsch, his sadistic streak, his compulsive need to torture.

Palitzsch's brutality extended to his womanizing. He didn't mind killing the women he slept with. But Katya, seven years his

© APMAB

Gerhard Palitzsch, feared SS officer and Katya Singer's lover, in an undated photo.

Auschwitz's infamous Black Wall, 1946 or 1947. Here, an unknown number of prisoners were executed by gunshots.

junior, believed their relationship was different. When she tried to talk him out of sending a Romani woman he'd been involved with to the gas chamber, he told her he couldn't help himself. Yet with Katya, he was tender. He told her she resembled his late wife, who had died of typhus soon after the epidemic of 1942. He told Katya she wasn't like other women. He sent her letters when he was away from Auschwitz. When a prisoner in the men's camp needed her help, Katya would ask Palitzsch to intervene. He never quite understood why she wanted to help, but he would do as she asked.

With Palitzsch's help, Auschwitz's buildup of corpses had become overwhelming. On September 21, 1942, the SS began burning corpses in the pine forest near the camp. Before then, the corpses had been buried, a practice that became untenable as the volume of dead bodies grew. So the *Sonderkommando* was assigned the grisly job of drenching some two thousand bodies with oil or methanol, stacking them in deep pits, and lighting them on fire. Once the corpses were reduced to ash and embers, two thousand more bodies were added to the pyre. Auschwitz's top brass began studying the technology of human cremation, seeking to maximize efficiency.

The stench of burning corpses pervaded the camp, another reminder of death for those who remained alive.

As Katya Singer's assistant, Zippi sported a striped dress, worn only by administrative workers, and a black apron with two pockets where she kept supplies handy. She continued to paint stripes on prisoners' uniforms, but in addition she helped Katya bring order to Birkenau. For her dual role, Zippi got a double ration of the worst bread she'd ever tasted—a combination of potatoes and sawdust—along with soup and rutabaga, the only truly edible part of the meal. Everything else seemed to be made of scraps of the Germans' discarded food. Zippi also got herself a pair of stockings—an illicit treasure that kept her warm—but it stuck to the pus that oozed from the boils on her legs, forcing her to wear the stockings for weeks until the abscesses dried up. Her treasured stockings finally crusted off on their own.

Zippi and Katya wasted no time as they concocted ways to improve conditions at Birkenau. They sat on benches, resting their feet on pallets to protect them from the muddy floors, and plotted a plan. First, Katya would recruit new barracks administrators. Most of the women in charge up to this point were the prisoners from Ravensbrück, who delighted in punishing those in their charge. Katya would train and assign capable, trustworthy, and kind women who would do as she asked.

In the meantime, Zippi tackled the unruly paperwork. She sifted through stacks of documents, trying to make sense of what she saw.

Zippi was responsible for the *Hauptbuch,* the number book—a general ledger of prisoners, identified by number. Each day, she recorded the numbers of those not present during the morning *Appell.* In a special column identified as "unknown corpses," she kept track of bodies that had purportedly disappeared; in reality, these were the prisoners selected for the gas chamber. When shown the book, Zippi immediately recognized some of the numbers as those of women with whom she narrowly avoided being transported, back when she'd been sick.

Scanning the numbers, Zippi remembered watching the women. Nearly too weak to stand, they'd been chased by guards and hauled into trucks. Zippi remembered seeing this and then being told to hold a pen, to write. She'd been delirious and yet, even then, she'd understood the girls' fates. None were spared. Just Zippi, the sole survivor among thousands.

Now she had this list, and those women's numbers had black crosses next to them. Numbers marked with a red cross meant death from any of a variety of causes—whippings, beatings, illness, starvation. The black cross meant "special treatment": code for the gas chamber.

Zippi didn't just see the numbers of the dead. Each day, she also saw the numbers of the doomed.

Before a selection, the SS provided Zippi with numbers of people who were still living, and sometimes she was told to mark them with a black cross. To her horror, Zippi was learning of inmates' deaths before they actually happened. Often, she'd list a number in the book and mark it with a black cross, only to pass the person later that day. Zippi imagined an invisible target on their back — she was encountering the walking dead. The job was gruesome and it wore on her, Zippi confided to her friend Magda Hellinger, a fellow Slovakian who'd worked briefly at the office.

Guards typically took new groups of women to be gassed in the evening. By morning, Zippi had a tally in her hands, the numbers of those who'd been killed overnight. She would update the book and all relevant files, transferring numbers from the column of the living to the column of the dead. If she thought about it too long, she might lose herself to despair and anger. And she knew herself well enough to realize that if she got depressed, she would not survive. So she tried to detach herself as best she could.

But sometimes it was impossible. Just before she'd gotten sick with typhus, Zippi had asked Katya to transfer a handful of women to Budy. She'd believed Budy was a safe zone, a subcamp surrounded by meadows and fields, where inmates needn't worry about selections or gas chambers. She'd been sure she was saving her friends.

Instead, she sent them to a new version of hell. The women were massacred days after Zippi had left the infirmary. SS guards and German prisoners later claimed that the inmates had tried to revolt. In retaliation, they said, guards used whatever weapons they could get their hands on — clubs, hatchets, and rifle butts — to murder ninety inmates. In the aftermath of what Höss called a bloodbath, corpses were strewn on the ground, flies swarming above them. The women's numbers were moved to the column of the dead. For the rest of her life, Zippi would endure sleepless nights thinking of them.

Zippi focused her energies on doing good. Together, she and Katya devised a "pre–roll call." For each block, there was now a book with three columns: names, numbers, and "remarks." Zippi employed an assistant who was specifically tasked with drawing lines for these book columns. The *Blockälteste* was responsible for filling in the remarks: whether someone had gotten ill during the day and transferred to the hospital, transferred to a different block, or died. They also kept a tally of any new prisoners who arrived during the day. Each evening, Zippi and Katya gathered these reports from administrators across the women's camp — from work sites, the hospital compound, the IG Farben factory, and the various living blocks. Each book listed its current prisoner roster. Zippi used the reports to create a pre–roll call for the SS to check off in the morning. The list had to be precise; it had to coincide exactly with the number of prisoners during the morning roll call.

This was a role made for Zippi, a perfectionist. She used a stopwatch to time roll calls and found that after the system was revamped, the entire process took just about three minutes. This meant inmates, guards, and the SS could all sleep a bit longer. Supervisors kept better control of their inmates and made fewer mistakes in their reports to Berlin. As far as Zippi could tell, everybody won. Now, with Katya overseeing roll call and overall organization, Zippi believed that inmates no longer had to suffer for days without enough rations, enough clothes, or substantial bedding. She was convinced that by providing the smallest comforts to inmates, she and Katya were making life slightly more tolerable.

Katya's bosses were pleased with her work. She took advantage of that momentum to convince Mandl to create a specialized office to track inmates through graphs and statistics. Seeking to satisfy the Nazis' desire for order, Mandl granted Katya permission to organize the office as she saw fit.

Around this time, Zippi and Katya developed a filing system they called a cardex. On index cards, they catalogued information collected about each inmate during registration—from their skills and professions, to the languages they spoke, their nationality, and their overall health. The *Stabsgebäude,* the main camp's administrative office, sent Birkenau a weekly list of factories that needed labor. Mandl gave the list to Margot Drechsel, who passed it on to Katya and Zippi. From there, they managed to transfer women to safer factory jobs.

This was a start. But Katya and Zippi wanted to do more.

As Zippi's role became more prominent, she had more freedom to move around the camp.

By the winter of 1942, Franz Hössler, head of the women's camp alongside Mandl, had come to appreciate Zippi's work, bestowing upon her more responsibility—and more leeway. Aside from having Zippi run roll call and track the camp's statistics, Hössler enlisted her to design insignias for armbands to distinguish prisoners' roles. Among the most common were the *Kapo*s, prisoners who helped supervised work crews and reported to the SS officers in charge of each *Kommando;* the *Blockälteste,* prisoners who oversaw barracks and answered to the *Rapportführer,* the SS officers who led roll call; and the *Lagerälteste,* prisoners who helped run the camp administration.

Hössler arranged for a small room within Katya's office to be Zippi's very own drafting room. Here, Zippi had a large drafting table, a stove, and benches. Hössler himself had installed the stove so Zippi could heat up glue and use it to mix paint. Now she had a door she could shut, a warm office that she could call her own.

Zippi had become the camp's one and only graphic designer. For her first assignment, Hössler asked for diagrams of the camp to illustrate daily life within the women's division. Her color-coded graphs illustrated the eighteen to twenty changes that took place in camp each day, including shifts in the labor force, new inmates, the types of jobs around camp, and the ever-growing ranks of the dead. The diagrams were produced monthly. Each color curve represented a shift in the population of a specific division for each day of the month. When officers wanted to know a statistic about the camp, they came to Zippi.

Zippi also made herself useful to the SS officers personally, widening her connections. When an officer passed by with a spot on her uniform, Zippi would offer to clean it up with turpentine. When their boots began to fade, she would volunteer to paint them with black lacquer. Zippi became known around camp as Zippi *aus der Schreibstube,* or Zippi of the office. Word got around that Zippi was handy; she could keep the SS neat and their uniforms pristine. The officers appreciated Zippi's work, and in return did her small favors, such as moving inmates to different details—and often saving their lives—when she asked.

In turn, Zippi used her growing influence to shield unhealthy prisoners by giving them positions inside her office. There, they could recuperate until she could get them safer *Kommandos*. In this manner, she kept them from being transported into worse conditions—or from being gassed.

She appreciated having her private little enclave within the camp. It sported windows, which the Nazis arranged to be outfitted with blue-and-white curtains woven with Hebrew lettering: prayer shawls confiscated from Jewish prisoners. In her former life, the thought of using these shawls as window dressing would have been inconceivable. But this was another world. At least, Zippi told herself, Orthodox women would not be affronted by the curtains as they never entered this room.

Her office also afforded ways to take better care of herself. She used her stove to cook potatoes for herself and her friends, quickly spilling glue into the fire afterward to mask the smell of food in case an SS officer came by. She used her ironing board to press her uniform. She continued to slather margarine on her face, convinced it was keeping her skin smooth and young. She'd heard that cod-liver oil was packed with vitamins, so she scavenged for it around the camp, even rifling through discarded parcels. She kept liters of cod-liver oil squirreled away inside her office and consumed a bottle a day. She realized that she stank of the oil, but that was nothing compared to the various confluences of smells in the camp—especially the inescapable stench of burned bodies. In the dead of winter, when women complained of frostbitten toes or nipples, Zippi relinquished some of her cod-liver oil and instructed them to rub it on their wounds. She'd always cared about her looks, and in Auschwitz especially, she knew how far a good impression could go.

Her transformation was incredible. Weeks earlier she'd been emaciated and bald, wearing rags and reeking of urine and diarrhea. Now she was clean and, she thought, even quite pretty. More importantly, she had earned some agency and respect—as well as new influential friends. Among these was the *Nachtwächter,* night watchman, who had become an informal doorkeeper for Zippi. Each evening before curfew, prisoners had a few moments of unofficial idle time, a rare opportunity to connect with one other. On the sly, Zippi admitted visitors into her office. She'd become popular with prisoners and even guards, who visited her office often, sometimes becoming a distraction during the day.

Zippi was now also allowed to leave the camp, provided she was accompanied by an SS officer, and only for the purpose of buying stationery and office materials from the town's stores. Likely, being outside the camp's gates felt nearly as oppressive as being inside. The few Polish citizens who were allowed to stay in town were civilian workers for German factories or in the homes of SS officers as maids or gardeners. They lived in fear of the Nazi occupiers and suspected at least a fragment of the atrocities taking place behind the barbed wire. Most did nothing to help; the few who did — finding ways to sneak food or information to the camp — faced torture and death if they were caught.

Beside her brief forays outside of the camp, Zippi found other opportunities to stretch her legs. She took frequent walks around the camp, meeting block administrators who had become her friends and would share the latest news from the outside world. When she learned of new arrivals from Slovakia, she would look for anyone she might recognize. She always left before selections took place — she couldn't bear to watch.

It was through her acquaintances from Bratislava that she learned that her father, stepmother, and stepbrothers had been shipped off on a "family transport" to the Majdanek camp in Lublin, some 125 miles south of Auschwitz. Himmler had originally earmarked Majdanek to become the largest concentration camp in German-occupied Europe. The plan went unrealized — that distinction fell to Auschwitz-Birkenau — but its inmate conditions were almost as dire as in Auschwitz.

The first mass deportation of Jews to Majdanek had just taken place that spring — 8,500 Jews from Slovakia. Only three months after Zippi had been at the old bullet factory in Patrónka, her father, stepmother, and stepbrothers reported there. Hlinka guards had told them that they were relocating for work and that families would stay together. But this was part of Nazi Germany's agreement to remove Jews from Slovakia. The three Spitzer men were sent to the Majdanek and Regina Spitzer went to Sobibór, a killing center outside of Lublin.

Zippi didn't know the details of what went on inside these camps, but she knew enough not to hold out hope of seeing her family again: her world outside Auschwitz had shrunk once more.

★   ★   ★

For fourteen months after arriving in Auschwitz, Zippi had stopped menstruating. Now, thanks to her larger rations, she was suffering from cramps once more. One morning, she decided to stay in her bunk and rest.

Maria Mandl was conducting one of her spontaneous checks that morning. Always eager for an opportunity to beat an insolent inmate, Mandl kept her baton and whip ready for use wherever she went.

When Mandl found Zippi, idle, she asked her why she wasn't at work.

She had bad cramps, Zippi explained to the Beast.

For such a response, a typical inmate could expect to lose teeth, or worse. But Zippi was no longer a typical inmate. Mere months ago, she'd been left to die on the dirty floor of an infirmary. Now things were different. Zippi's diagrams had earned accolades from Mandl's bosses in Berlin. The inmate was making Mandl look good.

Mandl reached for Zippi.

She placed a hand on Zippi's forehead. Her touch almost seemed maternal.

Sleep and get better, she said.

Zippi spent the afternoon in bed. That night, she stayed up late to finish her diagrams so she could turn them in on time.

She had no illusions: Mandl was no better than the others: an animal, a trained killer. But as long as Mandl was satisfied, Zippi was safe. Or so she thought.

As Zippi went about her traumatizing tasks, she had to appear unbothered. She'd known acute loss from a young age, and her grandmother had taught her not to give in to grief. Zippi was aware that now, more than ever, reacting would be fatal—that breaking down would be her downfall. So she took a clinical approach to her job, and to the camp itself. From the moment she'd set foot in the muddy grounds of Auschwitz and undressed, she'd told herself she must become stone.

Despite her dwindling connections to the world beyond Auschwitz, she continued to reach out. Her notes to her brother, Sam, expressed coded warnings. They passed through the censors and, she hoped, through the battlegrounds where the Germans continued to advance, and eventually into Sam's hands. He wrote her infrequently, also in code. They understood each other in a way that only the two of them could.

His postcards probably brought her some relief—confirmation that he was alive.

This time, though, the news was not good.

Tibor—her fiancé—was gone.

Dead.

The postcard didn't have details, just enough to let her know.

The news was devastating. It was more than another name on a list; this one was more familiar, more intimate. This one had been a promise of a new future.

Now more than ever, Zippi had to be stone. She had to control her grief, to keep the news about Tibor to herself. Most likely, she didn't tell anyone of the despair she felt. She swallowed this loss, like she had so many others.

Years ago in Bratislava, she'd decided to take his photograph. She'd been experimenting with a camera and he'd posed for her, her willing subject. Now these photos were lost to her, as was he. He'd left nothing behind.

Tibor was twenty-seven when he died. Zippi hadn't seen him in at least two years.

Now the only person she had left was Sam. They'd never been close growing up. Maybe that was for the best, Zippi thought. How much loss could one person take?

Save your heart, she thought.

★　　★　　★

From time to time, Zippi found herself at the Sauna. She might come to collect data, to drop off a report, or to clean herself. She had her reasons, her excuses. Sometimes she woke up extra early to shower before roll call began at four in the morning. She enjoyed those hot showers alone, in peace.

One day, she saw two horses. A man rode one, a woman the other. The animals galloped, the woman's hair blowing behind her.

Zippi stared at the beautiful riders, unable to look away. The pair was enchanting: they belonged in a movie scene. *Beauty still exists beyond these fences,* she realized then.

The woman was Maria Mandl. The man was her lover. The horses grazed; their riders glistened.

The image stayed with Zippi for days, weeks. Was such a life still possible? Did beauty deserve to exist in a place like this?

*S*he paused to look through a window inside a room where men sorted through clothing.

These bald skeletons, she thought, they could not be human. Their skin like wrinkled balloons, eyes bulging, bodies curved — the sight filled her with sorrow.

But among the walking corpses, one figure stood out: young, his chestnut eyes filled with vibrancy, life. His uniform was tailored and clean. Was he better fed than most? Could he be healthy, even?

Not long ago, she'd been a bald skeleton herself.

But not now.

Her hair was growing out, in thick, undulating waves. Now she was clean, she had curves: a real woman again.

Their eyes met and she saw a gleam of life inside a graveyard.

He smiled — at her.

PART III

DUET

CHAPTER TEN

The Hanging

David knew that Zippi was no regular inmate. He'd caught glimpses of her, heard the rumors. *Zippi of the office.* She came by frequently, finding excuses to be there—to see him, he suspected. When she appeared, he found reasons to brush past her. She was clean and neat. But it was her scent that was the most tantalizing. It was like nothing he could describe. Perhaps it was just that she was a woman, a rarity in his world; either way, she was new, refreshing.

For weeks after their first encounter, likely in early 1943, Zippi and David stole glances at each other, trying not to be obvious. Around them, the guards circled, eager to torture and destroy any inmates who stepped out of line. David would graze her sleeve; she'd murmur a soft hello.

She was pursuing him, he thought, elated. Imagine that: a woman. The very idea was outrageous; and yet. No doubt she'd noticed his tailored striped uniform. No doubt she saw that he was in good shape, healthy. She must've heard about him. The attractive, healthy young man at the Sauna. Yes, David was certain of it. Someone had told Zippi about him and now she had come to see for herself. She must've liked what she saw; she kept coming back.

After what felt like months, someone made an introduction. She was dressed better than any other woman there. She even wore a nice jacket. No one else seemed to be looking at them. David understood some Slovak, he could say a few words—it was close enough to Polish. They both also spoke Hebrew, and David understood some German, so perhaps their exchange was peppered with a bit of each language. But that first exchange was so brief—really just long enough to agree to speak again. Zippi would return to see him at the Sauna.

David was all nerves. *This was taboo!* How was it that he was speaking to a woman? *In here?* She knew people—he had heard, of course; but he hadn't realized the extent of her connections. She knew officials; she knew male inmates; she knew how to get the guards to look the other way. She was important, and she was experienced at getting what she wanted. She could've had anyone, but she'd chosen him. Out of every inmate in the camp, *she'd chosen him.*

David swooned at the thought. At seventeen, he'd already experienced so much, and yet nothing at all. When he was fourteen, he'd had one romantic liaison in Warsaw—a rite of passage. An initiation. He was ready for more. But could it really happen here, of all places?

The first time they spoke, David had felt it was just the two of them. Later, replaying the moment in his head, he would wonder about the other inmates, where they'd gone. In his memory, it felt as though they'd left the room—disappeared. But that couldn't be. He would try to remember what she'd said, what he'd said. But the words eluded him. A woman had been within his reach, her breath soft against his—that was all that mattered.

They began to send each other notes through messengers. Small scraps, nothing that might incriminate them. From time to time, by design, their paths would cross, their whispers hot against the fabric of their uniforms. In time, he'd forget the exact exchange, but her phantom breath against his cheek lingered, the light touch of a finger, a hidden smile, the hope for something more.

It was crazy to think it, but maybe they'd find a way to spend time together, truly alone.

Was it crazy to think it?

The longer they survived Auschwitz, the more they realized that anything was possible.

There was a moment that spring of 1943, just around the time David and Zippi first met, when inmates held out hope. The Sixth Army, the most decorated division of the *Wehrmacht,* Germany's armed forces, had recently fallen to the Soviet Union's Red Army after the torturous six-month Battle of Stalingrad. The Nazi surrender came at a steep Soviet sacrifice—more than seven hundred and fifty thousand Red Army soldiers died in action—but the Nazis also suffered significant bloodshed, with four hundred thousand German soldiers dead and the ninety-one thousand survivors taken as starved, frostbitten prisoners of war. The surrender had coincided with the Nazis' tenth anniversary in power. On February 3, 1943, the defeat was announced to the public over German radio, and Hitler declared four days of national mourning.

For opponents of the Nazi regime, the moment felt promising—but it didn't stop the transports from arriving at a steady clip. On February 2, the day of the Nazis' defeat at Stalingrad, 2,266 prisoners from various ghettos arrived in Auschwitz. Of those, 617 were admitted into the camp; the remaining 1,649 were sent straight to the gas chambers. Meanwhile, European refugees continued to lose their homes and were trying to escape a similar fate. That spring, American and British delegates convened in Bermuda for ten days of secret deliberations on how to help those displaced. Their proposals were almost immediately rejected by the representatives' respective governments. Although the American public had begun to learn about Hitler's massacre in November of 1942, only 11,153 Europeans had been allowed entry into the country. By the end of 1943, that number would drop to 4,920.

David's dream of going to America was increasingly improbable. He was, however, navigating Auschwitz with relative comfort—perhaps too much comfort.

It began with the weather. You could never get warm enough during the wintertime, when the frigid Polish wind burned through thin layers of clothes. Given the opportunity, the Sauna was among the few places inmates could warm up. David had learned to take these chances when he could. Even when he probably shouldn't.

One Sunday afternoon in March 1943, David woke in the Sauna with a start. He and the other workers had finished hanging the disinfected clothes by noon. Sunday's afternoon roll call was at 1 p.m. With less than an hour to lie down on the concrete floor and enjoy the rare warmth emanating from around him, David shut his eyes to rest in his sanitized, poisonous cocoon.

By the time he'd blinked the sleep out of his eyes, he'd realized that he was alone. Everyone else was lined up outside. His so-called friends could have woken him up, but they'd left him there. And now David was missing the *Appell*.

He looked out the window. Column after column of pale prisoners, row after row, always in fives, stood at attention. Guards paced dirt roads, batons in hand, and spat out commands under the gnarled trees. They'd clearly been standing in the bitter cold for some time now.

They were looking for him, David realized in a panic. He knew he had grown to be important, he thought, but he must be more important than he'd realized to have all these people stop on his behalf.

He crept outside, trying to make himself invisible. His gaze turned to his cellblock. Men stood in their familiar positions, cramped rows of tired, vacant eyes. David ran past the ditch in the middle of the campground—the same one where he'd labored with the *Leichenkommando*. He shuffled along the electric fence toward his barracks, trying to hide between inmates and slip in unnoticed. But no one would cover for him; the stakes were too high.

The guards spotted the latecomer. They pushed David to the front of the rows, sludge splattering underneath their feet. The ground was covered with the residue of the previous night's mix of rain and snow. A guard dragged David past the ditch from which David once hauled out fresh corpses—and deposited him in front of a syrup-brown puddle. *This is it,* David thought. *They're going to kill me—no doubt about it.*

As David faced the *Lagerführer,* the commander in charge of the warehouse, he felt the eyes of thousands of men—maybe even as many as fifty thousand—on him. Only one thing kept him from complete despair: if he had been an unknown newcomer, he thought, he'd be done for, executed on the spot. But he'd been there for almost five months. In Auschwitz, surviving this long should bode well—it suggested important connections. His ruby cheeks suggested he was healthy—useful. David, like Zippi, understood how much appearances mattered here.

You make one move and dirty my boots and you're dead, an officer said, loud enough for his boss to hear. He poked at David's ribs with a meat hook. *You're dead right here.*

David's shoes were covered in mud. Over the years, the earth below him had absorbed the blood of countless inmates. The infamous ditch had held bodies dead and alive. Now, staring at the sharp edge of a meat hook inches from his chest, he willed his body not to move.

The officer had winked at David—he was almost sure of it.

He sent David back to his bunk.

Back in the barracks, David was sure his punishment was not

over. It couldn't be. He'd seen the SS officer write down his number. His breathing was shallow. There was no way they'd let him off like that. His friend Szaja had missed roll call and for that had received fifty lashes on his backside and a permanent limp.

No, he thought, this wasn't over.

The next day, David woke up covered in sweat, burning with fever. The muscles along his thin arms and legs throbbed, his head ached, his stomach was sore. He was visibly sick and couldn't hide it. David had typhoid fever. He was sent off to the infirmary in Block 7.

Weak and dehydrated, all he got was the mystery tea-coffee concoction. There'd be no medicine, no such frills. Most prisoners came here to die.

But once again, David was in luck. Inmates he'd befriended at the Sauna smuggled over food and water. Within days he was healthy enough to return to his block and get back to work. He was mystified. He couldn't shake the feeling that he was in the eye of a storm.

He was sure an example would be made of him: the SS would not pass up the chance to showcase its power, to demonstrate the consequences of not living by its rules. David awoke each morning in dread. The reason behind the delay finally hit him: he had to be healthy enough to suffer.

A few days later, a guard slashed a whip across David's hands ten times. In the days that followed, his palms swelled, dripping with pus and burning with infection.

Next, an officer ordered David to follow him to a room. David saw a noose. Gallows had been set up. *This is it,* he thought; *this is how it ends.* A group of SS men stood by — an audience. One tightened the noose around David's neck as his buddies watched with giddy anticipation. An officer kicked a plank out from under David's feet.

His death would be a blur.

He dropped down into a hole that was at least six feet deep. The men around him guffawed at their joke: the noose around David's neck hadn't been tied.

Down on his knees, for better or for worse, David was very much alive.

David's mock-hanging was his initiation into the *Strafkompanie*, the penal colony, where he was admitted on March 19, 1943, and where he served for the next three months. Inmates who'd committed the most serious crimes but who'd been spared a public hanging landed here. The *Strafkompanie* was known for its brutal torture tactics. Earlier on it had been housed inside Block 11, known as the "death block" in the main camp, which contained "standing cells" in its basement, where prisoners suffering the most severe punishments were confined to sleep at night, and a dungeon.

By the time David was incarcerated, the *Strafkompanie* had been relocated to Block 1 in Birkenau, a dark, dusty overcrowded space where prisoners slept in bare beds of wooden boards. Inmates were isolated from the other prisoners and forbidden to have any contact with others. They worked longer, more grueling hours, pushing wheelbarrows of gravel and digging the central drainage ditch. Their work was more strenuous, and yet they received smaller rations. While prisoner functionaries ran much of the camp, SS officers took a special interest in supervising the *Strafkompanie*, where they would give random beatings, carry out torture, and enjoy shooting sprees. The *Kapos* directly supervising these inmates were among the most unscrupulous criminals, depraved outcasts who were said to enjoy crushing Jewish men's testicles with a wooden hammer on a board.

Day after day, David went out to dig ditches. He was whipped on the back when he moved too slowly, whipped again when he was too quick to pick up a shovel. He no longer received extra rations. He no longer sang. Supervisors smacked him across the face on a whim.

Six days passed—maybe more, maybe less. Days were no longer relevant. The warmth of the Sauna, the flicker of a connection with Zippi, was unthinkable. Survival was minute by minute. David was losing weight and strength. He was sure he was never going to leave the penal colony alive.

And then one day, without warning, he was ordered not to go to work.

CHAPTER ELEVEN

An Understanding

Thanks to her role under Katya, by May of 1943, fourteen months into her imprisonment, Zippi's living situation had improved dramatically. She moved to Block 4, which housed about a hundred women, a major upgrade from the other blocks, where eight hundred to nine hundred prisoners were often crammed together. The women of Block 4 had bedsheets and warmer blankets. They even had small cubbies to store personal items, like extra underwear. About 60 percent of the inmates were Jewish; the remainder was a mix of Poles, Ukrainians, and Yugoslavs. They spoke a variety of tongues. Most worked at the *Schreibstube*—the women's administrative office and the nerve center of their camp—where Zippi and Katya worked. Conveniently, the *Schreibstube* was in Block 4. A dayroom with long tables and benches separated the workspace and Katya's room from the sleeping quarters.

The women of Block 4 had Anna Palarczyk as their *Blockälteste*. A twenty-four-year-old Polish political prisoner who'd arrived in Auschwitz that August, Anna growled at her inmates and slapped them when the SS officers were in sight—but otherwise she was kind. The women she oversaw understood their supervisor's vacillating behavior, even appreciated it. Anna was handpicked by Katya to replace a brute from Ravensbrück, and Katya made it explicit to Anna that her chief responsibility was to take care of the women in her block, to treat them well. *We must get to an understanding, the Jewish women and the Polish women,* Katya said; they had to help each other to make life bearable.

Women from similar backgrounds tended to gravitate to one other—and help one another. It was simply a matter of practicality: they shared the same language and culture; they arrived together and tended to stick together. But this often bred resentment among different nationalities. Since the Slovakian women had arrived before the others, they'd managed to get the best posts, and more connections. It helped that as residents of the former Austro-Hungarian Empire, the Slovakian women typically spoke German and thus could communicate with the SS. Zippi epitomized this phenomenon. Polish women who arrived later on didn't have the same pull. In deputizing Anna Palarczyk as the new *Blockälteste* of Block 4, Katya was trying to expand the circle of women who had access to power—effectively increasing the number whom she could help.

Zippi had the same mindset. She admired women who'd been imprisoned for their politics and values. She respected fighters—and her new *Blockälteste* fit that mold. Anna had been in miserable shape when she first arrived in Auschwitz. Her wooden clogs fell apart almost as soon as she got them, and she trudged barefoot through whatever odd jobs she was assigned. She carried corpses and escorted sick women to the infirmary. She suffered from dysentery; she shriveled to just skin and bones. She was congested and despondent. Nevertheless, Mala Zimetbaum, a Jewish inmate from Belgium, had scolded Anna—to get a grip, to wash herself, to get better clothes and new shoes on the camp's black market. When Anna bemoaned her lack of money, Mala told her not to eat for three days and exchange her bread rations for shoes. *You must take care of yourself,* Mala chided. *Because otherwise, otherwise you will croak here.*

Mala's harsh advice probably saved Anna's life. Anna's transformation from a sickly inmate likely also helped her secure a better job. Anna was proof that appearances could change an inmate's life.

Mala was now among Anna's charges in Block 4, and one of Zippi's block mates. Zippi wasn't quite sure what to make of her. Mala had a strong personality, and Zippi was suspicious of where that might lead her.

Zippi had first met Mala in fall of 1942, when Zippi was registering a new transport from Belgium. Even in the dim light, Mala was hard to miss. She jumped on a table and tried giving the incoming Belgian women orders. This was problematic.

What are you doing? Get down! Zippi hissed at Mala. *You're in Auschwitz, you're not in Belgium. I don't want you to show off. The moment you show off, the SS will remember you. Get down from there; get off the table.*

Now here they were, sharing a barrack. Not only had Mala survived, but the SS had recruited her as an interpreter, since she spoke fluent French, German, and Polish. Mala was also among the dozen "runners" who roamed the camp, tasked with delivering messages. This meant she had extensive reach within the camp's grounds.

Mala could be a good friend to cultivate and to keep close — or a dangerous friend, one to keep at arm's length. Nevertheless, she was an ally. And here, Zippi didn't have the luxury of choice.

The little farmhouse in the middle of the woods seemed innocuous enough.

Mandl had wanted to extend a kindness to the inmates in exchange for their work in the administrative office: a special hike in the woods — good, fresh air. A Ravensbrück *Kapo* would accompany them, of course.

They came upon the peasant's cottage, made of brick layered with white plaster, its roof covered in straw, its windows barred.

Signs around the circumference read ZUM BAD ("to the bath"). This, the *Kapo* told them, is where the first transports were gassed. The needs of Auschwitz had long since outgrown the small house.

The women were led inside the relic. Zippi thought of the bright red flames, still visible from the women's camp. She already knew that more corpses than ever burned every night, but here was confirmation: no matter how much her life improved, she remained in an inferno. As she walked through the hut that was known throughout Birkenau as the Little White House, Zippi thought of those who lost their lives in this very spot.

Was it luck that was keeping her alive? Fate? Or was it only a matter of time?

Zippi's secrets were adding up.

By early 1943, she had begun duplicating each diagram that she created for her supervisors, hiding the copies in her office in hopes that one day they'd come in handy. These graphs documented the extent of the SS's crimes. If an officer caught her, she'd be killed, yes; but one day the world would know the extent of their barbarism—and if she could help that happen, it was worth risking her life.

All the while, Zippi had her post behind the registration desk, processing new arrivals. Zippi *aus der Schreibstube.* She felt comfortable whispering advice to wide-eyed newcomers who didn't yet know how to handle the camp. By then, prisoners were doing most of the work, including processing the newcomers, with the SS overseeing from the sidelines. This presented Zippi with opportunities to ask questions about the world outside, to find out about loved ones. And also to give warnings.

Don't say a word, she'd say, sometimes in German, sometimes in Polish or Slovak. *Just do what they tell you and you'll be okay.*

Some women resisted. *I'm married to an Aryan,* they wailed as clumps of their hair fluttered to the floor. *Be quiet,* Zippi would warn them. *Let them cut your hair. It's not the end of the world. It will grow back.*

Back at the office, she and Katya kept a ledger with multiple columns, tracking the inmates: the sick, those working in the fields, those in the staff office, in factories, and around camp. Their cardex system kept track of inmates' skills and professions, so the SS came to Katya and Zippi whenever they needed someone with a specific background around camp.

Zippi continued what had been her first role upon arriving at Katya's office: tracking the numbers of the dead for the SS's records. What the SS didn't know, though, was what Zippi and Katya did with those numbers. When a guard asked for a list of prisoners they had already condemned to death, Zippi would swap out several numbers with those of the already dead—numbers no longer in circulation. The Nazis never bothered to count the people they corralled to the gas chamber; if they asked for 500 prisoners, under Zippi and Katya's watchful eyes, fewer went. By recycling numbers, they could appear to satisfy the SS's death quota—when in fact they were saving women's lives.

Zippi and Katya did not stop there. With the help of other women in strategic positions, they extended their sphere of influence. Mala, Zippi's block mate and tentative friend, had become a part of their circle and often asked them to find better, safer jobs for her Belgian compatriots. As a camp runner, Mala had other methods of helping the women. She would look for ways to interact with the new Belgian arrivals, to give them some sort of hope and encouragement. Whenever the guards ordered her to take note of illnesses at the hospital, she identified weaker women, those in the greatest danger of being killed. Zippi would move these patients from the infirmary under the guise that they were assisting with her work. In this way, Mala and Zippi bought these inmates time to recuperate, safe from potential selection.

Meanwhile, Katya's role within the camp continued to

expand—as did her rewards. Prisoners took notice: there was her beautiful blue coat, her newly bleached hair, and rumors spread when Hössler, who ran the women's camp with Mandl, brought Katya a plate of cookies baked by his wife. Some inmates resented her, sure that she'd been corrupted by power. She had no qualms about giving prisoners orders, they said. Others felt she used her position to award special favors specifically to Slovakian women, rather than distributing her aid equally among the inmates. Even those who liked her felt she was getting a "swollen head."

Through her privilege and power, though, Katya sought creative ways to improve camp life. Early on, she replaced the most brutal Ravensbrück guards with Jewish and Polish inmates such as Anna Palarczyk, women who were decent—sympathetic to the inmates, even—and who wouldn't torture others. She selected women who had "human feelings"—who wouldn't steal rations from prisoners, who would help procure extra food and extra soap for the women in their blocks. While she couldn't replace the guards herself, she could whisper ideas into Mandl's ear. The Beast had grown to trust Katya and would often follow her advice.

Zippi realized that much of Auschwitz's infrastructure lay beneath the surface, outside the view of regular inmates, most of whom were focused on surviving from one minute to the next. Machinations were in place that they would never see, that they could never understand.

Knowledge was power and safety—sometimes. Zippi understood that in Auschwitz she had to straddle a thin line that demarcated empowerment from danger. When it came to certain goings-on within the camp, she stuck to another adage: the less she knew, the better.

Henryk Porębski, an electrician charged with checking the wiring throughout Birkenau, had become a frequent visitor at Zippi's office. Henryk was, as far as Zippi knew, the only man living inside the women's camp. His job gave him a pass to walk freely with the excuse that he was checking on wires. During his visits, Henryk asked Zippi for small favors, the kinds of favors she'd grown accustomed to doing for acquaintances and friends of friends, such as work assignment transfers. But he also came to her with more unusual requests—to write down special symbols and trademarks. Zippi granted these favors and didn't ask questions; it was wiser, she thought, not to get involved. All the while, her friends teased her about having a love affair with the Pole.

Henryk walked around camp collecting information and documents wherever he could. He gathered ID cards and photographs from the floor of the crematorium and buried whatever he got. One day, he hoped, these would be discovered and the truth about Auschwitz would come out. At first, he worked on his own; eventually Henryk was recruited by the underground resistance, which by this point was well established in the camp.

Outside the camp, Polish underground resistance rooted in youth movements like Hashomer Hatzair—the Zionist organization to which Zippi and Sam had belonged—had become more active than ever by 1943, with regular meetings taking place inside the Warsaw Ghetto. Clandestine newspapers circulated monthly, disseminating news on the travesties occurring across Poland. Eventually such information reached the walls of Auschwitz.

Within Auschwitz, too, similar movements had spread. These were out of sight of the SS and most prisoners. Although the camp had resisters of every nationality, the Poles were among the most organized. Perhaps the most famous was Captain Witold Pilecki, a thirty-nine-year-old soldier of the Second Polish Republic.

Three years earlier, on the dawn of September 19, 1940, Witold had deliberately walked into a Nazi roundup in Warsaw. He wanted the SS to arrest him. He wanted to be transported to Auschwitz. Witold's plan, executed with stoic efficiency, was to get caught and stuffed into a truck with other imprisoned civilians. From there, he'd register as an inmate in Auschwitz and organize a resistance group from the inside.

Witold had spent months creating a forged identity before he arrived in Auschwitz. His efforts paid off: he arrived without suspicion and was shaved, terrorized, and tortured like everyone else. He became Prisoner 4859: "Blinded by the lights, shoved, beaten, kicked, and rushed by the dogs, we had suddenly found ourselves in conditions which I doubt any of us had ever experienced," he later wrote. "The weaker ones were so overwhelmed that they simply fell into a stupor." Within days, Witold was on familiar terms with the three officers who'd earned the reputation for being the most dangerous and bloodthirsty within the camp—and Palitzsch, Katya's lover, was at the top of the list.

Witold's plan was fourfold: to inform the world of the reality inside Auschwitz; to supply camp prisoners with news from the outside; to gather extra food and clothing through the underground; and to prepare inmates to fight. He picked out inmates who would be loyal and active, who would be operating under the SS's nose. He knew that the SS had informants among the prisoners and that it was a gamble to trust anyone, so he had to be discerning. But he slowly built his network.

Early on, his network carried off what should have been a major coup. By a stroke of luck, one of Witold's early recruits, a political prisoner, became one of the few men officially released from the camp in October 1940. Until the summer of 1942, a very small number of prisoners were released—mostly Polish political prisoners who'd had some means of influence, either through connections in Berlin or bribery. The man memorized Witold's report, which detailed the conditions of the camp, and begged the Polish government to bomb Auschwitz and end the prisoners' torment. Through a courier system, he smuggled the information to the headquarters of the Secret Polish Army, the resistance group he'd founded. In March of 1941, the Polish government in exile in London shared this intelligence with the Allies. By the time the message reached the Royal Air Force, only the request to bomb Auschwitz had become the headline; the heart of Witold's report—the description of the camp and the prisoners' strife—was stripped down to a single line. The Air Ministry in London perceived the bombing as "an undesirable diversion and unlikely to achieve its purpose." The world did not react.

Later on, one of Witold's recruits who worked in Auschwitz's hospital laboratory took advantage of the typhus epidemic inside the camp in 1942 to breed typhus-infected lice. The group released them into the coats of the most egregious members of the SS and the most vicious guards. Palitzsch was targeted but survived; his wife caught typhus and died.

Witold and his growing number of recruits carried on, finding more creative ways to send out intelligence. Every so often a small trickle of political prisoners, usually Polish, would be released. Female inmates, mostly Polish Christians who worked inside a warehouse that held the personal effects of political prisoners, tucked small notes inside the linings of suitcases that would leave the camp when inmates were released.

Henryk Porębski, the electrician who had been burying messages on his own initiative, soon became one of Witold's recruits. He delivered messages between the men's and women's camps but, for his own safety, and for the safety of those involved, never asked questions about how the information would be used. He asked Zippi for data and figures, peeking at rough copies she'd kept of the diagrams and graphics she created for her bosses. One time, he asked her to paint the inside of an empty watch with miniature letters. Zippi was baffled by the odd request but did as he asked. She trusted him. In return, Henryk shared any news he had, which he received through a radio hidden by the resistance. He passed the information on to Anna Palarczyk at Block 4, who would then alert Zippi.

Sometimes Henryk or other members of the Polish underground would ask Zippi to "go for a walk." She would stroll around camp, visiting with the friends she'd made across the grounds—from guards to *Kapo*s to inmates—leaving her office free as a semisafe space for other prisoners. It was one of the few places in the camp where inmates could have relative privacy. Knowing how fortunate she was to have her own little enclave, Zippi was happy to share it.

Other times, she left her office for friends to rendezvous with their lovers. Everyone had needs; she knew this all too well. Though rarely acknowledged, affairs thrived in certain circles. While most prisoners struggled to find enough food to stay alive, a privileged few found love in Auschwitz. In Canada, especially, male and female prisoners had a greater opportunity to interact. They also had the currency to protect each other and exchange favors, which could get them a private corner of some storage room, with someone to guard the space while the lovers were inside. Payment to guards ran the gamut from soap to perfume to food. Usually, friends facilitated exchanges of notes and letters. Magda Hellinger, Zippi's friend, had received a love letter from a man who worked in the kitchen. Rudolph Vrba, a Slovak Jew who managed to escape Auschwitz, recounted helping a *Kapo* named Bruno send messages to another *Kapo, Hermione,* whom he'd been attracted to. Before long, the two had arranged a sort of love nest. When Rudolph asked a girl at the storeroom how they did it, she told him, "We've piled up a few thousand blankets to make a wall. After all, lovers need a bit of privacy, don't they?" Witold Pilecki, the resistance leader, recalled that SS authorities in the women's camp exchanged "knowing glances" with inmates marching back to their barracks from work.

AN UNDERSTANDING

A hint of an affair between or involving prisoners was risky—especially for the prisoners in the equation. Physical liaisons were not easy to hide, and the consequences of being discovered were severe. Inmates with the highest status sometimes avoided the penal colony; but most didn't. A romance would lead to torture, death.

And yet, for many these clandestine meetings were worth the risk. Prisoners understood their mortality in this place, where savage death was around every corner, almost unavoidable—a question of when, not if. And so the possibility to feel a tender touch, to experience something other than pain—actual pleasure—made for a powerful motive. Often the simple prospect of intimacy was worth the cost.

As summer crept over Auschwitz, David was toiling in the *Strafkompanie*. Zippi never saw David during her visits to the Sauna lately. They hadn't seen each other since early March. As always, Zippi focused on finding strategic ways to focus her attention.

A runner from the men's camp, really just a child, had begun to make daily visits to her office. He reported on the number of non-Jewish males under the age of five residing in the women's camp with their mothers. There weren't many, but Zippi kept track of those who survived. The information she provided the boy ingratiated her with his boss, the head of the men's work detail. After the boy collected his figures, Zippi left him alone in her office to meet with Polish women and relay information to them from the men's side. In exchange, he left Zippi with cigarettes and tobacco, which she would later exchange for food.

In her mind, Zippi didn't formally belong to the underground—her contributions were unofficial. She stayed away from her office for as long as they needed her to. She distributed whatever favors she could. All the while, she tried not to learn any more than was strictly necessary.

Zippi was balancing on a tightrope. When she was in her office, friends frequently came by to visit. She preferred to work at night, when she wouldn't be disturbed by "those little monkeys," as she called them affectionately. Sometimes she had to shout at her friends to leave her alone to do her work. Now and then she'd even throw out her *Blockälteste*—and now friend—Anna.

The flow of visitors to her office included a steady stream of Nazis—the ones she was officially working for, who would not be pleased to see inmates conspiring in her workspace. Outsiders from Berlin were directed to Zippi, too, when searching for particular people or buildings. Zippi had become the compass of the women's camp, and the SS could very well walk in at the wrong time.

This new role gave Zippi the seed of an idea.

She would build a three-dimensional model of the women's camp in Birkenau that would show exactly where everything was located. This model would encapsulate all buildings, barracks, and offices; it would serve as a visual directory of the camp. To build this, she would need access to every inch of the grounds. She would draw everything precisely to scale. To do that, she'd have to measure every surface, observe every detail. The model would be an exact replica of the women's camp.

Without seeking permission, she began to work.

When Hössler asked her what she was doing, she explained that it would help her better assist those who came to her office.

How can I carry on if I don't know the sizes properly? she asked him. *I would like to have permission to go get the barracks and the spaces between the barracks measured correctly. I do not want to ask for plans from the building office; I would rather do that myself.*

When Hössler asked her who'd given her permission, she said, *Nobody.*

Despite this—and perhaps as a testament to her growing influence—Hössler permitted her to pursue the project. She would have full, unrestricted access to the entire camp—but she was not to include the crematoria. As of June 25, 1943, four such facilities had been constructed and were fully functional, primed to burn at least 4,756 corpses a day.

Zippi acquiesced. She would collect information; she hoped it would fall into the right hands.

Sam's postcards to the *KZ*—the German abbreviation for concentration camp—were tapering off.

In June of 1943, soon after his birthday, she wrote him a postcard, using their nicknames for each other.

My dearest Schani,

I am happy that I can write to you. A long time has passed since we separated. You will be 21 by now. Every year on the third of May I [think] about you a lot. Be strong, my child. Keep your head up. You must never forget that you only have me and that should give you a lot of hope. Even if we as siblings had only a little time together, maybe it is better this way. Should we see each other again in this lifetime I hope, our relationship will be strong. Stay healthy. I feel very fresh and am working. In case you need anything, please write a letter to KZ. That is all for today. I am kissing you.

Your sister Hellay

Sam was still in prison in Bratislava. He'd been locked up for seventeen months by then and had seven more to go before he'd complete his sentence—but he was ill.

How much could Zippi have known? Did she wonder whether the one person she had left in the world was still alive? It is possible that she knew Sam was ill; news traveled quickly via the underground. Transports from Bratislava could have carried information to Zippi, or perhaps Sam had told her himself in an earlier letter.

Perhaps her own letter was an attempt to urge him to fight for his life. She'd long ago learned that there were very few things she could control in this tormented life.

She took charge where she could.

Zippi walked into the Sauna one afternoon as Josef Mengele stood in front of a group of inmates. Although he was known for being calm and enjoying jokes, in his brief time at the camp he had more than earned the nickname that the Auschwitz inmates had coined for him: the Angel of Death. Mengele began his Auschwitz career in May of 1943, at the age of thirty-two. Although at least fifty physicians performed selections and experiments in Auschwitz, he was perhaps among those most frequently found making selections. Often, when a new cattle train pulled onto the entrance ramp, Mengele would be waiting: a short, dark-haired officer standing erect and holding a baton. With a flick of a finger, he decided each inmate's fate: excruciating life or decisive death. Many of the inmates whom he spared on the train platform would suffer at his hands in other ways.

A proponent of eugenics, Mengele was keen on maintaining a "pure race." Any inmate could be subject to his pseudo-experiments, which ran the gamut from kerosene injections on pregnant women to agonizing experimental treatments on Romani children. But Mengele was most fascinated by twins. He was known to inject them with bacteria, remove their organs, and casually murder them in order to perform autopsies—all in the name of "science."

When it came to selections, Mengele's sadism was on full display. He did not limit himself to new arrivals. He held selections anywhere, on a whim. Sometimes he appeared in the barracks without notice, ordering everyone to undress and stand in line. His motorcycle waited outside while he paced the room, his trained eyes scanning the rows of five, his grip on a whip or club. Mengele had an easy, gap-toothed smile that gave him an air of nonchalance, but woe to the inmate who caught his attention: he was, in fact, cold and calculating. He rarely raised his voice; he didn't have to. He inspected each body and noted the weakest and oldest. Those whose numbers that he jotted down were sent to the ovens, making room for a fresh crop of younger, stronger prisoners.

When Zippi walked into the Sauna, he was in the midst of a selection.

Zippi saw Mengele before he noticed her. She came to a halt and quickly averted her gaze.

By the time he spotted her, she had already started to inch away.

Hey, you! he called. *Where are you going?*

Zippi looked straight ahead, continuing to exit the room. She was well-dressed; she wasn't a common prisoner, she told herself. Surely he saw that; surely she'd be safe. But she also knew that this was someone who casually castrated boys and drugged children, leaving them to writhe in pain until their deaths.

Zippi told herself to remain calm. No matter what, she couldn't betray her fear.

Hey! Mengele called again.

She had to get out of there. As she hastened away, she heard someone tell Mengele that she worked at the camp office.

Mengele had been running; now, he gave up the chase. Once again, she'd survived by a slender thread of chance.

But just how many threads were left?

CHAPTER TWELVE

"You Are My Sister-in-Law!"

Without reason or explanations, David was ordered to stay inside. He was not to join the others at the *Strafkompanie*. Not today, not tomorrow. From then on, David was relegated to simple indoor chores: no more beatings, no more back-breaking work.

Someone must have been looking out for him, he thought. Someone must have known that he was on the brink, that he wouldn't survive another day of hard labor. Perhaps Georg, his Sauna supervisor, was looking out for him. Georg liked him, he was kind. Yes, thought David, Georg probably found a way to bribe the SS.

David would spend what was left of his three-month sentence in the penal ward cleaning the barracks and enjoying the extra rations that had suddenly begun finding their way to him.

By June of 1943 he was back at work at the Sauna. David felt as though he'd become even more important, having survived the penal ward—no small feat.

It likely didn't take long before Zippi made an appearance at the Sauna. Supposedly for a shower. He soon realized she was taking showers almost every day. Their glances and brief exchanges continued, as though they'd never stopped. A note from Zippi made its way to him; he wrote her back.

Either now or in months to come, he would tell her about his visits to the opera with his father. They would share their love for music, memories of better times.

He would have never thought he'd be in a relationship with a woman here. Never. It was inconceivable. And yet here they were.

The sun had just about set and the town of Oświęcim was gray and choked in smoke. Scattered arc lamps illuminated columns of Birkenau prisoners as they returned to their barracks for roll call, weary after a long day's work.

Once again, David was missing.

He'd take small excursions by himself—aimless walks, small gasps of artificial freedom. He'd survived so much, and had kept surviving. He felt somewhat protected. By now, most people knew him, knew his voice.

But some did not.

Josef Schillinger, one of the many sadists among the SS, stopped David as he was walking in the middle of the road. He demanded to know where the inmate was headed. And why was he alone?

David tried to explain that he was running an errand. His excuse fell short. Schillinger instructed David to stick out his hands, bend his knees, and stay still. David was not to move until Schillinger told him he could do so—until Schillinger got bored.

David did as he was told. Schillinger struck him across his cheek. The force of his fist knocked out two of David's teeth.

Power intoxicated sadists like Schillinger, but despite what they might have liked to believe, it wasn't absolute. A few months later, when Schillinger was gathering prisoners to undress before a gassing, he would learn this. In the middle of barking orders, he would stop, attracted by an incoming inmate, who was slowly peeling a stocking from the arch of a foot. He watched as she gracefully shifted to lift her skirt, to hoist up her blouse. He was transfixed as she leaned against a pillar and bent down to take off a shoe. The woman, a Polish dancer named Franceska Mann, used the SS men's paralyzing fascination and struck her high heel against an officer's forehead, grabbed his pistol, and shot Schillinger, along with two other SS men. As he collapsed to the ground, Schillinger cried out. Moments later, he was dead.

For now, however, Schillinger was very much alive and his eyes were on David Wisnia. He ordered David, whose gums were bleeding, to return to his barracks. Three prisoners had attempted to escape, Schillinger said, and the SS had a show in store for him and the rest of the camp.

David returned to his block. All inmates in the men's camp were ordered outside for roll call. David joined them and watched in horror. Three shackled prisoners were ordered to stand on chairs. Gallows had been set up in front of the kitchen. One of the prisoners was a child. *Kapos* bound their ankles and thighs and tied nooses around their necks.

"Long live free Poland," one of the adults cried out before the chair was yanked from underneath him and he died alongside the others.

David forgot about the new gap deep inside his mouth, the metallic taste of blood coating his tongue, the imprint of a hand still burning on his cheek. All he could do was watch, along with a thousand other prisoners—forced to bear witness together, knowing that they, too, would perish if they dared look away.

Sometime in the late summer of 1943, David was standing outside the Sauna, staring past the electric wire that separated the women's camp from the men's. A column of Polish women marched past in rows of five. Among the shaved heads and gaunt faces, David thought he recognized a figure from his former life.

He squinted. Yes, there she was: Sara Lewin, his old friend and duet partner from Sochaczew, now an inmate, a walking matchstick, number 47100.

He needed to find a way to get her attention, to make her recognize him.

"Sara!" he yelled in Polish. "Remember, you are my sister-in-law!"

David hoped she would remember the roles they'd once played at the Sochaczew theater, back when they'd sung together, in freedom. If the guards and *Kapos* thought they were related, he reasoned, maybe she'd be safe; he did have some influence now, after all. And if word somehow got around about their past association, he didn't want the gossip to reach Zippi and for her to think Sara was a former girlfriend.

Sara continued to march. She didn't glance his way.

"Sarale," he tried again. This time, she turned around. David stood near the ditch in the men's camp across the road, by the barbed wire. Again he shouted: "David here! You are my sister-in-law!"

She recognized him, finally. But he could tell she didn't know what he was trying to say. Sara kept going; the guards were watching. David may have felt safe yelling to her, but she clearly didn't feel the same way.

Sara looked as though she might snap into pieces at any moment. She would never survive Birkenau like this, he thought. But he knew of one person who could help.

Sara had arrived in June of 1943, in a cattle car from Majdanek, the concentration camp in Lublin where Zippi's father and brothers were sent almost exactly a year earlier. Sara came with a preselected group of men and women deemed fit for "extremely hard labor." One of Sara's sisters had escaped from Warsaw with her husband; her youngest sister was separated from her at Majdanek. Her parents were long dead. Sara arrived at Auschwitz on her own and was immediately placed with the *Aussenkommando,* the outdoor squad, where she carried large stones from one place to another under the cold gaze of whip-bearing Nazis. In the evenings, she'd retreat to her bottom bunk, which she shared with seven women. She made do with rations that just barely kept her alive.

Sara was plucked out of roll call and ordered to see Zippi. She went along dutifully, unaware of who this petite Slovakian woman was. No doubt she was surprised when Zippi gave her extra clothes and bread. Soon after, Sara was moved to one of the camp's most desirable roles: a job at one of the Canada warehouses, where she sorted through piles of clothes confiscated from inmates—silk blouses, wool pants, and fine coats—creating stacks of beautiful garments that would be bundled and sent to Berlin. She'd been warned that anything of value belonged to the SS. Still, whenever she found cash inside the pockets, she hid it inside her uniform. She planned to ask David what she could do with the money the next time she saw him. He would know, she thought.

Occasionally David snuck visits to Sara. It wasn't unusual for men and women in Canada to interact; this was yet another privilege among the "elite" prisoners. They had access to more food, better work conditions, better clothes, better hygiene—and each other.

Sara came to rely on David and Zippi. On occasion, David would slip her an extra ration of soup or bread. Sara showed David the dollar bills she'd found, wondering what she could get for them. David warned her not to engage in Canada's black market. *This is the worst thing you could do. Never do it again.* He took the money on her behalf, exchanging it for a piece of bread. Now that Sara had a good job, he would try to watch out for her—all the while knowing there was only so much he could do. Zippi was keeping an eye on Sara, too.

David relied on Zippi. Every time he was afraid that he was in some kind of trouble, he would tell her about it—and somehow his troubles would evaporate. He never asked how—perhaps he was embarrassed, or perhaps he felt that their time was too short for him to wallow in hypotheticals. Perhaps he was afraid to know, or that his luck would run out.

In turn, he wanted to impress this woman who had power and confidence—this woman who'd chosen him. He saw all sorts of treasures at the Sauna, he told her—watches, jewelry, and more. He wanted to bring her gifts. Zippi refused; nothing good would come of that. Still, he would ask her again and again: he'd seen the most beautiful watch. Could he bring it to her? Each time, Zippi would decline.

If David was caught, Zippi knew, he could be tortured—at the very least. More likely he would be killed. Zippi had no patience for such frivolousness. David didn't seem to understand that their notes, their exchanges were the only risks she needed him to take.

CHAPTER THIRTEEN

Orchestra Girls

For Zippi, life in Auschwitz had become manageable—at least insofar as life in a death camp could be. She had a job that kept her relatively safe and gave her an outlet for her creativity and, better yet, the power to do some good. She had her flirtations with David. And now it looked like music might find a way back into her life as well.

Maria Mandl wanted to create an orchestra—a bona fide orchestra complete with violins, mandolins, cellos, guitars, and a percussion section. She wanted an orchestra that would ooze prestige and impress her bosses: a professional group made up of Birkenau's most talented female inmates.

Back in 1941, before Auschwitz had become a death factory—its transformation a key part of Himmler's solution to the Jewish Question—a group of male prisoners had convinced the SS to let them play music on the ground floor of Block 24. They had instruments from back home, and the SS liked the idea of creating a tempo as prisoners marched to their outdoor labor. Plus, they could always use the entertainment.

By May 1942, an orchestra of more than a hundred musicians regularly performed at Auschwitz's main gates: a collection of shaved men in striped uniforms, clean and ironed, with tailored trousers. Many wore caps. They sat facing music stands, performing German marches, Mozart's symphonies, and Beethoven's concerti. Eventually, a variety of ensembles emerged in the subcamps—male only—but this original orchestra remained the gold standard.

For months, Katya lobbied Drechsel for something similar, suggesting that an orchestra would benefit the women's camp. Drechsel jumped on the idea and easily convinced Mandl. A female orchestra would add to the camp's camouflage—the SS party line that Birkenau was a humane internment camp, and certainly not a killing machine. How could it be, when it provided such an outlet for its artists? What evil could possibly lurk in a place that allowed its prisoners to enjoy Mozart and Beethoven on their way to work?

A music lover herself, Mandl appreciated a good concert. And, as Katya and Zippi knew, she was eager to raise her visibility among the higher-ups in Berlin, to impress her bosses and rise through the ranks of the SS. An orchestra would add another notch to her belt. Katya, for her part, figured that it would be another opportunity to place women in safe jobs. It would also give her a chance to spend more time in the men's camp under the guise of learning how to form an ensemble. This would allow her more latitude to engage with the men's underground operations, which seemed to have more information about the outside world.

Mandl began by meeting with Katya and Zippi to discuss the best way to recruit women. They needed a conductor, someone to drive the orchestra. Katya and Zippi could easily identify a candidate by referring to their various cataloguing systems that categorized prisoners' professions and skills. But the Polish prisoners employed at the camp office pushed for Zofia Czajkowska, a music teacher and one of their own. Mandl assumed that Zofia was a relative of Pyotr Ilyich Tchaikovsky, the famous composer, because of the similarities in their surnames. In reality, Zofia had no connection with

Tchaikovsky. Moreover, Zippi felt she had little musical talent, certainly not enough to create and run an orchestra. The Polish prisoners encouraged Mandl's assumption, though; having a Pole in power would be helpful. Convinced, she handed Zofia the baton.

Zippi hadn't held a mandolin in years; she seized this chance to make music again. She convinced Mandl that she could play in the orchestra with little practice, and maintain her office job without interruption. Mandl gave her blessing and Zippi became an inaugural orchestra member. Not only did she have another artistic escape, but now Zippi also had another opportunity to expand her access within Birkenau and beyond it—to corners of the Auschwitz system she had yet to see.

But first, they needed more instruments. Zippi and Zofia secured permission to scavenge Auschwitz I, the main campus, to find instruments. Inside a warehouse, they stumbled onto riches from a far-gone world: mounds of precious stones, gold, money, and jewelry. But these days, a slice of bread was far more valuable than a diamond. The real treasure was the hundreds of instruments tossed in the jumble, confiscated from prisoners who had been encouraged to bring along their most precious possessions for resettlement. From this treasure trove, the men's orchestra had its choice of instruments, from mandolins and flutes to guitars and cellos. Now it was up to Zofia to negotiate for their share.

Within a matter of weeks, the women's orchestra had made a home in Block 12, which became known as the Music Block. The orchestra girls, or "Mandl's mascots," got better beds, better rations, and better clothing. Their full-time job was to rehearse and perform. Women who joined the orchestra were protected from selections and were treated relatively well. While Zippi continued to sleep in Block 4, she now had access to both office and orchestra rations. In addition, she'd also gained another excuse to recruit sick women from the hospital to help her. With Zippi, they secured jobs crafting sheet music paper, safely occupied while they recovered.

At first, the performers were mostly Polish recruits. They played small concerts at the women's hospital—simple Polish melodies. To Zippi, they sounded like *Katzenmusik*—a cacophony of howling cats. Zofia had no experience conducting, thought Zippi. She really had no business holding a baton.

Zippi worried that the amateur orchestra wouldn't survive long.

Block 10 needs a violin.

Katya received the odd message from a runner three months after the orchestra had been created. It didn't sound right. Block 10, an infamous building in Auschwitz I, had a reputation—and not for its music.

Back when most of Auschwitz was still under construction, back before the Final Solution had been authorized, Dr. Carl Clauberg, a German gynecologist sent a proposal to Himmler. Clauberg, a round-faced, balding professor who wore thick, bulbous glasses, specialized in female infertility. He told Himmler he wanted to develop new methods of mass sterilization. The proposal was in line with Himmler's interest in sterilizing enemies, especially Jews. Clauberg began his work in Birkenau, but as the women's orchestra was being assembled in April 1943, Clauberg secured a full research center in Block 10.

From the outside, the two-story barracks looked like any other stone building in Auschwitz I, except that some of its windows were boarded up so the women inside couldn't look out at the infamous Black Wall that faced it.

In the beginning, Clauberg needed ten women for his experiments. Desperate inmates who thought they had nothing to lose volunteered to join the block. There, they would have showers (though with cold water) and flushable toilets (though without privacy). The women were told that they wouldn't have to go outside for hard labor, that instead they'd have some work done to their bodies—for "medical purposes."

Each morning at roll call, a set of women from Block 10 were plucked out for research. Those who weren't selected spent the day picking leaves and flowers for tea, or filling rubber baskets with dirt from the road to fill in potholes. Those selected for experiments were examined, probed, and photographed in the nude with their legs spread wide on a gynecological chair. But the probing and the photographs were nothing compared to what followed.

Irreversible surgeries, without anesthesia, and severe radiation burns from X-rays were par for the course. Some women were artificially inseminated. Others were sterilized. Some had parts of their cervixes excised in the name of "cancer research." After Clauberg was done with them, they would never be able to conceive. Often, Höss came by to watch Clauberg inject a chemical substance into a woman's fallopian tubes.

The women who survived these depravities were released to another block, emotionally and physically scarred, yet forbidden to speak of their experience. Despite this, word got out and the horrifying experiments of Block 10 became common knowledge. Women stopped volunteering and had to be forcibly chosen through selections. Katya herself observed Clauberg, with his bulging stomach and pursed smile, pick out the youngest and most attractive newcomers to join his laboratory. Sometimes Clauberg enlisted Mandl to send him new subjects. Other times, Mengele ran the selection, often opting for married women. Before long, Block 10 was housing anywhere from three hundred to five hundred women at a time. Once they were no longer useful, the survivors from this cohort were either "discharged" back into Birkenau or sent off to the gas chamber.

What use could music possibly be in a place like this?

But now, according to the runner, a musical prodigy had landed among Block 10's inmates: Alma Rosé. And she was in need of a violin.

Katya asked Zippi if she knew the name.

Of course she did, Zippi said. Alma Rosé was a gifted, critically acclaimed violinist. She'd founded and led a Viennese women's orchestra that had toured Europe in the 1930s. She'd been briefly married to a notable Czech virtuoso and violinist, Váša Příhoda. Then there was Alma's uncle, the Austrian-Jewish composer and conductor Gustav Mahler—a living legend. To top it all off, Alma's father was a violinist and the famed concertmaster Arnold Rosé, who'd led the Vienna Philharmonic for more than half a century. Alma had spent the last decade building a name for herself; her cherubic face, coiffed brown hair, and inviting smile had been featured in international newspapers and publicity posters.

What's going on? Zippi asked Katya.

Katya conveyed the runner's message: Alma Rosé was in Block 10 and needed a violin.

Zippi was dumbfounded. What was Alma Rosé doing in Block 10? Alma was music royalty! Hearing her name in Auschwitz was jarring. Alma was from a different world. But in the Nazis' eyes, that didn't matter: she was Jewish. And although she'd briefly married a Christian and relinquished her faith, it was no use. She'd been born a Jew and, as far as the SS was concerned, she would always be a Jew.

Well, let's transfer her over here! Zippi said.

Zippi knew it was impossible to transfer women out of Block 10. For all the manipulating she and Katya did to the Nazis' lists and numbers, Clauberg's little empire was off limits. But this was no regular prisoner. Plus, the women's orchestra was a disgrace—run by an amateur, thought Zippi. Things could change. Alma could transform the orchestra into something to be proud of.

When Alma Rosé arrived in Auschwitz, in July 1943, she went through the typical registration procedures and was branded Prisoner 50381. But unlike most other inmates, she and about a dozen other women, presumably the most attractive and youngest, were selected for the experimental block. By then, nearly four hundred

Jewish women had become subjects for Clauberg's experiments, living with sixty-five prisoner-nurses and some two dozen women who'd been forced into sex work. Earlier on, Himmler had ordered bordellos to be formed across concentration camps to incentivize men to work harder. Auschwitz's first bordello was established in mid-1943. Jews weren't allowed inside them, but Germans and prisoners of high rank were sometimes rewarded with visits. Only Aryan women could "volunteer" for the job. These so-called volunteers were the ones who had the worst jobs outside, who lived in the worst facilities—and were promised food, cigarettes, their own rooms, and daily showers. Many ended up in Block 10.

Alma was stunned when she arrived. Before the war, she'd founded a touring orchestra. She'd posed for publicity photos and newspaper clippings, her dark, sultry eyes gazing confidently at her audience. She'd been intense about her art, strived for perfection. Now she was wearing an old Soviet POW uniform. Her porcelain face was bloated. She learned about the surgical procedures that might await her. She saw the X-ray machines, the haggard women, and knew she probably wouldn't survive. Still, she realized it would serve her best to remain calm.

As soon as Alma Rosé arrived, word spread around Block 10 that a genuine celebrity was among them. Magda Hellinger, the *Blockälteste* and a friend of Zippi's who'd worked briefly with her, instantly recognized Alma.

Back in Slovakia, Magda had been a kindergarten teacher. She'd arrived in Auschwitz in the same transport as Zippi and Katya and had witnessed how they used their powerful positions to save lives. One time, she'd seen Katya save some three hundred women who'd been selected for the gas chamber, somehow finagling their numbers and sending the girls back to their barracks when the SS wasn't looking. As the so-called senior of Block 10, Magda tried to help her fellow prisoners however she could. Her cropped blond hair was growing out. According to an SS physician, she "didn't look Jewish," and she used this to her advantage, making requests for the women in her block that would've otherwise been flat-out denied, securing nightgowns, pillows, soap, and towels. Whenever she could, she also found ways to lighten the mood for the women of Block 10. In the evenings, after the SS departed, she gathered a group of women to act and dance for one other. The women paraded around and laughed at their ridiculous, ill-fitting nightgowns; they found reasons to smile. On one occasion, she'd even allowed two girls to slip out of the barracks. Later, the girls were noted as missing at roll call and Magda was accused of sabotage. That she'd survived the incident was a miracle.

Alma's presence in Block 10 presented another opportunity for Magda to help the inmates in her charge. But she had to find a way to communicate with the main office.

It wouldn't be easy. Magda couldn't be caught writing a note or she'd end up in the penal ward. And so she sent an oral message to the camp office through a runner, the one Katya received.

Alma received a violin that same night. Behind locked doors, she performed for the prisoners of Block 10.

For a few days, Alma performed nightly cabarets for the women of her block. Eventually, the SS began to attend. These concerts, which took place inside one of the most notorious blocks of Auschwitz, were surreal—all the more so because they were being given by Alma, the darling of Vienna's violin virtuosos.

But these Block 10 performances were short-lived.

When Mandl got wind of Alma and her talent, she didn't waste time. Zofia, she'd decided, wasn't up to her standards. Within a month of Alma's arrival, she was transferred to Birkenau's Music Block, replacing Zofia as the women's orchestra conductor. Zofia was kicked upstairs, now serving as the Music Block's *Blockälteste*.

Alma quickly imposed on the orchestra a kind of order that had been lacking. She was a professional. For her, this was not a hobby;

there was no room for mediocrity. She demoted women who didn't play well, though she always found them other jobs within the Music Block to keep them protected. She made the case to Mandl for additional positions, from copyists to maintenance workers. She regularly tried out new musicians. Her auditions could save an inmate from outdoor labor, from having to stand in roll call in the freezing weather, from casual torture, and, of course, from gassing. Under Alma's tutelage, the "orchestra girls" were allowed daily showers and special uniforms for their concerts. They got socks and underwear, and even an iron stove that kept them warm during the bitter cold winter. They enjoyed extra rations, including a third of a loaf of bread, margarine, sausage, jam, and beets three days a week.

In exchange for these privileges, the women were expected to practice rigorously. They were held to a standard of discipline that Zippi had gotten used to—and appreciated—in the mandolin orchestra she'd performed with as a child. Alma warned them, over and over again: "If we don't play well, we'll go to the gas."

They all knew what going to the gas meant. Each of the four crematoria that had been completed the previous month contained its own gas chamber. Now, more prisoners could be exterminated at once—and they were. The chimneys were in constant use. When newcomers arrived in Auschwitz and underwent selections, they gazed in wonder at the smoke and fire polluting the sky. Well-meaning old-timers attempting to calm these inmates would suggest that the SS was burning old prisoners' clothes. But the stench of human ash gave the crematoria away; their purpose was unmistakable.

While there was no escape from reality, Zippi's moments practicing with the girls provided her a respite. She was elated by the challenge, feeling that Alma was performing a miracle. To Zippi's ear, the orchestra now played nicely—beautifully, even. And most crucially, in Alma's capable hands, the orchestra now had a chance to survive, and to create additional safe jobs.

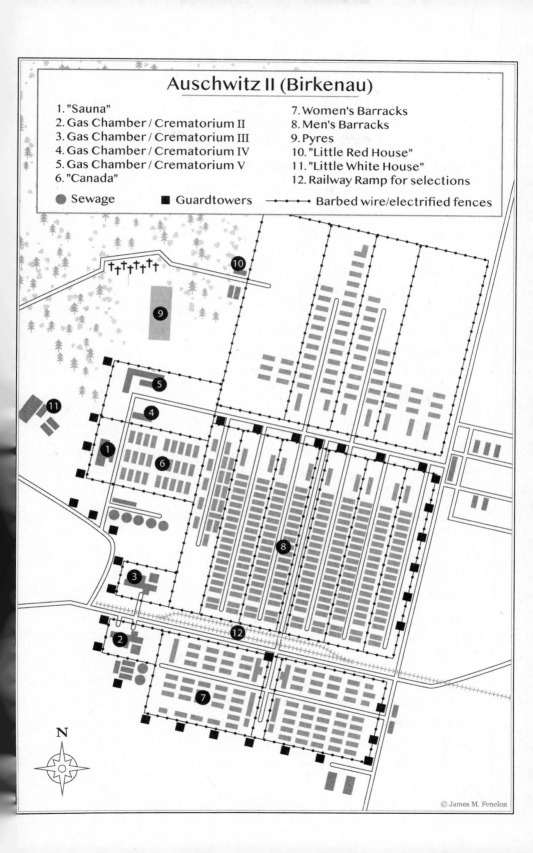

Now that they had professional panache, the women rose before dawn to perform as *Kommandos* marched out to work. Some were tasked with setting up music stands and stools at the camp's main gate. Then they would all stand for *Appell,* drink their coffee-tea concoctions, and, in rows of five, march back to the main entrance. They played German military marches that kept columns of women moving in tempo. In the evenings, they returned to the main gate and performed as the *Kommandos* returned in groups that were usually smaller than those that had set out in the morning.

The orchestra performed selections from Schubert, Bach, and others, always aware that the gas chamber was in near-constant use. For some, the beautiful music in such a murderous environment was jarring. But for Zippi, who only played during the morning and evening marches, the music was therapeutic. After the morning march, the women rehearsed operettas, arias from the Italian opera *Madama Butterfly,* popular songs, and even works by banned Jewish composers, like the first movement of Mendelssohn's Violin Concerto in E minor. SS officers would come by on a whim to demand performances.

Alma conducted in a calm, controlled manner, separating the camp from the music. One time, at the sound of an officer's voice or a guard's cackle, she stopped the players.

I can't make music that way, she said.

The guards quieted down.

Soon the orchestra accompanied an assortment of talented dancers and singers, all performing together around the camp. Höss enjoyed private concerts in the comfort of his villa. Mengele took breaks from experiments to watch trained dancers perform just for him. Among the performers was Edith Eva Eger, a trained Hungarian ballerina who'd dreamed of joining the Olympic team but was disqualified at age sixteen for being Jewish. She became one of Mengele's favorites. As Alma conducted the orchestra through Johann Strauss II's *Blue Danube* waltz, Edith shut her eyes and pirouetted. She imagined she was away from Auschwitz, on stage at the Budapest opera house where she'd once dreamed she would dance.

On Sunday mornings in the summer, the women performed out in the open air. They played upbeat classics while new arrivals went through selections and smoke rose from the crematoria chimneys. In the winter, they played at the Sauna, witnessing cruel punishments and the terror of inmates registering into their new home. They tried to stay focused on the music. Tears meant punishment; Alma would not stand for shows of emotion.

Some women felt Alma was nothing more than a *Kapo,* eager to exert her power over them, happy to demean them when she felt they underperformed. Others believed that Alma was fighting for them, that she pushed them and demanded their best to help them survive. All agreed that the orchestra had become Alma's obsession.

Anita Lasker-Wallfisch arrived in Auschwitz just as the orchestra needed a low-octave instrument. During registration, Anita offhandedly mentioned that she played the cello. The prisoner registering her told Anita to stand aside and wait in the shower room. She sent an inmate to get Alma.

Fantastic that you are here! Alma said to Anita, who stood before her in the nude. Eighteen-year-old Anita had just endured Auschwitz's ceremonial shaving. Her freshly tattooed forearm was red and swollen. *Where did you study?* Alma asked. She told Anita someone would get her for an audition. *You will be saved,* Alma said before she left.

Anita had dreamed of a career in music. At age thirteen, her parents had sent her from Wrocław (then Breslau) to Berlin, nearly two hundred and fifty miles away, to study the cello. She remained there for six months, renting a room in an older woman's apartment, until the violent pogroms of *Kristallnacht* made it clear that Berlin was no longer a safe place for Jews. Two years had passed since she'd touched a cello. Now, in Auschwitz, she secured an audition, playing one of Schubert's *Marches militaires,* soon after being clothed and quarantined. She was in.

The orchestra became one more avenue through which Zippi could disengage from death. *I can be half dead, but if I have a job to do, I'm doing it,* she thought. Despite everything she'd been through, everyone she'd lost, she focused on what beauty she could find. Her creative work — building models, designing graphs, and playing the mandolin — this was her therapy. Her art allowed her to lose herself, to forget where she was, even briefly. It allowed her to feel as though she were her own master.

Then there was David. Another reminder, her very own, that humanity could be beautiful, could be good — could be worth fighting for. Even if it meant losing everything.

CHAPTER FOURTEEN

"Evening in the Moonlight"

I t was likely around February of 1944, about a year after Zippi and David had first traded glances. A tumultuous year filled with death and close calls—from illnesses to imprisonment and beatings. They took whatever good they could—mostly in the form of music and love notes. And now, Zippi decided, it was time for more.

The new Central Sauna was ready, after nine months of construction. A state-of-the-art decontamination facility located in the Canada complex, it was the largest building in Birkenau. Men and women worked side by side, delousing inmates and clothing.

All her life, Zippi had been strategic in the kinds of risks she took. But when it came to David, she'd allowed herself an exception, a luxury. They had a shared loneliness, a shared need for tenderness. The possibility of prolonging their encounters was worth risking her life—and her heart.

And so Zippi took the reins.

The next time they saw each other, she told David where to go.

For the first time since he could remember, he looked forward to waking up.

He arrived at the designated spot in Canada, heart pounding, palms sweating. There, in the barracks near Crematorium IV and Crematorium V, he found walls made of packages. Behind them was an enclave, a space just for them. Inside, a structure like a ladder beckoned him: jackets, pants, and coats, all bound up, tight as bricks. He ascended. This was inmates' clean clothing, bounty confiscated upon arrival. A makeshift ledge that only he and Zippi would climb.

She'd built this sanctuary for them, he realized. Outside, snow met swamp, the smell of burning, the shadows of the dead. But inside, the space was their own: for their bodies and no one else's.

Fellow inmates stood guard. They were paid—perhaps in food, or in clothes, or in some sort of protection. While they waited, they might pace, eyes dart across the warehouse, a silent prayer for no trouble. Perhaps they sat on packages of clothes, thinking of their own loves lost.

While these tattooed guards kept watch, Zippi and David tried not to worry. The risk of being discovered was death. But for now, they had each other, this seventeen-year-old boy and this twenty-five-year-old woman.

She would teach him everything.

Before David and Zippi began their affair, he wouldn't have believed that such an arrangement was possible. Unlike Zippi, he didn't know of anyone else in Auschwitz who was having this kind of romantic liaison. The consequences would have been too horrific, he thought. Torture. Death. But David's boldness—and his recklessness—were growing, as was his desire for Zippi.

She arranged everything. About once a month, Zippi and David met at the same spot—their little hollow within a mountain of bundled clothing in the Canada warehouse. Each time, she paid off inmate guards to keep watch for them, and to warn them if the SS was nearby.

"EVENING IN THE MOONLIGHT"

Zippi and David limited their time at the nook to thirty minutes, an hour at the very most. They were as careful as they could be, all the while knowing they were being reckless.

After meeting a couple of times, David needed less instruction, but he still followed Zippi's lead. She was self-assured—experienced. They exposed little skin—holding back, removing only what they had to. Holding on, inside their cave.

At first, they didn't talk much. But slowly, they started.

He told Zippi about being a child star in Warsaw. He recalled his father's passion for opera. Zippi told him about her mandolin, the orchestra back at home, and now holding the instrument again.

Zippi wanted to hear him sing, and he happily obliged. Perhaps sometimes she sang or hummed along, harmonizing with this bright-eyed boy who, like her, still saw the possibility of music and beauty.

One day, she taught him a Hungarian song, *"Holdvilágos éjszakán"* ("Evening in the Moonlight"). It had a rhythm they could imagine themselves dancing to, in a different world, words that could transport them. Together, they sang:

Evening in the moonlight
What does she dream about in the night?
That a prince might arrive
Riding a steed of snow-white.

This dream is so wondrous
But waking up is too cruel, too vicious
The prince is fading away
His arrival, a misstep, a dance of disarray.

Yet how small are those clouds up there
Floating on the sky's rim slow
Gazing at them drifting in the air

Hoping forevermore
And the story goes on.

Evening in the moonlight
What does she dream about in the night?
That a prince might arrive
Riding a steed of snow-white.

A hundred thousand Cinderellas
A hundred thousand shoes looking for one gallant
The prince hides during the day
And the lady cannot wait
She may find someone new.

Evening in the moonlight
What does she dream about in the night?
That a prince might arrive
Riding a steed of snow-white.

Yet how small are those clouds up there
Floating on the sky's rim slow
Gazing at them drifting in the air
Hoping forevermore
And the story goes on.
That a prince might arrive
Riding a steed of snow-white.

That a prince might arrive
Riding a steed of snow-white.

Before they left their nook, cheeks flushed, they fixed themselves up as best they could. Hair in place, shirts straightened, they snuck back out, one at a time. The last one out rebuilt the wall.

CHAPTER FIFTEEN

"We Are Going to Play"

When Roza Robota showed up at Zippi's office one night, likely around the fall of 1943, Zippi felt an instant connection. Roza, a Polish Jew just about Zippi's age, had deep-set, downturned eyes that sparkled when she smiled. She was tall and wide-boned with a commanding presence.

Like Zippi, Roza had arrived in Auschwitz early on, back in 1942. She now worked at the *Bekleidungskammer,* a clothing storage room in Canada, across from Crematorium IV. During that initial visit, she told Zippi that she recognized her from a Hashomer Hatzair gathering in Poland. Roza had been a loyal member since childhood and had taken on various leadership roles.

That night, Roza and Zippi came to an arrangement: Roza, who had access to luxury items, would provide Zippi with underwear and bandages to distribute to women in need. In return, Zippi would place specific prisoners into whatever work positions or barracks Roza requested.

Zippi didn't think much of their first conversation. She understood that the Polish women in Birkenau were at a disadvantage compared to the Slovakians.

A few evenings later, Roza returned. This time, she brought

Zippi a gift: an apron. Usually Zippi wore a simple blouse and a skirt; few inmates had aprons. Zippi was touched by the small, thoughtful gesture.

Two weeks later, Roza came by again. She handed Zippi a new apron.

I don't need another, Zippi tried to tell her.

Roza wouldn't have it. She asked Zippi to return the old apron; she wanted to replace it with the new one. Zippi accepted. She'd had odder requests.

Two weeks later, Roza returned with yet another apron. Again, she exchanged the old one for the new one.

These exchanges continued every two weeks. They were bizarre, but Zippi shrugged them off. Later, she noticed small layers inside the aprons' seams. She wondered if something was hidden within the folds of fabric—it's unlikely she would have asked.

That May of 1944, under the sweltering heat, Zippi met a girl so small she almost disappeared in her clothes. She reminded Zippi of the days when she herself had been a walking skeleton, on the verge of death. The girl begged Zippi for help.

Two years before, Zippi had come to Eva Weigel, the German political prisoner she had befriended early on in the camp, with a similar plea. Eva, who had worked for a powerful Nazi, had told her to return to the barracks, that she'd be made *verfügbar*—available for an indoor position. Now Zippi was in a position to do the same.

She took the girl with her to the Sauna. There, Zippi undressed her and had her bathed. Handing the girl her cure-all remedy of cod-liver oil, Zippi then told the *Blockälteste* not to send her out to work—she was *verfügbar.*

Zippi arranged a job for the girl as a nurse's aide at the camp hospital, where she would be warm, have a bit more food, and start gaining back some weight and strength. There, she'd have a chance to survive.

Zippi and Katya took in prisoners in trouble at the office when they could. When an older Polish Jew arrived at camp and made it through the selection on what Zippi guessed must have been a particularly dark evening, Katya quickly took her into the office and created a job for her, duplicating cardex files. Whenever the SS stopped by, she hid her. Katya also arranged for an older Romanian woman, who'd lost both her breasts, either to cancer or an accident, to get an office job.

There were others. Zippi and Katya had done this before and they would do it again.

It was easier for them to save women, but every so often news would find its way to Zippi that a man was in danger of being sent on a transport or moved to an outside job. Sometimes the reports came from women who had discovered that a partner or friend had been threatened. Other times it even came from SS guards she'd bribed for this very purpose.

When this happened, Zippi would ask Mandl for permission to go to the men's camp. She had to collect missing statistical figures for her diagrams, she said. Mandl sent her off. Zippi asked to see the head of labor detail, a prisoner functionary. This man, whose runner made daily visits to Zippi's office, was familiar with her. He appreciated her dependable work. She gave him the numbers of the prisoner she wanted to help, and he obliged.

Zippi had also befriended a *Kapo* from the men's side of the camp, who delivered shoes for the women. At his request, she facilitated meetings for him to impart messages to the female inmates during his visits. In return, she asked him to look out for men she knew who could use the help.

During Zippi and David's monthly trysts in their Canada nest, they rarely spoke about goings-on inside the camp, preferring to focus on happier topics: the outside world, the past. But in their nook one day, Zippi told David about the day Mandl had sent her, along with some of the other office girls, on a hike in the woods. David listened in disbelief.

Zippi had gone inside the Little White House. He couldn't imagine.

As Zippi spoke, he thought of the transports going in and never coming out. The smoke that covered their skies. He listened to Zippi's voice and thought of the trap inside the Little White House, where so many inmates had died before the new gas chambers came online.

Somehow, they were both safe. But outside their cocoon, the thick smoke was overwhelming. The image of the Little White House, and all it represented, haunted David — haunted them both.

By 1944, the two farmhouses, the original temporary gas chambers, had long been replaced by the four larger gas chambers and crematoria. Larger numbers of inmates arrived daily, Birkenau expanded, and the chimney flames shot up higher.

If Zippi were to get pregnant, the repercussions would be catastrophic. Zippi and David did everything they could to avoid a pregnancy, but their methods were far from foolproof. There was a chance, they knew, that she would get pregnant.

Pregnant women often had forced abortions that killed both mother and child. Babies born in the camp were often poisoned, drowned, or gassed. Some blond-haired, blue-eyed children — the lucky ones — were sent away for "Germanization": their names were changed and they would be raised as ethnic Germans.

Gerhard Palitzsch, Katya's lover, was well known for murdering entire families at the Black Wall. One time, he lined up a unit of five and calmly shot an infant through the skull as she nestled in her mother's arms. He then shot the two older children before shooting their parents. On another occasion, he shot the father first, then the eldest child. Then, instead of pointing his gun at the youngest, a baby cradled in his mother's arms, he grabbed the infant and flung him against the Black Wall, shattering his skull. He killed the mother last.

Zippi had witnessed firsthand as Palitzsch executed an inmate at the wall. She and David must have willed the thought away, but also been plagued by the fact that, if Zippi did have a baby, it might well end up in the hands of a monster like Palitzsch.

Zippi could not abide Palitzsch's daily visits to Katya's office. After weeks of biting her tongue, Zippi couldn't hold back any longer.

What's he doing here? she asked Katya after Palitzsch left.

He's coming to visit me, Katya said.

Katya, that's a mass murderer! Zippi said, horrified.

She'd seen him orchestrate executions of hundreds of prisoners. Everyone in camp knew about his thirst for blood, his hunger for power, and, most of all, his sadism.

Katya didn't respond.

Do you love him? Zippi asked.

What is there to love about him? Katya said.

She tried to explain that she could help more people because of him, that he was a reason she could help prisoners in the men's camp.

Still, Zippi couldn't understand Katya. She recognized the need for companionship, but she couldn't forgive an affair with Palitzsch. She warned Katya to end the relationship, but Katya was too entrenched; there was no turning back. No matter how much she insisted otherwise, Katya was a Jewish prisoner. How does a Jewish inmate—no matter how high-ranking—end an affair with one of the Nazis' most notorious Jew-killers?

Katya and Palitzsch were becoming sloppy. Zippi's *Blockälteste*, Anna, also knew about the affair and was terrified for Katya. If high-ranking SS officials found out, Katya would most certainly be killed. For Palitzsch's part, any SS man who slept with a "subhuman" woman like a Jew or a Romani would be locked up in Block 11.

Palitzsch could have satisfied himself in a camp bordello, but perhaps he was attracted by the illicit nature of the affair. He was hardly the only SS man in Auschwitz who was carrying on an affair with an inmate. Even Höss was rumored to have a mistress among the inmates.

It didn't matter. Zippi could not come to terms with Katya's relationship. She'd once respected her friend so much. Now Katya seemed stupid. How could she risk everything for this killer?

Across occupied Europe, the underground resistance was abuzz with good news: 1944 had started off with word that the Allies were beating the Nazis. Around camp, the visible gloom of the SS officers confirmed what the inmates were hearing. In the east, a nearly 900-day siege of Leningrad had ended when the Soviets had forced the Germans to retreat. Hitler believed that Leningrad (known today as Saint Petersburg) was "the cradle of Bolshevism" and needed to be captured for the sake of the Nazi crusade. Some three million German soldiers, and more than a half-million non-German Nazi allies, advanced on the city in June 1942. To Hitler, a victory in Leningrad would've meant domination of the Soviet Union's mainland, and a necessary precursor to invading Moscow. Instead, the German army's surrender, on January 27, 1944, marked the beginning of Nazi Germany's collapse in northern Russia.

And yet inside Auschwitz, greater and greater numbers of inmates were arriving daily, Birkenau expanded, and more smog assaulted the skies.

Still, the resistance inside the camp had mustered a few victories. Information was trickling out of the camp in a variety of ways. On June 7, 1943, the Polish government in exile received a telegram from a source that called themselves Kazia. The message went so far as to state that sick inmates in Auschwitz were being killed with injections of lead to their hearts, that men and women

were being subjected to experiments involving castration, sterilization, and artificial insemination, and that a new subcamp had been
built for the Romani. Other telegrams listed the numbers of the
sick and inmates who'd "disappeared." Telegrams sent from another
source, with the code name Wanda, detailed gassings and selections. Neither source was ever identified, but their information
had, crucially, made it outside the walls of the camp. Zippi, who
had access to so much data herself, somehow provided the resistance with the number of women who'd died in Birkenau that July
(1,113). To top it off, since 1939, a British spy organization had
been intermittently intercepting radio communication between
Auschwitz and Berlin, in which the camp administration updated
Nazi headquarters about the number of incoming prisoners and
other increasingly detailed statistics.

Partly as a result of the recent leaks, Himmler officially discharged Höss. There'd been too much talk on the English radio
about the extermination of Auschwitz prisoners, Himmler had
explained to Höss as the men strolled in the gardens surrounding
Höss's villa. The evidence was too damning. Berlin leadership
needed to distance itself from the horrors of the camp. They needed
the support of the German public and wanted to avoid international interference. Hitler excused Germany's military aggression
by casting Germany as the victim of Jews and foreigners, even as
the Nazis' casual torture and murder proved otherwise. Blame for
Auschwitz's conditions was thrown on Höss, a rogue agent. By
November of 1943, he was gone.

But this was Auschwitz. Celebrations never lasted.

On March 6, 1944, Katya overheard an SS officer in a telephone
call with Berlin. The inmates at Auschwitz's Terezín family camp
were scheduled to be killed.

The Terezín family camp, made up mostly of Czech Jews, was
an unusual satellite within the system of camps and subcamps at

Auschwitz. Most of its inmates had arrived from the labor camp in the Theresienstadt ghetto, in Terezín, Czechoslovakia. Upon arrival in Auschwitz, they didn't have their heads shaved, they kept their luggage, and they wore civilian clothes. They lived in a special section of the camp, where children shared their own block, had lessons, and played games.

Denmark's government had expressed concern at the deportation and "resettlement" of Danish Jews to Theresienstadt, and planned to send a Red Cross delegation to the camp. The SS wanted to be prepared in the event that they followed Theresienstadt with a visit to Auschwitz. The Terezín family camp had been set up as a Potemkin village, a living diorama to fool any such inspectors. But the SS had clearly decided that it no longer needed to keep up this charade. And now Katya had learned that the inmates' demise was imminent. With urgency, she passed the information on to her underground connections. But it was too late.

Two days later, at around 8 p.m., the SS surrounded the Terezín family camp with its trained dogs. Officers ordered the Jewish men, women, and children into trucks covered in tarps. Their luggage, they were told, would follow them by train. At 10 p.m., twelve trucks set out, each carrying forty inmates. Men were dropped off at Crematorium III. Women and children went to Crematorium II. Around 2 a.m., while they waited for their death, the women sang Czech folk songs, the anthem of the Zionist movement, "Hatikvah," and the Czech national anthem. The sun was beginning to rise when the 3,791 Jewish men, women, and children were gassed to death.

Zippi felt sick when she heard the news. The resistance had failed. For days, she could think of nothing else, she couldn't see straight. In a daze, she walked straight into the door of her office. Blood trickled down to her eyes from a gash on her forehead. Zippi's friend, a former dentist, stitched up the wound.

When they could, she and Katya tried their hands at revenge. They now had a book tracking all prisoners within the penal ward. This presented an opportunity: they might not be able to strike back at the Nazis, but they could, at least, ensure that the worst of their collaborators—the camp's most vicious *Kapos* and *Blockälteste*—remained out of commission for as long as possible if they wound up in the penal ward for one infraction or another. When Katya and Zippi saw a number belonging to someone particularly cruel, they'd extend their time in the penal ward.

For months, Alma Rosé spent sleepless nights finding ways to improve her orchestra's repertoire. Her hair was graying—a dangerous problem for most, as signs of aging typically led to selections. Her mood vacillated between depression and elation.

Then, in April of 1944, Alma fell ill. She vomited, burned with a high fever, and suffered from chest pains. The root of her illness was mysterious, but many suspected poison. Others guessed she was suffering from botulism after ingesting spoiled alcohol or food.

The Queen of Birkenau, as she was known, received medical intervention that was unprecedented in Auschwitz. And yet within two days, Alma died.

Mengele ordered an autopsy and lab work to test for meningitis and food poisoning. Zippi was walking outside and happened upon the body. Crestfallen, Zippi noticed the crude way her abdomen had been stitched up after the autopsy.

The orchestra was permitted to mourn Alma. Even Mandl was openly devastated. A Russian prisoner replaced Alma as conductor, but the orchestra was never the same. Sunday performances were canceled. Members had other duties in addition to rehearsal: they now had to knit and mend prisoner uniforms.

Zippi stopped going altogether.

She later thought about Alma's pride at the orchestra she'd created from nothing. *I will never go back to my old times, to my old way of playing,* Zippi remembered Alma telling her troupe. *I will take you girls to Europe, all over Europe, and we are going to play.*

Together, Zippi and Alma had dreamed of a world beyond Auschwitz. Zippi remembered her pleasure in getting praise from the conductor, in being chosen by a world-renowned violinist. *Did she know what that meant to us?* Zippi wondered. *To get such an offer?*

CHAPTER SIXTEEN

"Long Live Poland"

The volume of bodies burned in Birkenau in the summer of 1944 created a stench so overwhelming that at times it felt impossible to breathe. While the Allied armies invaded Normandy, in what would become a turning point of the war, the SS ramped up its plans to exterminate all Hungarian Jews.

Auschwitz and its subcamps were brimming with new transports, and the Canada warehouses overflowed with confiscated goods. And still, David and Zippi managed to meet.

Their meetings had always been exciting, but now they were more of a challenge. With the constant smoke hovering, it became harder to distance themselves from the reality around them. If what they had heard about the war was true, the end of the Nazi regime was a distinct possibility. Yet death was moving closer, too.

Zippi told David about her brother, Sam. He was still alive, she told him, somewhere in Slovakia. David's own brothers were gone. One dead in Warsaw, the other—who knew? He had no idea.

David could not understand how it was feasible that he'd survived this long. He saw acquaintances and block mates disappear every day—either transported to other camps or sent to the gas chamber. When he and Zippi met, when she walked up to him, clean, wearing a jacket, always so well put together—well, he had his suspicions. This was a woman with access, he thought. And the more he thought about it, the prouder he felt, the more special that she had chosen him.

Music brought them pleasure. So they sang. Sometimes they even laughed.

And they kissed, always so tender. It was surreal, having these brief moments, these lulls from life outside Canada. Could they have been falling in love? They wouldn't dare say the words. Instead, they sang.

Evening in the moonlight
What does she dream about in the night?
That a prince might arrive
Riding a steed of snow-white.

Someone yelled from downstairs. One of their guards. It was safe to come down now.

And just like that—until, they hoped, the next time—their session was up.

Sirens blasted across the camp. Word quickly got around. Two inmates had run away: Mala Zimetbaum and her boyfriend, Eduard Galiński, known as Edek.

A couple of hours earlier, Zippi had been on her way to see a friend, a Slovakian *Blockälteste* she'd known from back home and whom she frequently visited in the camp. As usual, none of Zippi's supervisors seemed to care where she was on that searing summer afternoon, so long as her work was done. So she'd made herself scarce, loaning out her office to the resistance while she traipsed across camp on a social visit.

Zippi wandered into Block 6—but instead of her friend, she found Mala, the loud-mouthed Belgian runner and interpreter who'd once been her barrack mate. Mala had suffered several bouts of malaria and had since been transferred. Now Zippi found her lying in a bunk; her boyfriend, Edek, was standing near her. Concerned that Mala had had a malaria attack, Zippi walked over and asked how she felt. Realizing she was fine, Zippi left quickly; she was not one to infringe on a fellow prisoner's precious privacy.

Edek was a Polish political prisoner who had arrived in Auschwitz with the first transport of prisoners, back in 1940; he had the low prisoner number of 531. As a locksmith, he was allowed to move about in both the men's and women's camps. After their first meeting, Mala and Edek found reasons to bump into each other and eventually fell in love. Then they were gone.

Over the years, plenty of men had escaped Auschwitz. Few succeeded in getting far. Those who were caught suffered the perfunctory SS treatment: torture at Block 11, followed by death, often by hanging. Zippi had seen how reckless Mala could be. Less than a year before, she had seen Mala up on a table, trying to take charge of a group of Belgian prisoners. Reckless. And yet she'd made it out.

Mala had gotten her hands on papers stating that she was being transferred. Edek had somehow acquired an SS uniform and pretended to be her escort. She'd carried a washbasin on her head and followed behind Edek. The SS guard at the front gate didn't even bother to look at their passes. He simply opened the gate and let them through.

The sirens sounded hours later. When the inmates learned what the ruckus was about, most were giddy with joy. Two prisoners had met in Auschwitz, fallen in love, and escaped, in spite of everything. Theirs was a story of success, proof that it was possible to defy the odds.

The SS officers were furious. Escape attempts had become increasingly frequent. Even worse, elsewhere in Europe the Allies were beating the Germans. June 1944 had started with D-Day, when Allied forces had overwhelmed the Germans in Normandy. Later that month, a handful of Italian cities were liberated. By June 24, 1944, the day Mala and Edek escaped, the Red Army was inching closer to Poland.

The Nazis were relentless in their search for the lovers. Guards interrogated civilians and prisoners throughout the camp and in nearby towns. At first, they uncovered few clues—but that soon changed.

It is unclear what, exactly, gave the couple away. Some say they ran out of food and that an SS man recognized Mala when she walked into a store. Others say they were turned in by a local Polish girl. Regardless, the couple enjoyed only twelve days of freedom.

Once arrested, the lovers were as good as dead. One inmate recalled seeing Mala being returned to Auschwitz in a wheelbarrow, her head low to the ground, "going *clank, clank,* and banging into the asphalt."

Mala and Edek were locked inside the bunker of Block 11. They were interrogated, flogged, and tortured over and over again; the Gestapo was intent on tracking down anyone who'd helped them. But neither Edek nor Mala spoke. They were condemned to a public hanging.

On September 15, 1944, all prisoners were required to stand in roll call and witness the executions. Edek's hanging would take place in the men's camp in Birkenau; Mala's would take place at the women's camp. Zippi had the privilege of being able to avoid the sickening spectacle; she shut herself inside her office.

Afterward, she heard different versions of what happened out in the public square, on the Nazis' stage for hangings and other punishments. What seemed clear was that, as Mala stood by, hair tousled, eyes pale, Mandl had made a speech. The prisoners who applied themselves to their work would be treated well by the Ger-

The two lovers, Mala Zimetbaum and Edek Galiński, escaped camp and enjoyed twelve days of freedom before they were caught.

mans, Mandl said. As for those who betrayed the Germans—those who'd committed treason—well, they'd suffer for it.

The monologue had hardly ended when an inmate slipped a razor to Mala. Before anyone could stop her, Mala slashed both her wrists. Blood trickled down her palms. The SS noticed something was wrong.

From there, details grew murky. As she lost consciousness, Zippi later heard, Mala slapped Mandl across the face with her bloodied hand before she was shoved into a cart and brought to the crematorium. Some said an SS officer shot her dead before she made it. Another prisoner said that she saw Mala slap a different officer, whose face turned bright red at the horror of a Jewish prisoner daring to raise her hand against a German. There were rumors that Mala was thrown into a cart used to carry stones, and taken to the hospital so she could recover before being killed at the hands of the SS. Another prisoner claimed to have heard her scream, "Long live Poland, long live the [*sic*] freedom, long live the world without Hitler."

Whatever happened to Mala, everyone agreed that her suicide attempt caused a commotion unlike anything they'd seen before in the camp. At his own hanging, Edek called out "Poland lives!" as he kicked a stool from under him.

Selfish, stupid girl, thought Zippi. She'd gotten so many people in trouble because of this poorly planned escape, and to what end? She lost her life, and so did Edek. The thought of it made Zippi angry. Mala had held a good job; she had a chance to live, and to help others do the same. And she had squandered it.

Katya, too, was taking bigger risks. She wanted to send information to her sister, to let the free world know the truth of what was happening inside Auschwitz. She enlisted Zippi's help to write a message in German; Palitzsch had promised to mail it for her. Katya and Zippi did not mince words: they wrote about the hunger, the torture, and the gas chambers, about being surrounded by smoke and death.

It's unclear why Katya would have written the letter in German, and why she asked Palitzsch to send it for her—let alone whether he knew what was inside. If so, she could not have been surprised when, in the end, the letter wound up in the hands of the Gestapo. Katya's sister and her husband were arrested; their son was sent to an orphanage.

Zippi had warned Katya that Palitzsch was trouble. Yet Katya refused to believe that Palitzsch would have betrayed her. Perhaps he hadn't—but then again, perhaps he had. Later, he sent Katya a letter himself, writing that he'd finally realized that he was a murderer. He was a changed man, he told her. He would no longer carry out death sentences. Katya believed him. Perhaps she needed to.

In any case, these lovers' recklessness, too, soon caught up to them. When someone at camp denounced Katya and Palitzsch for their relationship, Zippi was not surprised.

Katya had been petitioning the SS to recognize her as an Aryan, to once and for all rid herself of the stigma of being a Jewish prisoner. Palitzsch had apparently been trying to help her campaign.

Josef Hustek-Erber—an SS officer who was dubbed "Franken-stein" for his long arms, crooked legs, prominent cheekbones, and two sets of false teeth—noticed Palitzsch's efforts. He initiated an investigation and quickly discovered the affair—although he may not have been the first person to drag the lovers out into the open. Zippi, for her part, believed that Margot Drechsel, jealous of the affair, had been the one to expose them.

Many SS officers who'd had relationships with prisoners in plain sight weren't necessarily denounced. For one, Officer Franz Wunsch—the same man who'd whipped David's friend Szaja Kalfus fifty times and left him permanently disabled—had fallen hopelessly in love with a Jewish inmate, Helena Citron, who had arrived from Slovakia in the first transport, before Zippi and Katya. Wunsch had removed Helena's sister from the gas chamber when he'd found Helena distraught. He'd fed and protected Helena herself in special quarters when she was suffering a bout of typhus. He helped her survive Auschwitz and carried a photograph of Helena in a locket around his neck for the rest of his life. At the camp, their romance had become an open secret, but Wunsch was not punished.

Palitzsch was a different case. Höss, who had returned to Auschwitz in May of 1944, had never liked Katya's lover. Perhaps Höss felt threatened by Palitzsch. In any case, now he had reason to get rid of him.

Both Katya and Palitzsch were sent to the penal ward, and in early September of 1944 Katya was transported out of the Auschwitz system, to a concentration camp in Stutthof. Here she found another overcrowded camp in the woods—but here she had no sway. Mercifully, she was told that the camp's gas chambers were out of order. She wouldn't be killed—not for now.

Palitzsch, meanwhile, remained in Auschwitz. He was accused of stealing clothing, money, and valuables from Jewish and Polish prisoners—a common practice and one that was usually ignored, but which technically was an infraction, given that such goods were officially expected to go to the Third Reich. Höss took the chance to blame Palitzsch for the "mistreatment" of prisoners, saying that any abuse they'd endured was due to Palitzsch's sadism rather than his own role in running the camp—much less the system of the camp itself.

Palitzsch landed in the penal ward alongside Poles he'd once tormented, prisoners whose friends and families he'd killed. Now, he groveled and beat his chest in atonement. He wrote the Polish prisoners a letter asking for forgiveness. "God help me leave this bunker, so that I can pay back Höss," he wrote, "because it was he who forced me to do all these things and often, despite his own rulings, demanded more and more victims." He then asked the Poles inside the bunker to share their bread with him.

After some time in the penal unit, Palitzsch was transported out of Auschwitz and disappeared. Many believe he died in battle on the Eastern Front.

Just like that, Zippi's closest friend and partner in resistance was gone. She and Katya had their differences, but they'd saved each other's lives countless times. Zippi now added yet another name to the tally of loved ones gone. She had long learned how to live with loss, to push on. But that could not have made it any more bearable.

Perhaps she masked her sadness with anger and disappointment. She remained incredulous that, like Mala, Katya had been stupid enough to risk her good life and important position in Auschwitz. Katya had saved thousands of prisoners and could have done so much more, she thought. Instead, she'd given up her life for a mass murderer.

By then, Zippi had proven herself to Mandl and Drechsel—the latter of whom didn't care much for Zippi but nevertheless saw the value of her work. In particular, the three-dimensional scale model of Auschwitz that Zippi had built was a hit. Zippi was especially proud of the model: aside from the gas chambers and crematoria (which she'd been forbidden from including), it was an exact replica, down to the barbed wire that lined the camp's borders. She'd used a stencil and oils to match the colors of the wooden barracks and approximated the precise shade of olive green for the roofs. She'd used glue and sand to replicate the texture of the dusty streets. Henryk Porębski, the Birkenau electrician who worked with the underground, had helped insert a battery-powered flashlight beneath the model. In the dark, the model's watchtowers lit up the front gate. Zippi signed the bottom of the model with her number—2286.

Mandl prominently displayed the scale model to her superiors. Officers from Berlin came to her office to gaze at the diorama, impressed. Zippi was told that Franz Hössler, a former head of the women's camp, had requested the model be placed in his office, under a glass case. Later, she heard that the model had been transferred to Berlin headquarters.

By then, Zippi's value to the camp administration may have saved her life again. Within a month of Katya's departure, the women who'd performed in Birkenau's orchestra had been transferred over to Bergen-Belsen, a small concentration camp in such deplorable conditions that most of its inmates succumbed to starvation or disease. But thanks to her office work, Zippi was spared the transport.

Despite the loss of her coconspirator, Zippi had reason to be optimistic. Since June 1944, cities in Italy and France had been liberated from the Nazis, one by one. That July, the Majdanek concentration camp in Lublin, where Sara had been imprisoned before her transfer to Auschwitz, and where Zippi's father and brothers had been sent to die, became the first camp to be liberated by the Red Army. And in Warsaw, Polish underground soldiers were gearing up to revolt against the Germans.

The 1944 Warsaw Uprising—not to be confused with the Warsaw Ghetto Uprising of 1943, the largest Jewish revolt of World War II, in which seven thousand Jews were killed—began that August, led by the Polish Home Army, and briefly saw resisters take control of the city. But by the end of the month, international newspapers reported that the Germans were "savagely annihilating whole districts of Warsaw, killing people by tens of thousands, burning all the principal buildings and mercilessly shooting down any who try to extinguish fires that are spreading unchecked because the city's water supply is wrecked." Indeed, Warsaw—already shattered and scarred by bombings back in the siege of 1939—had now burned almost completely to the ground. Once again, the resistance had failed.

Still, the SS were nervous. In Auschwitz, officers made plans to liquidate the camp and obliterate all evidence. The administrators at Majdanek hadn't destroyed evidence of their murder operations, and, when the Red Army had shown up, their actions had been exposed for the world to see. The SS would not make the same mistake in Auschwitz. So it was that, as resistance fighters inside the camp trained prisoners to escape and join partisans in the countryside, SS officers were burning documents.

Prisoners connected with the Polish Underground had good information that the Red Army was approaching Warsaw and in short order would take the city back from the Germans. Soon they'd find their way to Auschwitz—but, the underground feared, not soon enough.

When Höss returned to Auschwitz, he was put on a mission to eliminate all Hungarian Jews, the only Jewish community in occupied Europe that remained intact. Transport after transport kept the crematorium chimneys spouting fire and smoke, day in and day out. A small pond near Crematorium IV and Crematorium V was filled with human ashes. In order to keep up with the constant transport of Hungarian Jews arriving in Auschwitz, camp officials expanded the *Sonderkommando* from around three hundred to some nine hundred prisoners, while also putting Bunker II, the Little White House, back into operation.

But Höss was far from done, and was making preparations to expunge Auschwitz itself. He sought to eradicate all traces of people, barracks, gas chambers, and crematoria — to leave no evidence behind. Despite his best efforts, the resistance continued to smuggle out documents and photographs that showed inmates being forced into the gas chambers.

And still the ashes piled up.

CHAPTER SEVENTEEN

"Don't Give Up"

David and the others working at the Sauna were busier than ever disinfecting the piles of clothing that arrived each day. Zippi sometimes wore twelve pairs of underwear that Roza had given her, and later distributed them inside the barracks of the new arrivals, whose uniforms were increasingly spare.

At least, thought David, the SS was so busy with the constant stream of transports that they didn't focus as much on the old-timers. He and Zippi continued their monthly visits without incident. With each visit their conversations deepened, although they always reached a limit. Much of their past was too painful to talk about; and any future remained uncertain.

David had a friend, Ralph Hackman, who worked at the "dirty side" of the Sauna. These days, on the rare occasions when they could speak, they wondered at their circumstances. How was it that they hadn't been "eliminated" yet? Ralph didn't believe they would ever get out. Perhaps the SS had forgotten about them, he said to David.

But they wouldn't forget for long. On the afternoon of October 7, 1944, a Saturday, David was hanging disinfected clothing in the Sauna when he heard a loud explosion.

The loud bang was followed by the *ratatat* of machine guns. David tried to look out from the Sauna window. He'd heard some rumblings about a revolt; there was always talk of one thing or another. But now something was actually happening.

Months earlier, a plan had evolved inside the red, windowless Weichsel-Union-Metallwerke, known as the Union Factory, a few miles outside Birkenau. Here, Auschwitz prisoners, male and female, worked alongside civilians to manufacture armaments for the *Wehrmacht*. Amidst the hot machinery, rubber aprons, and thick yellow dust, the prisoners had silently united. Jewish and Polish resistance groups had intended to organize a revolt. In preparation, leaders had recruited Roza Robota, Zippi's Polish friend, to coordinate Jewish women within the union to smuggle gunpowder back to Birkenau.

Along the glass-paned hallways and assembly lines, under the watchful eye of the SS, men and women, Jews and non-Jews, found a way to plot. Men smuggled bread and fruit to the women. Those with access to tools and matériel pilfered matches, gasoline, gunpowder, and more. Each object had its purpose. A woman, for instance, would hide a wire cutter within a hollowed-out loaf of bread. She would then pass through inspection on her way back inside the camp. The wire cutter went under her mattress, to be used later. It was one small piece of the puzzle, one detail of many.

Meanwhile, Jewish women who worked in gunpowder manufacturing collected small bits of the coarse salt-like steel-gray powder and hid them inside tiny scraps of cloth that they knotted into small sacks. Two men would then transfer the contraband out of the factory and hide it inside the camp. Sometimes they used soup bowls with double bottoms; other times, they simply placed the tiny bags inside a prisoner's pocket and hoped they wouldn't be frisked. Sometimes they layered powder inside their uniform seams or bras. Once the gunpowder reached Birkenau, Roza was the link between *Kommando* leaders and the resistance groups. Members of the *Sonderkommando* picked it up from Roza, who worked in a Canada warehouse across from Crematorium IV, and hid the contraband inside a cartful of corpses.

Inside the same factory, prisoners sabotaged the machinery on which they worked. They failed to close fuses properly; they disposed of good material in the garbage; they tampered with machinery. Most were unaware of each other's work. But their combined efforts were having an effect. The *Wehrmacht* had begun complaining about artillery produced at the Union Factory.

Some of the workers took the efforts further. An inmate codenamed Prisoner T, a Jew and factory organizer, was recruited by a cell of the British Intelligence Service. He was asked to tinker with machines so they produced defective items, to sabotage the *Wehrmacht* war effort. Prisoner T had also been tapped by the resistance to join the revolt. He helped plan the smuggling of gunpowder from the factory into the camp. Eventually, perhaps inevitably, his path would cross with Zippi's.

On the morning of October 7, 1944, hours before David heard the explosion from the Sauna, word circulated around camp that Auschwitz's management planned to liquidate the *Sonderkommando* that very day. The men knew their day was coming. They were never meant to survive their jobs; they knew too much. But they hadn't thought the day would arrive so soon. As the Allies advanced and the Nazis began to destroy evidence, the resistance wanted to detonate the crematoria, eliminating at least some of the camp's killing apparatus. The resistance groups involved in the planning didn't have time to coordinate and send in help. The *Sonderkommando* at Crematorium IV couldn't afford to wait, so, at 1:25 p.m., they decided to act.

David heard the blast and gunfire and then saw people running—men and women in a jumble of stripes that made it difficult to tell anyone apart. Crematorium IV was within sight of the Sauna, a few hundred feet away and almost directly across from it. Dust and smoke filled the air. Almost immediately, the SS and their dogs arrived; the sound of machine guns and pistols was deafening. All David saw was a commotion; all he heard was the sound of artillery. Before he could react, the SS had locked the Sauna so that no one could come in or get out.

Later, David found out some of the details of what happened next door to the Sauna. The resistance fighters in the *Sonderkommando* had attacked an SS guard unit with hammers, axes, and stones. They'd detonated homemade grenades that they'd prepared and hidden inside Crematorium IV. Some used gas-soaked rags to set fire to the mattresses in the dormitory. The fire quickly licked through walls and spread inside.

When they had seen the dust rise above the Canada warehouses, the *Sonderkommando* attached to Crematorium II had scrambled to join in the resistance. They'd killed three SS officers, pushing two to roast in a flaming oven, then tore down a fence and fled. Meanwhile, caught by surprise, the *Sonderkommando* at Crematorium III and Crematorium V didn't have time to join in before the SS intervened. The prisoners' machine guns and artillery were no match for the Nazis. Four hundred and fifty-one prisoners died during the revolt; the *Sonderkommando* shrank from 663 to 212 prisoners.

There was one piece of good news: Crematorium IV, now a pile of charred wood and scattered stones, was out of commission.

After the revolt, irate SS officers interrogated prisoners and civilians alike. How did the *Sonderkommando* get their hands on the gunpowder? How did they make the grenades? And more to the point: who was involved? All evidence pointed to the Union Factory. Moreover, Berlin headquarters had long been complaining that grenades manufactured at the factory were faulty. They demanded an investigation. In the end, four women, including Roza, were accused.

How the women were caught remains a mystery. Some said they were mere scapegoats. Others believed a *Kapo* gave them away. Regardless, despite being savagely tortured, the women refused to give away names.

Zippi was caught off guard when she'd heard of Roza's involvement. Roza was a shrewd, skillful woman who'd helped so many Polish prisoners. Zippi was in awe of this woman, her friend.

Almost four months earlier, Zippi had shut herself in her office during Mala's execution. On January 3, 1945, the day of Roza's hanging, she did the same.

Outside, inmates stood in rows of five, watching. The SS organized two sessions. The first two women were hanged in front of night-shift workers at the Union Factory during evening roll call. The other two were hanged in front of the day-shift workers the following morning.

Roza held her head high to the end.

"Freedom!" she yelled out in Polish, before her body dropped. Almost immediately, blood seeped from her eyes.

Later, Zippi would think about the aprons that Roza had insisted on trading in every two weeks. There had been something about that practice, something she couldn't shake. Had she inadvertently helped transfer gunpowder to the various visitors in her office? Had the aprons served as storage until Roza could deliver the explosives to the *Sonderkommando*?

Zippi had no answers. Regardless, she was proud of the women who'd carried off the revolt. One crematorium was down—a huge win against the Nazis, a victory that would save countless lives.

On November 10, 1944, Maria Mandl approached Zippi. She needed her neat calligraphy. Mandl's friend and Birkenau commander Josef Kramer was celebrating a birthday, and she was gifting him a book.

It's my birthday, too, Zippi said as she inscribed the book for Mandl.

Apparently, Mandl was in a generous mood.

Go to the package room, she said, *and pick out the nicest package you can find for yourself.*

A smattering of parcels took up the package room—boxes and envelopes with medicine and food, addressed to female inmates. They were unclaimed, the intended recipients long dead. She found a package filled with chocolate and fruit. As she bit into an apple, she felt something hard. It was a strip of metal, razor thin and pliable, folded into a cone shape. Inside the cone, she found a one-inch slice of paper, folded. The entire contraption was small enough that it left just the slightest scratch on the apple's skin.

Zippi looked around, trying to hide her excitement. She needed a place to read the message alone. When she found a safe spot, she had to squint: the words were few and tiny, in German script.

Don't give up, it read. *The war could end any day.*

Zippi's eyes filled with tears. From the label, she recognized that the letter had been written by a German officer, though obviously not a Nazi. His neat, small handwriting was likely intended for his lover or fiancée, who Zippi was certain was dead. It occurred to her that, had a Nazi been the one to bite into the apple, the writer of the note probably wouldn't have survived.

She swallowed the message.

For weeks, she would think about the words she'd eaten. She carried their warmth inside her.

As the Soviets got closer, the Nazis' apprehension grew exponentially. The fighting was now happening in their backyard; they could hear shots fired from inside camp. SS officers began to disappear—some leaving to join the fight, others simply deserting.

At the end of November 1944, a month after the *Sonderkommando* revolt, Himmler issued an order: all of Auschwitz's gas chambers and crematoria would be shut down. Hammers and pickaxes at hand, a newly assembled workforce broke up the facilities' massive slabs of concrete. As prisoners cracked through the foundation of the crematoria, some found the pliers in the nearby earth that the *Sonderkommando* had used to pry out victims' golden teeth—buried evidence. Another *Kommando,* this one made up of women, cleaned up the bricks yanked from the crematoria walls and placed them in wagons in an orderly fashion. Nothing was wasted. The fragments of these buildings were preserved for later use. Yet another *Kommando* disassembled ventilators and furnace parts. Others dismantled the ovens and drilled holes into gas chamber walls to store dynamite. Just a few weeks later, in January 1945, the SS blew up whatever was left.

It was the end of an era: the camp's inmates would no longer be gassed. Instead, they were transferred to other camps. Auschwitz had entered its terminal phase.

Around the end of December 1944, the sounds of artillery changed. The inmates had long grown accustomed to the *ratatat* of machine guns firing and bombs detonating from afar, the never-ending thunder and crackles of lightning. But now something was different. David couldn't quite put his finger on it. The SS men were increasingly nervous, friendlier than usual.

David was working at the Sauna when his boss, Georg, came in, agitated.

We're going to lose the war, Georg said.

David had felt this for some time; Zippi had even told him as much recently. But coming from Georg, it was a confirmation. David thought about how long he'd survived. Most men who'd arrived in the cattle train with him two years earlier were long gone. He thought of the Nazis' obsession with getting rid of evidence and realized that he himself was a liability to them. He knew too much; he'd seen too much. They wanted to get rid of all the evidence—and *he* was evidence.

He threw himself into his work at the Sauna, always looking busy, hanging clothes. He hoped that the SS saw him as essential to the maintenance of the camp. Ever since he had discovered the bodies of his parents, little brother, and grandfather on a pile of other corpses, he'd promised himself he would survive. He'd lived through two and a half years in Auschwitz, thanks, he thought, to a combination of God and his voice. Now more than ever, he felt like his time was coming to an end.

How am I going to remember you if they separate us? Szaja Kalfus, David's friend at the Sauna, said to him one mid-December morning as they were hanging up uniforms.

Szaja had an idea. David was always tinkering with music; he'd even composed a couple of songs—one in Yiddish and another in Polish. Sometimes David hummed his songs and shared the lyrics with his friends. Szaja found a notebook and a blue pen and told David to write out his song "Little White House in the Woods." The song described the transports being taken to Bunker II.

Sitting inside the *Kapo's* office in the Sauna while Szaja kept watch, David wrote about the farmhouse where prisoners had been murdered before the crematoria had been built. He also wrote out the lyrics to a Polish parody he'd composed. When he was finished, he handed the sheets of notebook paper to his friend. In return, Szaja gave David a poem he'd written: "The Blessing of Hanukkah."

These mementos in hand, the two men returned to work, knowing their time together was nearing its end.

She arranged for them to meet at their usual spot. But this time was different.

Zippi told David that soon everyone would evacuate the camp. It was already happening; the transports were leaving every day.

This might be their final opportunity to be together.

They wondered: where would they meet again?

David could only think of one place: his former home.

He suggested they meet at the Jewish Community Center in Warsaw, or where it had once stood. Zippi agreed. After this was all over, they promised, after the Germans had lost the war, after they were free, they would find each other.

And so they left their nook for the last time, with a promise.

CHAPTER EIGHTEEN

"Always Forward"

I n the early morning of January 17, 1945, no one went to work.
Instead of inmates marching to their death, the camp was filled
with frenzied Nazis riding their bikes and motorcycles. Wary
prisoners watched, awaiting their fates. The entire day passed; in
the evening they stood for roll call.

Himmler had finally given orders to evacuate the camps. All those
in fit condition had to leave. They were told to prepare for a journey.

The men would leave first. Germany needed a workforce, as its
men were on the front lines of the war. The country needed cheap
labor to manufacture heating equipment and war material—and
nothing was cheaper than slaves. Further, Germany didn't want to
inadvertently supply the Allies with additional soldiers by leaving
capable men behind. The fates of the sick and the handicapped,
however, didn't figure into SS commanders' calculations. Those
inmates would remain in Auschwitz. The January cold, they thought,
would take care of the evidence—take care of those left behind,
those too weak to work.

Final arrangements were made. Prisoners and officers who
had the means would help themselves to extra clothing, extra food—
anything they could carry. Some thought about hiding and waiting

for the Russians to arrive, but the Nazis had their bloodhounds sniff out hidden prisoners, who were then shot on the spot. Before he joined the column of prisoners that was forming in the main road, David organized extra rations. He wore his uniform with civilian clothing underneath it. He hid bread and other sustenance inside his coat. He'd long since abandoned his awful wooden clogs; instead, he wore solid, sturdy shoes that he'd long ago "organized" for himself.

The first march began just before midnight. The winter winds blew the falling snow in every direction. The prisoners lined up side by side in rows that formed a long column, with armed SS men on the wings: they'd long ago grown accustomed to standing in order. So it was that they walked into the dark night, away from the gates that had confined them for so long.

David became just one more figure among the throng herded down the road. He walked alongside men whose eyes were hollowed out, whose cheeks were sunken, their spirits long shattered. He positioned himself in the middle of the crowd. The perimeters were more dangerous; it was safer to hide in the middle. His friend Szaja Kalfus marched next to him. They would walk for some thirty miles.

Men who fell behind were shot. When their cold, snow-flecked bodies obstructed the road, the SS ordered prisoners to toss them out of the way and into the forest. The march went on, with some men falling out of line, some dragged forward by fellow prisoners, and others dropping to the snow, where they would remain. They'd survived the camps only to succumb to this final, agonizing slog.

Meanwhile, Soviet propellers whirred above them. Whenever David caught glimpses of red stars on aircraft wings, he felt a tinge of hope. Everyone knew that the Germans were retreating. Air-raid sirens played a cacophonous symphony as the men trekked on into the darkness. Wounded German soldiers who'd survived the front walked alongside the prisoners. Some were missing legs; others were missing one or both arms.

They paused in Gleiwitz, a small Auschwitz subcamp near a train depot. The prisoners were loaded into an open train that had once transported coal and wood. Some 120 men climbed inside each compartment, packed in for a journey of nearly five hundred miles in chilling temperatures. They had no toilets, no buckets, no water, no blankets. David was lucky; he had pilfered two heavy jackets from Canada. Some men passed around cans of urine to quench their thirst; they were desperate, no longer thinking clearly. Every few miles the train stopped to unload the dead.

As David moved onward, his specialness fell away. Behind him, he left all his privileges, all of the things that had been keeping him alive. And, with them, Zippi.

Back in Auschwitz, the SS continued to destroy anything incriminating—anything that testified to their gruesome crimes. Documents, death certificates, and files went into a car belonging to the SS. Pages and pages containing diagrams and statistics were gathered up and burned. The first list to coil into fire held records of all the inmates who'd been gassed to death.

Zippi had been duplicating nearly every list, diagram, and sketch that she'd created, onto wax paper, and stashing them away with care. She knew that, were the SS to discover what she was doing, she would be killed. But if the Allies found her copies, the world would know the details of Auschwitz's depravity, the sheer volume of prisoners who'd been turned into numbers, into smoke. She stuffed everything she could fit inside tubes, burying a roll of documents behind a bookcase and another behind a wardrobe—hoping that in this small way, she could help bring the Nazis to justice.

One of Zippi's final assignments had been to label addresses on three heavy packages for SS officers Luise Helene and Elisabeth Danz, who was known for her particular cruelty; Danz had a penchant for hitting prisoners under their chins while kneeing them in the torso. Zippi was certain that the three parcels had contained some sort of precious metal, perhaps a block of gold made up from the dental fillings of murdered inmates.

The SS would ultimately torch the Canada warehouses, but not before they had sent various packages containing valuables ranging from clothing to gold to the Third Reich. Much of what was left behind was consumed in a blaze that would burn for five days.

On the eve of January 17, 1945, 67,012 Auschwitz prisoners in the main camp and the subcamps reported for a final *Appell*. From January 17 to 21, some 56,000 prisoners would evacuate on death marches.

Some began marching in the late afternoon. Others set out in the middle of the night. Tall mounds of snow hardened in the freezing snow that swarmed around them. Those who could walk were told to evacuate. One woman who had been sick in bed mustered up the strength to stand and leave alongside her barrack mates. She'd survived this long; she might as well try to survive another day, she thought, to witness Hitler's defeat.

Meanwhile, inside the camp hospital, inmates with broken legs, toothaches, or typhus awaited their death. The remains of prisoners' files—from the history of their illnesses to their fever tables—were scorched. Bonfires of burning barracks smoldered in muddy crevices throughout camp.

There was nothing left for Zippi; it was time for her to go.

They would leave in intervals. On January 18, 1945, as she joined the river of bodies, Zippi, like David, left behind her camp status and privileges, becoming just one more prisoner amidst a mass of nearly sixty thousand leaving. David's group would veer north; hers would inch south. They would each travel dozens of miles in opposite directions.

Somehow, Zippi and Sara managed to find each other in the chaos. The SS officers, martinets until the end, were still trying to keep the women in rows of five. Rain pounded down; some prisoners stood too close to the electric fences and were electrocuted before getting the chance to leave. Officers chased other inmates to make them move faster. Unprepared women sank bare feet inside mounds of snow that were at least three feet deep. Those in felt boots got frostbitten toes. They trampled over blankets strewn across the road, scraps given up by those who'd become too weak to carry them. Zippi and Sara kept pace; they would endure this together.

Where are we going? a woman dared ask a guard.

Always forward, he answered.

They marched westward, away from the Soviets. Those who tried to escape were accused of sabotage, shot on the spot.

The *bratatatatat* of machine guns that echoed around them was the new drumbeat by which they marched. The prisoners knew well that their lives were cheap in Nazis' eyes. One officer shot a woman for drinking from their canteen. Another woman, hiding beneath a stack of hay in a wagon, was killed with a pitchfork. Others were more fortunate: two sisters happened upon a bag of sugar, undetected—manna from the sky.

They forged ahead, shoes stuck inside ditches dyed maroon from blood-soaked mud. Their entire path was covered in red-streaked snow. They'd thought Auschwitz was hell, that it couldn't possibly get worse. But yes, they discovered; yes, it could.

Everywhere she looked, Zippi saw corpses—shot dead, or simply marched to death. Local residents gawked from their windows, horrified. One woman insisted on offering the prisoners water; an officer shot her through the back of her head. Other civilians were able to sneak bread and water to prisoners without being caught. A dozen Polish women in one small village stood by the side of the road, offering water to the parched skeletons they saw trudging down the road. The kind gestures gave prisoners hope to carry on.

That first night, some slept while standing up. The Red Army was three miles away, or so went the rumors.

On they dragged, for two or three days and nights. Always forward.

*T*hey hardly spoke—at first. They'd craved a reminder that pleasure can overcome pain. In their cave, they remembered. All breath and touch, they strove for silence.

But words swelled from sputters to streams and currents of music. In whispers, they opened themselves up. Another risk.

Their moment passed, and ended.

In spite of themselves, they made promises.

And when they descended the ladder, mere numbers again, they went their separate ways.

PART IV

INTERLUDE

CHAPTER NINETEEN

"You Are Free!"

Airplanes roared overhead, wingtip lights shining like fire-flies, as the women dragged themselves from the railway station in Breslau, Germany—a city once known as Wrocław, Poland. It was nighttime. They watched the silent silhouettes of SS officers as they jerked frozen corpses off compartments of the open freight trains, spines snapping like twigs when they hit the ice-bound mud. Zippi and some of the other women took over the compartment. Desperate for nourishment, they scavenged bits of relatively clean snow.

A winter storm brought numbing wind and blinding sheets of fresh snow, making for a bone-rattling ride. Despite the bombed-out railroad stations throughout the country, they made it through Berlin, evading fire. Inside her train compartment, Zippi's friend Susan Cernyak-Spatz watched the shadows of the city rush past. What a satisfying sight, she thought, to see the Nazi capital in ruins.

From her own vantage point, Zippi couldn't see but after a few stops, she suspected that they were headed to Germany. She'd learned the locations of various camps through her diagrams of prisoner transfers. Part of her job had included calculating locations of the various other camps and their distances from Auschwitz. She figured the Ravensbrück camp, in northern Germany, would be their final stop.

She was right. Some of the cruelest *Kapos* she'd met in Birkenau had been previously incarcerated in Ravensbrück. She'd befriended some kinder ones, who had revealed that there, the SS placed Polish women in isolation and surgically removed their ribs, which would somehow be used for the benefit of German soldiers who'd been crippled in the war.

Now Zippi and some twelve hundred other women disembarked just outside the camp to spend the night, packed in a single room. Unable to stretch their legs, they crouched on the floor, back to back. Lice nestled in every crevice of their bodies. Sleep was elusive, food even more so.

As they approached the camp's gates the following morning, Zippi recalled the filth, disorder, and devastating famine that had greeted her in Auschwitz back in 1942. Here too, roll call descended into disarray. Here too, the SS had no organized system in place.

The local inmates greeted the mob of new arrivals with anger. *You had gold, you had men! Go back to Auschwitz,* they said. At least the rooms had windows that could be opened — their chance to eat snow. The women threw themselves at stray scraps of food.

Sometimes, a cauldron materialized. Zippi stood in line, attempting to remain civilized. In a flash, someone pushed her to the ground. The heavy heel of a boot struck her jaw. Then everything went pitch black.

On January 27, 1945, nine days after Zippi had left Birkenau, a unit of the Red Army finally arrived at Auschwitz. A grenade exploded by the iron gates and the Soviet soldiers entered the camp. They found a scene that can only be described as hellish: pits of smoldering documents, charred buildings, buried bones. When the prisoners saw their liberators, they panicked and flung themselves against the once-electric fences — and survived.

Nearly seven thousand living, breathing corpses awaited freedom.

"Welcome, victors and liberators!" one called out in Russian.

"You are free!" a soldier responded.

Some survivors mustered tears of joy. Most seemed inhuman to the liberating soldiers. The inmates had lost the spark of life in their eyes. These were, by and large, the inmates who had been too sick or weak to march out of the camp. Many were listless, faces shriveled, bodies ragged, covered in filth.

Here and there were piles of shoes and clothing, small mountains on a field of mud. The Nazis had left in such haste that they hadn't had a chance to send all of their stockpiles of shorn human hair—shades of gold, auburn, brunette, and gray—to the Third Reich. About fifteen thousand pounds of Nazi victims' hair had been sent to German factories to make textiles and fabric, but much remained in Auschwitz. The soldiers found fragments of human bones, left by the *Kommandos* who had been charged to destroy them. Some six hundred charred corpses, many stacked between wooden logs, spread across the swampy land.

Here, among the living dead, the Red Army found traces of the 1.1 million who had perished in the Auschwitz camp system.

Medics arrived almost immediately, but how to conduct triage in a place infested with lice, disease, and human excrement? A place engulfed by starvation, diarrhea, tuberculosis, and acute trauma? A place without water, medicine, clean bedding, heat, or food?

A platoon of Soviet soldiers mustered the surviving children and the elderly around the gallows to record the pivotal moment on film. One of the youngest, a five-year-old, would remember that moment into old age: the moment his liberation was documented—at the same platform where others had been hung to die.

Patients bristled at the call for a "bath," a word that invoked the gas chamber. Medical injections were met with terror. Nurses handed out bread, which was promptly stuffed under mattresses with fear that none would come again. One survivor ravaged a slice of cheese that a soldier had given him. The next day, he died of a ruptured stomach; his body couldn't tolerate the volume of even such a small morsel.

A group of local volunteers emerged to dole out food and assist the medical staff. Some took former prisoners into their homes; a few even adopted children from the camp. Eventually, some of these survivors would manage to locate their families, although it would take years of searching.

Some survivors, of course, could never truly escape. They would spend years not talking about their pasts, suffering a lifetime of guilt, wondering why they'd survived when so many had not. In search of a new beginning, they would instead spend a lifetime grasping at what they'd lost.

Some four hundred miles away, in Ravensbrück, Zippi hadn't stayed unconscious for long. An inmate helped her get up and clean herself so she could stand with the masses of other prisoners awaiting food. Her head throbbed. Her jaw felt dislocated. She had no bandages, much less pain relievers or medicine. All she could do was wait—but for what, no one could be sure.

The next few weeks were a blur. The women were told they would move once more, to yet another satellite camp. Again they marched. Again they boarded a train. Again they had no food, no drink. They headed to Malchow, some fifty miles northwest of Ravensbrück.

Malchow was another overcrowded subcamp surrounded by an electric fence. But it was smaller than any they'd been to before. Zippi saw no guard towers. Again, organization was nil. The lucky inmates got three slices of dry bread a day, but for most, the pangs of hunger were so intense that they ate grass. The first women to arrive shared bunks or mattresses on the floor. Most lay on the bare ground.

Some prisoners worked at a subterranean ammunition factory, making bullets for the German war machine. Zippi worked in the kitchen. Her job was to count the cooking vats and clean the dishes used by the Nazi staff.

The prisoners grew thinner by the day. As the Russians drew closer, the corpses accumulated.

Hundreds of prisoners perished in Malchow. Not because of beatings or gunshots—Zippi never once saw anyone being murdered outright. Here, the cause of death tended to be hunger, dehydration, and the overall squalid conditions.

Nazi camp guards made themselves scarce. As far as Zippi could tell, they'd been replaced by the *Wehrmacht,* soldiers in the German army. Yet the German military was collapsing. Soldiers deserted their uniforms, terrified that the Red Army would take revenge on them for the atrocities they'd committed against Soviet POWs.

On May 1, 1945, Zippi watched a convoy of white buses arrive in Malchow. The White Buses, a rescue action of the Swedish Red Cross, had come to evacuate parts of the camp. First, they removed inmates who were sick. As Zippi looked on, the Polish *Rapport-schreiberin,* registration clerk, selected fellow Poles for evacuation. The Hungarian clerk picked out fellow Hungarians. Here, the Slovakians were not in charge—so Zippi didn't stand a chance.

At first, inmates were wary of the Swedish Red Cross. Back in the concentration camps, the Nazis had used the Red Cross name to deceive their victims. Prisoners saw gray ambulances, a Red Cross logo on the hood; but instead of carrying the sick, these ambulances transported cans of Zyklon B.

Eventually the Malchow inmates were convinced to board the buses, which would take them to Copenhagen, Denmark, and eventually to Lund, Sweden. The prisoners who didn't fit in the first convoy received packages of food. Some of these packages contained sardines; later, those who'd enjoyed them would suffer from diarrhea, their bodies unaccustomed to so much sustenance. For now, Zippi looked on as most of the rations went to the Poles and the Hungarians. She didn't get any of it. But it didn't matter: she finally allowed herself to believe that her own freedom was near.

Meanwhile, beyond Malchow's gates, masses of refugees marched. Prisoners on death marches, soldiers, and civilians were all intermingled. Somewhere along a highway, out of Zippi's earshot, a motorcycle with a sidecar roared by.

The Führer is dead! a soldier whooped.

The column stopped moving. *We're free!* some cried.

The celebration lasted only a moment, and then the marching began again.

The few guards who remained in Malchow announced: *Dead or alive, everyone must be counted.* They were leaving for a neighboring town. The Soviets were closing in, and the Germans needed to be gone by the time they arrived.

Together, the guards and inmates marched to the nearby highway, which was clogged with trucks, horses and buggies, motorcycles, and cars. The SS were different now. They weren't the typical trained camp guards. These were the *Waffen-SS.* Some seemed even more sadistic than the camp guards. A young boy had dared to kneel beside his dying father: a guard killed the child with the butt of his rifle.

Zippi felt responsible for Sara Lewin; she had promised David that she would take care of his friend. They would stay together, no matter what. Sara clung to Zippi, unaware that David was more than just a friend—that he was the lodestar guiding Zippi to the end of their ordeal.

The ordered columns had long disintegrated; the rows of five disbanded. As sunlight dimmed, some inmates slipped into the forests. Those with shaved heads and in uniforms were easily caught. They were skin and bones; boils and lice. The farther they walked, however, the less it mattered: *Wehrmacht* soldiers and Nazis began to shed uniforms for civilian clothes and they, too, tried to disappear.

Zippi had been looking for an opening—and now she had one. She grabbed Sara's hand. She'd concocted a plan in Auschwitz, while painting red stripes on clothes—the stripes that identified camp prisoners. Instead of the SS-approved paint, Zippi had used watercolor on their garments. Now she removed the stripes with ease, likely using water from melted snow, allowing her and Sara to slip away.

They walked until late afternoon, through frenzied streets, in gusts of snow and rain. Zippi and Sara were lost in a mob. How could they know whom to trust? French POWs, Soviets, and SS members who'd "lost" their insignias ambled down the road, side by side.

Finally they slipped to a field on the side of the road. Daylight was nearly gone when Zippi noticed a small, abandoned farmhouse in the fields. It seemed a good place to rest.

They were free.

Freedom, after years of enslavement, in the wake of a war that had created millions of homeless refugees, wasn't straightforward. They had no time to process the end of roll calls, electric fences, smoking chimneys. Or the loss of loved ones.

As she and Sara made their way to the barn, two men joined them. Perhaps they appeared to be Danish, or Dutch. Either way, they were just as lost. They debated their next move. Should they continue westward, toward the Americans? Or wait for the Soviets?

The Russians, the Americans, and the British were all the same, Zippi said. What mattered was their actual liberation. And Warsaw. She had to get to Warsaw. She had a promise to keep.

Zippi and Sara decided to spend the night in the barn. The two men wanted to keep moving, but Zippi talked them out of it. It wasn't worth their while; they could get shot by the Germans.

Zippi was so sure of herself that the men agreed. Befriending the men and convincing them to stay nearby was prudent: in the havoc of liberation, women were particularly vulnerable at the hands of drunken Allied soldiers and Nazis alike.

They were surrounded by chaos; they were still in mortal danger. Cannon fire in the nearby forest kept them up. Zippi wondered whether she also heard Katyushas, the Soviet rocket launchers known for their distinctive wail followed by a crushing snap. Those were popular, especially on the front lines. The howling blasts shook the forest until three or four in the morning.

Just before dawn, silence settled in.

CHAPTER TWENTY

White Star

D avid knew he was in trouble the minute he set foot in the Dachau concentration camp, in January 1945. Eager to get off the cattle cars, men pushed each other out. Some lay where they'd fallen, long dead. Others collapsed, alive but unable to move. The Nazis hit those with the butt of their rifles. It seemed to David that the Germans had brought every one of their prisoners to this filthy, disease-ridden strip of land.

Dachau was in the midst of evacuation. As new prisoners came in, old prisoners were sent out. Some newcomers were forced to surrender their clothes and were issued blankets instead of uniforms. They would live without garments for weeks. Inmates slept standing up in the corridors, crouched on cement floors or outside on mounds of dirt—wherever they found space. The bit of food that David had smuggled in from Auschwitz was running out.

The men in Dachau were living skeletons. Their eyeballs had just about disappeared inside their skulls; their dried-out lips were black. They moaned, unable to move. David would have to get used to the stench of the dead bodies slowly decomposing in the snow, a different olfactory horror from the ubiquitous smoke in Auschwitz.

In Auschwitz, David had contracted typhoid, witnessed epidemics and famine, and yet none of it compared to the squalor of Dachau. This was not a place one survived. He reminded himself that the Soviets were coming from the east and the other Allies from the west; all he had to do was stay alive a bit longer.

There was no roll call, no way to keep track of time, but after what must have been several days David noticed flyers posted all around the camp. The Germans were seeking volunteers to work in southern Austria. They needed able-bodied men to carry hundred-pound sacks of cement to build an underground hangar for airplanes.

For now, David thought, he was still fit. This was his ticket out.

David was one of close to a hundred of Dachau's strongest inmates who were herded into a closed cattle car and sent to Mühldorf, a satellite camp in Bavaria. As they traveled east, the Red Army inched ever closer.

The first time they heard an air raid, the Nazis rushed everyone off the train. They stood by a ravine for nearly an hour. After the sirens passed, they climbed back on. Moments later, it happened again. As air raids grew more frequent, so did their stops. The German army was in retreat and its units were attaching themselves to prisoner trains in an effort to protect themselves from Allied fire.

Again and again, the train was attacked by Allied aircraft: black airplanes with double tails that zoomed overhead. David recognized them as Russian—harbingers of liberation, so close yet still out of his reach. Over and over, the cattle car stopped, and prisoners and guards exited and stood by the ditches. German soldiers fired back at the attacking planes. One prisoner was accidentally shot in the hand. David watched the others wrap the wound with soiled rags. The German soldiers used their rifles and machine guns to herd the prisoners back onto the train.

We'd better get away from here, David said to a few men he'd recognized from Auschwitz. *Somewhere along the way we're going to get killed.*

The ground quivered beneath his feet and a tail of smoke rose from the back of the long train. Strangely, the German guards they encountered at each station seemed to age with each stop. *The Nazis must be in need of constant replenishments,* David thought. They were sending their young men to the front, and replacing them with older guards.

At the next stop, David and a group of men made a break for it. They sprinted to an open field, where they saw a farmhouse and a barn surrounded by gardens and enclosed by a wooden fence. The men leapt into the garden and lay down.

But a handful of armed SS guards had chased them down. David was sure his lucky streak was over.

Perhaps the guards didn't want to leave behind more dead bodies. Or they were that desperate for laborers. Whatever their reasons, they escorted the runaways back into the cattle car without punishment. Another close call. They were going to be killed at some point, David thought, either by the Germans or by the airplanes strafing them from above.

He had little to lose. The next time they stopped, he thought, he would try to escape again. He spoke with two other prisoners. They resolved to run, each in a different direction. If the Germans caught one of them, they might kill him—but at least the others might get away.

It was nearly an hour before the train stopped again. The men stepped out into a ravine and dozens of SS guards stood in a column parallel to the track, each about a hundred feet away from the others. With a start, David noticed that the guard nearest to him was flushed, sweating. The Nazi was more scared of the air raids than he was, he realized.

As David shifted on the spot, he stepped on something: a small shovel. *Either he kills me or I kill him,* he thought. He grabbed the tool, snuck up behind the soldier, gathered his strength, and smacked him over the head. The man slumped to the ground.

David dropped the shovel and bolted.

Perhaps the guard was chasing him. Perhaps he was dead. David didn't have time to consider. He ran into the dark of the night, grateful that the sun had set. He figured the drumming of artillery would lead him to the front lines. Eventually he heard his train chugging away and wondered whether the two other men had managed to escape, to survive.

He guessed he was at least ten miles from Dachau. He scurried through the dark fields. He stopped in front of a barn; it appeared to be empty. David wondered whether there was food inside. The door was open: an invitation. He didn't even have to break in. It was a large space, packed with hay and straw. A ladder led him to a second level, away from the animals. He lay down in the hay.

Where do I go from here? he thought, struggling to keep his eyes open.

Poland wasn't an option. His world had come to a devastating end in Warsaw; he didn't want to go back. When he'd suggested to Zippi that they meet in Warsaw, it had seemed like a natural destination, familiar. But now, with the reality of liberation looming before him, he felt repelled by the city. He wanted a fresh start, away from the horrors he'd experienced. He needed to leave behind the tragedy of his past.

He imagined the United States, his childhood dream. His mantra kept him going: *750 Grand Concourse, Bronx, New York, 723 Gates Avenue, Brooklyn, New York.*

David stayed in the barn until the following night. He didn't dare walk outside while the sun was out. That evening, the cold air struck him as he walked beneath the moonlight, toward the shots in the distance. He hadn't seen a single person since he left the train, and that was just fine with him. He skulked through the fields, avoiding roads. If he ran into someone, he'd say he was a German civilian worker.

At dawn, David found another abandoned barn. *This is my fate,* he thought. *That's what I'm going to be doing for the rest of my life. I'm going to be going from barn to barn.* He stayed for a day and a night.

The artillery stopped as the sun rose to kiss the sky. David peeked outside. The world was quiet. He wondered—could the war be over? A hill dotted with trees stood about five hundred yards away. He set out for it and began to climb.

The faint rattle of tanks interrupted the silence. Maybe the war really *was* over, he thought, although he didn't quite believe it. A magnificent highway gleamed below him and the grating of tanks grew louder. A column of fifteen or twenty tanks materialized, rolling down the highway.

David strained to spot an insignia—a black cross or a swastika. He was certain the tanks were German. But maybe not; maybe his luck had turned. As long as he didn't see a swastika or black cross, he'd be okay.

As the tanks got closer, David spotted the outline of a white star.

David took a breath. It had to be the Soviets. *Oh God, Wisnia, you've made it!* He scrambled down the hill, elated.

The silence returned. The column of tanks, interspersed with trucks and jeeps, had abruptly stopped. They were stopping for him, David realized. *I'm important,* David thought. *The war stopped for Wisnia!* He tore down the hill to stop at a ravine by the highway. Tripping over the edge, he caught his breath.

The hatch of the leading tank opened and a soldier climbed out.

The man spoke and David quickly grew confused. David spoke German, Polish, Hebrew, some Yiddish, and understood some English. He didn't recognize this language.

Where'd ya come from? the soldier asked.

David recalled his lessons in school and realized this was some sort of accented English. He became suspicious. He'd heard about

Germans posing as Americans—even going so far as to wear American uniforms.

The man pointed at David.

You escape where? he asked.

Train, said David.

What's the train? the man asked. *SS?*

Yes, said David.

Show me, said the soldier. *We'll go.*

David wasn't convinced.

You Russian? David asked. *Russkiy?*

No, American, the man answered.

No, no, star Russian, David said.

He'd seen stars on the airplanes as he'd left Dachau. They had been Soviet planes.

No, no, no, American, the man said.

David was incredulous. The soldier insisted.

Slowly, David began to understand more of the man's South Carolina drawl. He asked if anyone spoke Polish. The man consulted with other soldiers, then called out to the back. A jeep pulled up and an unassuming soldier stepped out. Ferdinand "Ferd" Wilczek stood five feet five inches tall and spoke just enough Polish for David to understand him.

Leery, David asked if anyone was Yiddish, a term then interchangeable with Jewish. Again the soldiers conferred and yelled out to the back of the column.

Another jeep pulled up, and a soldier introduced himself as Harry Weiner. Harry said a few words in Yiddish. David was amused—this man's Yiddish was worse than Ferd's Polish. But David decided to trust them.

Well, Wisnia, you made it, he thought again. And not only that: *You got to the Americans.*

And as he soon discovered, these were not just any Americans.

The boys of the 506th Infantry, a regiment of the 101st Airborne Division of the United States Army, were tired. It had been a dark, brutal winter. It was April of 1945, and they'd experienced devastating losses. As they advanced through southern Germany and Austria, liberating town after town, they were relieved to see rolling lands, and finally some green. Spring was coming.

They had trained at Camp Toccoa, in Georgia, beginning in 1942. Until Japan's surprise attack on Pearl Harbor, the great majority of Americans didn't want to engage in what they considered a foreign war. But Pearl Harbor changed everything. Within a week of the December 7, 1941, attack, the country unified: a Gallup poll found that 91 percent of Americans agreed that the US should declare war on both Germany and Japan. Louis Vecchi, a twenty-one-year-old draftee from California, explained to his mother—as she shook her head in exasperation—that he wanted to be a paratrooper because they were "the best-trained fighters in the army."

At Camp Toccoa, the young soldiers underwent grueling runs, rope climbs, punishing exercises, and endless drills. There, for the first time, the paratroopers stepped off a thirty-four-foot tower into thin air. They completed their parachute-jump training on American soil at Fort Benning, with initial jumps of at least fifteen hundred feet.

At Fort Benning, the men got their "wings"—a silver pin that they displayed proudly on their jump jackets. In the summer of 1943, they boarded troopships to England, where they spent another nine months training. They put on parachuting shows for Winston Churchill, and simulated missions and jumps.

In June of 1944, after a weather delay, they finally got the go-ahead from General Dwight Eisenhower. Thousands and thousands of troops—British and American—prepared to take to the skies. At the airfield, they celebrated the long-awaited order, loading into the C-47 aircrafts known as gooney birds, ready to fight the Nazis in occupied France.

Most gooney bird pilots had never been in combat before. Now they were maneuvering crowded skies at night, into dense clouds crammed with thousands of paratroopers aimed at Normandy.

It was one in the morning when they started to jump. The sky was so dark that they couldn't tell if their parachutes had opened or not. Louis Vecchi, by then a corporal, landed waist-deep in a flooded field. He was soaked, carrying at least 110 pounds of ammunition and mortar rounds on his 138-pound frame. Fred Bahlau, a lieutenant, thought he jumped some twelve hundred feet—but it was hard to tell for sure. He landed right next to a waterway known as the Douve. As he hit the ground, he clutched his Thompson submachine gun to steady himself.

It was June 6, 1944—D-Day—and the Germans were waiting for them.

The 101st Airborne lost a lot of men during the invasion of Normandy. Company H, a unit within the 506th Regiment, was supposed to be in Normandy for four or five days; instead, they stayed a full month to aid other units. Surviving soldiers crawled over bridges as they tried to avoid mortar and artillery rounds and machine-gun fire. Some made it; many didn't. By then, the Allies were no longer taking prisoners: any German who stood in their way would be shot. They were determined—and angry. They'd lost too many of their own to show mercy or slow down.

American newspapers touted D-Day as a "decisive battle" and saluted the "critical scenes of action by air." But more than sixty-five hundred American soldiers died on June 6 alone, and 41 percent of Americans were not clear on why the US was at war. They'd heard about the Nazis' persecution of the Jews, and yet they didn't want to take in refugees. Many Americans believed that the stories of concentration camps were propaganda. How could such horrific tales be real?

The soldiers who survived D-Day prepared for yet another test: liberating Western Europe. In Normandy, they'd experienced some of the worst tragedies they could've imagined: their comrades were mowed down in droves, drowned, disintegrated by land mines, and torn apart by artillery; some died immediately, others much too slowly. The survivors were gutted. And still they forged on. They cleared German towns, one after another, using their rifles without hesitation.

By August of 1944, Paris was liberated—but the work wasn't done. The troops returned to London for reinforcements and started training once more. That September, they parachuted into Holland, but this time the jump was different. They descended during the day, when they had a clear view from the skies, into a seventy-two-day battle. Finally, they were furloughed in Paris.

Then, in December 1944, the men of Company H were told to grab a rifle and move quickly. They slept on the open ground and were on the move at dawn. It was so cold they could hardly think. Their jump boots weren't thick enough to insulate them from the cold, but they couldn't build fires, lest they give away their positions. All they could do was rub their hands together, massage their frozen toes, and wrap their boots in blankets.

In what came to be known as the Battle of the Bulge, at the Belgian town of Bastogne, the Germans hit them hard, with tanks and snipers especially taking a terrible toll. The 101st Airborne emerged from the Battle of the Bulge scarred but not broken. In the end, they hadn't just liberated Paris; they'd liberated all of France, Belgium, and Holland. Afterward, they pushed through Germany to Austria, liberating town after town along the way.

The paratroopers had been as prepared as one could be to experience horrific combat. But as they walked into Kaufering, one of the subcamps of Dachau, they saw skeletons and decomposing corpses strewn about like scraps. The living and the dead were almost indistinguishable. The soldiers were stunned. This was a different sort of killing, nothing they could ever have prepared themselves for.

These were the men David stumbled across: members of Company H, a unit of the 506th Parachute Infantry Regiment attached to the 101st Airborne Division—these were among the American soldiers whose service in Europe is the stuff of legend. But he had no way of knowing this. All he knew was that he was finally safe. Also this: his aunts in New York felt closer than ever.

The soldiers asked David to walk into a Red Cross truck for a medical checkup. David refused.

No, no, no, he said, shaking his head. Unspoken, the thought: *That's where they asphyxiate people.*

The men didn't push him. David was not underweight; his privileged position back in Auschwitz had afforded him extra pounds, some of which he had retained in the weeks since he'd left the camp. He still wore the clothing he'd smuggled out of camp—a short warm jacket, long pants, a shirt, and regular shoes. But the soldiers could see his tattoo, his buzzed hair. They probably understood that David had survived a concentration camp. They didn't ask any questions of this scared eighteen-year-old who'd materialized from nowhere, seeming to have weathered the camps better than most.

The troops had work to do. Before taking off, they fed David Spam and chocolate until he couldn't eat any more of it. The rations he'd received in Birkenau had kept him healthy enough that the food wasn't a shock to his system.

At some point in their stopover, the soldiers had made a decision—and so had David. They would take him with them. Already David felt like the unit mascot, the little brother the soldiers wanted to protect. And to him, they were not only his saviors; they were also his adopted family.

David hopped inside Harry Weiner's jeep. As he rode off with his new American friends, Auschwitz dissolved into another life, one he was eager to leave behind. Already Zippi was dissolving, too, fading away with the other ghosts from his past.

On April 29, 1945, around the same time that David was adopted by the 101st Airborne, the US Seventh Army liberated thirty-two thousand inmates who'd managed to survive Dachau's main camp. Nearly ten thousand prisoners had perished there after David had left.

The soldiers were flabbergasted—and so was the American press, which finally published proof of the crimes being committed in the heart of civilized Europe. A correspondent for *Time* magazine described the coal cars filled with skeletons on his way to the camp. Inside the camp, he met the liberated prisoners, and later wrote that "they began to kiss us, and there is nothing you can do when a lot of hysterical, unshaven, lice-bitten, half-drunk, typhus-infected men want to kiss you. Nothing at all."

A group of editors and publishers from across the United States flew to Europe to see for themselves whether the horror was as bad as had been reported. "We found they were not exaggerated," said Joseph Pulitzer, publisher and editor of the *St. Louis Post-Dispatch.* "As a matter of fact, they were understated." The journalists agreed that the American public should be more exposed to the reality in Europe. "If some people have to endure these atrocities, certainly other people can look at them," said William L. Chenery, publisher of *Collier's* magazine. Dachau, they agreed, had exposed them to the worst of the depravity they'd seen.

At last, Americans might come to see what many couldn't yet believe. Perhaps, once they saw, the doors to immigrants might open up a tad. To David, the United States felt closer than ever. He listened to the easy English flowing between the soldiers and tried to absorb every word. He was determined to become one of them.

He couldn't stay with them for long: the troops had to return to battle. They'd been ordered to assemble in Starnberg, a town about thirty miles south. They promised they'd come back for him—and in the meantime, they'd find a safe space to leave him.

Harry found a house with a shield on its door, the symbol that indicated a German doctor's residence. David would have to wait for them there, with the man and his family, Harry told him.

David watched, dubious, as Harry marked the doorframe with a Star of David. *The young boy will not be harmed in any way,* Harry warned the doctor, *or I'll shoot you when I get back.*

The 101st would return for him, Harry assured David.

He'd come so close to America—or so he'd allowed himself to hope. And now here he was, delivered to a German home.

CHAPTER TWENTY-ONE

"Are We Free?"

The women didn't get much sleep in the barn, even as the shrieks of Soviet rockets subsided. In the morning, stomachs rumbling, they grabbed the potatoes they'd seen in the garden. A soldier passed by. Zippi noticed the red Soviet star on his cap.

Who are you? she asked in Russian.

He didn't answer.

Are you a Russian soldier? she tried again.

Yes, he said.

And are the Russians here already? Zippi asked.

Yes, he said.

Zippi offered him some of her food but he declined. The army was returning with candy, he said.

And are we free? she asked.

Yes, he said.

He and another soldier moved along to survey the space, inspecting for hidden Nazis.

It was May 3, 1945, already a significant date to Zippi: Sam's birthday. And now they were finally, truly free: liberated. She'd been out from under German supervision for less than twenty-four hours, but this, now, was the moment her freedom became official.

This was the moment to jump up gleefully, dance with joy, yell out in revelry. But how could they celebrate? She had no energy, blistered feet, a bruised face, and probably fractured bones. Most of their loved ones were gone. They had no home. They had nothing. They had to figure out where to go, where to sleep that night and all the nights following.

Within moments, a column of tanks, horses, and soldiers emerged on the main highway, near the woods. As Zippi and her friends walked by the barn, Soviet soldiers handed them candy. Former prisoners lined up along the road, half-naked and shriveled, on the brink of death. The Soviets took food and supplies from German villages they now occupied and passed it on to them. Many of the former prisoners ate with reckless abandon; some would get sick, inevitably: too much nourishment, much too soon.

It was her brother's birthday, Zippi told Sara. They had been liberated on his birthday, she marveled. She needed to locate him. If she were to find him anywhere, she thought, it would likely be back home in Bratislava.

First, though, they would go to Warsaw.

Postwar pandemonium spread from Germany to Poland. Villagers flung white sheets down from their windows in surrender as the Red Army liberated town after town. Thousands of displaced persons, or DPs, searched for family and friends. They contended with slow trains, tracks that came to sudden ends, locomotive breakdowns, and overcrowding. Many Soviet soldiers who'd liberated Germany celebrated their victory with outbursts of sexual violence and rape, mostly toward German women, but sometimes others, too.

To get to Warsaw, Zippi and Sara would have to travel some 435 miles east through this mayhem — a significant detour on their way to Bratislava. The deviation would cost them time and come at a terrible risk. The two women would travel through countries whose governments and societies had been upended, places where the embers of war were still smoldering. Zippi and Sara would be easy targets for desperate refugees and savage soldiers.

But Zippi had made a promise: she would go to the Jewish Community Center in Warsaw. With Sara, she would find David.

They decided to hitchhike. Zippi stopped a car driven by a Soviet soldier and asked him for a ride. He took the women as far as Waren, a small town in northern Germany, where he dropped them off with food and found them a room to spend the night. He warned them to get to the American zone as soon as possible, where they'd be safer, and advised them to rest up; a Soviet army vehicle would come by in a few hours to transport survivors.

In Waren, liberated prisoners from all over Europe congregated in the bedlam of freedom. Zippi approached men in uniforms she didn't recognize, curious. The men explained that they were American prisoners of war liberated by the Soviets. Zippi introduced herself. She said that she'd been imprisoned for being a Jew, and that she was from Slovakia. A soldier told her that his parents, too, were from Bratislava. There was still fighting there, someone else said. They exchanged stories, tips on where to go, places said to be safe, places to avoid. Zippi spoke with refugees and soldiers, easily switching from one language to another.

She needed a map, she said. Once she had one, she'd feel more confident moving about in this unfamiliar landscape. And the next morning, she got one.

Map in hand, Zippi felt prepared to continue toward Warsaw. The Polish capital was more than four hundred miles east of Waren. She and Sara got a ride to a railway junction, then took a cattle train. The trip would take days. There was no straightforward route; destruction was everywhere.

When Zippi finally arrived in David's hometown, she found a city hollowed out by war. The Germans had systematically eviscerated the once-glittering Polish capital, "street by street, block by block, building by building," reported the *New York Times*.

The destruction had begun with the Nazis' takeover in 1939; it continued with the Warsaw Ghetto Uprising in 1943, and culminated in the unsuccessful Warsaw Uprising in the summer of 1944. Even in early January 1945, a news correspondent observed that artillery shelling was still being lobbed across the Vistula River at regular intervals. According to the reporter, every single building in the city was gutted. He could see no sign of human life. Days after his account was published, the Red Army broke through the German lines, finally taking over the bombed-out metropolis.

By the time Zippi and Sara arrived in Warsaw, thousands of Polish Jews had been liberated from a smattering of camps, and all were in search of other survivors. Refugees weren't just emerging from the camps; they came out after years spent hiding in cellars, or from the forests where they'd fought as partisans and soldiers, or from the homes of gentiles who'd risked their lives to save them. They converged in Warsaw, hoping to find anyone else who'd survived. The American Jewish Joint Distribution Committee, informally referred to as the Joint, set up soup kitchens around town where the displaced could circulate, search, and wait.

Some streetlights remained erect, elegant and untouched, on streets that ended with cavernous holes. People gathered inside near roofless buildings, former homes with broken windows, no doors, and floors covered in shards of glass, and pieces of stone and wood. Hardly any structure had been spared; even those that had survived the fighting had been plundered, looted, then set on fire.

Refugees set up booths and shacks made of broken bricks and traded whatever food and clothing they had. Some cafés had miraculously survived and were coming back to life. One still had a grand piano, where people congregated and sang. They gathered in hope.

Zippi and Sara navigated the crumbling city and quickly realized there was no longer anything resembling a Jewish community center. Instead, the soup kitchens funded by the Joint served as gathering points where refugees exchanged information.

One man found his wife, whom he thought he'd lost after the Warsaw Uprising. But another woman went on to spend years waiting before an older sister finally materialized. Many feared what they might learn. They could stumble upon a loved one by pure chance, but they might just as easily find confirmation of their death. The glimpse of a tattoo on a man's forearm might lead to a family reunion, or to the impartation of devastating news.

In the end, finding a loved one took a combination of patience, persistence, and pure luck.

Zippi was patient.

She waited for David. And she waited.

Each day, she waited.

But David never came.

CHAPTER TWENTY-TWO

Little Davey

The doctor's daughter wanted to know what happened, how David had ended up among the Americans. So he told her and her father what he had been through. He told them everything.

He had some Jewish blood in him, the German doctor told David. His ancestors, from way far back — there'd been a Jew among them. David couldn't know whether this was true, whether they were trying to reassure him or protect themselves, but clearly they wouldn't harm him. The Americans had taken the town. They had marked the doorframe with a Star of David. For once, the sign would protect him.

The doctor offered him food, but David's stomach ached from all the Spam and chocolate he'd eaten with the troops. So instead, his host gave David a toothbrush, and for the first time since he could remember, he brushed his teeth and took a real shower.

The doctor's wife led David to a small room with a bed. The family's home was spare and very clean. Quiet. David climbed into the bed. It had been four years since he had laid his head on a soft pillow. A clean, white sheet and a heavy blanket covered him.

Finally, he slept.

*   *   *

David slept, ate, and slept some more. Within days, Harry returned for him, as promised.

Back in the fold of Company H, David felt protected. At eighteen, he was sure that he was the youngest in the group. The soldiers had affectionately dubbed him Little Davey.

He listened to how the troops spoke English. David was amused by Captain Walker's South Carolina drawl, the way his vowels extended when he said *Ca-roh-laaah-nah,* compared to Ferd's Rhode Island accent; how his *r*'s dropped from some words and appeared on the end of others. David's musical ear helped him pick up English quickly. He forced himself to swallow any hint of a European accent. He was meticulous in his reinvention.

Within a week of their reunion, the men of Company H put David in an olive-green American uniform. He'd shed his rags from

David Wisnia in his US Army uniform after being "adopted" by troops of the 101st Airborne Division, 1945.

Auschwitz weeks earlier and now here he was, clad in an Eisenhower jacket with cuff buttons and a woolen inseam, and a parachute infantry garrison wool cap angled ever so slightly on his forehead.

He couldn't shed his old skin, his old life, fast enough.

By the time the soldiers from the 101st Airborne adopted David, the heavy artillery of war was mostly over. The Nazis had, for the most part, stopped shooting.

But the soldiers still had work to do. In late April, General Eisenhower had ordered them to make their way to Berchtesgaden, a resort town on the Austrian border. Hitler had an idyllic mountaintop home just outside town, perched on the top of the Kehlstein peak, eight thousand feet above sea level. Bunker complexes had been dug underground as a refuge of last-resort for party leaders— the Third Reich's final holdout. Because Berchtesgaden was known as a central artery of the Nazi system, American commanders were dedicating thousands of paratroopers from various companies, with extra ammunition and rations, to taking this mountain stronghold.

The men of Company H, along with the rest of the 101st Airborne, were going to empty out the Eagle's Nest. And David was going with them.

David's fluent German and his growing comprehension of English made him an ideal interpreter. He took on an unofficial, unpaid role as a civilian auxiliary of the US Army, and felt empowered for the first time in years. Now, instead of being interrogated by the Nazis, he was the one asking questions. Instead of cowering in front of SS soldiers, he was the one standing tall, watching as they trembled at the sight of the Americans. He remembered the morning he'd spent with his father taking in Hitler's victory parade in Warsaw. Back then, David could not believe that anyone could beat the Nazis. Now, witnessing their defeat, he felt fulfilled.

David rode in a jeep at the back of the convoy, yelling through a loudspeaker at the Germans they'd pass: *Wirf deine Waffen runter!*

Throw down your arms! He smirked at them as they groveled. He no longer worried about being shot — not least because the men of Company H were doing their best to protect him. Each time they jumped out of a truck for a skirmish, a wall of American soldiers kept guard, ensuring that David remained in the back. When they weren't fighting, David helped Ferd, who was a supply-room sergeant charged with organizing clothing and various items for the soldiers. David kept the room tidy and clean. At night, he slept in the barracks, near Ferd.

By May of 1945, they'd moved eastward toward Austria, past Landsberg in Germany, where scorched cars and discarded weapons littered the roads. Thirty-foot-high piles of abandoned German helmets lay on the fields. Across Europe, roads were congested with nearly twenty million wanderers, including troops of various nationalities, prisoners of war, former soldiers, and camp survivors.

As they neared the Eagle's Nest, the men of Company H readied for their mission. A sergeant handed David a Thompson submachine gun. He needed to know how to protect himself. The sergeant taught David how to assemble, disassemble, load, and shoot. David wrapped his fingers around the walnut grip, reveling in the ten-pound heft of aluminum, steel, and wood.

He could kill somebody, David realized. He thought back to Hebrew school and the Ten Commandments — lessons from a bygone time.

Holding the Thompson, he yearned for revenge.

By the time Company H arrived in Berchtesgaden, most of the Germans in town had already conceded. The Allies had begun to draw up surrender terms for the Nazis. A message arrived on May 6: American troops were not to fire on Germans unless they were fired upon first. German troops had been ordered to give up their weapons, and those west of the surrender line became prisoners of war, sequestered in barns and schools to await their fate.

The 101st Airborne companies spent much of the time at Berchtesgaden collecting Nazi loot—from jewelry to art, cigars, and vintage wines. Troops discovered roomfuls of priceless artwork and lavish, gold-encrusted candelabras and vases. One general replaced his jeep with Hitler's four-ton armored Mercedes-Benz. American soldiers stumbled across literal buried treasures, including more than $4 million in different currencies inside a barn. Technically, this bounty was off-limits. Still, the troops helped themselves to cameras, shotguns, and binoculars—"souvenirs" to bring home. The various divisions of the 101st scavenged the blown-out buildings around town. David didn't know where to start.

Come on, David, take what you want, called out one of the soldiers. The man opened a door and let him peek into the room.

David examined the assorted weapons, some of which may well have been the same types that the Nazis had once used against him and his family. He grabbed a small Walther pistol. Then he grabbed a camera—never before had he seen such a gorgeous camera. Last, he took a larger, semiautomatic pistol. David grinned. It was one of the best days of his life.

The biggest prizes, however, were the most notorious Nazi leaders, who were hiding throughout the local German villages. They took cover in abandoned barns, in farmhouses, in civilians' homes. Among those captured around the time David was in Berchtesgaden were Hermann Göring, the highest-ranking Nazi military leader; Robert Ley, leader of the German Labour Front; and Franz Xaver Schwarz, national treasurer of the Nazi Party.

Finally the Allied troops could celebrate. After a long winter and spring, they had their pick of luxury hotels circling the shoreline of the crystalline Königssee, one of Germany's most beautiful lakes. They enjoyed the liquor that flowed throughout the resort town. They killed local cows and made themselves steaks and roasts, savoring the food that had once belonged to the SS. David sipped the wine and champagne—courtesy of his Nazi captors—and, best of all, he enjoyed it with the Americans. Whenever a piano was in sight, David performed and sang, pleased to provide music, to entertain—on his own terms.

After a few days of heavy drinking, festivities, sleeping in proper beds, and eating hearty meals, the 101st scattered around the local towns. Still with Company H, David's next stop was Zell am See, Austria, about twenty miles to the south.

David was riding in a jeep with Ferd, en route to Zell am See, when Ferd spontaneously pulled to a stop in the middle of the road. He got out.

Come out, Little Davey, he said.

David stepped out, confused, not understanding what was happening.

Ferd grabbed David and pulled him into a tight hug. He kissed him. *You made it, you son of a gun,* Ferd said.

What happened? David asked, confused.

The war's over!

They hadn't had the opportunity to stop, to think, to understand. They hadn't processed any of it, despite the Champagne, the wine, the celebration. Now, at last, it had dawned on them. Ferd needed to say the words out loud, to acknowledge what they'd lived through.

The odds had been overwhelmingly against David. And yet he had made it.

The moment ended as abruptly as it had begun. They climbed back into the jeep and continued on their way.

In Zell am See, Company H discovered another charming resort town on a magnificent lake. Once-expensive hotels had been converted into military hospitals crammed with German soldiers. American soldiers took over. The 101st had a pointed assignment: to collect the hidden Nazis. They did this while enjoying the town and the service of fallen German soldiers and refugees who did their cooking and cleaning.

Little Davey sang and played the piano at every opportunity. He also did more serious work, helping the GIs collect any German weapons they could find. As an informal interpreter, he knocked on doors and asked the residents questions about people they'd seen, hidden Nazis, any information that might help in their mission.

One afternoon, a Polish man answered the door. David, hearing a fellow countryman, immediately switched from German to Polish as he asked his usual questions.

This time, the man's response sparked a fire in David.

There's a Nazi hidden near here, the Pole said. *He was in charge of a camp. He'd been in charge of torturing prisoners.*

The Pole pointed toward a barn.

David walked to the building on his own, without telling any of his friends.

He took his Walther with him.

CHAPTER TWENTY-THREE

"How Are You Still Alive?"

After days of waiting for David, Zippi and Sara finally admitted to themselves that he wasn't coming. Was he dead? If not, why didn't he come? Where was he? They had no way of knowing.

The two now found themselves adrift in Warsaw, an eddy in the vast river of displaced persons (DPs) coursing throughout central Europe in the final days of World War II. It was May 1945; the Germans had just surrendered. The only place Zippi and Sara could think to go to was back to what had once been "home."

Zippi had seen a building with a large flag of the Czech Red Cross hanging outside. There she found an acquaintance willing to lend her enough money to make the trip to Bratislava. For the first time in years, Zippi and Sara weren't treated like cattle. There was no stray hay caught in their hair, no lice crawling on their skin, no smell of urine permeating their compartment. But in other ways, the past still clung to them like smoke. Some travelers still wore their flea-infested uniforms, heads shaved, unrecognizable. They all traveled light.

Zippi arrived in Bratislava with the shoes on her feet, the clothes on her body, a map of Germany in her hand, and the ache in her heart of another love lost.

Months earlier, Bratislava had been a ghost town. Liberation had transformed it, but not entirely for the better: Soviet soldiers roamed the streets; women feared being raped. Apartments that had once belonged to Jews were abandoned or occupied by gentiles. Jews who returned to town found former neighbors out on the street, wearing their old winter coats. One woman saw a stranger in her mother's dress—a dress her mother had sewn herself. Many locals weren't eager to see their old neighbors returning: they didn't want to give up the confiscated homes, stolen clothing, and plundered furniture they'd been enjoying.

Each day, survivors gathered at the railroad station in search of lost faces. There they confronted the arrival of unrecognizably bare-boned bodies. Freshly liberated, these new arrivals reported to a Jewish bureau run by the United Nations Relief and Rehabilitation Administration (UNRRA), where they stood in a long line, waiting to register their names and look for relatives and housing.

A man and a woman in line struck an all-too-common conversation:

Where were you? she asked.

In Auschwitz, he said.

Me too.

Did you find any family when you came back? he asked.

I found a sister, she said.

You're lucky.

UNRRA helped some refugees reconnect with lost family members, and others found new roommates, struck up new friendships, or met partners with whom to create a new life.

It was likely through UNRRA that Zippi discovered the one person from her old life who survived the war was Sam. She'd kept tabs on him through acquaintances from Bratislava, and through their correspondence, but up until then she couldn't have known for sure whether he had made it through the final throes of the war.

But now she learned the happy truth: Sam was alive. It couldn't have been too difficult to find him—he was helping displaced people like herself. Neither sibling left a record of how or where they discovered each other. But after more than three years apart, of corresponding through coded postcards, of long silences that left them wondering if this moment would ever come, their relief must have been overwhelming. They were orphans; their family was dead. But at least they had each other.

Sam could finally tell Zippi details he hadn't been able to convey in his postcards.

He had been released from prison in Bratislava a few months early, for good behavior, only to be met by two officers waiting outside his cell. Now that he was no longer a prisoner of war, he was back to being something worse—a Jew. The Nazis had come for him.

They took Sam to the Sered' labor camp, which manufactured coffins for the German army, as well as other goods for the general public. At first, Sam worked with the camp's fire brigade. Then he became the camp's undertaker. When typhus broke out, Sam washed the dead bodies and wrapped them in sheets, trying to contain the disease. Inevitably, Sam was infected and quarantined at a nearby convent.

As he recovered, the underground was abuzz with plans of resistance, and Sam kept himself informed. In 1943, Slovakian forces who wanted to overthrow Jozef Tiso and the Nazi regime established the Slovak National Council, with its own underground partisan movement and army. The Czechoslovak government in exile and the Slovak National Council were now fighting the same opponent. At the Sered' camp, Slovak guards looked the other way as prisoners mobilized for an uprising. Sam was given a mission: to make his way out of the labor camp and report to resistance organizers, whereupon he would join the Slovak military resistance and fight against the Axis. The underground got him enough money for a train ride—and the rest was up to him.

It sounded like an impossible task, but none of the guards tried to stop him from leaving. Breaking out of the convent was as simple as walking out the door, Sam chuckled. By now, it was 1944 and half the guards seemed ready to join the resistance. He found it surprisingly easy to hop on a train and disappear. He met with organizers at an arranged location in Prievidza, a large metropolis in western Slovakia, and received a new identity, including a new name and official fingerprinted identification papers. Sam Spitzer was no more; that June he'd become Jan Maslonka, no longer Jewish—a safer identity among resisters, even if they were fighting the same opponent. Sam kept his birth date and birth city the same to prevent more confusion than necessary; he had to keep his new story straight.

As Jan Maslonka, Sam reported to military barracks and joined dissidents of the Slovak army who'd been working with the Czechoslovak government in exile, based in London, the same entity that had overseen Tibor Justh's mission two years earlier. Their first stop was the military airport in central Slovakia, Letisko Tri Duby, where the British and Americans provided supplies for the resisters.

Soon after Sam joined, Germany formally occupied Slovakia with the approval of the country's puppet president, Jozef Tiso. The Slovak National Uprising began on August 29, 1944, a day after the occupation. The Slovakian forces, including Sam, became part of a formal army called the 1st Czechoslovak Army Corps. They joined the Allied forces, keeping in touch with the other fighters through a radio connection.

"We were armed up to our teeth," Sam remembered later. They had clothing, ammunition, tanks, cannons—and "it all fell in our hands."

The Slovak National Uprising ended in defeat, with towns and villages burned to the ground, and casualties on all sides. Some of the barbarism Sam witnessed remained etched in his memory forever. But it was stumbling upon the family of a friend who'd apparently gone into hiding to escape the Germans that truly shook him to his core. He recognized the man — his friend's father — hugging his grandson. An entire family were huddled together, their faces fresh-looking; all frozen to death.

Shortly after that, the Germans captured Sam and a few other Slovak soldiers, took them to a guest house, and locked the doors. *This is it,* Sam thought. *I'll be executed in the morning.*

The Germans spent the night drinking. Sam noticed an open window. It must have been around four in the morning when he slipped out, made his way to the nearest town, and talked his way onto a train to Bratislava. Somehow, he reestablished contact with the underground and once again became Jan Maslonka.

In the hinterlands of Czechoslovakia, the fighting continued. Sam and some twenty thousand Slovak fighters were now partisans. Along the Low Tatras mountain range, day after day, he walked about three miles from his base to position himself as a sniper by the ruins of a medieval castle. Despite the frigid weather and layers of snow, his vantage point was good: he was at the apex of a rocky limestone cliff overlooking the Danube, the longest river in Slovakia.

Sam shot down at German soldiers with machine guns and anti-tank guns; he tossed grenades and used whatever ammunition he had at his disposal. On the banks of a creek some five hundred meters away from where he slept, the Nazis had slaughtered a group of French partisans. The Nazis had left their footprints. Sam and his companions followed the footprints and avenged the partisans' deaths. He made sure that when he returned to the base each morning, he had no leftover bullets.

On April 4, 1945, the Slovak partisans, with the help of the

Sam Spitzer, identified as Jan Maslonka in a false ID issued by the underground movement, June 1944. Jews received forged papers with a non-Jewish identity for additional protection.

Soviets, finally forced the German army to retreat from Bratislava. By then the Red Army had liberated most of the country. Sam returned victorious to his birthplace, wearing his partisan uniform and carrying a semiautomatic pistol.

The feeling didn't last long. Almost immediately Sam saw a Red Army soldier shove a local Jewish man who'd managed to survive in hiding. The Jew looked at Sam and took a gamble. *Help,* the man mouthed.

There's something about Jews, Sam later mused. *They recognize one another by the sadness in each other's eyes.*

Sam approached the Soviet soldier, eyes blazing. "That's not a German — that's a Jew," he said, willing to give the soldier a chance to step away.

Instead, the soldier cursed at him. Sam pushed his pistol against him. The military police came to see about the commotion and Sam explained what had happened. The police were Jewish. They took the Soviet soldier away and—"Goodbye, Charlie, you know?" Sam remembered later.

This was a defining moment in Sam's life. Up until then, he had believed in the principles of the Communist regime—he'd been fighting for them. Now he came to a sad realization: the idea of Communism was only beautiful on paper, he decided. It wouldn't work in the real world, a world where prejudice would always stand in the way of true cooperation.

Sam's return to Bratislava wasn't as triumphant as he'd hoped. Still, he wanted to make himself useful. He volunteered to help distribute blankets that the UNRRA provided.

After a few days at work, he recognized a girl from his Hashomer Hatzair days. Her name was Margaret. She'd grown up into a beautiful woman.

"My God, you're alive?" came the now-familiar question, uttered in disbelief and joy. "Where did you survive the war?"

"Prison," he answered.

"What did you steal?" she teased with a smile.

They fell in love almost immediately. Neither of them had anyone left that they knew of; Sam hadn't heard from Zippi and could only imagine what had befallen her.

With each day that passed, Sam reconnected with more fellow survivors from Hashomer Hatzair. Through them, he met a Polish Palestinian Jew who'd come to Europe to help displaced Jews immigrate to Palestine, still an illegal proposition under the British Mandate. The man was also organizing a supply chain of armaments to the Palmach, a Zionist military defense force in Palestine that was fighting the British for an independent Jewish state. Sam wanted to help—and he was well connected. So he used his network to help the Palmach.

★　　★　　★

The revelation that Sam had fallen in love—that he had found his new beginning—must have been bittersweet for Zippi, whose romantic plans dissolved over the days she'd spent waiting for David in Warsaw. But her brother was happy, and she focused on that.

She also focused on finding a purpose. As teenagers, Zippi and Sam had seen firsthand the trickle of Jewish refugees who had slipped through Bratislava en route to Palestine. Now that the war had ended, a large number of displaced Jews had nowhere to go. Like her brother, Zippi wanted to help.

Zippi Spitzer soon after her liberation in 1945.

In the postwar world, borders had been redrawn. Occupied Germany was now split into four Allied zones: British, French, Soviet, and American. Camps for displaced persons had been hastily built throughout each region, many in former concentration camps, and run by the military. Chaos and panic swept the nation as DPs found themselves trapped once again: Polish Jews who tried to return home found they were not safe in Poland, but borders across zones had become heavily guarded.

Many refugees managed to escape through the Brichah (from the Hebrew word for flight), a clandestine movement started by a group of war survivors to smuggle Jews across borders. Some DPs wanted to go to Palestine; others wanted to go wherever they had any family link left. Most wanted to flee westward and leave the suffering and calamity of Europe behind them. The continent, these survivors felt, was indelibly stained with the blood of their families and friends. There was nothing left here for the living.

The Brichah had unofficial connections with various local governments and funding from the American Jewish Joint Distribution Community, which Zippi had first encountered in Warsaw. The group organized identity cards and money for refugees, whose journeys often lasted several weeks. A Brichah leader would escort refugees from border to border, often late at night. Sometimes the refugees fled by train, trying not to give themselves away when guards passed by and asked for identification. Sometimes they traveled in trucks driven by other Brichah members. Wherever they headed, most passed through Bratislava, a central hub.

The Czech government allowed Jewish transients inside its borders and even agreed to provide them with food and transportation. The supposed generosity came with two caveats, however: Jews agreed not to stay permanently, and the Czech government was to be reimbursed for all its expenses. Antisemitism remained rampant across the continent, often escalating, even as the truth about the Holocaust was finally coming out.

Zippi found a purpose in escorting DPs across borders through the Brichah. She escorted them westward from Vienna to Munich, then to Feldafing, the first all-Jewish displaced-person camp in

Europe. A former Hitler Youth summer camp on the scenic shores of a Bavarian lake, it had been set up after the war for Jews to live in freedom while avoiding antisemitism and neighbors who'd been complicit in torture and murder. During one of her first clandestine trips across the borders of Czechoslovakia, Austria, and Germany, Zippi guided a Polish-Jewish family disguised as Greeks. She warned them not to speak as they traveled through Austria. It's possible that, along the way, Zippi also helped forge identity cards for those she smuggled.

Following an upsetting interaction in her hometown, Sara made the journey, too. Before they'd arrived in Bratislava, Zippi had accompanied her to Sochaczew, the small village where Sara and David had grown up and sung together. Perhaps Zippi expected to find David walking along the streets where he'd grown up. Perhaps she toured the town of the boy she had loved in Auschwitz and worried that he was no longer alive. Sara had hoped to see her old home, to look for anything that had once belonged to her family. But her hope faded when she bumped into her former cleaning lady on the street.

How are you still alive? the woman asked Sara, her distaste obvious. Sara was shaken. They'd left Poland immediately, Sara vowing never to return. She had one sister who was likely still alive, and she found her eventually—in Feldafing.

Zippi herself wasn't entirely sure she wanted to stay in Feldafing. Perhaps part of her hoped that David would come looking for her in Bratislava. Or, she thought, maybe they hadn't agreed to meet in Warsaw, after all. Could it have been Bratislava all along? Could one of them have misunderstood?

In late September of 1945, Sam and Margaret married. Zippi remained in Bratislava for a few months, mostly working with the Brichah. Ultimately she decided the time had come to move on. Her brother and new sister-in-law were eager to start their own family, and Zippi didn't want them to feel responsible for her. Besides, she'd waited long enough. She'd helped dozens of DPs start anew; it was time for her to forge her own path.

During one of her trips to Feldafing, Zippi reconnected with acquaintances from Birkenau, many of whom she'd once protected. They told her that her organizational skills were badly needed at the burgeoning DP camp, where hundreds of survivors were arriving each day. She also got to know Dr. Henri Heitan, a French UNRRA physician in charge of patient care at the camp. He told her he could use her help distributing food to pregnant women, babies, and the chronically ill.

By then, she'd made several trips back and forth. It was time to make the leap. Besides, so many Auschwitz and Birkenau survivors were beginning anew in Feldafing. Who knew whom she might run into?

CHAPTER TWENTY-FOUR

An Example for the Rest of the World

Gun in hand, David approached the barn. He pushed the door open and slid inside, quiet as falling snow.

A man stood alone. He saw David—a determined, 175-pound soldier in American uniform—and backed away.

"Where's your uniform?" David asked in German. He wanted proof, although he knew what the man was.

At first, the Nazi feigned ignorance. He quickly changed tactics.

I was just working, he told David. *It was the government. I was fulfilling duties. I had nothing to do with it.*

Sure, David thought.

He saw the man's motorcycle inside the barn. He saw the man's uniform in a corner. He had no doubts.

This was no regular German soldier. He was SS.

The Nazi was about to bolt. David felt the gun against the palm of his hand. The pistol had been designed and developed for the *Wehrmacht.* His souvenir from Berchtensgaden. All it would take was his finger on the trigger.

Here's your payback for your duties, David thought.

He shot the man in the chest. Then he shot him again.

It was quick, expedient.

Afterward, David would tell himself that it was possible he hadn't killed the man. Sure, he'd shot him twice, point blank. But maybe—

Inescapable, though, was this: this was the first time he'd shot a person on purpose. Because yes, even if the Nazi had somehow survived, David had meant to kill him.

David felt sick. He wanted to get out of there. But before he left, he took the SS officer's motorcycle out of the barn. He rode it around the bend of the road to meet up with the rest of his group— and lost control.

He crashed into a pile of hay and tumbled off the bike.

David's body was stiff, and for a moment he wondered if he was dead. But he picked himself back up and brushed off the hay, watching the bike's wheels still spinning in the air. He lifted it up, got the wheels on the ground.

David revved the engine. It still worked. It was fine; he was fine.

He didn't tell anyone what he'd done. Instead, he rejoined his friends as though nothing had happened. No one asked any questions about the bike. They'd grown accustomed to helping themselves to abandoned treasures.

David tried to tuck the incident in the back of his mind, nauseated by what he'd done. It wasn't guilt, exactly—but something was churning in his stomach. He'd be happy never to think of it again.

At eighteen years old, David had quite a few lost years to make up for. While David and the troops of the 101st Airborne had been stationed in Zell am See, Austria, they'd enjoyed the thrills of being the victors about town. When it came time to move again, their convoys went on to Paris.

Until just recently, Paris had been a mere shadow of the grand city it once was. Shops shuttered, bakeries closed, nightclubs gone dark. Only the subways, still moving underground, seemed alive.

But by the time David and his regiment made their way over in June of 1945, the city of light was sparkling back to life.

American troops had been told that, after a brief furlough, they'd be redeployed to the Pacific for more fighting. David would remain in uniform, still an unofficial member of Company H, for as long as he could. He had no home to return to. Poland was out of the question. Zippi was nothing more than a memory—a shadow from a past life that he was eager to leave behind. And he had no intention of leaving his adoptive family. His Yankee accent was practically perfect. His future was in the United States.

David needed to get in touch with his aunts in New York; surely they would help sponsor him. In the meantime, he remained in his 101st Airborne garb with his GI friends. David felt powerful in uniform. Sure, he wished he'd collected the impressive insignias that his buddies wore on their jackets—but still, he was one of them, at least until they shipped out for the Pacific and he was left on his own.

But on August 6, 1945, an atomic bomb dropped on Hiroshima—and everything changed.

Company H's fighting days were over.

American troops received a *Pocket Guide to Paris and the Cities of Northern France,* issued by the US military. "So far as your military duties permit, see as much as you can," the guide advised. "You've got a great chance to do now, major expenses paid, what would cost you a lot of your own money after the war. Take advantage of it."

And they did. The spirit of hedonism raged, particularly among the city's liberators. "From early evening to the wee hours of the morning, the GIs in Paris usually flock to the Montmartre cabaret district to make merry with pretty French girls," the army newspaper, *Stars and Stripes,* reported. A men's nightclub opened atop the Eiffel Tower for the exclusive pleasure of Allied troops in uniform, who were permitted to bring along one civilian guest.

For the first time in his life, David got soused. With his buddies, he went to Folies Bergère, a cabaret featuring nude women. He enjoyed too much Benedictine, an herbal French liquor, and cut off all his buddies' ties. David was a happy drunk. He fixed up his American friends with French women, since he spoke the language, considering himself the group's "procurer" of girls.

GIs also took in the city culture by day. In July of 1945, they celebrated Bastille Day, dancing in the streets for the first time since Paris had been occupied five years before. Cafés and restaurants remained open late and loudspeakers played music on every street corner. When they weren't dancing, US troops were among the first to take in the return of masterpieces like the *Mona Lisa,* the *Venus de Milo,* and *Mercury Fastening His Sandal,* all of which had been evacuated from the Louvre to provisional hiding places before the war.

Every so often David ran into Jewish survivors who tried to convince him to go to Palestine with them. But David was part of the US military now, he tried to explain. He was an American. He had a new life.

Paris wasn't all play. David had a military job in Versailles, about ten miles outside of Paris, managing a gift warehouse in an Army Post Exchange, informally known as the PX, a marketplace exclusive to American soldiers, where they bought drinks, snacks, cigarettes, and even clothing imported from the US at marked-down prices.

By now David was on the US military's payroll. In addition, he was well positioned to amass a small fortune by participating in the rampant postwar black market. He made more money than he'd dreamed possible buying a carton of cigarettes from the American PX for 50 francs and reselling it elsewhere for a thousand francs.

The black market extended well beyond cigarettes. Postwar Paris was short of goods ranging from coal to housing to food and clothing. Shady dealings plagued the entire continent—and nearly every facet of life. This led to surges in food prices for middle-class citizens, who already lived off government-subsidized bread and rationed wine, sugar, and meat. In the United States, contraband had become a problem, too. Cigarettes practically became currency. Those who dealt in the black market extended from the lone GI to sophisticated gangs. Both the attorney general and the FBI warned war profiteers that they would suffer consequences. But that didn't faze David or the thousands of others who were happy to put a few extra dollars in their pockets after years of deprivation.

Even as he enjoyed this unimaginable new life, David's aunts' addresses drummed inside his head. *750 Grand Concourse, Bronx, New York, 723 Gates Avenue, Brooklyn, New York.* He needed them now more than ever.

Immigration into the United States was far from a slam dunk, even for a refugee in a GI uniform. A national debate was raging over how to handle Europe's displaced people. While some six million DPs were repatriated by September of 1945, one million remained in the American and British zones alone. Six million Jews had been murdered in Europe and more than half a million were left without a home. These Jewish survivors hoped that the DP camps would eventually lead them either to the west or to Palestine.

Despite having seen the photographs from Europe and heard Nazi victims' horrific accounts, most Americans did not want to take in refugees. By 1945, the United States had spiraled into a recession. Returning GIs were having trouble finding employment and housing. Antisemitism remained widespread.

But in a move against popular opinion, President Harry Truman issued the Truman Directive in December of 1945. While his executive order maintained the existing immigration quotas, it gave visa preference to Nazi victims, underscoring that the majority of refugees coming in should be orphaned children.

The directive would facilitate immigration, particularly for the displaced persons in the American zones of occupied Europe. "This is the opportunity for America to set an example for the rest of the world in cooperation towards alleviating human misery," President Truman stated.

David was an orphan, but according to the birth date he'd given himself when he arrived in Auschwitz, he was twenty-one. In reality, he had just turned nineteen. Regardless, he was no longer a child. He needed to ask his aunts in New York to sponsor him, to guarantee that he wouldn't be a financial burden to the nation.

When a GI friend mentioned he was returning home to New York, David gave him Aunt Helen's address: *750 Grand Concourse, Bronx, New York,* each word and number a well-worn talisman after all those nights in Auschwitz.

David had been close to both of his mother's sisters, but far closer to Helen than to Rose; Helen had helped raise him and his brothers, after all. She had nourished them, and the memories of her chicken soup—like the mantra of her New York address— had helped him to endure the long, difficult nights in the camp. She would get David to America; he just knew it.

He asked his friend to tell Aunt Helen that David was alive, that he was stationed in Versailles—reborn from the ashes as an American soldier.

David's aunt, it appeared, was an American herself now, too—at least in a sense. The woman at 750 Grand Concourse in the Bronx wanted nothing to do with her refugee nephew.

His friend had called her, had stopped by her building, to no avail. She kept insisting that she didn't know any David Wisnias.

Outraged, the friend gave her a piece of his mind—how could she abandon her nephew, who'd lost his entire family?—but it didn't help. David's friend spent four months reaching out to her, trying to change her mind. She repeated each time that she didn't know who David was.

The message couldn't be clearer.

They don't want to know you, kid, his friend told him. *You're on your own.*

David was in utter disbelief. How could it be? After all those nights of repeating her address—*750 Grand Concourse, Bronx, New York*—how could Aunt Helen, of all people, reject him? And to think—she was, presumably, still close to Aunt Rose. This meant Helen hadn't been the only one to turn him away—both aunts were part of the decision. He was devastated. Where would he go? At some point after the war, he learned that his eldest brother, Moshe, had been killed. He had no family left in Europe.

David wrote a letter with his information to the *Jewish Daily Forward,* a Yiddish newspaper that was printed in New York and connected to a radio station, WEVD. On Friday afternoons the station aired a reading of the names of war survivors who were looking for family. He hoped his aunts were listening. Maybe they would change their minds. One way or another, he told himself, he would get to the United States.

In the meantime, his army duties had expanded to helping to supply DP camps. The wide network of camps was managed by the UNRRA and to a large extent the US military. Americans had committed to caring for destitute war victims. While some soldiers expressed resentment toward DPs, most were empathetic. Jewish soldiers, especially, wanted to do what they could to help. Some went so far as to find ways to adopt orphans to bring them to the United States; others served as honorary parents at bar mitzvahs and weddings celebrated in the DP camps.

The army ensured that the camps were well run, had ample supplies, and were safe. It coordinated with Jewish organizations, especially the Joint Distribution Committee and the Hebrew Immigration Aid Society (HIAS), which provided funding and helped with logistics. But when bureaucracy slowed down the response of these welfare agencies, the brunt of the work fell on the military.

And as a civilian aide to the American military, it often fell on David.

One of his main jobs, as it transpired, would be to drive ten hours in an army jeep to deliver supplies to a DP camp outside Munich—a camp called Feldafing.

*S*he'd first seen him at the Sauna. A glance was all it took. For months, they'd waited. They'd been patient. Notes, brief mumbles, nothing else. Finally, in their nest, they'd held each other in defiance.

But he'd been born to be a soloist. And in her own way, she was, too. They had waited and waited — the waiting thrilling, then.

PART V

CADENZA

CHAPTER TWENTY-FIVE

"The Loneliness of Survival"

Zippi prided herself in fattening up the many babies being born daily in the DP camp. She spent her days distributing food to a boom of pregnant women. What could be more gratifying for a peaceful new beginning? The setting helped. Feldafing was a "beautiful rolling country, small lakes, small hills," Katie Louchheim, an American diplomat who'd helped form the UNRRA, wrote, describing her initial arrival just outside the camp. "A truck full of American soldiers shout 'Come play,' wave baseball bats. They are singing."

To Zippi and her friends, though, Feldafing's best features were outside the camp. The main attraction was the idyllic Lake Starnberg, where the body of the Bavarian king Ludwig II had mysteriously washed ashore in 1886.

Decades later, it was also here that, according to Zippi, she saved Erwin Tichauer's life.

The balmy summer days were a perfect occasion for DPs to frolic in the cool, crystalline lake. But in this tranquil oasis, Zippi noticed a figure struggling in the water. Her days as a champion swimmer in the Danube were long gone, but Zippi still knew how to handle herself. She dived in and hauled the man—tanned, muscular, with dark eyes and curly hair—back ashore. Little did she know where this rescue might lead.

Erwin had heard of Zippi long before he arrived in Feldafing. When he was a prisoner in Auschwitz, he heard of a "peculiar" and "moody" woman who was the graphic designer at the women's camp in Birkenau. This woman, he heard, was very exact in her work. In fact, he nearly became her boss at the ammunitions factory. Franz Hössler, who supervised the women's camp in Birkenau with Maria Mandl, proposed the idea. He went so far as to tell the factory's civilian engineers at the factory to expect the draftswoman to begin work soon, and that Erwin would be her supervisor. But Zippi insisted that Katya and Margot Drechsel not let her go. She'd been trained as a graphic designer, she argued, not as a draftswoman. She didn't know the first thing about technical drafting.

Zippi, for her part, had never heard of Erwin until she arrived at Feldafing, where he was relatively well known. There, he was the camp's police chief and a security officer employed by the UNRRA, in charge of the entire region's security. He also liaised with the American military, ensuring that the camp had all the supplies it needed.

Erwin was a Berliner through and through. And in the DPs' self-assigned class structure, Berliners topped the pyramid: in general, Germans were considered among the most cultured, while the Yiddish-speaking Jews from Lithuania and Poland were often looked down on as "shtetl Jews."

Erwin's arrival in Feldafing was a bit of a mystery, much like his existence in Auschwitz. Back in Berlin, he'd grown up tinkering with clocks—disassembling and reassembling them and learning their mechanics. The son of a well-regarded Berlin law professor, Erwin had studied at a German high school where military training was a part of the curriculum. He spent his time outside of school scrutinizing animals' movements at the zoo and observing brewery horses pulling heavy loads in the city streets. He amused himself by studying the Paleolithic man and the prehistoric stone tools at the Museum für Völkerkunde, the Ethnological Museum of Berlin. As Erwin got older, he wanted to pursue science and mechanical engineering or surgery. During the prewar years, he earned a bachelor's degree, postgraduate honors, and a doctorate from the University of Königsberg, in East Prussia, where he later became a lecturer.

When the Nazis came to power, Erwin's academic work was cut short. Instead of teaching, he was forced to work at a German carton factory, where he was responsible for machinery maintenance, regularly lying down naked under filthy cutting machines to clean and oil its sharp blades. "The surgeon-to-be literally lay down 'under the knife,'" a friend would later recall. Rather than sit down with the other workers during their few breaks, Erwin spent the time on his own, reading books. By night, he led the illegal Zionist HeHalutz ("Pioneer") group and trained young Jews for agricultural work in Palestine. Before he left the carton factory, Erwin apparently detonated a homemade bomb that destroyed most of it, according to his friend's memoir. He was never caught.

Erwin was arrested during what came to be known as *Fabrik-Aktion,* or factory action, a final major deportation of German Jews to Auschwitz during the first weeks of March of 1943, during which eleven thousand other Berlin Jews were rounded up. The Gestapo yanked Jews from their jobs and homes, and from the streets, and shoved them in trucks to Auschwitz. But his entrance into the notorious concentration camp may have been closer to that of the Polish resistance fighter Witold Pilecki than to the experiences of Zippi, David, and the majority of other Auschwitz inmates. According to rumors among those who knew him, he was a member of the foreign legion, a group of Polish and French underground fighters who were resisting the Nazis. The legion, they said, had sent him to Auschwitz as a mole.

In Auschwitz, Erwin donned the red triangle that identified him as a political prisoner, despite being Jewish. At first, he'd been assigned to a subcamp, Jawischowitz, where he worked in a coal mine, one of the most punishing and physically exhausting jobs in Auschwitz. Later, he was transferred to the Union *Kommando,* the Auschwitz munitions factory. He later claimed that he helped plan the *Sonderkommando* revolt there, and once again he evaded capture for his role in the sabotage.

Erwin had left Auschwitz on a death march to Dachau with thousands of men—a group that included David. Like David, he'd volunteered to leave Dachau and carry concrete for the Nazis in the subcamp Mühldorf. In a remarkable coincidence, Erwin, like David, had also been among the prisoners who managed to escape the transfer to Mühldorf. Might they have plotted their getaway together? In any case, Zippi may never have known of the men's close encounters.

From there, the details grew murky. Some have said Erwin was a spy for MI5, the British counterintelligence agency. If that's true, he may have been the so-called Prisoner T, the worker recruited by the British to sabotage machinery at the Union Factory in Auschwitz. Other survivors maintain that he'd worked for the US Army's Counterintelligence Corps (CIC) all along.

Erwin does seem to have had a connection to the US armed forces. Erwin's postwar records state that upon his escape, like David, he joined an American military unit that liberated him. Erwin would later be alleged—by Zippi herself—to have been key to the US Army's capture of the Ludendorff Bridge over the Rhine. The conquest was a breakthrough moment that may have helped shorten the war. Erwin, Zippi later said, met and befriended

General George Patton during this operation, where he earned himself the nickname *Eisenbrecher,* or Iron Breaker. By the summer of 1945, under the jurisdiction of General Patton's XX Corps in the Third US Army, Erwin had landed the job as a top brass in the Feldafing DP camp.

It was around this time, in August 1945, that Earl G. Harrison, US representative to the Intergovernmental Committee on Refugees, an international organization that had been created in 1938 to assist political refugees in Germany and Austria, published a document now known as the Harrison Report. In it, Harrison described refugees in DP camps living "under guard behind barbed-wire fences [...] amidst crowded, frequently unsanitary and generally grim conditions, in complete idleness, with no opportunity, except surreptitiously, to communicate with the outside world, waiting, hoping for some word of encouragement and action in their behalf." Further, after years of inhumane treatment, the war survivors had to readapt to a social environment, and that was not simple. The camp was in dire need of organization, of discipline.

Like Zippi, Erwin had an innate sense of organization. He also had military training, making him an ideal candidate to bring structure to the camp. Erwin was tasked with building up the camp's police force and maintaining law and order inside its parameters. He worked closely with the head of the American military police.

Erwin was also charged with combatting the camp's wildly popular black market, which was wreaking havoc on local currencies. His department performed daily raids and staged honor court tribunals, which adjudicated on everyday crimes as well as any Jew who'd aided a Nazi. DP lawyers served as defense and Erwin served as prosecutor. Trials were often held outside in fresh air, within sight of any interested spectators.

Feldafing, wrote the American diplomat Katie Louchheim, had become "a town of hospitals, dreary and off-limits," with

Zippi in Tutzing, spring 1946, in the fenced-in chicken coop in the house she and Erwin lived in.

"wooden barrack buildings that are battered by bombs." Survivors wanted to forget their pasts and enjoy the hope of a new beginning. In his campaign for lawfulness and dignity, Erwin gave them these things, too.

Zippi and Erwin began to date soon after she'd saved him from drowning. They both had a love for learning. Like Zippi, Erwin spoke multiple languages, including Hungarian, Spanish, English, and their mother tongue, German. They'd also both lost most of

Erwin and Zippi relaxing by Lake Starnberg, near Feldafing, June 1946.

their families. In Feldafing, Erwin and Zippi enjoyed some levity after seemingly countless years surrounded by death, spending much of their free time enjoying the waters of Lake Starnberg with their new friends.

In September of 1945, Erwin led General Eisenhower and General George Patton on a tour of the camp. The duo had come in response to the Harrison Report, at President Truman's request that they visit a displaced persons camp within American jurisdiction. After the tour, Erwin detailed the DPs' experiences under the Nazi regime, giving special attention to the atrocities in Auschwitz. General Eisenhower then addressed Feldafing residents.

Zippi stood among the crowd. Later, she heard Erwin's personal take on General Patton. The two men had known each other since March, when they'd captured the Ludendorff Bridge at Remagen. According to Zippi, General Patton regarded Erwin as a war hero. The men had developed a friendship, and at one point General Patton called Erwin over for an informal chat.

Erwin Tichauer leading General Dwight Eisenhower on a tour of the DP camp in Feldafing, 1945.

Let's talk, General Patton began. He asked Erwin whether he had a girlfriend.

Yes, Erwin said.

Where's she from? General Patton asked.

She's from Slovakia, Erwin told him.

General Patton asked Erwin whether his girlfriend liked chocolates or cigarettes.

She won't accept any of those gifts, Erwin told him.

Then grab her, General Patton responded, apparently hinting that Erwin had found an honest woman.

Erwin had every intention of doing just that.

Zippi's new boyfriend was infatuated with this self-assured and stubborn woman who kept refusing his gifts of nylon stockings and chocolates. They understood, like most survivors around them, that time was a luxury not to be taken for granted. Zippi was twenty-six, considered old for a single woman who'd survived the war; Erwin was also in his mid-twenties. Most camp survivors were in their teens or early twenties, since the Nazis had a predilection for keeping the young and able-bodied alive as long as they stayed productive.

Despite having been an ambitious career woman, Zippi hadn't intended to remain single until age twenty-six. But Tibor Justh, her resistance fighter, the man she once thought she'd spend her life with, had died under the blade of a guillotine. Then, of course, David had come along. David, her young lover, her temporary escape from the horrors of Auschwitz. David, who'd left her waiting, who'd abandoned her.

David, who'd broken her heart.

David, who, unbeknownst to both of them, had been running errands to Feldafing since Zippi relocated to the camp. Somehow their paths never crossed.

A few months earlier, however, Zippi *had* run into a friend who had news of David. Relief, curiosity, and incredulity must have overwhelmed her at the revelation that her old lover was alive. Maybe David had a good reason for not showing up to meet her.

But no. David was in Paris, her friend had said. He'd joined the US Army and had been in Paris for months. He was having a very good time, her friend added.

Zippi absorbed this news. So, while she'd been in Warsaw waiting and waiting, hoping that David would turn up, he'd been gallivanting in Paris. While she'd been taking care of his friend Sara, making sure she was fed, dressed, and alive, David didn't give either of them a second thought.

It became all too clear: David was no longer a part of her life.

Yet she didn't intend to be alone.

Erwin cared for her. He was brilliant, courageous, and kind—
a leader. Plus, he was handsome. Young female officers and aid
workers vied for Erwin's attention, envious of Zippi. They urged
him not to marry a displaced person. But their efforts were lost
on him.

In February 1946, Zippi and Erwin married in Tutzing, a resort
town sporting scenic views of the Bavarian Alps. In the previous
century, the beauty of Tutzing had inspired Johannes Brahms to
complete his string quartets *Opus 51 and the Variations on a Theme
by Haydn*. This was a fitting locale for the wedding of a woman
who'd grown up loving music, whose household had been inspired
by the arts.

Tutzing was three miles south of Feldafing, and because of
Erwin's official position, Zippi and her new husband could live in
the resort town, outside the DP campgrounds. They settled into a
villa that had been requisitioned by the military for American and
UNRRA personnel. A German family was employed as their
housekeepers. A chauffeur-driven jeep brought them to camp
every day. Erwin was paid in US dollars and the couple did their
shopping at the PX in Munich. Instead of dining with the DPs,
they ate at the American mess hall.

Once again, Zippi was enjoying a life of relative privilege—
and as before, she gave back in the best way she knew how. She
continued to distribute rations to pregnant women and described
her position as "top management." Years later, she recalled that one
of the first babies she'd seen born in Feldafing had a Greek father
and a Hungarian mother—"two people who shared no language
but an urgent need to escape the loneliness of survival."

And indeed, Jews married and had babies at record numbers in
postwar Germany. In 1946, the country boasted the highest Jewish
birth rate in the world.

*   *   *

That summer, a Latvian American Jew showed up in Feldafing with a recorder and two hundred spools of wire. David Boder, a psychologist by training, was collecting stories from survivors across Europe. He interviewed Erwin. Then he approached Zippi.

Zippi participated eagerly. She and Boder spoke in German for nearly two hours. During their conversation, she spoke of her deportation to Auschwitz, the ins and outs of the camp, and her liberation. She spoke energetically and with detail—but she was far from maudlin. Her goal was not to mourn, but to distill what she'd seen, especially given her unusual vantage point from both the prisoners' and the Nazis' perspectives.

This interview, it turns out, would mark the beginning of her role as a historian's guide to Auschwitz.

Zippi didn't want to be defined by her ties to Auschwitz, but neither did she try to escape her past. It was imprinted on her in ways that went beyond the number inked into her forearm. She suffered from chronic pain in her face, which had never been properly cared for after the savage kick she'd suffered in Ravensbrück. She'd ignored the pain until she stumbled in the snow that winter and was hospitalized with a fractured fibula—serendipitously, as it turned out, since it put her in front of doctors who could treat her other injuries. On December 30, 1946, Zippi began treatment at the UNRRA hospital in Feldafing. She was admitted for nearly a month, then again for four days the following February. In addition to treatment for her broken leg, Zippi also underwent emergency reconstructive surgery to remove broken bones from her face.

Around mid-1947, Zippi and Erwin decided it was time to leave Germany. They couldn't stay there forever; they'd had enough of a life in limbo. All around them, refugees were moving on—to the United States, Canada, Australia, and Palestine.

Erwin had no desire to return to Berlin. But he had a couple of

Zippi enjoying a happier moment amidst an often painful postwar period.

uncles who'd left the city shortly before the war and now lived in Chile. Before meeting Erwin, Zippi had considered returning to Bratislava, to be near her brother. But the prospect of Chile excited her: she was eager to travel somewhere unknown, learn a language, meet new people, absorb a new culture. And in Chile, they would have family that could help them and sponsor them. To get there, however, they had to fly through Argentina or Brazil—and neither country would grant a visa to those traveling without an international passport. Various refugee commissions worked to obtain the necessary documents on their behalf. In the meantime, like most other refugees, they waited.

CHAPTER TWENTY-SIX

"That's an American"

One by one, the American soldiers whom David had gotten to know were returning home. David wondered about his own future. Eventually, he would either have to apply for a visa elsewhere, return to Poland, or go to a DP camp. But he refused to consider any of these options. He would find a way to go to the United States. He had to.

These days, David worked primarily at the PX in Bar-le-Duc, where the army had a base. He took the occasional trip to Feldafing—not once running into Zippi—and continued to visit Paris when he had time off. He was working at the PX one day when he was summoned.

Wisnia, report to the captain's office, came the order.

What did I do now? David wondered as he went.

We have a telegram here with a $25 money order from the United States, the captain told him.

Immediately David knew. His letter to the *Jewish Daily Forward* must have worked. They must have read his name out loud on the radio in New York, and his aunts must have heard it and reconsidered. Of course, of *course* they hadn't abandoned him. David was thrilled—

285

and relieved. Something must have changed their mind. But it didn't matter. They'd responded.

But then there was the matter of the money order. By then, he'd amassed a large sum of money through his cigarette business in the black market—he didn't need it at all.

David returned to the PX and told a buddy about the telegram and the cash.

I think I should send it back, he said.

Don't do that, his friend said. *You'll insult them.*

But I don't need it, said David. *They probably need it more than I do.*

What mattered to David much more than money was reconnecting with his family. He began corresponding with Aunt Helen, who said she'd immediately begin the paperwork for the sponsorship process: soon he would be on his way to the United States. He'd always had a premonition that the day would come. And sure enough, he anticipated that soon he would be an American on US soil.

At the Port of Bordeaux in February 1946, David Wisnia boarded the SS *Monarch of the Seas,* bidding goodbye to his life in Europe. He set sail with twenty-three passengers that included an assortment of French, Spanish, and Austrian citizens—a group that comprised students, a mechanic, a chauffeur, and a housewife. David was among the youngest aboard, and the only passenger in an American soldier's uniform.

For David, the two-week voyage across the Atlantic Ocean seemed endless, prolonged by pure anticipation. Finally, on a frosty Wednesday afternoon, David set foot in the land he'd been wishing to see ever since he could remember.

His American family awaited him at the Hoboken terminal.

Davidja! Aunt Helen called out when she saw him from afar. She was the one who'd seen him last, who'd fed him chicken soup on Fridays. She recognized him almost immediately.

No, that's a GI, said Aunt Rose, the older sister, who'd emigrated to the United States before David was born and had only seen his pictures. *That's an American.*

That's him! Aunt Helen insisted.

As the boy walked toward them, his aunts were floored. It was indeed their David. They watched him in wonder, the sole survivor of their European family. His American family learned through his radio message that he was the only survivor, so he was spared having to tell them now. They embraced their soldier, their boy.

How could they ever have rejected him?

As it turned out, they hadn't.

On a Friday night just a few months prior, one of his aunts had been cooking a Shabbat meal while listening to WEVD, the radio arm of the *Forward,* when she'd heard David's letter. She'd dropped the fish, his aunt later recounted to David; she'd dropped everything. She'd quickly alerted the family that their little David was alive.

In a bizarre twist of fate, after repeating his aunts' addresses to himself for so many years, David had accidentally misremembered their information. The woman he had directed his GI friend to was not his aunt, but a different woman altogether, with the last name Borenstein. And so the person his friend had approached and chased for months had truly not known who David was. Later, David would laugh at himself for making such a mistake. It was a miracle he'd remembered an address at all, he would say.

When David's real Aunt Helen had learned that he was alive and stationed at the US army base in Bar-le-Duc, she immediately sent him the telegram with the $25 money order. But her nephew really hadn't needed the money. By the time David arrived in New Jersey, he'd accumulated some $5,000.

After an emotional reunion at the Hoboken port, David needed proper civilian clothes; all he had was his uniform. His aunts returned home and David's uncle Izzy, Rose's husband, took David on the New Jersey PATH and the two men set off for Manhattan.

David could not believe Uncle Izzy's accent-laden English — he'd been living in the US for decades now. How did he not speak better English? Meanwhile, David could tell that his uncle was impressed by his vocabulary and impeccable American accent. They rode to Sixth Avenue, where Uncle Izzy introduced David to the great American department store. David was not impressed.

Uncle Izzy, they have big department stores in Paris, said David. *And I don't come from a little shtetl town. I come from Warsaw, you know. It's a big city.*

David felt that he had been primed for New York City his entire life. Right away, he got himself a suit. Aunt Rose had insisted David stay with her and Izzy in Brooklyn. Izzy owned two millinery factories and they were doing quite well financially. Meanwhile, Aunt Helen and Uncle Sam had two small girls at home, including a newborn. But the arrangement didn't sit well with David. Aunt Helen had practically raised him, she was familiar; he wanted to be with her. He would live in Aunt Helen's apartment in the Bronx and sleep on the couch.

David didn't plan to spend much time on that couch. On his very first night in the US, he went out dancing in Manhattan. He informed his aunt and uncle that he was going to the Palladium Ballroom. The Palladium had just recently opened in Midtown and was quickly becoming a mecca of Latin music. Aunt Helen protested that he'd literally arrived in the country just a few hours before, but David assured her that he spoke English well and would find his way around. David didn't want to waste any more time — and off he went.

David spent his first night in the United States dancing the mambo at the Palladium Ballroom. When he'd had enough, he treated himself to coffee and cake at Hector's Cafeteria, on Fiftieth Street and Broadway. He was right at home. He'd brought along one of his Nazi souvenirs, the camera that he'd taken at Berchtesgaden, and set it down at the counter. But the moment he looked away, the camera had vanished.

At first, David was distraught—but, just as he had before, he told himself that he didn't need reminders of his past. The tattoo etched on his forearm was enough. Auschwitz—and everything that had happened there—was behind him now.

Life in America was everything he'd hoped it would be. At first, David worked with Aunt Helen's husband, Sam, at a small food center in the Bronx. Together, they manned the shop until a Safeway store opened nearby; they were unable to weather the competition. David was hardly upset, though; he'd never envisioned a future shelving groceries. It was too late for a career in the opera, but at the very least, he wanted to earn more money.

David scanned the classified ads for a palatable position until a posting at a publishing company caught his eye. The Wonderland of Knowledge Corporation, an encyclopedia maker, was in search of book salesmen.

David got the job. He was charismatic, friendly, and ambitious. He quickly built himself a good reputation, rising through the company ranks, carving out his own American dream.

A year after arriving in the United States, David met Hope, a third cousin, at a wedding in Manhattan. David was struck by the brown-haired, hazel-eyed girl with the sparkling smile; Hope was attracted to the confident man with dimples and smooth dance moves. They spent the evening talking and dancing.

David and Hope went on a date. Again, they danced the mambo. David fancied himself a sophisticated dancer; his friends had begun to call him Mambo Dave. Hope was smitten by the handsome European who had such zest for life. She'd been born and bred in Brooklyn, and she now studied at Brooklyn College and taught high school students. David, though, didn't talk much about his past.

Each weekend, David drove his black Chevy from Queens to the Bronx to see Hope. Within months, the couple married.

"Really, if I have to say why I married him, he was a good kisser and a good dresser and a good dancer," Hope would say later. A year after their wedding, the couple had their first son.

In 1952, the Wisnias moved to Levittown, Pennsylvania, where David managed the local branch of the Wonderland of Knowledge Corporation, now as a vice president of sales. The family lived in a two-story home in a predominantly Jewish planned community. Soon after, the Conference on Jewish Material Claims Against Germany, a nonprofit organization, began negotiating reparations from Germany for the Jewish people's stolen property and the suffering and losses endured at the hands of the Nazis. David used the money to buy himself a Jaguar.

Now David had a growing family, a beautiful house, a lawn, and his own luxury car on his very own driveway. He had secured his very own slice of America.

Early every Monday morning, David would hop on an airplane to sell encyclopedias across the country. Like his father years before, he returned home on the weekends. David jumped at the opportunity to volunteer as a cantor at the local synagogue, where he led the congregation in prayer and sang liturgical verses. Now he had a regular gig sharing his passion for music and prayers from his childhood, what he called Jewish soul music. David always tried to return to Levittown in time to join the services on Friday and Saturday nights. Hope raised their four children — two boys and two girls — largely on her own, while David became more of a family figurehead. His children found him happy and benevolent, if often physically distant.

Since his arrival in the United States, David had been known simply as the European wunderkind who'd survived the war — the handsome polyglot with a beautiful voice. No one ever asked about his background, the details of his life in Europe. And that was just fine, as far as he was concerned. When he wore short-sleeved shirts, people asked about the digits on his left forearm. David felt that if he told them the truth, they'd regret the question. He'd give the stock response that had become a popular joke with other survivors: "That's my phone number." He was tired of living with the tattoo, though, and fed up with the question that invoked the life he'd so purposefully left behind. More than anything, David wanted to blend into this world that he'd worked so hard to find a place in.

He was naturalized in 1951; he was finally a full-fledged American. It was time, he decided, to erase 83526—and Auschwitz—once and for all. David found a surgeon on Roosevelt Boulevard in Philadelphia and told him to cut the numbers out—and the surgeon did just that, carving the numbers out of his forearm and pulling the skin back together around the incision. David couldn't have imagined the burning, throbbing pain that he'd suffer as a result of this procedure—the price, in a sense, of trying to forget.

For a year after his surgery, David had trouble falling asleep. The gap that was sliced into his forearm seared; the agony was almost unbearable.

And still, a curve of the number six remained.

Meanwhile, back in June of 1950, Sara Radomski had arrived in the United States—also in a boat filled with survivors. She came with her husband, whom she'd met through friends in Feldafing. Their wedding in Munich was small and sad, with few friends, no family, and no frills.

Like David, Sara had grown tired of being asked about her tattoo. Each day, she covered it up with a new Band-Aid: her own perpetual wound, one that refused to heal.

Through a thriving network of survivors Sara learned that David was alive and married, and that he now lived in Levittown, Pennsylvania. She called him. The two had sung together as children in Sochaczew, and the last time they'd seen each other was behind the gates of Auschwitz. Sara called David and they caught up on their new lives, exchanging tidbits of their past.

Zippi was alive, too, Sara mentioned. She told David they had gone to Warsaw together to find him after the war; when he never turned up, they'd left.

If David felt a stab of regret when he heard this, he never admitted it. But David did want to hear more about his former lover. Sara told him what she knew; the two women had drifted apart but still spoke sporadically. Zippi's husband, Sara told David, was a gifted scientist who worked for the United Nations. Last she'd heard, they were living in South America. They'd all moved on and left their bleak history behind in Europe. And though they ached to forget the past, they nevertheless kept in touch. Theirs was a lifelong bond, a shared trauma that no one would ever understand.

Before she hung up, Sara gave David Zippi's contact information.

After their conversation, David thought more about Zippi. There was a question that had nagged at him during these recent years—a question he finally allowed himself to ask: How was it that he'd survived Auschwitz for so many years when most people lasted mere weeks?

He could sing, sure. He'd entertained the Nazis, yes. But looking back, it almost seemed as though a guardian angel had looked after him. Each time he got into trouble, he somehow made it out alive.

He knew without a doubt that, at his request, Zippi had saved Sara's life, perhaps more than once. He wondered: had Zippi kept him alive, too?

David decided to give his old girlfriend a call.

CHAPTER TWENTY-SEVEN

"Just the Ticket"

When David first telephoned Zippi, she didn't know what to say. She hadn't heard his voice in years. What's more, during all the time they'd spent together—all those secret hours in Canada—she'd mostly heard him speak in whispers. Now he sounded louder, confident. The same voice, but with gravitas. Grown up.

It was soon after the war was over, but not soon enough—late 1949, early 1950. By then, David was married, and so was Zippi. Later, she wouldn't remember where she was when she'd taken that phone call.

As they spoke, Erwin Tichauer listened in from the other line. *And why shouldn't he?* she'd thought. She had nothing to hide.

David wanted to meet, but it didn't feel right to Zippi. He had left her waiting in Warsaw. He'd made a conscious decision: he had abandoned their plans. He had abandoned *her.* And she couldn't forget the broken promise. Besides, they'd both built new lives for themselves. Why reunite now—what for?

David told Zippi about himself as though he were casually catching up with an old friend. He spoke about his immigration to

America, his wife, how he was doing well, living the life he'd always dreamed of.

Not once did he ask Zippi how she was doing.

Not once did he apologize for not coming to Warsaw.

Does he feel any remorse?

Zippi tried to shrug it off. *Most people are only concerned about themselves these days,* she tried to tell herself. It was nothing personal. Still, did he think of her just as an old acquaintance, a casual fling? He hadn't been that to her.

And so, when David asked if he could visit her, she said no; an emphatic no. He could not visit her. She was not interested.

They hung up. Disappointment lingered on both sides.

Zippi decided then that she would have no more contact with him.

It's better this way, she thought. She and her husband were embarking on their new life.

Zippi and Erwin had arrived in Chile just a few years prior, in 1947. By then, Erwin had already secured various engineering positions at manufacturing companies. He was smart and charismatic, the kind of person who captured an audience simply by entering a room. He also knew how to market himself, and so his reputation as an accomplished engineer spread quickly.

Zippi understood that her husband was gifted—and so was she. She was fascinated by the field and knew she could enrich his work with her own skills. She'd continue to dabble in graphic design where she could; but she decided to focus primarily on helping to catapult her husband's career. They were a team and she would ensure his success. She would become Erwin's partner and collaborator.

Initially, Erwin worked for a manufacturer of specialized machinery in Chile. He looked for ways to redesign everyday tools for manual laborers and rehabilitate those entering the workforce. Zippi's innate curiosity and design skills were the perfect complement to Erwin's engineering background. Together, husband and wife conducted research and wrote papers. Zippi studied ergonomics and drew diagrams to accompany her husband's work. Erwin began to make a name for himself in the field of occupational biomechanics and ergonomics. As his partner, Zippi participated in nearly all his research, contributing diagrams and ideas. When she saw her illustrations and graphics in print, in the scientific literature, she was tickled. She never received official recognition for it, although Erwin acknowledged the fact to friends and colleagues.

Her entire life, she had operated this way: Zippi never asked for credit for her help with the underground in Bratislava, in Auschwitz, or with the Brichah—if anything, she preferred not to speak about her part in it. All she wanted was to keep herself busy in a way that was useful and helpful to others.

While Zippi refused to put her own story to paper, she pushed her husband to share his. Perhaps her wounds were still too fresh; perhaps she saw more value in being a source to historians. During stolen moments, Zippi coaxed Erwin to reveal his war story to her, and eventually he did. She urged him to allow her to write it down—he agreed, on the condition that he would change people's names and certain details—she agreed.

And off they went. He spoke; Zippi typed.

In 1950, Erwin and Zippi were offered a new home in Australia, where the government had welcomed more Holocaust survivors than any other country, as a proportion of its total population. An agricultural equipment company in Brisbane hired Erwin to take on a managerial role as design engineer. In addition, the University of Queensland offered him a lecturer position.

For months, she suffered debilitating headaches, another consequence of the injuries she'd sustained in Auschwitz and Ravensbrück. Before the move to Brisbane, Zippi flew to Munich to undergo yet another operation.

While in Munich, Zippi was in a post office and caught the eye of a couple whom she recognized. At first, she thought they might be old friends. She had a strong feeling of déjà vu, but couldn't quite place where she knew them from.

Then it dawned on her, a visceral realization. She understood from the couple's facial expressions that they had had the same realization, perhaps simultaneously.

These were former SS members. She knew them from Auschwitz. Her legs felt as heavy as iron, like she was stuck in quicksand. Before she could even react, the couple ran out the back door of the post office. She thought of chasing them but was too afraid.

The incident would haunt her for years.

Europe also had some welcome surprises. Through the survivor network, Zippi discovered that her beloved Uncle Leo was alive. This was the man who'd doted on Zippi after her mother died, after her father effectively abandoned her. This was the man who'd taken Zippi under his wing, who'd introduced her to the mandolin and to Hashomer Hatzair. He'd made music a centerpiece of her life. She was thrilled by the news that he had not only survived the war, but he was married and living in Prague.

Zippi and Uncle Leo connected as soon as they could. After he'd fled to Palestine in 1933, he went to France to join the Czechoslovak government in exile. He wanted to fight for the country he loved, which was being destroyed by extremists. When he wasn't in combat, he played the mandolin in an orchestra, like Zippi— but with the Czechoslovak government in exile.

Zippi and Leo met in Prague. For years, she would make a point of meeting him there periodically, and they would walk through the city together, arm in arm. Uncle Leo and Sam were now Zippi's sole connections to her past. She relished having these reminders of who she was and where she came from.

★   ★   ★

When Zippi and Erwin settled in Australia at last, they found their new home beautiful, clean, and modern—worlds away from Europe, where a heavy past hung in every corner. This was not a bad place for a new beginning. Brisbane offered the two qualities that Zippi had loved about Bratislava: a diverse population and a beautiful waterfront. Even better, Sam, his wife, and their daughter had also immigrated to Brisbane just the year before.

Sam and his family had left Bratislava in 1949, after a series of pogroms made them realize that they would never feel safe in Europe. Fed up with the endless persecution, Sam decided he wanted to get as far away from Europe as he could, and Australia was "just the ticket." He took on a series of odd jobs there, from working as a kitchen hand to working in a rubber factory. He also studied English. Sam worked long hours; he wanted to start his own business. He and Zippi saw each other on occasion, but not often; they were both busy rebuilding their lives.

Zippi and Erwin were hard at work cementing Erwin's career. He traveled around the world to conferences, and on occasion Zippi went along with him. The International Labour Organization (ILO), a UN agency focused on improving labor practices in developing countries, recruited Erwin. For several months, he served as a technical consultant in industrial productivity in Lima, Peru. Erwin advised government organizations, universities, and businesses on how to conduct vocational training. He gave technical advice and made recommendations to employees. Erwin and Zippi also spent time in La Paz, Bolivia, where Erwin worked with the country's ministry of labor. Zippi continued to do whatever she could to help women improve their lives: when she discovered a community of struggling breastfeeding mothers, she designed cans that would preserve milk for their babies.

Erwin wrote research papers; Zippi illustrated them. In his

field, illustrations and diagrams were paramount to the research conducted. In 1960, Erwin was invited to be a senior lecturer on industrial engineering and ergonomics at the University of Sydney. The couple moved a ten-hour drive down the coast from Brisbane. Sam and his family followed soon after. By then, Sam had established a successful real estate company. For a brief time, the siblings enjoyed living near each other. But soon Erwin and Zippi were once more on the move.

In 1963, Texas Tech University recruited Erwin to join the faculty as a visiting professor and develop graduate courses in biomechanics. The job came with prestige and an opportunity for Erwin to expand the university's research facilities, and so the couple moved to the United States, settling in Lubbock, Texas. Within a year, he was a full-fledged professor of industrial engineering.

But Zippi was unhappy. Lubbock felt small. Racism against the Black and Latino populations was rampant. Almost no Jews lived in the city. Zippi felt like a foreigner in her new home. She couldn't believe the bigotry and ignorance surrounding her. She'd endured discrimination in Europe; she'd thought America was better than this.

And so, when she could, she traveled.

It was around then that Sara reached out to Zippi again, telling her that David still hoped to meet. And it just so happened that Zippi and Erwin were planning a trip to New York City. This could be an opportunity.

Zippi hesitated. But David had been so insistent. It had been around ten years since he'd last called her. Perhaps enough time had passed; perhaps the conversation would be different this time.

All right, she told Sara. She would meet him in Manhattan.

CHAPTER TWENTY-EIGHT

"Ask Me Anything"

David steered north onto the interstate highway. The drive was roughly an hour and a half from Levittown to Manhattan. He sat alone in his Jaguar; perhaps the convertible top was down, the wind blowing against his hairline, just beginning to recede. It was the mid-1960s and David was in his late thirties. The last time he'd seen Zippi, they'd been some twenty years younger.

Perhaps he was nervous. Excited. They'd only seen each other as slaves, as prisoners. They'd only *known* each other in uniform. Back then, he'd been a boy, naive. He'd learned so much since. She hadn't seen the man he'd since become. What would she think of him now?

David drove through the Lincoln Tunnel, under the Hudson River. Traffic always picked up in Manhattan, but nevertheless, he now was mere minutes away. Did he grip the steering wheel, white-knuckled? Did he hum an old tune?

Finally, arriving at Central Park, David found a spot for his car near the hotel they'd settled on for their reunion. Probably, he'd dressed up for the occasion: slacks, a freshly ironed button-down shirt, a blazer. Possibly, Hope had seen him off.

David sat down in a hotel lobby across from Central Park. And he waited.

Businessmen, families, and couples—tourists from around the world passed through. David looked up expectantly, searching for that familiar face. Would they recognize each other immediately? How much could she have changed in the span of ten years? Did he experience a moment of panic?

He searched faces. And he waited. The minutes added up.

Zippi never showed.

David had wanted a clean break from his past—but Zippi was different. She'd comforted him when he was alone, a slave in an inferno, his parents gone. More than that, she was at the center of a mystery that was burning more and more hotly in his mind: he'd seen death all around him—and he'd survived. As much as he tried not to think of it, he couldn't help it. How had he lived when so many others had perished? He was certain Zippi knew the answer.

Not long before David was hoping to have met Zippi, he had returned to Auschwitz. It was 1957, ten years after a memorial and museum opened up at the site of the former main camp. The camp was open, and he wanted to visit. After years of turning away, he couldn't help but look.

"I just wanted to see," he would later say with a shrug. "Life pulls you back."

He couldn't explain the appeal. He walked through the field of overgrown grass in Auschwitz's main camp. Birkenau was still recovering from the disarray the Nazis had left behind—a couple of years earlier, the roof of the Sauna had collapsed, not long after a group of visitors passed through. The better-preserved blocks at the main camp were being used for exhibitions.

David entered Block 15. Once crowded beyond belief, it was now empty, dank. He climbed onto the middle bunk of one of the triple-deckers and leaned on the wooden planks. Probably using a key, he scratched his name in block letters, white gashes on the gray stone. There. Now he'd left *his* mark. It was the first time he went back as a free man, and it wouldn't be the last.

Back home with his young family, he refused to speak of his past. Just around then, David's oldest son, Eric, about seven or eight years old, asked why he didn't have any grandparents on his father's side. They were dead, his parents told him, and that was the end of the conversation. Sometimes, instead, David told Eric about being a veteran of the American army.

It was only at Eric's bar mitzvah, in 1962, after performing the song he'd written in Auschwitz, that David told Eric he wasn't born in America—that he was from Poland, and that his parents and grandparents had been killed there. Eric was astonished. David had a perfect American accent and it had never occurred to Eric that his father wasn't born and bred in the United States.

It would take another four years for David to get into details. When Eric's rabbi realized that Eric knew nothing about his father's past, he arranged a conversation. One summer afternoon in 1966, Rabbi Hendel drove sixteen-year-old Eric to Pete Lorenzo's Cafe, near the Trenton train station. There, they met David and sat down for lunch in a booth. David spoke for two hours. He looked at the rabbi as he talked, unable to face his son.

Eric didn't say a word. He was stunned. Neither David nor Hope had ever told their children anything about the war. Eric wondered how much his mother knew.

It would take several more years for David to speak freely about his past. In 1974, he and Eric—by then a twenty-four-year-old rabbi—began to talk about the Holocaust without too much trepidation. David began to take regular trips to Warsaw, where he visited synagogues and recounted his story to members of the city's Jewish community, and once again felt the adulation he'd enjoyed as a child. Before the war, about three million Jews had lived in the Polish state; more than three hundred thousand survived.

During those trips, David would usually visit Auschwitz, too. To see; to try to understand.

By then, David had pivoted careers. For decades, he'd volunteered as a cantor while having a high-earning job in sales. But when Books of Wonder downsized, David lost his job. He'd attempted to open his own book business from home, but that wasn't panning out. He needed to get paid. He took a cantorial test in New York and was officially ordained. Soon after, he became a bona fide cantor, earning a regular paycheck at his local temple. David was beloved by his fellow congregants, who lined up to have him perform b'nai mitzvahs and weddings.

By this time, the world was more prepared to face the Holocaust, too. For decades, it had been a taboo subject around the globe. Most survivors avoided the topic altogether; some felt guilty for surviving when so many had perished, and others were embarrassed to have been victims. Often, they just wanted to move on, to forget the sordid details of their past, to protect their family from their trauma. But in the 1970s, around the time that David began to share more about his life, many other survivors around the globe were beginning to open up about their experiences. Eventually they began to publish memoirs, often to acclaim. Elie Wiesel, a Hungarian survivor, is perhaps the most famous among them. His memoir about Auschwitz, *Night,* was first published in English in 1960 and later became a commercial success, and Wiesel went on to win scores of medals and literary awards, including the Nobel Peace Prize in 1986.

David was, at first, ashamed to speak about his past. But once he felt the admiration and curiosity among students and congregants, he grew increasingly comfortable sharing his story. Eric later joked that after his father realized that people were interested in hearing about his past, he wouldn't stop talking about it. It had likely been their conversation in that New Jersey café that had opened the floodgates. David gave interviews to local newspapers, to museums, and at his kitchen table; he even made a documentary, sponsored by a local Levittown air-conditioning company. All of a sudden, he realized there was value in sharing his story.

Most of all, David sang. One grandson, Avi, a musician, became his partner. The duo performed at synagogues and libraries; David sang and Avi accompanied him on the piano. Afterward, David, a charismatic speaker and a natural performer, would share some of his story.

David also told nuggets of his past at Eric's temple. Congregants who heard him speak were amazed. One congregant, Robin Black, was so taken by David that she suggested that he write a memoir. David refused. Robin insisted, adding that she would help him write it. She finally wore him down. Robin and David spent months exploring his past—together, they went to Warsaw and Auschwitz, where he showed her the site of his old bunk, the Sauna, and Canada.

As he finally allowed himself to revisit his past, David relived flashes of his time in Auschwitz. Every so often, he would remember details about his parents. Over dinner one night, he suddenly recalled the color of his mother's coat in that pile of corpses. Brown. He couldn't get the fabric out of his mind. That evening, he didn't finish his meal.

Before then, he'd rarely talked about Zippi. But as he opened up to Robin, he began to open up to his family, too. There had been that time around 1965 when he'd mentioned Zippi to Hope, back when he'd expected to meet his old girlfriend in that Manhattan hotel lobby. Now he told his family about her, how powerful she'd been in Auschwitz.

Eventually David even included Zippi in his memoir, *One Voice, Two Lives*. He gave her the pseudonym Rose. Within its pages, Rose has a mysterious allure; she appears gentle and sophisticated. She'd chosen him, and he still marveled at his luck. Still, though, Rose turned up only in a couple of pages out of a much longer book. David insisted that the affair was more physical than emotional.

"We were at the right place at the right time at the right moment for one another, and that was it," he told Robin.

Except that wasn't it.

David's growing suspicion that Zippi had somehow helped him survive Auschwitz was overpowering. His family was intrigued. They wanted to help find this mysterious woman—the one who, they were beginning to suspect, had made their lives together possible.

To Zippi's delight, her stint in Lubbock was brief. In 1967, she and Erwin moved to Manhattan. New York was nothing like Texas. In Lubbock, Zippi had felt claustrophobic; she felt more at home in Manhattan. The city's diversity and culture made her feel like she belonged.

At New York University, Erwin had the resources and the time to develop his research in anatomical engineering. He and Zippi often had students and faculty over for dinner at their home in Kips Bay, on East Thirty-Third Street between First and Second Avenues, where they enjoyed the kind of intellectual conversations that Zippi had relished even as a child. International media featured Erwin and his research on a regular basis. By 1969, at the age forty-nine, Erwin had become a tenured professor at NYU. That same year, *Time* magazine ran a two-page feature on Erwin that included illustrations that Zippi had likely created. She was in her element.

The couple enjoyed the thrill of academia, until Erwin was diagnosed with Parkinson's disease in the 1980s. The illness advanced quickly, and before long, they rarely left the house.

Joan Ringelheim, a prominent historian who focused on women and the Holocaust, first visited Zippi around these years. At the time, Joan oversaw the oral history archives of the United States Holocaust Memorial Museum, in Washington. Before Zippi would let Joan up into her apartment, though, she wanted to prepare her: her husband was suffering from Parkinson's disease, she said. He had difficulty speaking and was physically handicapped. But she would not have her husband ignored, Zippi warned Joan. If the historian couldn't handle his condition, she couldn't come up.

Zippi also wanted to make sure that Joan had proper knowledge of the Holocaust, that she was smart enough to understand the nuances of Auschwitz. Zippi was not above throwing historians out of her apartment if they seemed frivolous or uninformed. She'd done it before and would do it again.

Joan was taken aback. She'd interviewed dozens of people and had never before felt intimidated like this. But she agreed, and Zippi welcomed her into the apartment. Joan was relieved when she realized, at the end of the interview, that she'd passed Zippi's test.

Joan went on to interview Zippi for many hours over the following decades, often by phone. She would also meet the couple together in person several more times. On one occasion, Erwin shuffled over to Joan while Zippi was out of the room.

Do you want to hear what happened to me? he asked.

Joan was surprised. Although he could walk and participate in conversations, Erwin's health had been deteriorating quickly and it was becoming difficult for Erwin to speak. Before she could respond, he continued.

I was a spy, he slurred with a minimal German accent.

Joan was shocked; she didn't know how to respond. The moment passed and Zippi returned for her interview. Joan asked her about what Erwin had just shared with her. Zippi shrugged. Was she surprised that Erwin had shared such a thing with Joan? If so, she didn't show it, but neither would she elaborate, instead pivoting back to their own interview. She would only speak of her own expertise. Back in 1950, Erwin had submitted a finished manuscript based on his life to a publishing house. But the work had been rejected—he was told that readers had no interest in literature about concentration camps.

"Maybe he just felt he needed to say it to somebody," Joan later wondered. Perhaps Erwin had seen her so often that he'd felt comfortable saying it to her.

Whether it was true or not, Zippi feigned ignorance.

"There's something about her that kept her at arm's length," said Joan. The two women eventually became friends and spoke on the phone two or three times a week. Invariably, Zippi would wind up talking about Auschwitz. She'd collected a variety of books on the Holocaust, many of which she complained had mistakes. She felt a need to correct these errors, no matter how big or small they might be. On one occasion, when she noticed a mislabeled photograph in a book about Auschwitz, she tracked down the author's phone number and called him at home. The author, Peter Hellman, felt sheepish as the woman on the phone pointed out his mistake. He went on to become one of Zippi's closest friends. Years after her stint in Auschwitz, Zippi remained the consummate connector, building bonds of friendship through her candor and bottomless loyalty.

By the late 1980s, Erwin could no longer walk, or feed or dress himself. He retired from NYU in 1988 as professor emeritus and Zippi took on a new, final role in their relationship: his full-time caretaker. Friends recall her petite frame raising her husband in the hospital bed that now occupied the middle of their living room, as well as dressing him and feeding him. She refused to allow others to take care of him.

Zippi herself was becoming more fragile. She rarely left their apartment. The beatings she'd taken during the war had come back to haunt her in her old age. She was losing her eyesight and her hearing. Still, she devoured new literature on the Holocaust, collected documents, and built her own personal archives. She helped dozens of historians who were authoring essays and books about

Auschwitz. She dreamed of one day re-creating some of the diagrams that she'd designed in that office all those years ago, the diagrams that she'd gone through the trouble of duplicating but which had yet to be found. She wanted scholars to understand what she'd seen. No one, it seemed to her, had a full understanding of the complex camp system that had been Auschwitz.

Over the years, Zippi had been in touch with Uncle Leo's twin granddaughters, Petra and Hana Nichtburgerova, both of whom lived in Prague. In the summer of 2001, nineteen-year-old Petra visited New York City and stayed with Zippi. She didn't know much about the Holocaust; their family had never spoken about it. Before Petra arrived at Zippi's home, her family warned her not to ask about her past.

"In Europe, it feels like Jews don't exist anymore," Petra said years later. "As a teenager I had the feeling it wasn't appropriate to say to people I was Jewish—I mean half-Jewish. It wasn't a topic."

But a few minutes after arriving at her great-aunt's house in Manhattan, she recalled, this changed.

You can ask me anything, said Zippi, as soon as Petra sat on the sofa.

She spent hours recounting her past. She did the same with Hana, over the phone. Thanks to Zippi, Hana became a Holocaust scholar.

While she was visiting, Petra got the sense that Zippi was always in the midst of organizing her paperwork and books. She was nearly blind, but for at least a couple of hours a day Zippi used a magnifying glass that lit up, and she read and organized. Petra wondered why Zippi never wrote down her story. She guessed that it was because Zippi was too much of a perfectionist.

"She was really tough on people," remembered Petra. "But she was really tough on herself, too."

A few years after Erwin's death in 1996, Zippi took over the hospital bed that he'd been in for so long. She was seventy-eight years old and her body was in near-constant pain. Zippi moved as little as possible and required a walker when she did. This did not prevent her from organizing Erwin's study, where they had accumulated mountains of research, journals, and reports. They had owned books on subjects ranging from art to the Jews of Czechoslovakia, and what seemed like everything that had ever been written about Auschwitz. Alone in her apartment, she sifted through her papers, using the magnifying machine to read.

She was determined to publish Erwin's story, and would eventually achieve this goal: Jürgen Matthäus, head of the research department of the United States Holocaust Memorial Museum, who was also a loyal friend and confidant, helped Zippi find a German publisher for the book *Totenkopf und Zebrakleid: Ein Berliner Jude in Auschwitz* (*Skull and Zebra Suits: A Berlin Jew in Auschwitz*), published in 2000. Erwin is credited as the book's author.

By then, a group of historians she respected and spoke with weekly had become a sort of extended family. Konrad Kwiet, a historian at the Sydney Jewish Museum who'd gotten to know her brother, Sam, became a surrogate son who called her every Friday. Michael Berkowitz, a professor of Jewish history at University College London, was another surrogate son, to whom she gifted her husband's old camera, as well as his unopened packages of underwear. (*Why should I throw them out or give them to a stranger when they are brand new?* she'd told Michael.) Zippi had also helped Wendy Lower, a prominent historian, write a brief on Feldafing. In the process, Wendy became Zippi's surrogate daughter, even helping Zippi obtain her marriage certificate, and bringing her jars of pickled sardines—a favorite—when she traveled to Germany.

In 2009, Zippi finally authorized a group of historians, led by Jürgen Matthäus, to publish a book about her experiences in Auschwitz. The book, *Approaching an Auschwitz Survivor: Holocaust Testimony and Its Transformations,* offers a unique lens into memory and is told solely from Zippi's perspective. Five scholars each wrote an essay based on multiple interviews each of them had had with Zippi over many years. Every piece focuses on a different aspect of her experiences during the war.

Throughout her interviews, she never once mentioned David or their affair.

David discovered Zippi's book in 2011 and reached out to her again.

Again, Zippi answered the phone. Again, she let him speak. David wanted to know if he could visit her.

This time, Zippi wasn't against it. So much time had passed—she supposed he'd had to find his own path. Perhaps more to the point, Erwin was no longer alive, so she didn't have to worry about disrespecting her husband.

Still, she wasn't in a rush. Perhaps she still wanted to punish David. Or she was protecting herself. Regardless, if David really did want to see Zippi, he'd have to wait.

David Wisnia in his later years, at the home where he raised his family, in Levittown, Pennsylvania.

CHAPTER TWENTY-NINE

Isn't Life Strange

Five years later, on a sunny afternoon in August 2016, David and two of his six grandchildren embarked on the nearly two-hour drive from Levittown to Manhattan. David was quiet during most of the ride. He didn't know what to expect. The whole situation was surreal: he was going to see an old girlfriend whom he had barely spoken with for more than seventy years.

Once the three Wisnia men arrived, they were surprised by the darkness of Zippi's apartment, by the shelves filled with books and documents. A frail, gray-haired woman lay in a hospital bed, with an aide at her side assisting her. Zippi could hardly move. She didn't seem to understand who they were. David's grandchildren feared that their grandfather would be distraught. What if Zippi didn't remember him? She was almost ninety-eight years old. What if they were too late?

As his grandchildren stood by, holding their breath, David inched closer to the small, silent figure. He leaned in and said his name.

David Wisnia.

Zippi lit up.

The connection was instantaneous. She knew exactly who he was.

A flow of words followed, in their adopted English language.

Over and over, she repeated: *I waited for you in Warsaw. I waited and waited and waited.*

David tried to explain. *I drove to Feldafing but I didn't know you were there, I was an American soldier.*

Isn't life strange, she said with wonder.

I would drive back and forth to Feldafing, he said. *And I had no idea you were there.*

I was waiting and waiting and waiting, she added. *I didn't know if you were alive.*

Again, Zippi told him that she'd waited for him. Didn't he remember their promise?

David tried to explain, again and again. He'd been just an ordinary soldier, but it was an extraordinary opportunity. He was eighteen years old, a kid. Poland had symbolized the death of his immediate family, the death of his childhood. When the chance for a new life — a new life in *America* — materialized, he grabbed it and held on as tightly as he could. To survive, he needed a clean slate far away from Poland. She had to understand.

David reminded Zippi that he'd tried to see her many years ago in New York. She hadn't shown up.

It was brave of me, not to go to you, Zippi answered. To break a promise was against her character, but most importantly she had to respect her husband. He was the one she shared a life with, who deserved her utmost loyalty. Did she fear that David still had a hold on her?

Zippi told David about her Erwin, his battle with Parkinson's disease, how difficult that period of their life had been for them both. And she was beginning to forget things, she said. She was, after all, older than David.

You are a young rock star, said Zippi.

You were a young chick, too, I remember it well, David said, laughing, not missing a beat.

For a brief moment, they were back in Auschwitz, remembering their secret getaways.

Do you remember our meetings? David asked.

Of course! said Zippi. *We went in an opening inside a room. I remember the little window; so much climbing to get there. And then we kissed.*

David chuckled, sheepish, not forgetting that his grandchildren were listening.

For a few moments they caught up on the past seven decades. Zippi told David that she'd traveled quite a bit with her husband. David told Zippi about his children and grandchildren, his pride and joy. He gave her a bouquet of yellow zinnias.

David's grandson Avi, who'd been listening in the background, handed her the flowers.

Zippi admired the bunch before her aide took them away and put them in water. There was so much to catch up on. David showed Zippi old photographs he'd brought along with him. He showed her a picture of him with a machine gun, in uniform.

Zippi strained at the photo with the scarce eyesight she had left.

How was I in Birkenau? Do you remember what I looked like? she asked, still the sprightly young woman who'd thought so much about appearances, who'd tried so hard to take care of herself— qualities that had saved her in camp, and in turn saved so many others.

David shuffled, awkward, a teenager again.

You were good-looking! he said, laughing.

From her pillow, Zippi smiled.

David couldn't contain himself any longer. He had to ask the question that had been haunting him for all these years.

How had he made it out of Auschwitz? Was it she who was responsible for his survival in Birkenau?

Zippi held up her hand to display five frail fingers.

I saved you five times, she said.

David gasped.

He'd never been quite sure—but deep inside, he'd always known.

He looked at his grandchildren, making sure they understood what this woman had done for him.

Whenever they selected prisoners, I looked for you, she said.

You got me out of trouble, said David.

I did, she said. *I didn't know why, but I did. I did it for others, too. So many people needed help.*

You saved Sara, too, said David. *She wouldn't have lived without you.*

Zippi didn't respond. Instead, she asked about Sara's daughter; the two women had long lost touch. He'd lost touch with her, he said.

David explained that he'd always wondered how he had survived the camp.

Most people who came to Birkenau died, he said. *When I overslept and ended up in the* Strafkommando—*you're the one who took my name out,* he said, more of a question than a statement.

How did you know? she asked, surprised.

I had a feeling, he said.

Yes, she told him now. It had been her.

How do you thank someone for saving your life, so many times, so many years ago?

I loved you, Zippi admitted softly, almost a whisper.

Me, too, David whispered back.

During their visit, Zippi pressed David more than once about why he hadn't come to find her after the war. Didn't he know her name? He could have asked survivors; he could have looked her up. She would not let him off the hook, even now.

Each time Zippi pressed David about why he'd abandoned her in Warsaw, he did his best to explain. He'd been a lost boy. Couldn't she see? Perhaps she finally did. She stopped asking.

Instead, Zippi asked David if there was anything she could do for him or his grandchildren.

Nothing, said David.

All he wanted was to show Zippi his grandchildren, the lives she'd made possible.

Before he left, Zippi asked David to sing to her. As his two grandchildren looked on, he chose the Hungarian song she'd taught him all those years ago. He reached out for her hand and for one last time they were at peace together.

Evening in the moonlight
What does she dream about in the night?
That a prince might arrive
Riding a steed of snow-white.

He hadn't shown up in Warsaw. But he hadn't forgotten, either.

EPILOGUE

How can anyone survive the trauma of seeing their family lying in a pile of corpses? Of writing down a list of numbers representing humans designated to be murdered? Of enduring a life of daily torture and enslavement, with no end in sight?

How can anyone possibly move forward from these moments? Live a normal life, let alone function at all?

When you're a survivor, as David and Zippi were, you keep finding ways.

By the end of his life, David had grown accustomed to sharing his story on a pulpit; the arc of his narrative had become a performance that he'd perfected. Zippi, meanwhile, would spend a lifetime zeroing in on the details of her past. She would become a historian's historian, trying to help scholars make sense of Auschwitz—trying to make sense of it herself.

As much as they wanted to forget, David and Zippi both were haunted. But that did not stop them from living—or from leading extraordinary lives.

★ ★ ★

Eric Wisnia once said that his father had the emotional maturity of a thirteen-year-old whose youth had been brutally cut short. He enjoyed a hedonist's lifestyle, in part because he had learned to lean into the qualities that had saved him—his voice, his charisma, his good looks. Yet David's joie de vivre masked a depth of character that resonated with those who met him.

A few years after David made it to the US, he looked up Ferd Wilczek, the GI who had taken him under his wing when David joined the 101st Airborne. Ferd's wife and young daughter were surprised when David appeared at their doorstep in Rhode Island—as was Ferd. They didn't know who he was. David came bearing a volume of encyclopedias in his hands as a gift.

Ferd had never spoken with his family about his service in the military. The only reason his daughter even knew that Ferd had been a soldier was that she'd seen his uniform in his closet. He'd held on to his boots, his silver rings, and his uniform, but never attended reunions or talked about that time in his life.

David invited him to Eric's bar mitzvah, and the two men stayed in touch until Ferd's death in 2013.

The military was a reminder of entirely different experiences to Ferd and David. Ferd had been in combat; he'd seen friends die. But to David, the army was his salvation, the family who'd adopted him with open arms. In 2008, David began to attend "snowbird reunions" in Florida for members of the 101st Airborne Division. There he would connect with veterans and their families and ask to lead them in singing the national anthem during closing night of the reunions. David would always say that he was "110 percent American." Outside his home of nearly seven decades, two flags—an American flag and a Screaming Eagle flag—waved proudly from the front yard.

Despite his allegiance to the United States, and his disdain for Poland immediately after the war, David would always be drawn back to the glamour of Warsaw, where he'd once felt his star begin to rise. As the years passed, he returned often. He reveled in the crowds that formed around him to hear his story, his voice. He enjoyed Warsaw's nightlife well into his eighties. In 2015, a reform synagogue in Warsaw invited him to teach lay cantors the music he'd learned at Warsaw's Great Synagogue back in the 1930s. David's grandson Avi accompanied him on the piano. During that same trip in 2015, David attended the seventieth anniversary of Auschwitz's liberation.

Five years later, in 2020, David returned once again to Auschwitz. He was ninety-four years old. By then, only two thousand survivors of the camp were still alive. This time he brought his grandchildren as well as his children and took them to see the sites of his childhood home in Sochaczew, his family's last home in Warsaw, and where he once was forced to sing in Birkenau. In Auschwitz, David sang a prayer for the departed in a ceremony that commemorated seventy-five years since the camp's liberation. His health had been failing for months but he'd insisted on this last trip to the camp. With his family surrounding him, David sang in Auschwitz — of his own volition.

Before her death, Zippi continued to have regular conversations with the circle of historians that had become her family. She spoke with them from her hospital bed at home, with the help of two Hungarian aides who took care of her around the clock. She could no longer read without the help of a magnifying machine and could not hear without her hearing aids. The phone, historian Atina Grossmann recalled, became Zippi's lifeline to the outside world.

"I don't need fame and I don't need glory," Zippi said. However, she did feel a burning responsibility to speak about what she knew about Auschwitz and to preserve the truth about this most notorious death camp.

It pained Zippi that scholars had searched unsuccessfully for the documents that she'd painstakingly duplicated and hidden before evacuating. To her great frustration, the large three-dimensional model that she'd built had also disappeared. Until her death, Zippi obsessed over trying to find that work. Scholars believe that the documents are either within inaccessible Russian archives or were discovered and destroyed by the Nazis.

It also mystified and annoyed Zippi that she was never asked to speak out in a court case against Nazi criminals. The one and only time she testified was in 1971, regarding the Ravensbrück subcamp Malchow. True to form, she focused on the technical details of the camp, especially its layout and size. In her testimony she said she had no memories of prisoners being shot in the evacuation march from Malchow. Further, she stated that only once in Birkenau was she an eyewitness to a murder. It's baffling to consider this, given all her years there. Perhaps she managed to look away from the killings that were perpetrated daily, as she did during Roza Robota's hanging and Mala Zimetbaum's botched hanging. Or maybe she had erased those moments from her memory. It's possible, too, that detail-oriented Zippi was simply hung up on semantics: that she'd seen many other dead bodies but, in those cases, didn't explicitly witness the act of a murder.

Zippi refused to proclaim that she belonged to a resistance movement, and this seems to be a matter of semantics, too. Whether she cared to admit it, Zippi was very much part of the resistance. From copying documents to manipulating numbers on lists, Zippi was resisting the Nazis whenever she could. Ultimately, it is unclear whether the aprons that Roza Robota gave Zippi were connected to the *Sonderkommando* revolt. Perhaps they were just innocent gifts, but this was unlikely. And beyond potentially carrying gunpowder, Zippi had helped Roza place the right people in the right jobs. In the end, Zippi's life, too, was on the line.

Zippi did not give interviews to the media or have speaking engagements. Her role, she insisted, was to set the record straight. Scholars and historians had inadvertently spread countless misconceptions about the camp, she said. She had the best vantage point to relate the truth about Auschwitz: she had lived through the worst conditions of the camp, yet also had enjoyed direct access to the highest ranks within the SS. Most important, she'd been in Auschwitz from close to its inception to its end. Survivors misremembered things or misconstrued what had happened, she claimed. She insisted that she knew better. Both she and Sam worried about antisemitism and Holocaust denial, one of the main reasons she fought so vehemently against inaccurate testimonies.

On more than one occasion, Zippi debunked a fabricated survivor story before it was published.

Given Zippi's rigid stance on separating fact from fiction, the very premise of her husband Erwin's memoir is surprising. A hybrid of fiction and memoir, the book features a protagonist named Herbert Stein—obviously a stand-in for Erwin—who is imprisoned in an Auschwitz subcamp in 1943. Herbert becomes a supervisor at the Union munitions factory and is involved in a plot to smuggle gunpowder to blow up the crematoria. This haze between fiction and nonfiction could be born of Erwin's desire to protect his mysterious background, or to allow him the freedom to make embellishments that he didn't want to be portrayed as fact.

Plenty of Erwin's life was documented in the media, though none of it related to the war. In 1973, the British trade publication *Safety & Rescue* marveled that "Professor Erwin Tichauer has so many qualifications, so many commitments, so many undertakings that he should be two or three men, perhaps four." A thick folder resides in New York University's Special Collections & Archives under the label "Erwin Tichauer," filled mostly with international news coverage of his research. Newspaper and magazine clippings and NYU press releases expound on the various awards that he collected over the years. Erwin did not mention his war experiences in a single interview. Perhaps the trauma made talking about it too difficult. After the war, Erwin spent two years searching for his parents and younger sister. In September of 1947, he received a letter from the Central Tracing Agency Bureau that his sister had died in Auschwitz—the same camp where Erwin had spent so much of the war, and which he of course had survived. His search turned up no trace of his parents.

Conversations regarding the Holocaust were, for the most part, his wife's domain. At most, he occasionally chimed in when Zippi yelled from across the room during a conversation with a historian, to confirm a date or figure. His one testimony, recorded by David Boder in 1946, disappeared soon after it was made. It remains lost as of this writing.

He did have his silent collaborator, Zippi, at his side, writing with him, talking through his research, illustrating his work, and hosting students and faculty in their home. Those who knew the couple knew that Zippi, from the shadows, made Erwin's accomplishments and accolades possible.

Sam Spitzer died of cancer in a Sydney hospice in 2009. Before his death, he and Zippi took to singing for each other over the telephone—their voices carrying across the Pacific, from Sydney to Manhattan. According to Sam's granddaughter, the siblings shared many traits—from their obsession with details and accuracy, to their demands for attention to themselves and their desire to champion those who needed help.

Over the years, Sam devoted much of his energy to fighting for the restitution of confiscated assets of Slovakian Jews. "It was Slovakia who supplied the first Jewish inmates to Auschwitz!" Sam wrote in an emotional plea to the World Jewish Congress in New York. But his claims against the corrupt Slovakian nation were unsuccessful.

A year before his death, Sam dedicated the Roza Robota Gates at the Sir Moses Montefiore Jewish Home in Sydney. The gates honored the woman whom his sister had told him about so many years ago—a woman whose courage and strength they both admired.

EPILOGUE

★   ★   ★

Katya and Zippi reconnected after the war. Katya had gone on to live a quiet life in Prague, where she and Zippi met for a final time in 1975. Katya rarely spoke about her war experience, instead referring anyone interested to Zippi. Katya gave her testimony only once, for the criminal proceedings against Dr. Carl Clauberg, the German gynecologist who set out to develop methods of nonsurgical mass sterilization. He was the man behind the notorious Block 10, where Alma Rosé had initially landed and where hundreds of women and girls in Auschwitz were forced to endure horrific experiments. In her testimony, Katya described how Clauberg's block had grown from ten women; she outlined his gruesome experiments on unsuspecting victims, and how his survivors were isolated and cast off to gas chambers. She estimated that at least a thousand women had died as a result of his experiments.

In 1991, Zippi convinced Katya to sit down for an interview with Susan Cernyak-Spatz, a friend of Zippi's. For the first time on record, Katya spoke with a fellow Auschwitz survivor, regarding her experiences. The conversation, published in *Jewish Currents,* is the only known interview that Katya gave in her lifetime.

"After liberation, Singer resumed civilian life and successfully buried her past," the article states. "She married a Christian, had children, and worked for the Czech government as an art gallery curator. None of the people with whom she spent the last fifty years of her life knew anything of what she had done."

Katya died in 1995 of kidney failure.

It's unknown how many people Katya helped save through her work as *Rapportschreiberin,* or how many lives Zippi saved as Birkenau's graphic artist. But according to women who knew them in Auschwitz, they saved at least sixteen hundred women.

Zippi tried to improve the lot of the women around her; she saved them when she could.

She did her best to rescue and sustain the men she'd loved.

Erwin she saved once, from drowning.

David she saved five times.

It was Tibor alone, her first love, whom she could not save.

On July 6, 2018, Zippi passed away at the age of ninety-nine. She died in a New York hospital with a caretaker by her side. Zippi and Erwin never had children; Sam's granddaughter helped to coordinate a modest funeral. Zippi had outlived most of her friends. Peter Hellman, the journalist whose book on Auschwitz she had once corrected, gave a heartfelt eulogy.

David died almost three years later, on June 15, 2021, with his family at his side. Shortly following his return to the United States after his final trip to Auschwitz, he had moved into a senior living community. Within weeks, a global pandemic meant no in-person visits with his family for a year—but they were able to be with him when he passed.

David's family held a public memorial. Dozens of guests attended. Framed newspaper clippings and photographs of David in his GI uniform lined the entryway to the auditorium where he was honored. Family and friends told tales of a life well lived—and now they sang prayers, for him.

*S*even decades before their Manhattan reunion, a boy saw a girl.

That first glance was fraught from the start. They were inside the Sauna, where the fumes were poisonous. Outside, gusts of wind had carried thick smoke from fires too horrible to describe.

The boy was younger; she was older. He was inexperienced; she was confident, wise. They locked eyes and she chose him. In a world of death and destruction, they climbed a makeshift ladder and found a window. Together, they were no longer numbers; they were no longer alone.

It had been wintertime in Birkenau, the largest and deadliest subcamp of Auschwitz.

Together, they survived.

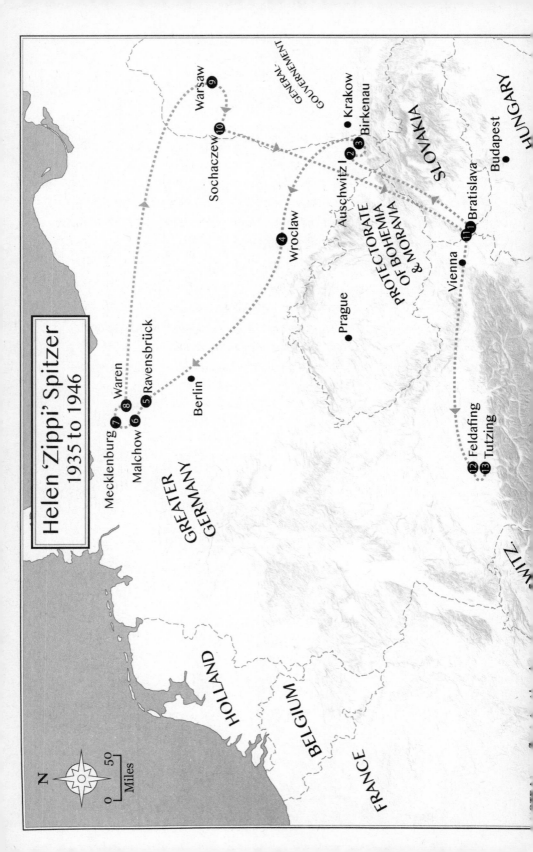

Helen 'Zippi' Spitzer
1935 to 1946

N

0   50
Miles

HOLLAND

BELGIUM

FRANCE

GREATER
GERMANY

Berlin

Mecklenburg 7
Waren 8
Malchow 6
Ravensbrück 5

Wroclaw 4

Sochaczew

Warsaw 9

10

GENERAL-
GOUVERNEMENT

Krakow
Birkenau
Auschwitz 2 3

PROTECTORATE
OF BOHEMIA
& MORAVIA

Prague

Vienna

Bratislava 1 11

SLOVAKIA

Budapest

HUNGARY

Feldafing 12
Tutzing 13

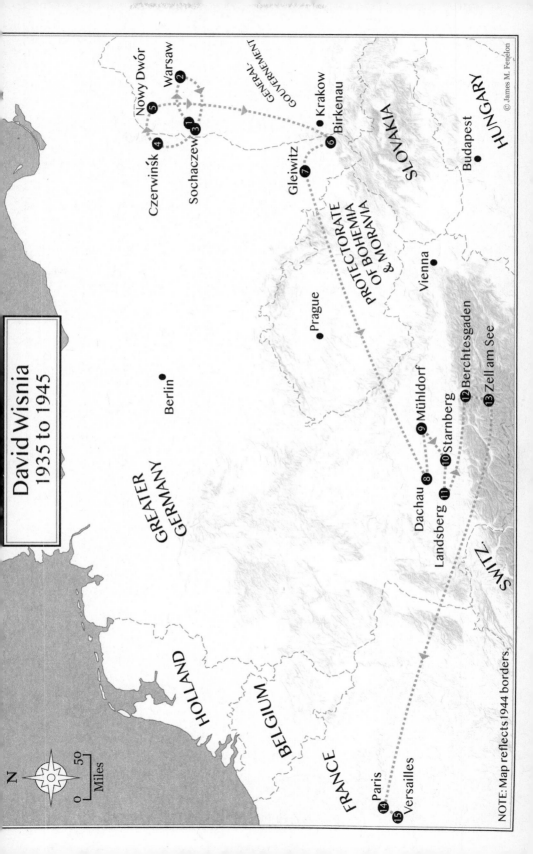

David Wisnia
1935 to 1945

N

0 50
Miles

© James M. Fenelon

NOTE: Map reflects 1944 borders.

GREATER
GERMANY

Berlin

HOLLAND

BELGIUM

FRANCE

Paris ⑭
Versailles ⑮

SWITZ.

Dachau ⑧
Landsberg ⑪
Mühldorf ⑨
Starnberg ⑩
Berchtesgaden ⑫
Zell am See ⑬

Prague

PROTECTORATE
OF BOHEMIA
& MORAVIA

Vienna

SLOVAKIA

HUNGARY

Budapest

Nowy Dwór
Warsaw ②
⑤
Czerwińsk ④
Sochaczew ③①
Gleiwitz ⑦
Krakow
Birkenau
⑥ Birkenau

GENERAL-
GOUVERNEMENT

ACKNOWLEDGMENTS

I owe my deepest debt of gratitude to the late David Wisnia, who invited me into his home and recounted so many of his life stories. David's dignity and his ability to find humor and beauty in life are lessons on the power of optimism. I'm honored to share his story.

I'm also extremely grateful to the Wisnia family, particularly to Avi Wisnia and Rabbi Eric Wisnia, for helping to coordinate interviews, for sitting down with me for interviews, and for sharing photographs of their patriarch. Thank you also to Sarah Taksler, who suggested I get in touch with Avi when I was investigating a book on World War II refugees.

In researching Zippi's life, I got to know a loyal circle of friends that remained close to her during her final years. They are proof that Zippi was adept, to the end, at surrounding herself with brilliant and generous confidantes.

I'm grateful to Jürgen Matthäus, editor of *Approaching an Auschwitz Survivor,* who indulged me with his time and formidable knowledge through every step of this project, and to Konrad Kwiet, who took regular morning calls in Sydney and shared his wisdom and unwavering enthusiasm for this project. Both Jürgen and Konrad's insights into Zippi's life and the broader context of the Holocaust were invaluable.

To the late Joan Ringelheim, who in the span of two decades recorded hours of interviews with Zippi. Joan's insights on Zippi and Erwin, our lively discussions on philosophy, and her scholarship on women and the Holocaust, all left a mark in these pages. To Michael Berkowitz, for sharing his time and vast knowledge of postwar Germany and photography—and for digging up newspapers, microcassette tapes and those early photographs of Zippi and Tibor.

To journalist extraordinaire Peter Hellman, who shared his interview notes, myriad anecdotes, and his beautiful eulogy to Zippi. Also to Wendy Lower, who shared her experiences with Zippi, as well as interviews and videotapes. To Atina Grossmann, whose insights into Zippi's postwar life, and into Feldafing and postwar Germany, were extremely illuminating. I also thank Joseph Toltz for shedding light into Zippi's musical upbringing and the world of Jewish music, and for sharing his unpublished interview with her.

Thank you to Robin Black, who helped David Wisnia author his memoir, *One Voice, Two Lives,* and years later reached out to me and generously shared tapes of their interviews. Speaking of unexpected treasures, I'm extremely appreciative of Anabel Aliaga-Buchenau of UNC Charlotte, who discovered Zippi's long-lost manuscript. Thank you also for a beautiful translation of Erwin Tichauer's book. To Susan Cernyak-Spatz's daughter, Jackie Fishman, for putting us in touch; and to Ilana Abramovitch for leading me to Jackie.

I'm deeply appreciative of Hana and Petra Nichtburgerova, Edvard Nichtburger, and Lisa Jacobson, who shared their experiences with Zippi, Sam, and Leo. Also to Alice Tyroler, one of Zippi's earliest childhood friends from Bratislava, for taking the time to answer questions about her past.

ACKNOWLEDGMENTS

I am indebted to the staffs of various libraries and archives and whose assistance was invaluable. To Steven Vitto, Elliott Wrenn, and James Gilmore at the United States Holocaust Memorial Museum, in Washington, DC; to Christine Schmidt and Barbara Warnock of the Wiener Holocaust Library; to Crispin Brooks, Jenna Leventhal, and Zach Larkin at the USC Shoah Foundation; to Sima Velkovich at Yad Vashem; to Janet Bunde at New York University Special Collections; to the Pilecki Institute; to the Arolsen Archives; to the staff of Butler Library at Columbia University; to Stephen Naron at the Fortunoff Video Archive for Holocaust Testimonies at Yale University; to the Imperial War Museum; to Piotr Setkiewicz at the Auschwitz-Birkenau State Museum; to Adam Strohm and Mindy Pugh at the Illinois Institute of Technology's Voices of the Holocaust; to Holly Rivet of the National Archives; to Nancy Toff of the Oxford University Press; and to Jason Dawsey at the Institute for the Study of War and Democracy, the National World War II Museum. I also appreciate Brad Zarlin, who donated many hours of interviews with both David and Sara to the USHMM.

I'm indebted to countless survivors whose powerful oral testimonies and memoirs shed light into unimaginable worlds. In particular, *The Nazis Knew My Name* by Magda Hellinger and Maya Lee with David Brewster; *Protective Custody: Prisoner 34042* by Susan Cernyak-Spatz; *I Escaped Auschwitz* by Rudolf Vrba and Alan Bestic; *The Auschwitz Volunteer* by Witold Pilecki; and *Inherit the Truth*: 1939–1945 by Anita Lasker-Wallfisch.

To my exceptional fact-checkers, Sue Carswell and Beatrice Hogan: they saved me from myself again and again. Any mistakes are my own. For various reasons spanning from interviews to research and translations, thanks are due to Arielle Goren, Betty Taylor Hill, Ralph Hakman, Leonora Franzke, Luca Makai, and Lori Miller of Red Bird Research.

To Erika Storella, Rebecca Gardner, Will Roberts and Nora Gonzalez, who tirelessly championed this project, and to the wonderful

ACKNOWLEDGMENTS

team at The Gernert Company, for their expertise and encouragement. In particular, I'm deeply indebted to Erika for getting this project into Alexander Littlefield's masterful hands.

When I first spoke with Alex, I knew I'd be fortunate to have him shepherd this book to fruition. I'm immensely grateful to him for sharing in my vision and for helping to transform a sea of reporting into a cogent narrative structure. I couldn't have hoped for a more sensitive, creative, and skillful editor. To Morgan Wu for her keen eye to details and for getting the manuscript across the finish line. To Albert LaFarge, whose meticulous copyediting smoothed out so many rough edges. To Ian Gibbs and Linda Feldman, gifted proofreaders, who improved each page they touched. Also, to Lucy Kim for the gorgeous book cover, and Elizabeth Garriga, Danielle Finnegan, Linda Arends and the fantastic team at Little, Brown. Thank you also to Fariza Hawke and Jessica Vestuto for their spot-on comments and feedback on early drafts of this book.

A huge thank you to Bill Ferguson at the *New York Times,* for his brilliant guidance throughout my reporting and writing of *Lovers in Auschwitz*. Thank you also for originating what would become the title of this book.

To my dear friend, and talented cousin, Maya Barkai, for taking my author photo. To Marcia Butler, who offered meaningful input, endless encouragement, and whose creativity inspires me daily. To Duy Linh Tu, my teaching partner and life coach. To Michelle Falkenstein, who helped open up this world of journalism to me. To David Andelman and Matt Schifrin, who took a chance on me as a reporter and have been cheering me on since. Thank you also to Amir Shaviv, for being a mentor and for his sage advice over the years. Also to Tom Post, Joseph Berger, Annalisa Birdsall, and Charles Salzberg for their encouragement.

To Dawa Choezom, Sharon Moreno, and Emanuele Oliveira for taking care of my boys when I was writing.

ACKNOWLEDGMENTS

And finally, I thank Tali and David, for our sib-night chats and laughter, for their boundless enthusiasm and love. To Orli, who's been lighting up rooms since joining the world. Thank you to Michael and to Lloyd for helping us decamp from Brooklyn when we realized life had changed.

In March of 2020, our family of three flew from New York to Texas for what we thought would be a few weeks. During the following seven months, my parents, Max and Desirée, lovingly put us up. I can't begin to express my gratitude to my mom for her boundless support: taking Rafa on daily visits to the neighborhood peacocks, playing Legos to the tune of *Mary Poppins* for hours, *and* cooking up delicious meals. Also to my dad, who perfected his challah recipe, played with Rafa, and encouraged me to keep on writing. Both remain my enthusiastic first readers. This book is dedicated to them.

In November of 2020, now a family of four, we drove an RV to California. I couldn't have hoped for warmer and kinder in-laws to bubble up with during the next five months: thank you to Rachelle, Murad, Yael, and Jeremy for all your care and support, and especially for your company and friendship. Also to "Kai-Noah-Liv," who made our bubble especially lively.

I'm eternally grateful to my boys, Rafael and Samuel. I spent countless mornings focused on some of the darkest moments in recent history. When I came out of my cave, your smiles and laughter drew me back into the light. You *are* the light.

And to Jonathan: my partner and advocate. Whether we're traveling the world or isolating from it, there's no one I'd rather share life with.

All four of my grandparents lost most of their families to the Holocaust. Displaced from Eastern Europe, my grandparents found their way to Brazil. This book is in memory of my two beloved grandmothers, Helena and Zipora—I see their verve and grit in Helen Zipora ("Zippi") Tichauer. It's also in memory of my

ACKNOWLEDGMENTS

grandfather, Eliezer, a journalist, pianist, and charismatic romantic who fought for his beliefs.

My living grandfather, Dov, survived heinous tragedies, fought back, and persevered with optimism and a passion for life. He remains a force, his story is an inspiration. A month before this book publishes we will celebrate his 98th birthday together.

NOTES ON SOURCES

Zippi Tichauer did not want to dwell on her relationship with David Wisnia. That's the inescapable conclusion of the gaps in the records that she left behind. Her reminiscences filled entire books—yet in all of the dozens of formal interviews that she gave to historians and scholars after the war, even in her own unpublished memoir, Zippi never mentioned David.

She did acknowledge her relationship with David on separate occasions to at least two historians I spoke with. Both instances were outside the scope of formal interviews. She briefly recounted the affair to Jürgen Matthäus, but offered few details, displayed little emotional involvement, and shrugged off its significance, saying that romances were commonplace among privileged prisoners. She conceded that she'd saved David's life, but downplayed this fact, explaining that she also helped others, and that anyone in her position would've done the same. Beyond that, Zippi had no desire to linger on that particular slice of her history.

I never got a chance to meet Zippi, so beyond corroborating their relationship, I leaned on David for details. David first told me about his former girlfriend in 2018. I'd been interviewing European refugees who'd immigrated into the United States during

World War II in unusual circumstances. I was told about a cantor who'd joined the 101st Airborne after surviving Auschwitz. By then, David was not shy about his past; he'd published a memoir, he'd spoken about his stint with the 101st Airborne to *BuzzFeed* and other media outlets.

We met at his home in Levittown, where we spoke for hours inside his office, a room with shelves filled with framed family pictures, a wall covered in photographs of his students and one large glass-framed poster of the 101st Airborne that had been autographed to him by dozens of veterans. He sat on a black office chair facing a mahogany desk strewn with thank-you letters from students, with papers, pencils and files, a couple of eyeglasses and a desktop monitor. He told me about his childhood in Europe, about his family in the ghetto, how singing had saved his life in Auschwitz, and about joining the 101st Airborne. Occasionally, he swiveled to check his laptop for email, or answered the cell phone he had hanging from a cord around his neck.

Before I left, I interviewed David and his grandson Avi, together at his living-room table, and we looked at photographs. I had stood up, ready to leave, when David said something that stopped me: *I had a girlfriend at the camp.* I sat back down.

David was proud of his relationship with Zippi. He also recounted it in oral testimonies and in his memoir. I reconstructed the scene of David and Zippi's New York reunion by conducting several interviews with him and Avi, relying on photographs and a recording. Within Auschwitz, however, I relied on David's memories.

I was fortunate to meet David for extensive interviews before he passed away in 2021. He was ninety-two years old when we first met, and more than seventy years had passed since he'd been incarcerated in Auschwitz. A natural storyteller, David was by then remarkably at ease sharing his life's story. He obviously cared for Zippi. But his eyes had a particular sparkle when he spoke of "the boys" of the 101st Airborne.

Human memory is, of course, delicate. Might David have mis-remembered moments? Of course. Within the endnotes I point to the few instances where David's memory didn't quite match other sources. For example, David believed he saw Sara as she was first entering Birkenau; Sara recalled having already been in Birkenau for some time. He also wasn't quite sure exactly when he and Zippi first connected, beyond that he was still at the "old Sauna" and it preceded having recognized Sara. In addition, it's unclear exactly where David ran into the 506th Parachute Infantry unit that adopted him. International Tracing Service documents from the Red Cross note there are no documents regarding his whereabouts beyond May 8, 1945.

In writing this book, I've tried to fill in the blanks by corrob-orating facts using as many interviews, archival documents, record-ings and oral testimonies as possible. Times when David was alone, such as his postwar encounter with a Nazi inside a barn, are impos-sible to corroborate, as are many of the moments David spent with the 506th Infantry, since his closest friends from Company H are no longer alive. Morning Reports, daily military records that highlight changes in personnel status, sometimes unit locations, and often significant events within the troop unit, show no record of David's encounter with Company H (searched from February 1 through June 15, 1945). However, one of Ferd Wilczek's daughters was able to confirm the two men's relationship in the army. More-over, according to Holly Rivet, a specialist at the National Archives, it was not unusual for refugees to be picked up and informally "adopted" by the military. Finally, David's role as a PX manager is confirmed in the manifest of passengers coming to the United States in the SS *Monarch of the Seas*.

Despite not having met Zippi, I've heard dozens of hours of inter-views and testimonies that she recorded. As I researched her life, I tried to contact anyone alive who'd known her. I immersed myself in academic literature about Auschwitz and tracked down memoirs and testimonies. In doing so, I found Susan Cernyak-Spatz's memoir, *Protective Custody Prisoner 34042,* which references Zippi. Susan also penned the *Jewish Currents* article, "Record-Keeping for the Nazis—and Saving Lives" with Joel Shatzky, the only interview Katya Singer ever granted in her lifetime. Within both works, Susan, who died in 2019, alluded to an unpublished manuscript by Zippi Tichauer from October 1991. None of the historians within Zippi's inner circle had heard of this manuscript.

In June of 2022, after more than a year searching for this phantom manuscript, I received an email. Anabel Aliaga-Buchenau, associate chair of the Department of Languages and Culture Studies at the University of North Carolina at Charlotte, had just discovered an unpublished manuscript inside a box; she immediately sent me a copy.

The Women's Camp at Auschwitz-Birkenau: Method Within Madness, purportedly written by Zippi and edited by Susan Cernyak-Spatz and Joel Shatzky, confirms many of the stories Zippi relayed in interviews and testimonies. It's also robust with additional details, names, and previously unknown information from inside Auschwitz. The historians who knew Zippi—including Wendy Lower, Michael Berkowitz, and Konrad Kwiet—agree that the text reads remarkably as her voice, and that it helped them understand nuances from their conversations, and shed light into Auschwitz's machinations. But the question remains: why was this document buried unpublished inside a cardboard box?

Zippi was a perfectionist. According to Jürgen Matthäus, she was skeptical of anyone other than herself writing a book about her experiences in Auschwitz. We don't know how much of the text was edited. Perhaps she disagreed with some of the edits. Not knowing how much her words were edited, I opted not to use direct quotes from the manuscript.

In writing this book, I've grappled with the responsibility of representing someone whom I've never met. Zippi was a tough critic with a high bar for authenticity. She likely would have been skeptical of this book. But I believe that her story of strength and self-sacrifice deserves to be told. In addition, the story of her romance with David in Auschwitz offers a spark of hope in a world of darkness—and the richness of their lives beyond Auschwitz is every bit as much of an inspiration.

Abbreviations in Notes:

AJDCA: American Jewish Joint Distribution Committee Archives, New York

LBI: Leo Baeck Institute, New York

UNRRAA: United Nations Relief and Rehabilitation Administration Archives, New York

USHMM: United States Holocaust Memorial Museum, Washington, D.C.

VHA/USC-Shoah: Visual History Archive, USC Shoah Foundation

Wiener-HL: The Wiener Holocaust Library Archives

NOTES

Prologue

p.1   *saw each other:* Unless otherwise noted, descriptions come from David Wisnia from two lengthy interviews conducted with the author at his home in Levittown, Pa., on January 19, 2018, and June 24, 2019.

p.1   *steam kettles:* Andrzej Strzelecki, "The History, Role and Operation of the Central Camp Sauna in Auschwitz II-Birkenau," in *The Architecture of Crime: The "Central Camp Sauna" in Auschwitz II-Birkenau,* ed. Teresa Swiebocka, trans. William Brand (Oswiecim: Auschwitz-Birkenau State Museum, 2001), 15.

p.1   *At four feet and eleven inches:* Helen Tichauer, unpublished video recorded by Wendy Lower, November 2013.

Chapter One: "Small Stuff"

p.5   *The frigid fall air:* Robert DeCourcy Ward, "Weather Controls over the Fighting During the Autumn of 1918," *The Scientific Monthly* 8, no. 1 (1919).

p.5   *looted shops and restaurants:* Pieter C. van Duin, *Central European Crossroads: Social Democracy and National Revolution in Bratislava (Pressburg) 1867–1921* (New York: Berghahn Books, 2009), 172.

p.5   *"national rebirth":* Mark Cornwall, "Apocalypse and the Quest for a Sudeten German Männerbund in Czechoslovakia," in *Sacrifice and Rebirth: The Legacy of the Last Habsburg War,* ed. Mark Cornwall and John Paul Newman (New York: Berghahn Books, 2016), 100.

p.6   *blamed their misfortunes:* Mark Cornwall and John Paul Newman, eds., *Sacrifice and Rebirth: The Legacy of the Last Habsburg War* (New York: Berghahn Books, 2016), 83.

p.6   *chanted "Down with the Jews!":* Van Duin, *Central European Crossroads,* 172.

p.6   *agents provocateurs, spies:* Aharon Moshe Rabinowicz, "The Jewish Minority," in *The Jews of Czechoslovakia* (New: The Jewish Publication Society of America, 1968), 1:226.

NOTES

p.6   *Vojtech:* This name has been documented as Vojtech in Slovak documents, and he's documented as Adalbert and Wojciech in documents filed with the International Tracing Services, but Sam and Helen both referred to their father as Albert. Rosa has also been documented as Roza.

p.6   *call her Hilanka:* Hana Nichtburgerova (Helen Tichauer's great-grandniece), interview with author, October 27, 2021.

p.6   *at a crowd:* "Pressburg Rioters Shot Down," *New York Times,* February 17, 1919.

p.6   *social democrats:* Van Duin, *Central European Crossroads,* 202.

p.6   *now called Bratislava:* Frank Reichenthal, "Jewish Art in Slovakia: A Personal Recollection," in *The Jews of Czechoslovakia* (New York: The Jewish Publication Society of America, 1971), 2:500.

p.6   *Slovak People's Party:* Van Duin, *Central European Crossroads,* 283.

p.7   *hundred-foot-long river pool:* Jana Liptáková, "Bathing in Danube Has Its Charm as Well as Its Downside," *Slovak Spectator,* August 11, 2017.

p.7   *squinted at a camera:* Konrad Kwiet, "Designing Survival," in *Approaching an Auschwitz Survivor,* ed. Jürgen Matthäus (Oxford: Oxford University Press, 2010), 10.

p.7–8   *went to a specialized sanitarium:* Helen Tichauer, unpublished interview with Konrad Kwiet, September 15, 2005.

p.8   *down the hall:* Helen Tichauer, unpublished interview with Konrad Kwiet, August 9, 2006.

p.8   *Zippi's grandmother, Julia:* H. Nichtburgerova, interview with author, October 27, 2021.

p.8   *local antiques dealer:* Tichauer, interview with Kwiet, September 15, 2005.

p.9   *used to loneliness:* The interviews undertaken by Dr. Joseph Toltz with Helen Tichauer took place in 2009 and 2010. They formed part of the ethnographic component of Toltz's doctoral dissertation, which was successfully defended in 2011, and remain the copyright of Dr. Toltz and Mrs. Tichauer's family. This material has been used with permission by both parties. Dr. Joseph Toltz is research manager at the Sydney Conservatorium of Music and adjunct researcher at the Department of Hebrew, Biblical and Jewish Studies at the University of Sydney.

p.9   *odd one out:* Lisa Jacobson (Helen Tichauer's great-grandniece), interview with author, October 5, 2020.

p.9   *A string quartet:* Joseph Toltz, interview with author, June 23, 2020.

p.9   *another played a mandolin:* Helen Tichauer, oral testimony, Imperial War Museum Archives, 2003.

p.10   *easy to lug around:* Helen Tichauer, unpublished video recorded by Wendy Lower, November 2013.

p.10   *Leo introduced Zippi:* Toltz, interview with author, June 23, 2020.

p.10   *the lone child:* Tichauer, Lower video, November 2013.

p.10   *celebrate Purim:* Joseph Toltz, interview with author, July 8, 2020.

p.10   *Zámocká Street:* Hana Nichtburgerova, email to author, June 24, 2020.

p.10   *the Zámocká Street Synagogue:* "Sitzbuch (Book of Seats) of the Zámocká Street Synagogue," Jewish Community Museum, Bratislava, http://www.synagogue.sk/collection/sitzbuch, accessed April 2, 2023.

p.11   *say the kaddish:* Kwiet, "Designing Survival," 11.

p.11   *playing soccer:* Samuel Spitzer, interview with D. I. Ritch, March 7, 1996, VHA/USC-Shoah.

p.11   *seventy thousand members:* Robert Buechler, "The Jewish Community in Slovakia Before World War II," in *The Tragedy of the Jews of Slovakia,* ed. Jarek Mensfelt (Oswiecim: Auschwitz-Birkenau State Museum/Museum of the Slovak National Uprising), 41.

p.11   *being a botanist:* Helen Tichauer, "The Women's Camp at Auschwitz-Birkenau: Method Within Madness," ed. Susan Cernyak-Spatz and Joel Shatzky (unpublished manuscript).

p.11   *Julia impressed on Zippi:* Helen Tichauer, interview with Joseph Toltz, December 10, 2010.

p.11   *cultural equality:* Monika Vrzgulová, "Holocaust in Women's Lives: Approaching a Slovak Oral History Archive," in *Women and the Holocaust,* ed. Andrea Petoő, Louise Hecht, and Karolina Krasuska (Warsaw: Instytut Badán Literackich PAN, 2015), 106.

p.12   *some three million:* Ihor Gawdiak, ed., *Czechoslovakia: A Country Study* (Washington, D.C.: GPO, 1987).

p.12   *dreamed of a nationalist state:* Cornwall and Newman, *Sacrifice and Rebirth,* 53.

p.12   *press off-limits:* William L. Shirer, *The Rise and Fall of the Third Reich: A History of Nazi Germany* (New York: Simon & Schuster, 2011), 65.

p.12   *embroidery, drawing, and painting:* Tichauer, interview with Kwiet, August 9, 2006.

p.12   *Zippi stopped:* Tichauer, "Women's Camp."

p.13   *She demanded:* Michael Berkowitz, interview with author, February 19, 2021.

p.13   *ranging from barbers:* Gabriel Drimer, interview with Sue Rosenthal, "Philadelphia Gathering of Survivors," April 21, 1985, USHMM.

p.13   *to kindergarten teachers:* Magda Blau, interview with Linda Kuzmack, June 11, 1990, USHMM.

p.13   *engaging discussions:* Helen Tichauer, "Ladies First," *Voice of the Woman Survivor* 6, no. 2 (1989).

p.13   *from business and finance:* Buechler, "Jewish Community," 33.

p.13   *convey messages:* Kwiet, "Designing Survival," 30.

p.13   *didn't care for:* Nechama Tec, "Recapturing the Past," in Matthäus, *Approaching an Auschwitz Survivor,* 29.

p.14   *took off for Palestine:* H. Nichtburgerova, interview with author, October 27, 2021.

p.14   *required attendance:* Spitzer interview.

p.14   *no reason to leave:* Kwiet: "Designing Survival," 29.

p.14   *ruin her hands:* Tichauer, "Women's Camp."

p.14   *not allowed inside:* Victor Klemperer, *I Will Bear Witness, 1933–1941: A Diary of the Nazi Years,* trans. Martin Chalmers (New York: Modern Library, 1999), 8–11.

p.15   *dragged out of his bed:* "Violence in Germany Again in the Ascendant: Attacks in Berlin, Frankfurt, Munich," *Jewish Daily Bulletin,* May 20, 1933.

p.15   *drink castor oil:* "Jews Flee Germany as Hitler Menace Grows: Terror and Panic Follow," *The American Israelite,* March 16, 1933.

p.15   *their welcome wore off:* Ferdinand M. Isserman, "Rabbi Isserman Sees Doom of German Jewry Brought Nearer," *The American Israelite,* September 27, 1934.

p.15   *spurned the thought:* Adam Hudek, "Between Czechs and Hungarians: Constructing the Slovak National Identity from 19th Century to the Present," *History Compass* 9, no. 4 (April 3, 2011): 263.

p.15   *primarily of Catholics:* Yeshayahu Jelinek, "Nationalism in Slovakia and the Communists, 1918–1929," *Slavic Review* 34, no. 1 (March 1975): 70.

p.16   *They yearned:* Matej Hanula, "The Pittsburgh Agreement and Its Role in the Political Life of Interwar Slovakia," *Kosmas: Czechoslovak and Central European Journal* 2, no. 1 (2019): 120.

p.16   *small eastern villages:* Akiva Nir, "The Zionist Organizations, Youth Movements, and Emigration to Palestine in 1918–1945," in Mensfelt, ed., *The Tragedy of the Jews of Slovakia,* 37.

p.16   *antisemitic demonstrations:* Miloslav Szabó, " 'Golemiáda': Odkaz protižidovských demonštrácií v Bratislave z apríla 1936," *Denník N,* March 19, 2016.

p.16   *smashed windows:* Miloslav Szabó, "From Protests to the Ban: Demonstrations Against the 'Jewish' Films in Interwar Vienna and Bratislava," *Journal of Contemporary History* 54, no: 1 (2017): 5–29.

p.16   *"small stuff":* Spitzer interview.

p.16   *enfant terrible:* Konrad Kwiet, interview with author, 2020.

p.16   *the less he knew, the better:* Spitzer interview.

p.16   *Tibor Justh:* Tibor Justh Indictment, Der Oberreichsanwalt beim Volksgerichtshof, Anklageschrift, Berlin, March 4, 1942.

p.16   *longstanding Jewish Community:* Yehoshua Robert Buchler and Gila Fatran, "A Brief History of Slovakian Jewry," JewishGen, https://www.jewishgen.org/yizkor/pinkas_slovakia/Slo0XI.html, accessed February 13, 2023.

Chapter Two: The End of an Era

p.18   *a little boy*: Unless otherwise noted, descriptions come from David Wisnia from two lengthy interviews conducted with the author at his home in Levittown, Pa., on January 19, 2018, and June 24, 2019.

p.19   *freshly paved:* "Warsaw Opens New Boulevard," *New York Times,* October 18, 1935.

p.19   *"Paris of the North":* "Warsaw Regains Title 'Paris of the North,' " *New York Times,* November 27, 1927.

p.19   *intimate playhouses:* "Direct from Old Warsaw," *New York Times,* March 15, 1931.

p.19   *playing the harmonica:* Photos from "Vintage: Poland During Interwar period (1918–1939)," *Monovisions Black and White Photography Magazine,* https://monovisions.com/vintage-poland-during-interwar-period-1920s-1930s/, accessed February 13, 2023.

p.19   *attendance shot up:* H. Howard Taubman, "The Opera in Paris and Warsaw," *New York Times,* September 29, 1935.

p.19   *Eliahu:* David referred to his father as Eliahu. His name has also been documented as Elias and the surname Visnia.

p.19   *age eight:* David Wisnia, interview with Joseph Toltz (transcript), April 7, 2011, USHMM.

p.20   *biggest arena:* Sara Lewin Radomski, interview with Brad Zarlin, 2007, USHMM.

p.20   *Shnei Michtavim:* The poem was written by Israel's first poet laureate, the Hungarian-born Avigdor Hameiri.

NOTES

p.20   *"The Two Letters":* "A Hebrew Liederabend" (program), June 4, 2019, YIVO, https://yivo.org/cimages/6-4-19_program.pdf, accessed February 13, 2023.

p.20   *a "lasting peace":* "The British War Bluebook: Text of German-Polish Agreement of Janurary 26, 1934," Yale Law School, https://avalon.law.yale.edu/wwii/blbk01.asp, accessed February 13, 2023.

p.21   *brush in hand:* David Wisnia, interview with Brad Zarlin, 2006, USHMM.

p.21   *town's only synagogue:* "The Sochaczew Yeshiva," Virtual Shtetl, https://sztetl.org.pl/en/towns/s/607-sochaczew/102-education-and-culture/27268-sochaczew-yeshiva, accessed February 13, 2023.

p.21   *he'd sing again:* Wisnia, interview with Zarlin.

p.21   *taunted Jews:* Yitschak Brzezowski (also Eddie Ilan), interviewed by Leonia Kurgan, VHA/USC-Shoah.

p.21   *Hasidic center:* Y. Trunk, "The History of the Community," trans. Jerrold Landau, Jewishgen, https://www.jewishgen.org/yizkor/Sochaczew/so601.html#History, accessed February 13, 2023.

p.21   *population of 13,500:* "History," Sochaczew.pl, https://www.sochaczew.pl/home/languageversion/4?filterId=1, accessed February 13, 2023,

p.21   *quarter Jewish:* "The Sochaczew Yeshiva," Virtual Shtetl, https://sztetl.org.pl/en/towns/s/607-sochaczew/99-history/138045-history-of-community, accessed February 13, 2023.

p.22   *Only peasants left Poland:* David Wisnia, taped interview with Robin Black, August 13, 2007.

p.22   *staged hunger strikes:* "Warsaw Students Strike," *New York Times,* November 25, 1936.

p.22   *sirens and drumrolls:* "War Games Darken Warsaw," *New York Times,* October 3, 1935.

p.23   *Krochmalna Street:* Isaac Bashevis Singer grew up here shortly after World War I and would memorialize the street decades later in his books.

p.23   *Eliahu's upholstery shop:* Wisnia, interview with Toltz, April 7, 2011.

p.23   *five biggest:* "The Nozyk Synagogue, Warsaw, Poland," https://www.bh.org.il/nozyk-synagogue-warsaw-poland/.

p.23   *wider exposure:* Wisnia, interview with Toltz, April 7, 2011.

p.24   *Moshe Koussevitzky:* "Moshe Koussevitzky," Milken Archive, https://www.milkenarchive.org/artists/view/moshe-koussevitzky, accessed April 10, 2023.

p.24   *A 1939 Gallup poll:* Frank Newport, "Historical Review: Americans' Views on Refugees Coming to U.S.," Gallup, https://news.gallup.com/opinion/polling-matters/186716/historical-review-americans-views-refugees-coming.aspx, accessed February 13, 2023.

p.24   *a North Carolina senator:* See Congressional Record, May 11, 1939 for the Senate's discussion on immigration. Senator Robert Reynolds introduced Reynolds-Starnes Bill bill. Furthermore, he stated: "I am proud that North Carolina has fewer aliens than are found in any other State in the entire Union—less than one-half of 1 percent and I hope always to keep it as it is."

p.26   *or so hoped many:* Wisnia, interview with Black, August 13, 2007.

p.26   *ages of twenty-one:* Jerzy Szapiro "Poles Mobilizing Army of 2,500,000," *New York Times,* August 31, 1939.

p.27   *he repeated, animated:* Wisnia, interview with Zarlin.

p.27   *the ruse:* Associated Press: "Bulletins on Europe's Conflict," *New York Times,* September 1, 1939.

p.27   *"meet force with force":* Otto D. Tolischus, "Hitler Gives Word: In a Proclamation He Accuses Warsaw of Appeal to Arms," *New York Times,* September 1, 1939.

p.27   *Overhanging mist and clouds:* Jerzy Szapiro, "Hostilities Begun: Warsaw Reports German Offensive Moving on Three Objectives," *New York Times,* September 1, 1939.

Chapter Three: "He Was Bluffing"

p.28   *engaged to be married:* Jürgen Matthäus, interview with author, July 7, 2020.

p.28   *uncomplicated death:* Nechama Tec, "Recapturing the Past," in *Approaching an Auschwitz Survivor,* ed Jürgen Matthäus (Oxford: Oxford University Press, 2010), 30.

p.28   *some 2.8 million:* William L. Shirer, *The Rise and Fall of the Third Reich: A History of Nazi Germany* (New York: Simon & Schuster, 2011).

p.29   *mobilizing its men:* "Order of Battle Handbook Czechoslovak Army," CIA Declassified Document Number: CIA-RDP81-01043R002800140007-5, August 1, 1958, 10, https://www.cia.gov/readingroom/docs/CIA-RDP81-01043R00 2800140007-5.pdf, accessed June 13, 2023.

p.29   *"he was bluffing":* "Czechoslovakia," *Fortune,* August 1, 1938.

p.30   *five hundred Jewish students:* "Anti-Semitism Has Free Rein in Slovakia; 500 Jews Expelled from Bratislava U," Jewish Telegraphic Agency, November 10, 1938.

p.30   *licensed graphic designer:* Tec, "Recapturing the Past," 29–30.

p.30   *Slovak People's Party:* "U. S. Protests Curb Slovak Violence," *New York Times,* December 8, 1938.

p.30   *"rightly blame them":* Ivan Kamenec, "The Deportation of Jewish Citizens from Slovakia in 1942," in *The Tragedy of the Jews of Slovakia,* ed. Jarek Mensfelt (Oswiecim: Auschwitz-Birkenau State Museum/Museum of the Slovak National Uprising), 111.

p.30   *were vandalized:* Peter Salner, "Ethnic Polarisation in an Ethnically Homogenous Town," *Sociologický časopis / Czech Sociological Review, IX,* (2001): 235–46.

p.30   *comic-opera version:* Yeshayahu Jelinek, "Storm-Troopers in Slovakia: The Rodobrana and the Hlinka Guard," *Journal of Contemporary History* 6, no. 3 (1971): 97–119.

p.30   *a bloody nose:* Alice Tyroler interview with Ina Navazelskis, May 18, 2013, USHMM.

p.31   *the only woman:* Konrad Kwiet, "Designing Survival," in Matthäus, *Approaching an Auschwitz Survivor.*

p.31   *twelve-person:* Tec, "Recapturing the Past," 30.

p.31   *fled to Paris:* J. R., "Czechoslovakia During the War: I—The Policy of the Government in London," *Bulletin of International News* 21, no. 22 (October 28, 1944): 897–906.

p.32   *a dilapidated building:* Samuel Spitzer Restitution papers (Annex: Commentary Without Prejudice, note 2). Courtesy of Konrad Kwiet.

p.32   *political prisoners:* Raanan Rein and Inbal Ofer, "Becoming Brigadistas: Jewish Volunteers from Palestine in the Spanish Civil War, Palestine in the Spanish Civil War," *European History Quarterly,* 46, no. 1: 92–112.

p.32   *pamphlets with updates:* Samuel Spitzer, interview with D. I. Ritch, March 7, 1996, VHA/USC-Shoah.

p.32   *Having been a driver:* Indictment, Der Oberreichsanwalt beim Dolksgerichtshof, Anklagefchrift, Berlin, March 4, 1942.

p.33   *non-Jewish Czechoslovaks:* Hana Kubátová, "Jewish Resistance in Slovakia," *Jewish Studies at the Central European University* 7 (2013).

NOTES

Chapter Four: "No One's Going to Beat Them"

p.34   *drawers full of clothes:* "Ruins Mark Line of Nazi Advance," *New York Times,* September 14, 1939.

p.34   *where they hoped:* Yisrael Gutman, *The Jews of Warsaw, 1939–1943: Ghetto, Underground Revolt,* trans. Ina Friedman (Bloomington: Indiana University Press, 1989), 4.

p.34   *endless artillery:* David Wisnia, taped interview with Robin Black, August 13, 2007.

p.34   *solution was the Gulag:* Anne Applebaum, *Gulag: A History* (New York: Anchor, 2003). See also Vera Golubeva's excellent oral-history series, "Generation Gulag," Coda Story, https://www.codastory.com/series/generation-gulag/.

p.35   *Most Jews believed:* Anne O'Hare McCormick, "Gambler's Throw Threatens the Crash of a Continent," *New York Times,* September 1, 1939.

p.35   *The altar was split:* Periscope Film, "Julien Bryan's 'Siege' 1939 German Invasion of Poland and Destruction of Warsaw 34444," YouTube, January 5, 2019, https://www.youtube.com/watch?v=SV4_-R-dZMw, accessed February 13, 2023.

p.35   *built barracades:* Gutman, *Jews of Warsaw,* 5.

p.35   *told a reporter:* "Saw Warsaw Bombed Hourly for Four Days," *New York Times,* September 11, 1939.

p.35   *Jewish Quarter was bombarded:* Gutman, *Jews of Warsaw,* 6.

p.35   *could no longer find:* Boleslaw Brodecki, interview with Linda Kuzmack, September 19, 1989.

p.35   *A third of Warsaw:* "Julien Bryan 'Siege' 1939."

p.36   *David and his family:* Unless otherwise noted, descriptions come from David Wisnia from two lengthy interviews conducted with the author at his home in Levittown, Pa., on January 19, 2018, and June 24, 2019.

p.36   *building next door:* Wisnia, interview with Black, August 13, 2007.

p.36   *remained undisturbed:* David Wisnia, interview with Brad Zarlin, USHMM.

p.36   *a bit longer:* Wisnia, interview with Black, August 13, 2007.

p.36   *tripled or quadrupled:* Gutman, *Jews of Warsaw,* 25.

p.36   *five hundred fires burned:* "20-Day Siege Ends," *New York Times,* September 28, 1939.

p.36   *No one's going to beat them:* Wisnia, interview with Black, August 13, 2007.

p.37   *they ordered:* Stanislaw Sznapman, in Michal Grynberg, ed., *Words to Outlive Us: Eyewitness Accounts from the Warsaw Ghetto,* trans. Philip Boehm (New York: Metropolitan/Henry Holt, 2002).

p.37   *were a threat:* Gutman, *Jews of Warsaw,* 55.

p.37   *off-limits:* Stanislaw Soszynski, transcribed interview, October 6, 1985, 5, USHMM.

p.37   *were designated:* Emmanuel Ringelblum, *Notes from the Warsaw Ghetto,* trans. and ed. Jacob Sloan (1958; repr., Potomac, Md.: Pickle Partners Publishing, 2015), 89, 104.

p.38   *was loot:* Helena Gutman-Stszewska, in Grynberg, *Words to Outlive Us.*

p.38   *abandoned relics:* Ringelblum, *Notes from the Warsaw Ghetto, 91.*

p.38   *375 acres:* Gutman, *Jews of Warsaw,* 60.

p.38   *ten-foot-high walls:* Ringelblum, *Notes from the Warsaw Ghetto,* 60.

p.38   *They took in:* David Wisnia, interview with Joseph Toltz (transcript), April 7, 2011, USHMM.

p.38   *become a repository:* "The History of the Great Synagogue," Jewish Historical Institute, https://www.jhi.pl/en/articles/the-history-of-the-great-synagogue,113, accessed February 17, 2023.

p.39   *he'd learned carpentry:* Wisnia, interview with Black, August 13, 2007.

p.39   *back and forth:* Wisnia, interview with Toltz, April 7, 2011.

p.39   *he brought home:* David Wisnia, interview with Brad Zarlin, 2006, USHMM.

p.39   *sworn an oath:* William L. Shirer, *The Rise and Fall of the Third Reich: A History of Nazi Germany* (New York: Simon & Schuster, 2011).

p.39   *responsibilities grew:* Adrian Weale, *Army of Evil: A History of the SS* (New York: NAL Caliber, 2012), 43.

p.40   *the Gestapo ruled:* Gutman, *Jews of Warsaw,* 94.

p.40   *appointed a Judenrat:* Ibid., 14.

p.40   *executing SS directives:* Ringelblum, *Notes from the Warsaw Ghetto,* 35.

p.40   *getting food:* Chaim Hasenfus, in Grynberg, *Words to Outlive Us.*

p.40   *a hundred and fifty Jews from Berlin:* Ringelblum, *Notes from the Warsaw Ghetto,* 126.

p.41   *ten centimeters wide:* Gutman, *Jews of Warsaw,* 29.

p.41   *dirty or wrinkled:* Ringelblum, *Notes from the Warsaw Ghetto,* 50.

p.41   *David wore his with pride:* Wisnia, interview with Zarlin.

p.41   *2.4 percent:* Gutman, *Jews of Warsaw,* 62.

p.42   *witty sayings in exchange:* Chaim Hasenfus, in Grynberg, *Words to Outlive Us.*

p.42   *Ghetto dwellers:* Gutman, *The Jews of Warsaw,* 68.

p.42   *particularly harsh winter:* Anonymous woman, in Grynberg, *Words to Outlive Us.*

p.43   *dragged out:* Natan Zelichower, in ibid.

p.43   *an uncle lived:* Wisnia, interview with Toltz, April 7, 2011.

Chapter Five: The Jewish Codex

p.44   *turn Tibor over:* Tibor Justh Indictment, Der Oberreichsanwalt beim Volksgerichtshof, Anklageschrift, Berlin, March 4, 1942.

p.45   *not yet considered:* Hana Kubátová, "Jewish Resistance in Slovakia," *Jewish Studies at the Central European University* 7 (2013): 509.

p.45   *nearly 90 percent:* Samuel Spitzer Restitution papers (Annex: Commentary Without Prejudice, note 2). Courtesy of Konrad Kwiet.

p.45   *new regime's secret services:* Ibid, files from Ústredňa štátnej bezpečnosti ("State Security Office of Bratislava"), January 24, 1942.

p.46   *In his mugshot:* Samuel Spitzer, interview with D. I. Ritch, March 7, 1996, VHA/USC-Shoah.

p.47   *a "colonization fee":* Ivan Kamenev, "The Deportation of Jewish Citizens from Slovakia in 1942," in *The Tragedy of the Jews of Slovakia,* ed. Jarek Mensfelt (Oswiecim: Auschwitz-Birkenau State Museum/Museum of the Slovak National Uprising), 116.

p.47   *He was wrong:* Spitzer, interview with Ritch, March 7, 1996.

p.47   *placards materialized:* Deborah Dwork and Robert Jan Van Pelt, *Auschwitz: 1270 to Present* (New York: W. W. Norton, 1997), 300.

p.47   *no more than 110 pounds:* Helen Tichauer, "The Women's Camp at Auschwitz-Birkenau: Method Within Madness," ed. Susan Cernyak-Spatz and Joel Shatzky (unpublished manuscript).

p.47   *saw her as merchandise:* Helen Tichauer, oral testimony, Imperial War Museum Archives, 2003.

p.47   *make this sacrifice:* Helen Tichauer, interview with David Boder, "Voices of the Holocaust," Illinois Institute of Technology, September 23, 1946. See *Approaching an Auschwitz Survivor,* ed. Jürgen Matth.us (Oxford: Oxford University Press, 2010) for most accurate translation.

p.48   *seemed plausible:* Helen Tichauer, interview with Joan Ringelheim, 2000, USHMM.

p.48   *mass conversions:* John S. Conway, "The Churches, the Slovak State and the Jews, 1939–1945," *The Slavonic and East European Review* 52, no. 126 (January 1974): 85–112.

p.48   *Der Grenzbote, reported:* "German Priests in Slovakia Baptize Jews to Save Them from Deportation," Jewish Telegraphic Agency, April 17, 1942.

p.48   *it wouldn't help:* Konrad Kwiet, interview with author, 2020.

p.48   *Nuremberg Race Laws:* "The Nuremberg Race Laws," Holocaust Encyclopedia, USHMM, https://encyclopedia.ushmm.org/content/en/article/the-nuremberg-race-laws, accessed April 3, 2023.

p.48   *"A Jew remains a Jew":* Conway, "The Churches, the Slovak State."

p.48   *made all the difference:* Tichauer, Imperial War Museum.

p.49   *bullet-producing factory:* "Bratislava During the Holocaust," Yad Vashem, https://www.yadvashem.org/yv/en/exhibitions/communities/bratislava/deportations.asp, accessed February 13, 2023.

p.49   *tailored wool winter coat:* Tichauer, "Women's Camp," 7.

p.49   *hardly anyone:* Yehoshua R. Büchler. "First in the Vale of Affliction: Slovakian Jewish Women in Auschwitz, 1942," *Holocaust and Genocide Studies* 10, no. 3 (1996): 299–325.

p.49   *resembled a soldier's dormitory:* Jeannette (Janka) Nagel (née Berger), in *Secretaries of Death,* ed: Lore Shelley (New York: Shengold Publishers, 1986), 23.

p.49   *surrounded by Hlinka guards:* Nechama Tec, "Recapturing the Past," in *Approaching an Auschwitz Survivor,* ed. Jürgen Matthäus (Oxford: Oxford University Press, 2010).

p.49   *not to speak:* Nagel in Shelley, *Secretaries of Death,* 23.

p.49   *a textbook:* Tichauer, "Women's Camp."

p.49   *instructed to probe:* Helen Tichauer, "Ladies First," *Voice of the Woman Survivor* 6, no. 2 (1989).

p.50   *hands inside her:* Tichauer, "Women's Camp," 7.

p.50   *narrow, bare rooms:* Nagel in Shelley, *Secretaries of Death,* 23.

p.50   *cold stone floor:* "Else Kellner," in Shelley, *Secretaries of Death,* 81.

p.50   *windows and gates locked:* "Rivka Paskus," in ibid., 205.

p.50   *blonde:* David Wisnia, interview with Brad Zarlin, 2006, USHMM.

p.50   *she was a Christian:* Susan Cernyak-Spatz and Joel Shatzky, "Record-Keeping for the Nazis—and Saving Lives," *Jewish Currents,* May 1, 2011.

p.50   *Katya Singer:* Her first name has also appeared as Katja, Katka and Katia, and her surname as Singerova.

p.51   *parched:* Tichauer, interview with Ringelheim, 2000.

p.51   *Dear Schani:* Postcard from Helen Tichauer to Samuel Spitzer, 1942. Courtesy of Konrad Kwiet.

p.51   *avoid transports:* Kwiet interview with author.

p.51   *a Saturday morning:* Buchler, "First in the Vale of Affliction."

p.51   *Head outside!:* Janka Nagel oral testimony, August 13, 1985, USHMM.

p.52   *798 women:* Danuta Czech, *Auschwitz Chronicle 1939-1945: From the Archives of The Auschwitz Memorial and The German Federal Archives,* (New York: Henry Holt and Company, 1990), 150.

p.52   *from a crack:* Tichauer, "Women's Camp," 7.

p.52   *find its way:* Nagel interview, USHMM.

p.52   *out of food:* Tichauer, interview with Ringelheim, 2000.

p.53   *train had arrived:* Tichauer, "Voices of the Holocaust."

Chapter Six: "You Go"

p.54   *Eliahu asked David:* David Wisnia, taped interview with Robin Black, August 13, 2007.

p.54   *tattered shoes:* "Warsaw's Jewish Quarter," USHMM Gallery, https://encyclopedia .ushmm.org/content/en/gallery/warsaw-photographs, accessed February 14, 2023.

p.55   *from a gramophone:* "Poverty in the Warsaw Ghetto," USHMM Gallery, https:// encyclopedia.ushmm.org/content/en/photo/poverty-in-the-warsaw-ghetto, accessed February 14, 2023.

p.56   *Epidemic Quarantine Area:* "Entrance to the Warsaw Ghetto," USHMM Gallery, https://encyclopedia.ushmm.org/content/en/photo/entrance-to-the-warsaw -ghetto, accessed February 14, 2023.

p.56   *he saw a pile:* Unless otherwise noted, descriptions come from David Wisnia from two lengthy interviews conducted with the author at his home in Levit-town, Pa., on January 19, 2018, and June 24, 2019.

p.56   *flung himself:* Wisnia, interview with Black, August 13, 2007.

p.57   *abrupt ends:* "250,000 in Poland Reported Killed," *New York Times,* July 27, 1942.

p.57   *working to "germanize":* "Nazis to Germanize Area of Poland," *New York Times,* August 18, 1942.

p.59   *the Jews of Sochaczew:* "Icek Brzezowski," Museum of Tolerance, http://www .museumoftolerance.com/education/teacher-resources/holocaust-resources /children-of-the-holocaust/icek-brzezowski.html, accessed February 13, 2023.

p.59   *resettle in the ghetto:* Sara Lewin Radomski, interview with Brad Zarlin, July 15, 2007, USHMM.

p.59   *had built:* David Wisnia, interview with Joseph Toltz (transcript), April 7, 2011, USHMM.

p.60   *one o'clock in the morning:* Wisnia, interview with Black, August 13, 2007.

p.61   *would take the floor:* Wisnia, interview with Toltz, April 7, 2011.

p.61   *surrounded by a wooden fence:* Geoffrey P. Megargee and Martin Dean, eds., *The United States Holocause Memorial Museum Encyclopedia of Camps and Ghettos, 1933—1945,* vol. 2, *Ghettos in German-Occupied Eastern Europe* (Bloomington: Indiana University Press, 2012), pt. A, 5.

p.62   *count for something:* Wisnia, interview with Zarlin.

p.62   *took to the streets:* Wisnia, interview with Toltz, April 7, 2011.

p.63   *some fifteen hundred others:* Danuta Czech, "Origins of the Camp, Its Construc-tion and Expansion," in *Auschwitz: Nazi Death Camp,* ed. Franciszek Piper and Teresa Swiebocka, trans. Douglas Selvage (Oswiecim: Auschwitz-Birkenau State Museum, 2009), 285.

p.63   *heard of a man:* Wisnia, interview with Zarlin.

p.64   *encircled by fire:* Helen Tichauer, interview with David Boder, "Voices of the Holocaust," Illinois Institute of Technology, September 23, 1946.

p.64   *wonder about self-sacrifice:* Richard Newman with Karen Kirtley, *Alma Rosé: Vienna to Auschwitz* (Pomptom Plains, Cambridge: Amadeus Press, 2003), 270.

Chapter Seven: An Ordinary Affair

p.67   *Los, los heraus und einreihen:* Helen Tichauer, interview with David Boder, "Voices of the Holocaust," Illinois Institute of Technology, September 23, 1946.

p.67   *the first time:* Helen Tichauer, "The Women's Camp at Auschwitz-Birkenau: Method Within Madness," ed. Susan Cernyak-Spatz and Joel Shatzky (unpublished manuscript), 7.

p.67   *an open field:* Deborah Dwork and Robert Jan Van Pelt, *Auschwitz: 1270 to Present* (New York: W. W. Norton, 1997), 301.

p.68   *she'd be among them:* Tichauer, "Voices of the Holocaust."

p.68   *massive steel gate:* Dwork and Van Pelt, *Auschwitz: 1270 to Present,* 169.

p.68   *She'd arrived:* Helen Tichauer, interview with Joan Ringelheim, 2000, USHMM.

p.68   *unremarkable city:* Rudolf Höss, *Death Dealer: The Memoirs of the SS Kommandant at Auschwitz,* ed. Steven Paskuly, trans. Andrew Pollinger (Buffalo: Prometheus, 1992), 118.

p.68   *at least three times:* "The History of the City of Oswiecim," Auschwitz-Birkenau Memorial and Museum, https://web.archive.org/web/20080202044740/http://www.auschwitz-muzeum.oswiecim.pl/html/eng/historia_KL/oswiecim_ok.html, accessed February 14, 2023.

p.68   *ravaging the region:* "About Castle Museum," Muzeum Zamek Oswiecimiu, https://muzeum-zamek.pl/strona/about-castle-museum.

p.69   *twelve thousand Polish residents:* William L. Shirer, *The Rise and Fall of the Third Reich: A History of Nazi Germany* (New York: Simon & Schuster, 2011), 936.

p.69   *Polish artillery barracks:* Danuta Czech, "Origins of the Camp, Its Construction and Expansion," in *Auschwitz: Nazi Death Camp,* ed. Franciszek Piper and Teresa Swiebocka, trans. Douglas Selvage (Ocwiecim: Auschwitz-Birkenau State Museum, 2009), 21–23.

p.69   *transit camp:* Dwork and Van Pelt, *Auschwitz: 1270 to Present,* 173–74.

p.69   *IG Farben:* "IG Farben," Auschwitz-Birkenau Memorial and Museum, http://auschwitz.org/en/history/auschwitz-iii/ig-farben, accessed February 13, 2023.

p.69   *would pay the SS:* Shirer, *Rise and Fall,* 937.

p.69   *Rudolf Höss:* The name is also sometimes spelled Rudolf Hess or Rudolf Höss.

p.69   *a loyal Nazi:* Höss, *Death Dealer,* 97.

p.70   *twenty brick barracks:* Tadeusz Iwaszko, "The Daily Life of the Prisoner," in Piper and Swiebocka, *Auschwitz: Nazi Death Camp,* 71.

p.70   *those around him:* Höss, *Death Dealer,* 118.

p.70   *could quarantine:* Danuta Czech, *Auschwitz Chronicle 1939-1945: From the Archives of The Auschwitz Memorial and The German Federal Archives,* (New York: Henry Holt and Company, 1990), 9-10.

p.70   *first group of Polish inmates:* Ibid., 13.

p.70   *renovate existing ones:* Czech, "Origins of the Camp," 21–23.

p.70   *they helped organize:* Bolesław Bicz, testimony, July 11, 1946, "Chronicles of Terror," Witold Pilecki Center for Totalitarian Studies, Warsaw.

p.71   *a special roll call:* Czech, *Auschwitz Chronicle 1939-1945,* 17-33.

p.71   *two letters a month:* Michael Berkowitz, interview with author, 2020.

p.71   *March of 1941:* Czech, *Auschwitz Chronicle 1939-1945,* 50.

p.71   *impressing IG Farben officials:* Dwork and Van Pelt, *Auschwitz: 1270 to Present,* 254.

p.72   *Himmler invited Höss:* Details surrounding Himmler's orders stem from Höss's memoir. Dwork and Van Pelt question the chronology of these events, given inconsistencies in Höss's testimonies; for further details, see *Auschwitz: 1270 to the Present.*

p.72   *the prime setting:* Höss: *Death Dealer,* 27.

p.72   *ninety-minute meeting:* Katrin Bennhold, "80 Years Ago the Nazis Planned the Final Solution. It Took 90 Minutes," *New York Times,* January 20, 2022.

p.72   *"Jews within our reach":* Höss, *Death Dealer,* 28.

p.72   *intended to wipe out:* Jacek Lachendro, in *Voices of Memory II: Soviet Prisoners of War in Auschwitz, trans. William Brand,* (Oswiecim: Auschwitz-Birkenau State Museum, 2016).

p.72   *the new subcamp:* Dwork and Van Pelt, *Auschwitz: 1270 to Present,* 255.

p.72   *brick by brick:* Ibid., 272.

p.73   *ease mattered:* Höss, *Death Dealer,* 28–29.

p.73   *about 10,900 prisoners:* Czech, "Origins of the Camp," 27.

p.73   *the ones to build them:* Höss, *Death Dealer,* 32.

p.73   *would run inside:* Dwork and Van Pelt, *Auschwitz: 1270 to Present,* 220.

p.74   *Soviet prisoners of war:* Höss, *Death Dealer,* 30.

p.74   *cellar of Block 11:* Czech, *Auschwitz Chronicle 1939-1945,* 85.

p.74   *Bunker I:* Franciszek Piper, "The Mass Extermination of Jews," in Piper and Swiebocka, *Auschwitz: Nazi Death Camp,* 167. See also Czech, *Auschwitz Chronicle 1939-1945,* 146; Dwork and Van Pelt, *Auschwitz: 1270 to Present,* 302.

p.74   *an electrified fence:* Sarah Helm, *Ravensbrück: Life and Death in Hitler's Concentration Camp for Women* (New York: Anchor, 2016), 181.

p.74   *exclusively female Ravensbrück:* Czech, *Auschwitz Chronicle 1939-1945,* 148.

p.75   *considered "asocials":* Helm, *Ravensbrück,* 24.

p.75   *carte blanche:* Höss, *Death Dealer,* 145.

p.75   *Slovakian Jewish women:* For a detailed account on these women's horrific journey, see Heather Dune Macadam, *999: The Extraordinary Young Women of the First Official Jewish Transport to Auschwitz* (New York: Citadel Press Books, 2020). According to Dune's extensive research only 997 girls were on that first transport.

p.75   *commands continued:* Tichauer, "Voices of the Holocaust."

p.75   *Blood seeped:* Magda Blau, interview with Linda Kuzmack, June 11, 1990, USHMM.

p.75–76   *Eyebrows and pubic hair:* Tichauer, "Voices of the Holocaust."

p.76   *stood on chairs:* Blau, interview with Kuzmack, June 11, 1990.

p.76   *disinfected, then stockpiled:* Tichauer, "Voices of the Holocaust."

p.76   *Who are these lunatics:* Blau, interview with Kuzmack, June 11, 1990.

p.76   *Russian POW uniforms:* Helm, *Ravensbrück,* xvii.

p.76   *cotton scraps:* Tichauer, "Voices of the Holocaust."

p.76   *caked with the blood:* Konrad Kwiet, "Designing Survival," in *Approaching an Auschwitz Survivor,* ed. Jürgen Matthäus (Oxford: Oxford University Press, 2010), 14.

p.76   *perforated with bullet holes:* Susan Cernyak-Spatz, *Protective Custody Prisoner 34042* (Cortland, NY: N and S Publishers, 2005).

p.76   *her feet were so small:* Tichauer, interview with Ringelheim, 2000.

p.76   *layer of old straw:* Tichauer, "Voices of the Holocaust."

p.77   *Zippi wondered:* Tichauer, "Voices of the Holocaust."

p.77   *Johanna Langefeld:* Czech, "Origins of the Camp," 148.

p.78   *twirled on the spot:* Blau, interview with Kuzmack, June 11, 1990.

p.78   *Zippi despaired:* Tichauer, "Voices of the Holocaust,"

p.78   *Prisoner 2286:* Tichauer, interview with Ringelheim, 2000.

p.78   *her left elbow:* Tichauer, "Voices of the Holocaust."

NOTES

p.78   *Block 9 in Auschwitz I:* Tichauer, interview with Ringelheim, 2000.

p.79   *twelve hundred inmates:* Blau interview with Kuzmack, June 11, 1990.

p.79   *twenty-two toilets:* Iwaszko, "Daily Life," 73.

p.79   *They'd been upgraded:* Tichauer, "Voices of the Holocaust."

p.79   *78 by 31 inches:* Iwaszko, "Daily Life," 72 (which uses 200 by 80 centimeters).

p.79   *chaos seemed total:* Höss, *Death Dealer,* 148.

p.79   *drank infected water:* Tichauer, interview with Ringelheim, 2000.

p.79   *they collected rainwater:* Tichauer, "Women's Camp," 103.

p.79   *Lice and bedbugs:* Höss, *Death Dealer,* 147.

p.79   *frozen urine:* Marie Schwartzman, interview with Gail Schwartz, August 23, 1994, USHMM.

p.79   *A rusty barrel:* Ruth Krautwirth Meyerowitz, interview with Linda G. Kuzmack, February 20, 1990, USHMM.

p.80   *rumors spread:* "Irene Schwarz," in *Secretaries of Death,* ed. Lore Shelley (New York: Shengold Publishers, 1986), 14.

p.80   *gassed to death at Birkenau:* Tichauer, interview with Ringelheim, 2000.

p.80   *it might be laced:* Blau, interview with Kuzmack, June 11, 1990.

p.80   *spiked with bromide:* Jeannette (Janka) Nagel (née Berger), in Shelley, *Secretaries of Death,* 25.

p.80   *daring to approach:* Helen Tichauer, unpublished interview with Konrad Kwiet, June 4, 2007.

p.80   *coming to realize:* Nechama Tec, "Recapturing the Past," in Matthäus, *Approaching an Auschwitz Survivor,* 37.

p.80   *sought companionship:* Tichauer, interview with Kwiet, June 4, 2007.

p.81   *part of a hunt:* Tichauer, interview with Ringelheim, 2000.

p.81   *using the stumps:* Blau, interview with Kuzmack, June 11, 1990.

p.81   *death certificates:* Schwarz, in Shelley, *Secretaries of Death,* 13.

p.81   *the real killer:* Blau, interview with Kuzmack, June 11, 1990.

p.81   *an agricultural estate:* Dwork and Van Pelt, *Auschwitz: 1270 to Present,* 191.

p.81   *clean muddied bricks:* Nagel, in Shelley, *Secretaries of Death,* 25.

p.81   *work with steamrollers:* Meyerowitz, interview with Kuzmack, 1990

p.82   *paid off:* Piper, "Prisoner Labor," in *Auschwitz: Nazi Death Camp,* 107.

p.82   *flogged, then killed:* Wilma Steindling, "A Miracle Saved Me from the Gas at Auschwitz," Wiener-HL, Index Number: P.III.g. (France) No. 791, February 1958.

p.82   *volunteered to join:* Tichauer, "Women's Camp," 12.

p.83   *one of her professors:* Katerina Singer, "Testimony in the criminal proceedings against the late Prof. Carl Clauberg," Wiener-HL, Index Number: P.III.h (Auschwitz) No. 881, June 4, 1957.

p.83   *he recognized Katya:* Susan Cernyak-Spatz and Joel Shatzky, "Record-Keeping for the Nazis—and Saving Lives," *Jewish Currents,* May 1, 2011.

p.84   *Katya's bookkeeping training:* Tichauer, interview with Ringelheim, 2000.

p.84   *creating order within the chaos:* Cernyak-Spatz and Shatzky, "Record-Keeping."

p.84   *she was just twenty-two:* Singer's KL Stutthof Registration card states date of birth as March 12, 1920.

p.84   *Langefeld was struggling:* Helm, *Ravensbrück,* 180–81.

p.84   *sneaking around:* Höss, *Death Dealer,* 149; see also Helm, *Ravensbrück.*

p.84   *senior prisoner:* Iwaszko, "Daily Life," 70.

p.84   *she was put in charge:* Tichauer, interview with Ringelheim, 2000.

p.85   *14,624 prisoners:* Czech, *Auschwitz Chronicle 1939-1945,* 161.

NOTES

p.85   *nearly two miles:* Czech, "Origins of the Camp," 30.

p.85   *on their bare feet:* Tichauer, interview with Ringelheim, 2000.

p.85   *on the wooden clogs:* Erwin Tichauer, *Skull and Zebra Suits: A Berlin Jew in Auschwitz,* ed. Jürgen Matthaus, trans. Anabel Aliaga-Buchenau (Berlin: Metropol, 2000), 70.

p.85   *eleven hours:* Czech, *Auschwitz Chronicle 1939-1945,* 151.

p.85   *With bare hands:* Dwork and Van Pelt, *Auschwitz: 1270 to Present,* 272.

p.85   *with leather whips:* Józef Garliński, *Fighting Auschwitz: The Resistance Movement in the Concentration Camp* (Los Angeles: Aquila Polonica, 2018).

p.85   *253 prefabricated wooden huts:* Dwork and Van Pelt, *Auschwitz: 1270 to Present,* 272.

p.85   *toss down bricks:* Blau, interview with Kuzmack, June 11, 1990.

p.86   *dying by the thousands:* Czech, *Auschwitz Chronicle 1939-1945.*

p.86   *had to exhibit health:* Tichauer, interview with Ringelheim, 2000.

p.86   *"you ugly Jew":* Tichauer, "Women's Camp," 108.

p.86   *instructed to return:* Ibid., 19.

p.87   *she only wanted a reprieve:* Tichauer, interview with Ringelheim, 2000.

p.87   *Zippi told Eva:* Helen Tichauer, unpublished interview with Peter Hellman, November 11, 2019.

p.87   *Stay at home:* Tichauer, interview with Ringelheim, 2000.

p.88   *mix paint from dry material:* Helen Tichauer, unpublished interview with Peter Hellman, November 19, 2010.

p.88   *the perfect job:* Tichauer, interview with Ringelheim, 2000.

p.88   *they were getting into:* Tichauer, "Women's Camp," 15.

p.88   *brushes and drying agents:* Tichauer, interview with Hellman, November 19, 2010.

p.88   *moving fast enough:* Tichauer, "Women's Camp," 15.

p.89   *the ragged dresses:* Tichauer, "Voices of the Holocaust."

p.89   *two-centimeter-thick line:* Kwiet, "Designing Survival," 17.

p.89   *strip of clothing:* Tichauer, "Voices of the Holocaust."

p.89   *single prisoners to 1,004:* Czech, *Auschwitz Chronicle 1939-1945,* 191.

p.89   *Juden raus schnell!:* Hermann Langbein, *People in Auschwitz,* trans. Harry Zohn (Chapel Hill: University of North Carolina Press, 2004).

p.89   *holding their dogs:* Michael Vogel, interview with Linda G. Kuzmack, July 14, 1989, USHMM.

p.91   *her dead children:* Tecia Grynberg, interview with Jill Margo, June 6, 1991, USHMM.

p.91   *greenery would conceal:* "The Death of Silent Witnesses to History," Auschwitz–Birkenau Memorial and Museum, March 27, 2007, http://auschwitz.org/en/museum/news/the-death-of-silent-witnesses-to-history,466.html, accessed April 10, 2023.

p.92   *Zippi heard:* Tichauer, "Voices of the Holocaust."

p.92   *eight thousand had vanished:* Czech, "Origins of Camp," 31: According to camp documents, 36,285 Polish and Soviet prisoners had been held at the camp between May 20, 1940, and January 31, 1942. According to reports, 2,435 were transferred, 76 were freed, 5 escaped, and 1,755 were killed. But only 11,449 were accounted for.

p.92   *apple and pear trees:* "The Death of Silent Witnesses to History."

p.92   *a gas chamber:* Piper, "Mass Extermination of Jews," 168.

p.92   *permission to enter:* Tichauer, "Voices of the Holocaust."

NOTES

p.92 *that exact distance:* Anna Palarczyk Testimony, First Frankfurt Auschwitz Trial, "Criminal Case Against Mulka and Others," 4 Ks 2/63 Frankfurt am Main District Court, October 15, 1964, p. 11.

p.93 *each day at noon:* Stanisława Rachwał, testimony, July 25, 1945, "Chronicles of Terror," Witold Pilecki Center for Totalitarian Studies.

p.93 *combs and compacts:* Meyerowitz, interview with Kuzmack, February 20, 1990.

p.93 *covered in pus:* Tichauer, interview with Ringelheim, 2000.

p.93 *collected "goodies":* Tichauer, interview with Ringelheim, 2000.

p.94 *pushed her off:* Tichauer, "Women's Camp."

p.94 *fresh data was necessary:* Tec, "Recapturing the Past," 40.

p.94 *a "bad assignment":* Michael Berkowitz, interview with author, February 19, 2021.

p.95 *move to Budy:* Tichauer, interview with Ringelheim, 2000.

p.95 *one prisoner's salvation could be another's damnation:* Atina Grossman, interview with author. See also my "Lovers in Auschwitz, Reunited 72 Years Later," *New York Times,* December 8, 2019.

p.95 *the cleanest quarters:* Tichauer, "Voices of the Holocaust."

p.95 *around four o'clock:* Iwaszko, "Daily Life," 81.

p.96 *She tried:* Tichauer, "Women's Camp."

p.96 *sent from the infirmary:* Czech, *Auschwitz Chronicle 1939-1945,* 229.

p.96 *first official gas chambers:* "Little White House," Auschwitz-Birkenau Memorial and Museum, http://70.auschwitz.org/index.php?option=com_content&view=article&id=304&Itemid=179&lang=en, accessed April 2, 2023.

p.96 *two thousand prisoners:* "Gas Chambers," Auschwitz-Birkenau Memorial and Museum, http://auschwitz.org/en/history/auschwitz-and-shoah/gas-chambers, accessed February 14, 2023.

p.96 *hundred death certificates:* Schwarz, in Shelley, *Secretaries of Death,* 12.

p.96 *Selections were routine:* Czech, *Auschwitz Chronicle 1939-1945,* 191-237.

p.96 *likely contagious:* Tec, "Recapturing the Past," 41.

p.97 *water or nourishment:* Tichauer, "Voices of the Holocaust."

p.97 *brought Zippi polluted water:* Tichauer, "Women's Camp," 20.

p.97 *sick with typhus:* Tichauer, "Voices of the Holocaust."

p.97 *another eight hundred women:* Czech, *Auschwitz Chronicle 1939-1945,* 233.

p.97 *in his own hell:* Indictment, Der Oberreichsanwalt beim Volksgerichtshof, Anklageschrift, Berlin, March 4, 1942.

p.97 *Stadelheim Prison:* Tibor Justh Death Certificate, the Arolsen Archives, formerly the International Tracing Service archive (ITS), located in Bad Arolsen, Germany.

p.98 *carrying out executions:* See, for example "Hans Scholl's Execution" and "Sophie Scholl's Execution," White Rose History, https://whiterosehistory.com/1943/02/22/hans-scholls-execution/ and https://whiterosehistory.com/1943/02/23/execution-record-sophie-scholl/, accessed April 1, 2023.

Chapter Eight: "God Is with Us"

p.99 *December of 1942:* Danuta Czech, *Auschwitz Chronicle 1939-1945: From the Archives of The Auschwitz Memorial and The German Federal Archives,* (New York: Henry Holt and Company, 1990), 285.

NOTES

p.100   *Gott ist mit uns:* The inscription that David recalled would have been on the belt buckle of a Wehrmacht soldier. An SS-man's belt buckle inscription would have read *Meine Ehre heisst Treue* ("My honor is loyalty").

p.100   *The unintended provocation:* David Wisnia, interview with Brad Zarlin, 2006, USHMM.

p.100   *soon raw and bloody:* David Wisnia, interview with Joseph Toltz (transcript), April 7, 2011.

p.101   *publicly executed:* Czech, *Auschwitz Chronicle 1939-1945.*

p.101   *as best they could:* Wisnia, interview with Toltz, April 7, 2011.

p.101   *yelled out a quick Hier!:* Witold Pilecki, *The Auschwitz Volunteer: Beyond Bravery,* trans. Jarek Garlinski (Los Angeles: Aquila Polonica, 2014).

p.101   *chopping down trees:* Anonymous eyewitness account, "The Terrors of the Evacuation of Auschwitz in January 1945," Wiener-HL, Index Number: P.III.h. No. 653, 1957.

p.102   *water covered the floor* Erwin Tichauer, *Skull and Zebra Suits: A Berlin Jew in Auschwitz,* ed. Jürgen Matthäus, trans. Anabel Aliaga-Buchenau (Berlin: Metropol, 2000), 30.

p.103   *As far as he knew:* Wisnia, interview with Toltz, April 7, 2011.

p.103   *the Sonderkommando:* "Shoah Resource Center," Yad Vashem, https://www .yadvashem.org/odot_pdf/microsoft%20word%20-%206031.pdf, accessed April 28, 2023.

p.103   *innocuous enough:* Franciszek Piper, "The Mass Extermination of Jews," in Piper and Swiebocka, *Auschwitz: Nazi Death Camp,* 167.

p.103–104   *in a special locker:* Henryk Mandelbaum, testimony, September 25, 1946, "Chronicles of Terror," Witold Pilecki Center for Totalitarian Studies, Warsaw.

p.104   *two large handles:* Szlama Dragon, testimony, May 10 and 11, 1945, "Chronicles of Terror." Witold Pilecki Center for Totalitarian Studies.

p.104   *nailed shut with boards:* Zalmen Gradowski, *From the Heart of Hell: Manuscripts of a Sonderkommando Prisoner, Found in Auschwitz,* trans. Barry Smerin and Janina Wurbs, (Osweicim: Auschwitz-Birkenau State Museum), 125.

p.104   *Scheinmetz, mach das fertig:* Dragon testimony.

p.104   *before the gas was released:* Jakub Wolman, testimony, April 13 and 14, 1945, "Chronicles of Terror," Witold Pilecki Center for Totalitarian Studies.

p.104   *basement of Block 11:* Piper, "Mass Extermination of Jews," 169.

p.104   *the physically strongest:* Gradowski, *From the Heart of Hell,* 9.

p.104   *cleaning up the gas chambers:* Dragon testimony.

p.105   *With each moment:* Wisnia, interview with Zarlin.

p.106   *"Joseph! Joseph!,":* Music by Nellie Casman, Saul Chaplin, Sammy Cahn, and Samuel Steinberg.

p.106   *the name of his Blockälteste:* Wisnia, interview with Zarlin.

p.106   *all that mattered was his voice:* Wisnia, interview with Toltz, April 7, 2011.

p.106   *sometimes tapped by guards:* Anonymous, "The Terrors of the Evacuation."

p.107   *bathhouses with showers:* Andrzej Strzelecki, "The History, Role and Operation of the 'Central Camp Sauna' in Auschwitz II-Birkenau," in *The Architecture of Crime: The "Central Camp Sauna" in Auschwitz II-Birkenau,* ed. Teresa Swiebocka, trans. William Brand (Oswiecim: Auschwitz-Birkenau State Museum, 2001), 13.

p.107   *called Canada:* Tadeusz Iwaszko, "Deportation to the Camp and Registration of Prisoners," in Piper and Swiebocka, *Auschwitz: Nazi Death Camp,* 59.

p.107   *"clean side," disinfecting uniforms:* Strzelecki, "The History, Role and Operation," 14.

p.108   *strap on a gas mask:* Wisnia, interview with Toltz, April 7, 2011.

p.108   *200-gram cans:* Jean-Claude Pressac, *Auschwitz: Technique and Operation of the Gas Chambers,* trans. Peter Moss (New York: Beate Klarsfeld Foundation, 1989), 27.

p.108   *still worn out and dirty:* Strzelecki, "The History, Role and Operation," 14.

p.108   *devoured a salami slice:* Wisnia, interview with Toltz, April 7, 2011.

p.108   *swapped the bill:* Ibid. David said he had a tailored suit. According to Dr. Piotr Setkiewicz, head of Auschwitz research at the Auschwitz-Birkenau State Museum, it was likely a better quality, cleaner uniform than most others.

p.109   *a collective silence:* Wisnia, interview with Zarlin.

p.109   *disabled for life:* Jeshayahu Kalfuss, interview with Peter Wortsman, February 28, 1975, USHMM. Name has also been documented as Szaja and Isaiah Kalfus.

p.110   *some of his own rations:* Wisnia, interview with Zarlin.

p.111   *Officers lined up:* Wisnia, interview with Robin Black, August 13, 2007.

Chapter Nine: The Number Book

p.113   *drive in, drive out:* Helen Tichauer, interview with David Boder, "Voices of the Holocaust," Illinois Institute of Technology, September 23, 1946.

p.113   *secretary to Paul Heinrich Müller:* Helen Tichauer and Anna Palarczyk. joint interview with Joan Ringelheim, August 16–17, 1996, USHMM.

p.114   *took her to the barracks:* Helen Tichauer, interview with Joan Ringelheim, 2000, USHMM. See also Tichauer, "Voices of the Holocaust."

p.114   *two thousand prisoners:* Danuta Czech, *Auschwitz Chronicle 1939-1945: From the Archives of The Auschwitz Memorial and The German Federal Archives,* (New York: Henry Holt and Company, 1990), 247.

p.115   *shoes they left behind:* Helen Tichauer, "The Women's Camp at Auschwitz-Birkenau: Method Within Madness," ed. Susan Cernyak-Spatz and Joel Shatzky (unpublished manuscript), 20.

p.115   *She made herself:* Tichauer, "Voices of the Holocaust."

p.115   *and found Katya:* Tichauer, interview with Ringelheim, 2000.

p.115   *barely even recall moving:* Tichauer and Palarczyk, interview with Ringelheim, August 16–17, 1996.

p.115   *an extra helping:* Tichauer, "Women's Camp," 24.

p.115   *bouillon cubes:* Ibid., 113-115.

p.116   *Zippi followed Katya:* Tichauer, interview with Ringelheim, 2000.

p.116   *look the part:* Konrad Kwiet, "Designing Survival," in *Approaching an Auschwitz Survivor,* ed. Jürgen Matthäus (Oxford: Oxford University Press, 2010), 16.

p.116   *she was Frau Singer:* Richard Newman with Karen Kirtley, *Alma Rosé: Vienna to Auschwitz* (Portland: Amadeus Press, 2000), 287.

p.116   *registration clerk:* Nechama Tec, "Recapturing the Past," in Matthäus, *Approaching an Auschwitz Survivor,* 40.

p.116   *reassigned to Ravensbrück:* Czech, *Auschwitz Chronicle 1939-1945,* 251.

p.116   *minor offenses:* Zofia Woźniak, testimony, September 16, 1947, "Chronicles of Terror," Witold Pilecki Center for Totalitarian Studies, Warsaw.

p.117   *She kicked prisoners:* Stanisława Rachwał, testimony, July 25, 1945, "Chronicles of Terror," Witold Pilecki Center for Totalitarian Studies.

p.117   *until they were unconscious:* Stanisława Marchwicka, testimony, August 5, 1947, "Chronicles of Terror," Witold Pilecki Center for Totalitarian Studies.

p.117   *victims were subhuman:* Susan Cernyak-Spatz and Joel Shatzky, "Record-Keeping for the Nazis—and Saving Lives," *Jewish Currents,* May 1, 2011. See also Maria

Gątkiewicz, testimony, August 5, 1947, "Chronicles of Terror," Witold Pilecki Center for Totalitarian Studies.

p.117 *torture prisoners:* Pola Blum, testimony, April 4, 1947, "Chronicles of Terror," Witold Pilecki Center for Totalitarian Studies.

p.117 *scalding soup:* Genowefa Ułan, testimony, June 3, 1947, "Chronicles of Terror," Witold Pilecki Center for Totalitarian Studies.

p.117 *took all the female inmates:* Anna Palarczyk, interview with Joan Ringelheim, 1996, USHMM.

p.117 *each block's Rapportführer:* "Prisoner Functionaries—Positions," Wollheim Memorial, Frankfurt am Main, http://www.wollheim-memorial.de/en/funktionshaeft linge_en, accessed April 28, 2023.

p.118 *very own chambermaid:* Susan Cernyak-Spatz, *Protective Custody Prisoner 34042* (Cortland, N.Y.: N and S Publishers, 2005), 86.

p.118 *gifts from prisoners:* Cernyak-Spatz and Shatzky, "Record-Keeping."

p.118 *Gerhard Palitzsch:* Hermann Langbein, *People in Auschwitz,* trans. Harry Zohn (Chapel Hill: University of North Carolina Press, 2004), 427.

p.118 *red with blood:* Karel Sperber, testimony, May 16, 1946, "Chronicles of Terror," Witold Pilecki Center for Totalitarian Studies.

p.118 *back of each prisoner's skull:* Tadeusz Bałut, testimony, August 18, 1945, "Chronicles of Terror," Witold Pilecki Center for Totalitarian Studies.

p.118 *"the true boss":* Rudolf Höss, *Death Dealer: The Memoirs of the SS Kommandant at Auschwitz,* ed. Steven Paskuly, trans. Andrew Pollinger (Buffalo: Prometheus, 1992), 309.

p.120 *she tried to talk him:* Cernyak-Spatz and Shatzky, "Record-Keeping."

p.120 *died of typhus:* Czech, *Auschwitz Chronicle 1939-1945,* 264.

p.120 *On September 21, 1942:* Ibid., 242.

p.120 *in the pine forest:* "The Death of Silent Witnesses to History," Auschwitz-Birkenau Memorial and Museum, http://auschwitz.org/en/museum/news/the-death-of -silent-witnesses-to-history,466.html, accessed February 15, 2023.

p.120 *technology of human cremation:* Frantiszek Piper, "The Mass Extermination of Jews," in Piper and Swiebocka, *Auschwitz: Nazi Death Camp,* 169.

p.120 *pervaded the camp:* Czech, *Auschwitz Chronicle 1939-1945,* 242.

p.120 *a striped dress:* Tichauer, "Women's Camp."

p.120 *on prisoners' uniforms:* Tichauer, "Voices of the Holocaust."

p.120 *discarded food:* Tichauer, "Women's Camp," 25, 115, 26.

p.121 *the number book:* Tichauer, "Voices of the Holocaust."

p.121 *"unknown corpses":* Tichauer, "Women's Camp," 75.

p.121 *None were spared:* Tichauer, "Voices of the Holocaust."

p.122 *the walking dead:* Tichauer, interview with Ringelheim, 2000.

p.122 *her friend Magda Hellinger:* Magda Hellinger and Maya Lee with David Brewster, *The Nazis Knew My Name: A Remarkable Story of Survival and Courage in Auschwitz* (New York: Atria, 2022).

p.122 *transferring numbers:* Tichauer and Palarczyk, interview with Ringelheim, August 16–17, 1996.

p.122 *she would not survive:* Tichauer, interview with Ringelheim, 2000.

p.122 *prisoners later claimed:* Michael Berkowitz, *The Crime of My Very Existence* (Berkeley: University of California Press, 2007), 101.

p.122 *murder ninety inmates:* Czech, *Auschwitz Chronicle 1939-1945,* 249.

p.122–123 *called a bloodbath:* Höss, *Death Dealer,* 145.

p.123   *strewn on the ground:* Berkowitz, *Crime of My Very Existence,* 99.

p.123   *a "pre–roll call":* Cernyak-Spatz and Shatzky, "Record-Keeping."

p.123   *three columns:* Helen Tichauer, interview with Joan Ringelheim, August 6, 2005, USHMM.

p.123   *had to be precise:* Cernyak-Spatz and Shatzky, "Record-Keeping."

p.123   *just about three minutes:* Tichauer, interview with Ringelheim, 2000.

p.123   *Zippi believed that inmates:* Tichauer asserted this in various interviews with both Ringelheim and Kwiet. Susan Cerynak-Spatz was skeptical.

p.123   *enough clothes:* Tichauer, interview with Ringelheim, 2000.

p.124   *a specialized office:* Tichauer, "Women's Camp," 33.

p.124   *permission to organize:* Tichauer, interview with Ringelheim, 2000.

p.124   *transfer women:* Cernyak-Spatz and Shatzky, "Record-Keeping."

p.124   *bestowing upon her more responsibility:* Tichauer, "Voices of the Holocaust."

p.124   *run the camp administration:* Tichauer, interview with Ringelheim, 2000.

p.124   *a stove, and benches:* Tichauer, "Women's Camp," 28.

p.124   *heat up glue:* Ibid., 46.

p.125   *Hössler asked for diagrams:* Tichauer, "Voices of the Holocaust."

p.125   *eighteen to twenty changes:* Tichauer, interview with Ringelheim, 2000.

p.125   *officers wanted to know:* Cernyak-Spatz and Shatzky, "Record-Keeping."

p.125   *widening her connections:* Tichauer, "Women's Camp," 29.

p.125   *Zippi aus der Schreibstube:* Tec, "Recapturing the Past."

p.125   *small favors:* Tichauer, "Women's Camp," 29-48.

p.126   *rub it on their wounds:* Tichauer, interview with Ringelheim, 2000.

p.126   *On the sly:* Tec, "Recapturing the Past," 44.

p.127   *in the homes of SS:* Piotr Setkiewicz, *The Private Lives of the Auschwitz SS,* trans. William Brand, (Oswiecim: Auschwitz-Birkenau State Museum, 2014).

p.127   *look for anyone:* Tichauer, "Women's Camp," 90-94.

p.127   *had originally earmarked:* "General Information," The State Museum at Majdanek, https://www.majdanek.eu/en/history/general_information/1, accessed April 2, 2023.

p.127   *The three Spitzer men:* Samuel Spitzer restitution records. Courtesy of Konrad Kwiet.

p.127   *seeing her family:* Tichauer, "Voices of the Holocaust."

p.128   *she decided to stay:* Helen Tichauer, interview with Peter Hellman, November 19, 2010.

p.128   *a trained killer:* Tichauer, interview with Ringelheim, August 6, 2005.

p.128   *Zippi was safe:* Tichauer, interview with Ringelheim, 2000.

p.129   *take his photograph:* Michael Berkowitz, interview with author, 2021.

p.129   *Maybe that was for the best:* Postcard from Helen Tichauer to Sam Spitzer, June 1943.

p.129   *Save your heart:* Tichauer, interview with Ringelheim, 2000.

p.130   *hot showers alone:* Tichauer, "Women's Camp," 34.

p.130   *she saw two horses:* Ibid., 41–42.

p.131   *filled her with sorrow:* Tec, "Resilience and Courage," 127.

Chapter Ten: The Hanging

p.135   *David knew:* Unless otherwise noted, descriptions come from David Wisnia from two lengthy interviews conducted with the author at his home in Levittown, Pa., on January 19, 2018, and June 24, 2019.

p.135   *likely in early 1943:* David was not sure of exactly when he and Zippi made their initial contact. Given the timing of when he was sentenced to the Penal Ward, it's likely they began speaking with each other before March of 1943.

p.136   *one romantic liaison:* David Wisnia, taped interview with Robin Black, August 13, 2007.

p.137   *seven hundred and fifty thousand Red Army soldiers:* John Spencer and Jayson Geroux, "Urban Warfare Project Case Studies Series: Case Study #1—Stanlingrad" Modern War Institute at West Point, June 28, 2021, https://mwi.usma.edu/urban-warfare-project-case-study-1-battle-of-stalingrad/, accessed January 4, 2023.

p.137   *ninety-one thousand survivors:* William L. Shirer, *The Rise and Fall of the Third Reich: A History of Nazi Germany* (New York: Simon & Schuster, 2011), 1306.

p.137   *2,266 prisoners from various ghettos:* Danuta Czech, *Auschwitz Chronicle 1939-1945: From the Archives of The Auschwitz Memorial and The German Federal Archives,* (New York: Henry Holt and Company, 1990), 321.

p.137   *to help those displaced:* Cordell Hull, "The Secretary of State to President Roosevelt," May 7, 1943, Department of State, Office of the Historian, 548.G1 /201, https://history.state.gov/historicaldocuments/frus1943v01/d141, accessed February 16, 2023.

p.137–138   *11,153 Europeans:* "Historical Statistics of the United States, 1789–1945," United States Census Bureau, https://www2.census.gov/library/publications /1949/compendia/hist_stats_1789-1945/hist_stats_1789-1945-chB.pdf, accessed January 4, 2023.

p.138   *realized in a panic:* David Wisnia, interview with Brad Zarlin, USHMM.

p.139   *mix of rain and snow:* Wisnia, interview with Black, August 13, 2007.

p.139   *as many as fifty thousand:* David Wisnia, interview with Joseph Toltz (transcript), April 7.

p.139   *willed his body:* Wisnia, interview with Zarlin.

p.139   *winked at David:* Wisnia, interview with Black, August 13, 2007.

p.141   *Strafkompanie:* Wisnia, interview with Zarlin.

p.141   *on March 19, 1943:* United Restitution Organization documentation from May 23, 1958.

p.141   *the next three months:* Wisnia, interview with Zarlin.

p.141   *the most serious crimes:* Anonymous eyewitness account, "The Terrors of the Evacuation of Auschwitz in January 1945," Wiener-HL, Index Number: P. III.h. No. 653, 1957.

p.141   *brutal torture tactics:* Józef Kret, testimony, August 20, 1947, "Chronicles of Terror," Witold Pilecki Center for Totalitarian Studies, Warsaw.

p.141   *"standing cells":* Franciszek Piper, "Living Conditions as Methods of Exterminating Prisoners," in *Auschwitz: Nazi Death Camp,* ed. Franciszek Piper and Teresa Swiebocka, trans. Douglas Selvage (Oswiecim: Auschwitz-Birkenau State Museum, 2009), 148.

p.141   *had been relocated:* The Penal Company," Auschwitz-Birkenau Memorial and Museum, https://www.auschwitz.org/en/history/punishments-and-executions/the -penal-company/, accessed April 10, 2023.

p.141   *more grueling hours:* Piper, "Living Conditions as Methods of Exterminating," 149–50.

p.141   *Jewish men's testicles:* Witold Pilecki, *The Auschwitz Volunteer: Beyond Bravery,* trans. Jarek Garlinski (Los Angeles: Aquila Polonica, 2014), 65.

p.141   *whipped on the back:* Wisnia, interview with Black, August 13, 2007.

NOTES

Chapter Eleven: An Understanding

p.143   *by May of 1943:* Helen Tichauer and Anna Palarczyk, joint interview with Joan Ringelheim, August 16–17, 1996, USHMM.

p.143   *the nerve center:* Susan Cernyak-Spatz, *Protective Custody Prisoner 34042* (Cortland, N.Y.: N and S Publishers, 2005).

p.143   *their Blockälteste:* Anna Palarczyk, interview with Joan Ringelheim, 1996, USHMM.

p.143   *women she oversaw:* Nechama Tec, "Recapturing the Past," in *Approaching an Auschwitz Survivor,* ed. Jürgen Matthäus (Oxford: Oxford University Press, 2010), 42.

p.144   *treat them well:* Tichauer and Palarczyk, interview with Ringelheim, August 16–17, 1996.

p.144   *congested and despondent:* Palarczyk, interview with Ringelheim, 1996.

p.145   *wasn't quite sure:* Helen Tichauer, interview with Joan Ringelheim, 2000, USHMM.

p.145   *dim light:* Helen Tichauer, "The Women's Camp at Auschwitz-Birkenau: Method Within Madness," ed. Susan Cernyak-Spatz and Joel Shatzky (unpublished manuscript), 127.

p.145   *jumped on a table:* Tichauer, interview with Ringelheim, 2000.

p.145   *sharing a barrack:* Palarczyk, interview with Ringelheim, 1996.

p.145   *fluent French, German, and Polish:* Tichauer, "Women's Camp," 127.

p.145   *roamed the camp:* Tichauer, interview with Ringelheim, 2000.

p.145   *a special hike:* Tichauer, "Women's Camp," 35.

p.146   *from the sidelines:* Anita Lasker-Wallfisch interview, USHMM via Imperial War Museum, March 19, 1991.

p.147   *It will grow back:* Carola Steinhardt, interview with Joan Ringelheim, June 3, 1996, USHMM.

p.147   *their cardex system:* Tichauer, interview with Ringelheim, 2000.

p.147   *appear to satisfy:* Susan Cernyak-Spatz and Joel Shatzky, "Record-Keeping for the Nazis—and Saving Lives," *Jewish Currents,* May 1, 2011.

p.147   *hope and encouragement:* Anonymous testimony, "Mala Zimetbaum: An Appreciation of a Historic Resistance Fighter," Wiener -HL, 1957.

p.148   *felt she used her position:* Stanisława Rachwał, testimony, July 25, 1945, "Chronicles of Terror," Witold Pilecki Center for Totalitarian Studies, Warsaw.

p.148   *"swollen head":* Palarczyk, interview with Ringelheim, 1996.

p.148   *"human feelings":* Vera Alexander, witness, the Trial of Adolf Eichmann, sess. 71, part 1, June 8, 1961, USHMM.

p.148   *another adage:* Tichauer, interview with Ringelheim, 2000.

p.148   *Henryk Porębski, an electrician:* Henryk Porebski, testimony, February 28, 1947, "Chronicles of Terror," Witold Pilecki Center for Totalitarian Studies.

p.148   *as far as Zippi knew:* Tichauer, interview with Ringelheim, 2000.

p.149   *with regular meetings:* Yisrael Gutman, *The Jews of Warsaw, 1939–1943: Ghetto, Underground Revolt,* trans. Ina Friedman (Bloomington: Indiana University Press, 1989), 178–79.

p.149   *the Poles were among:* Tichauer, interview with Ringelheim, 2000.

p.150   *he later wrote:* Pilecki, *The Auschwitz Volunteer.*

p.150   *top of the list:* Józef Garliński, *Fighting Auschwitz: The Resistance Movement in the Concentration Camp* (Los Angeles: Aquila Polonica, 2018).

NOTES

p.150   *a very small number:* "Releases from the Camp," Auschwitz–Birkenau Memorial and Museum, https://www.auschwitz.org/en/history/life-in-the-camp/releases -from-the-camp, accessed April 10, 2023/.

p.150   *end the prisoners' torment:* Jack Fairweather, *The Volunteer: One Man, an Underground Army, and the Secret Mission to Destroy Auschwitz* (New York: Custom House, 2019), 188-199.

p.151   *typhus-infected lice:* Pilecki, *Auschwitz Volunteer.*

p.151   *his wife caught typhus:* Garliński, *Fighting Auschwitz.*

p.151   *a small trickle:* "Releases from the Camp."

p.151   *inmates were released:* Rosalie (Chris) Laks Lerman, interview with Joan Ringelheim, December 1, 1998, and January 13, 1999, USHMM.

p.151   *for the safety:* Porebski testimony.

p.151   rough copies *she'd kept:* Tec, "Recapturing the Past," 44.

p.151   *baffled by the odd request:* Tichauer and Palarczyk, 1996.

p.152   *she left her office:* Palarczyk, interview with Ringelheim, 1996.

p.152   *affairs thrived:* Rudolf Vrba and Alan Bestic, *I Escaped from Auschwitz: The Story of a Man Whose Action Led to the Largest Single Rescue of Jews in World War II* (New York: Racehorse, 2020).

p.152   *received a love letter:* Magda Hellinger and Maya Lee with David Brewster, *The Nazis Knew My Name: A Remarkable Story of Survival and Courage in Auschwitz* (New York: Atria, 2022) 104.

p.152   *recounted helping a Kapo:* Vrba and Bestic, *I Escaped from Auschwitz.*

p.152   *"knowing glances":* Pilecki, *The Auschwitz Volunteer,* 282.

p.153   *for many these clandestine meetings:* Vrba, *I Escaped from Auschwitz.*

p.153   *to make daily visits:* Tichauer, "Women's Camp," 45.

p.154   *preferred to work at night:* Tichauer and Palarczyk interview, 1996.

p.154   *Hössler permitted her:* Tichauer, "Women's Camp," 39.

p.155   *4,756 corpses:* Franciszek Piper, "The Mass Extermination of Jews," in *Auschwitz: Nazi Death Camp,* ed. Franciszek Piper and Teresa Swiebocka, trans. Douglas Selvage (Oswiecim: Auschwitz–Birkenau State Museum, 2009), 169–70.

p.155   *My dearest Schani:* Postcard from Helen Tichauer to Samuel Spitzer, June 1943. Courtesy of Konrad Kwiet.

p.155   *he was ill:* Samuel Spitzer, interview with D. I. Ritch, March 7, 1996, VHA/ USC-Shoah.

p.156   *walked into the Sauna:* Tichauer, "Women's Camp," 140.

p.156   *at least fifty physicians:* "Joseph Mengele," Holocaust Encyclopedia, USHMM, https://encyclopedia.ushmm.org/content/en/article/josef-mengele, accessed April 10, 2023.

p.156   *kerosene injections:* Alexandra Gorko, interview with Eileen Steinberg, August 19, 1985, USHMM.

p.157   *rarely raised his voice:* Nina Kaleska, interview with Linda G. Kuzmack, January 3, 1990, USHMM.

p.157   *inspected each body:* Sigmund Schwarzer, interview with Mitchell Schwarzer, June 1, 1986, USHMM.

p.157   *casually castrated boys:* Michael Vogel, interview with Linda G. Kuzmack, July 14, 1989, USHMM.

p.157   *he gave up the chase:* Helen Tichauer, interview with Peter Hellman, November 19, 2010.

Chapter Twelve: "You Are My Sister-in-Law!"

p.158   *someone must have:* Unless otherwise noted, descriptions come from David Wisnia from two lengthy interviews conducted with the author at his home in Levittown, Pa., on January 19, 2018, and June 24, 2019.

p.158   *another day of hard labor:* David Wisnia, interview with Brad Zarlin, 2006, USHMM.

p.158   *Supposedly for a shower:* Helen Tichauer, "The Women's Camp at Auschwitz-Birkenau: Method Within Madness," ed. Susan Cernyak-Spatz and Joel Shatzky (unpublished manuscript), 116.

p.159   *two of David's teeth:* Wisnia, interview with Zarlin.

p.159   *attracted by an incoming inmate:* Filip Müller, *Eyewitness Auschwitz: Three Years in the Gas Chambers,* ed. and trans. Susanne Flatauer (Chicago: Ivan R. Dee, 1999).

p.160   *Franceska Mann:* Ofer Aderet, "The Jewish Dancer Undressed Slowly. Then She Shot an SS Soldier to Death," *Haaretz,* August 27, 2019. See also Danuta Czech, *Auschwitz Chronicle 1939-1945: From the Archives of The Auschwitz Memorial and The German Federal Archives,* (New York: Henry Holt and Company, 1990), 513.

p.160   *watched in horror:* Wisnia, interview with Zarlin.

p.160   *a child:* It's unclear when this event took place. It is possible this was the "sad-eyed angel" who years later would be memorialized in Elie Wiesel's *Night* (New York: Hill and Wang, 2006), although Wiesel recalls the two adult men yelling, "Long live liberty!" Dov Edelstein, an Auschwitz survivor, also remembers a similar scene. See Shahar Ilan, "Auschwitz Survivor: A Living Witness," *Haaretz,* July 25, 2006.

p.160   *bound their ankles:* Rudolf Vrba and Alan Bestic, *I Escaped from Auschwitz: The Story of a Man Whose Action Led to the Largest Single Rescue of Jews in World War II* (New York: Racehorse, 2020), 179.

p.160   *A column of Polish women:* Sara Lewin Radomski, interview with Brad Zarlin, July 15, 2007, USHMM.

p.160   *Sara Lewin, his old friend:* David was certain that he saw Sara just as she first arrived into Birkenau, before she even got tattooed. If indeed David saw Sara as she first marched in, he wasn't yet meeting Zippi privately. In this case, he would've slipped Zippi a note, or sent a message through a friendly guard. Or, perhaps, David saw Sara as she marched with her *Kommando* after having already lived in Birkenau for a few months.

p.161   *number 47100:* Sara Lewin's Konzentrationalager (KZ) Auschwitz Registration record, The Arolsen Archives, formerly the International Tracing Service archive (ITS), located in Bad Arolsen, Germany.

p.161   *you are my sister-in-law!:* Wisnia, interview with Zarlin.

p.161   *June of 1943:* Lewin, KZ Auschwitz Registration record.

p.161   *"extremely hard labor":* Czech, *Auschwitz Chronicle 1939-1945,* 428.

p.161   *escaped from Warsaw:* Radomski, interview with Zarlin.

p.162   *It wasn't unusual:* Jean-Claude Pressac, *Auschwitz: Technique and Operation of the Gas Chambers,* trans. Peter Moss (New York: Beate Klarsfeld Foundation, 1989).

p.162   *Never do it again:* Radomski, interview with Zarlin.

p.163   *his troubles would evaporate:* Helen Tichauer, unpublished interview with Jürgen Matthäus, March 5, 2011.

NOTES

Chapter Thirteen: Orchestra Girls

p.164   *had convinced the SS:* Danuta Czech, *Auschwitz Chronicle 1939-1945: From the Archives of The Auschwitz Memorial and The German Federal Archives*, (New York: Henry Holt and Company, 1990), 44.

p.164   *By May 1942:* James A. Grymes, *Violins of Hope: Violins of the Holocaust* (New York: HarperPerennial, 2014).

p.165   *Many wore caps:* Kazimierz Albin, "The Baton of Franciszek Nierychło, the First Conductor of the Auschwitz Camp Orchestra Now in the Collections of the Memorial," Auschwitz-Birkenau Memorial and Museum, http://www.auschwitz .org/en/museum/news/the-baton-of-franciszek-nierychlo-the-first-conductor -of-the-auschwitz-camp-orchestra-now-in-the-collections-of-the-memorial ,1335.html, accessed February 16, 2023.

p.165   *for something similar:* Helen Tichauer, "The Women's Camp at Auschwitz-Birkenau: Method Within Madness," ed. Susan Cernyak-Spatz and Joel Shatzky (unpublished manuscript), 131.

p.165   *provided such an outlet:* Susan Eischeid, *The Truth about Fania Fénelon and the Women's Orchestra of Auschwitz-Birkenau* (New York: Palgrave Macmillan, 2016).

p.165   *Mozart and Beethoven:* Richard Newman with Karen Kirtley, *Alma Rosé: Vienna to Auschwitz* (Portland: Amadeus Press, 2000), 262.

p.165   *the ranks of the SS:* Helen Tichauer and an unknown former member of the women's orchestra in Auschwitz, Richard Newman Collection, 1983-1994, USHMM.

p.165   *another notch:* Eischeid, *The Truth about Fania Fénelon*.

p.165   *more time in the men's camp:* Tichauer, "Women's Camp," 131.

p.165   *professions and skills:* Tichauer, Richard Newman Collection, USHMM.

p.166   *an inaugural orchestra member:* Helen Tichauer, interview with Joseph Toltz, USHMM.

p.166   *opportunity to expand her access:* Tichauer, Richard Newman Collection, USHMM.

p.166   *confiscated from prisoners:* Eischeid, *The Truth about Fania Fénelon*.

p.166   *up to Zofia:* Newman, *Alma Rosé*, 231-234.

p.166   *crafting sheet music paper:* Tichauer, Richard Newman Collection, USHMM.

p.167   *simple Polish melodies:* Newman, *Alma Rosé,* 233.

p.167   *a cacophony:* Tichauer, "Women's Camp," 135.

p.167   *for "medical purposes":* Judith Antelman, Sandra Bendayan, Jake Birnberg, and Zuzana Goldstein, interviews with Renee L. Duering, 1992, USHMM.

p.167   *Block 10 needs a violin:* Newman, *Alma Rosé*, 223.

p.168   *severe radiation burns:* Irena Strzelecka, *Voices of Memory 2: Medical Experiments in Auschwitz,* trans. William Brand (Oswiecim: Auschwitz-Birkenau State Museum, 2019).

p.168   *Katya herself observed:* Katerina Singer, "Testimony in the criminal proceedings against the late Prof. Carl Clauberg," Wiener-HL, Index Number: P.III.h (Auschwitz) No. 881, June 4, 1957.

p.168   *for married women:* Antelman, Bendayan, Birnberg, and Goldstein, interviews with Duering, 1992.

p.168   *according to the runner:* Tichauer, interview with Newman.

p.168   *Of course she did:* Helen Tichauer, oral testimony, Imperial War Museum Archives, 2003.

p.169   *led the Vienna Philharmonic:* "Arnold Josef Rosé," Mahler Foundation, https://mahlerfoundation.org/gt-member/arnold-josef-rose/, accessed February 16, 2023.

p.170   *forced into sex work:* Newman, *Alma Rosé,* 218.

p.170   *first bordello:* Hermann Langbein, *People in Auschwitz,* trans. Harry Zohn (Chapel Hill: University of North Carolina Press, 2004), 406. See also Robert Sommer, "Forced Prostitution in National Socialist Concentration Camps—The Example of Auschwitz," in *Forced Prostitution in Times of War and Peace,* ed. Barbara Drink and Chung-noh Gross, (Bielefeld: Kleine Verlag, 2007).

p.170   *face was bloated:* Alice Jakubovic, interview with Joan Ringelheim, August 27, 2002, USHMM.

p.170   *had witnessed how:* Magda Blau, interview with Linda Kuzmack, June 11, 1990, USHMM

p.171   *Magda couldn't be caught:* Newman, *Alma Rosé,* 223-224.

p.171   *Zofia was kicked upstairs:* Tichauer, "Women's Camp," 135.

p.172   *enjoyed extra rations:* Eischeid, *The Truth about Fania Fénelon.*

p.172   *standard of discipline:* Newman, *Alma Rosé,* 235.

p.172   *performed with as a child:* Tichauer, Imperial War Museum, 2003.

p.172   *"we'll go to the gas":* Newman, *Alma Rosé,* 278.

p.172   *that had been completed:* Czech, *Auschwitz Chronicle 1939-1945,* 295.

p.172   *Well-meaning old-timers:* Armando Aaron and Rebecca Aaron, interview with Jasa Almuli, November 13, 1996, USHMM.

p.172   *To Zippi's ear:* Tichauer, Imperial War Museum, 2003.

p.174   *setting up music stands:* Anita Lasker-Wallfisch, *Inherit the Truth, 1939–1945: The Documented Experiences of a Surivivor of Auschwitz and Belsen* (Paris: Giles de la Mare, 1996).

p.174   *usually smaller:* Anita Lasker-Wallfisch interview with Joanna Buchan, VHA/USC-Shoah, December 8, 1998.

p.174   *Bach, and others:* Newman, *Alma Rosé,* 262.

p.174   *murderous environment was jarring:* Carol Stern Steinhardt, interview with Joan Ringelheim, June 3, 1996, USHMM.

p.174   *the women rehearsed:* Lasker-Wallfisch, VHA/USC-Shoah.

p.174   *Violin Concerto in E minor:* Newman, *Alma Rosé,* 263.

p.174   *I can't make music that way:* Langbein, *People in Auschwitz,* 146.

p.174   *Edith Eva Eger:* Edith Eva Eger with Esmé Schwall Weigand, *The Choice: Embrace the Possible* (New York: Scribner, 2017).

p.174   *Blue Danube waltz:* Edith Eva Eger, interview with Marci Jenkins, August 14, 1992, USHMM.

p.175   *witnessing cruel punishments:* Stanisława Rachwał, testimony, July 25, 1945, "Chronicles of Terror," Witold Pilecki Center for Totalitarian Studies, Warsaw.

p.175   *nothing more than a Kapo:* Newman, *Alma Rosé,* 269.

p.175   *Alma said to Anita:* Lasker-Wallfisch interview, USHMM, 1991.

p.175   *You will be saved:* Lasker-Wallfisch, *Inherit the Truth.*

p.175   *Kristallnacht:* Kristallnacht ("Crystal Night"), also known as the Night of the Broken Glass, took place on November 9, 1938. Jews across Germany, Sudetenland, and Austria were targeted. Thousands of Jewish-owned businesses, homes, and schools were plundered, 1,200 synagogues were desecrated, and 91 Jews were murdered. On the days that followed, more than 25,000 Jewish men were arrested and sent to concentration camps.

p.175   *Two years had passed:* Lasker-Wallfisch interview, USHMM, 1991.

p.176 *Schubert's Marches militaires:* Lasker-Wallfisch, *Inherit the Truth.*
p.176 *I'm doing it:* Helen Tichauer, interview with Joan Ringelheim, 2000, USHMM.
p.176 *allowed her to feel:* Wendy Lower, "Distant Encounter," in *Approaching an Auschwitz Survivor,* ed. Jürgen Matthäus (Oxford: Oxford University Press, 2010), 109.

Chapter Fourteen: "Evening in the Moonlight"

p.177 *around February of 1944:* Unless otherwise noted, descriptions come from David Wisnia from two lengthy interviews with the author conducted at his home in Levittown, Pa., on January 19, 2018, and June 24, 2019.
p.179 *"Holdvilágos éjszakán"* by Mihály Eisemann, printed with permission © István Zágon, 2024. Translation by Luca Makai.

Chapter Fifteen: "We Are Going to Play"

p.181 *she told Zippi:* Nechama Tec, "Recapturing the Past," in *Approaching an Auschwitz Survivor,* ed. Jürgen Matthäus (Oxford: Oxford University Press, 2010), 46.
p.181 *loyal member since childhood:* "Roza Robota," Yad Vashem, https://www.yadvashem .org/odot_pdf/Microsoft%20Word%20-%205831.pdf, accessed April 28, 2023.
p.181 *came to an arrangement:* Tec, "Recapturing the Past," 45–46.
p.182 *She reminded Zippi:* Helen Tichauer, "The Women's Camp at Auschwitz-Birkenau: Method Within Madness," ed. Susan Cernyak-Spatz and Joel Shatzky (unpublished manuscript), 49–50.
p.183 *an older Polish Jew:* Ibid., 56–58. According to Zippi, the woman, Salomea Rineck, went on to live in England past the age of ninety. She volunteered at a hospital and maintained contact with Katya to the end of her life.
p.183 *Zippi told David:* David Wisnia, interview with Joseph Toltz (transcript), April 7, 2011.
p.184 *poisoned, drowned, or gassed:* Hermann Langbein, *People in Auschwitz,* trans. Harry Zohn (Chapel Hill: University of North Carolina Press, 2004), 233.
p.184 *in his mother's arms:* Christopher Buckley, "My Visit to Hell," *The Daily Beast,* July 14, 2017, https://www.thedailybeast.com/my-visit-to-hell, accessed February 15, 2023.
p.184 *shattering his skull:* Witold Pilecki, *The Auschwitz Volunteer: Beyond Bravery,* trans. Jarek Garlinski (Los Angeles: Aquila Polonica, 2014).
p.185 *witnessed firsthand:* Helen Tichauer, interview with Joan Ringelheim, 2000, USHMM.
p.185 *his sadism:* Rudolf Höss, *Death Dealer: The Memoirs of the SS Kommandant at Auschwitz,* ed. Steven Paskuly, trans. Andrew Pollinger (Buffalo: Prometheus, 1992), 311.
p.185 *Katya didn't respond:* Tichauer, interview with Ringelheim, 2000.
p.185 *What is there to love:* Susan Cernyak-Spatz and Joel Shatzky, "Record-Keeping for the Nazis—and Saving Lives," *Jewish Currents,* May 1, 2011.
p.185 *Zippi couldn't understand:* Tichauer, interview with Ringelheim, 2000.
p.186 *a "subhuman" woman:* Pilecki, *Auschwitz Volunteer.*
p.186 *rumored to have a mistress:* Statement of E.H., "Dachau, Concentration Camp, CIC Detachment, Seventh Army 1933—1945" Eisenhower Presidential Library, https://

www.eisenhowerlibrary.gov/sites/default/files/research/online-documents /holocaust/report-dachau.pdf, accessed July 17, 2023.

p.186   *Katya seemed stupid:* Tichauer, interview with Ringelheim, 2000.

p.186   *"the cradle of Bolshevism":* Harrison E. Salisbury, *The 900 Days: The Siege of Leningrad* (1969; repr., Cambridge, Mass.: Da Capo Press, 2003), 92–94.

p.186   *Nazi Germany's collapse:* Ralph Parker, "Rail Center Falls," *New York Times,* January 22, 1944.

p.186   *more smog assaulted the skies:* Tichauer, "Women's Camp," 93.

p.186   *called themselves Kazia:* Barbara Rogers, "British Intelligence and the Holocaust: Auschwitz and the Allies Re-examined," *The Journal of Holocaust Education* 8, no. 1 (Summer 1999): 89–106.

p.187   *code name Wanda:* Richard Breitman, *Official Secrets: What the Nazis Planned, What the British and Americans Knew* (New York: Hill and Wang 1999), 161.

p.187   *so much data herself:* Richard Newman with Karen Kirtley, *Alma Rosé: Vienna to Auschwitz* (Portland: Amadeus Press, 2000), 246.

p.187   *intercepting radio communication:* Breitman, *Official Secrets,* 8.

p.187   *explained to Höss:* Stanisław Dubiel, testimony, August 7, 1946, "Chronicles of Terror," Witold Pilecki Center for Totalitarian Studies, Warsaw.

p.187   *scheduled to be killed:* Newman, *Alma Rosé,* 296.

p.188   *Theresienstadt:* For details on this original "model camp" and its "beautification" campaign, see Geoffrey P. Megargee and Martin Dean, eds., *The United States Holocause Memorial Museum Encyclopedia of Camps and Ghettos, 1933—1945,* vol. 2, *Ghettos in German-Occupied Eastern Europe* (Bloomington: Indiana University Press, 2012), 180.

p.188   *didn't have their heads shaved:* Dina Gottliebova-Babbitt interview with Hilary Adah Helstein, VHA-USC/Shoah, September 26, 1998.

p.188   *Red Cross delegation:* Michal Aharony, "Meet Fredy Hirsch, the Unknown Holocaust Hero Who Saved Children at Auschwitz," *Haaretz,* April, 2018.

p.188   *3,791 Jewish men, women, and children:* Danuta Czech, *Auschwitz Chronicle 1939-1945: From the Archives of The Auschwitz Memorial and The German Federal Archives,* (New York: Henry Holt and Company, 1990), 595.

p.188   *stitched up the wound:* Tichauer, "Women's Camp," 98.

p.189   *extend their time:* Tichauer, interview with Ringelheim, 2000.

p.189   *was graying:* Newman, *Alma Rosé,* 291-308.

p.189   *Zippi stopped going:* Helen Tichauer, oral testimony, Imperial War Museum Archives, 2003.

Chapter Sixteen: "Long Live Poland"

p.191   *it felt impossible:* Anna Palarczyk, interview with Joan Ringelheim, 1996, USHMM.

p.191   *ramped up its plans:* Danuta Czech, *Auschwitz Chronicle 1939-1945: From the Archives of The Auschwitz Memorial and The German Federal Archives,* (New York: Henry Holt and Company, 1990), 562-564.

p.192   *a Slovakian Blockälteste:* Helen Tichauer, "The Women's Camp at Auschwitz-Birkenau: Method Within Madness," ed. Susan Cernyak-Spatz and Joel Shatzky (unpublished manuscript), 129.

p.193   *Zippi left quickly:* Helen Tichauer, interview with Joan Ringelheim, 2000, USHMM.

NOTES

p.193   *found reasons:* Pawel Sawicki, "They Simply Fell in Love," *Oś — Oświęcim, People, History, Culture,* no. 9, September 2009, Auschwitz-Birkenau State Museum.

p.194   *twelve days:* Czech, *Auschwitz Chronicle 1939-1945,* 651.

p.194   *low to the ground:* Dora Freilich, interview with Helen Grassman, October 24, 1984, USHMM.

p.194   *locked inside the bunker:* Czech, *Auschwitz Chronicle 1939-1945,* 651.

p.195   *Zippi had the privilege:* Tichauer, interview with Ringelheim, 2000.

p.195   *who'd committed treason:* Henja Frydman, interview with David Boder, "Voices of the Holocaust," August 7, 1946, Illinois Institute of Technology.

p.195   *SS noticed something:* Rose Szywic Warner, interview with Randy M. Goldman, September 12, 1994, USHMM.

p.195   *her bloodied hand:* Tichauer, interview with Ringelheim, 2000.

p.195   *could recover before being killed:* Frydman, "Voices of the Holocaust."

p.195   *"Long live Poland":* Szywic Warner, interview with Goldman, September 12, 1994.

p.196   *"Poland lives!":* Czech, *Auschwitz Chronicle 1939-1945,* 710.

p.196   *Selfish, stupid girl:* Tichauer, interview with Ringelheim, 2000.

p.196   *wound up in the hands:* Susan Cernyak-Spatz and Joel Shatzky, "Record-Keeping for the Nazis—and Saving Lives," *Jewish Currents,* May 1, 2011.

p.197   *trying to help her:* Aleksander Górecki, testimony, March 22, 1947, "Chronicles of Terror," Witold Pilecki Center for Totalitarian Studies, Warsaw.

p.197   *dubbed "Frankenstein":* Stanisława Rachwał, testimony, July 25, 1945, "Chronicles of Terror," Witold Pilecki Center for Totalitarian Studies, Warsaw.

p.197   *Helena Citron:* See the extraordinary documentary with interviews with both Helena Citron and Franz Munsch, *Love It Was Not (Ahava Zot Lo Hayta),* directed by Maya Sarfaty (Israel, 2022).

p.197   *concentration camp in Stutthof:* Katya Singer Transport Record, The Arolsen Archives, formerly the International Tracing Service archive (ITS), located in Bad Arolsen, Germany.

p.197   *she was told:* Cernyak-Spatz and Shatzky, "Record-Keeping."

p.197   *He was accused:* Rudolf Höss, *Death Dealer: The Memoirs of the SS Kommandant at Auschwitz,* ed. Steven Paskuly, trans. Andrew Pollinger (Buffalo: Prometheus, 1992), 309.

p.198   *groveled and beat his chest:* Górecki testimony.

p.198   *she'd given up her life:* Tichauer, interview with Ringelheim, 2000.

p.199   *texture of the dusty streets:* Tichauer, "Women's Camp," 40.

p.199   *Zippi signed the bottom:* Helen Tichauer and Anna Palarczyk, joint interview with Joan Ringelheim, August 16–17, 1996, USHMM.

p.199   *transferred over to Bergen-Belsen:* Newman, *Alma Rosé,* 308.

p.200   *largest Jewish revolt:* "Warsaw Ghetto Uprising," Holocaust Encyclopedia, USHMM, https://encyclopedia.ushmm.org/content/en/article/warsaw-ghetto-uprising, accessed July 17, 2023.

p.200   *newspapers reported:* "Warsaw Debacle Laid to 'Politics,'" *New York Times,* August 30, 1944.

p.200   *administrators at Majdanek:* Czech, *Auschwitz Chronicle 1939-1945,* 561-564.

p.200   *had good information:* Anna Heilman, *Never Far Away: The Auschwitz Chronicles of Anna Heilman* (Calgary: University of Calgary Press, 2001), 126.

p.200   *eliminate all Hungarian Jews:* Czech, *Auschwitz Chronicle 1939-1945,* 702.

p.200 *only Jewish community in occupied Europe:* "German Troops Occupy Hungary," Holocaust Encyclopedia, USHMM, https://encyclopedia.ushmm.org/content/en /timeline-event/holocaust/1942-1945/german-troops-occupy-hungary, accessed April 10, 2023.

p.200 *A small pond:* Gideon Greif, *We Wept Without Tears: Testimonies of the Jewish Sonderkommando from Auschwitz* (New Haven: Yale University Press, 2014), 18.

p.201 *nine hundred prisoners:* Franciszek Piper: "The Mass Extermination of Jews," in Piper and Swiebocka, *Auschwitz: Nazi Death Camp,* 169-172.

p.201 *eradicate all traces:* Czech, *Auschwitz Chronicle 1939-1945*, 701-702.

Chapter Seventeen: "Don't Give Up"

p.202 *busier than ever:* David Wisnia, interview with Brad Zarlin, 2006, USHMM.

p.202 *twelve pairs of underwear:* Helen Tichauer, "The Women's Camp at Auschwitz-Birkenau: Method Within Madness," ed. Susan Cernyak-Spatz and Joel Shatzky (unpublished manuscript), 125.

p.202 *thought David:* Wisnia, interview with Zarlin.

p.202 *Ralph Hackman:* Ralph Hackman, interview with author, fall 2019.

p.202 *a loud explosion:* Wisnia, interview with Zarlin.

p.203 *ratatat of machine guns:* David Wisnia, interview with Joseph Toltz (transcript), April 7, 2011, USHMM.

p.203 *red, windowless Weichsel-Union-Metallwerke:* Anna Heilman, *Never Far Away: The Auschwitz Chronicles of Anna Heilman* (Calgary: University of Calgary Press, 2001), 101.

p.203 *recruited Roza Robota:* Gideon Greif, *We Wept Without Tears: Testimonies of the Jewish Sonderkommando from Auschwitz* (New Haven: Yale University Press, 2014).

p.203 *glass-paned hallways:* Heilman, *Never Far Away,* 101, 128.

p.203 *uniform seams:* "Herman Haller," in *The Union Kommando in Auschwitz: The Auschwitz Munition Factory Through the Eyes of Its Former Slave Laborers,* ed. and trans. Lore Shelley (Lanham, Md.: University Press of America, 1996), 167.

p.203 *or bras:* "Noah Zabludowicz," in ibid., 294.

p.203 *Roza was the link:* Nechama Tec, *Resistance: Jews and Christians Who Defied the Nazi Terror* (Oxford: Oxford University Press, 2013).

p.204 *inside a cartful:* "Zabludowicz," 294.

p.204 *They failed to close fuses:* "Gizella Mozes," in Shelley, *Union Kommando,* 27.

p.204 *disposed of good material:* "Flora Neumann," in ibid., 33.

p.204 *Prisoner T:* "Erich Kulka," in ibid., 305.

p.204 *British Intelligence Service:* According to Kulka, Prisoner T was recruited by a cell of the 1,200 British POWs who lived at subcamp Monowitz and were employed at IG Farben (see Deborah Dwork and Robert Jan Van Pelt, *Auschwitz: 1270 to Present* [New York: W. W. Norton, 1997], 233). Prisoner T declined to use his name with Kulka, but this story is corroborated in testimony from another survivor, which identifies Prisoner T as Erwin Tichauer (Erna Elerat interview, March 28, 1993, USHMM).

p.204 *had also been tapped:* "Paula Stern," in Shelley, *Union Kommando,* 100. See also Erwin Tichauer, *Skull and Zebra Suits: A Berlin Jew in Auschwitz,* ed. Jürgen Matthäus, trans. Anabel Aliaga-Buchenau (Berlin: Metropol, 2000), chapters 13–14.

p.204 *On the morning:* Danuta Czech, *Auschwitz Chronicle 1939-1945: From the Archives of The Auschwitz Memorial and The German Federal Archives*, (New York: Henry Holt and Company, 1990), 725.

p.204 *didn't have time:* Greif, *We Wept Without Tears.*

p.204 *couldn't afford to wait:* "Zabludowicz," 295.

p.204 *At 1:25 p.m.:* Czech, *Auschwitz Chronicle 1939-1945*, 725.

p.204 *a jumble of stripes:* Greif, *We Wept Without Tears.*

p.205 *almost directly across:* "Virtual Tour," Auschwitz–Birkenau State Museum, https://panorama.auschwitz.org/tour2,3007,en.html, accessed April 23, 2023.

p.205 *locked the Sauna:* Wisnia, interview with Toltz, April 7, 2011.

p.205 *homemade grenades:* Greif, *We Wept Without Tears.*

p.205 *two to roast:* Czech, *Auschwitz Chronicle 1939-1945*, 725-726.

p.205 *Four hundred and fifty-one prisoners died:* Barbara Jarosz, "Organizations of the Camp Resistance," in Piper and Swiebocka, *Auschwitz: Nazi Death Camp,* 233.

p.205 *out of commission:* Tec, *Resistance.*

p.206 *two sessions:* Czech, *Auschwitz Chronicle 1939-1945*, 775.

p.206 *blood seeped from her eyes:* Ruth Barr-Shway, 1997, VHA/USC-Shoah.

p.206 *something about that practice:* "I was probably like a live bomb," Zippi said to Nechama Tec. "It could be that when she brought the apron, she had powder in it. It just could be that way."

p.206 *deliver the explosives:* Tichauer, "Women's Camp,"124.

p.206 *a huge win:* Helen Tichauer, interview with Joan Ringelheim, August 6, 2005, USHMM.

p.207 *It's my birthday, too:* Tichauer, "Women's Camp," 63.

p.207 *the package room:* Dune Macadam, *999: The Extraordinary Young Women of the First Official Jewish Transport to Auschwitz* (New York: Citadel, 2020), 101.

p.207 *carried their warmth:* Tichauer, "Women's Camp," 64.

p.208 *end of November:* Czech, *Auschwitz Chronicle 1939-1945*, 565.

p.208 *a newly assembled workforce:* Philip Goldstein, interview with Sharon Tash, June 2, 1992, USHMM.

p.208 *preserved for later use:* Erich Kulka, interview with Linda Kuzmack, 1990, USHMM.

p.208 *holes into gas chamber walls:* Andrzej Strzelecki, "Evacuation, Liquidation and Liberation of the Camp," in Piper and Swiebocka, *Auschwitz: Nazi Death Camp,* 272.

p.208 *increasingly nervous:* Filip Müller, *Eyewitness Auschwitz: Three Years in the Gas Chambers,* ed. and trans. Susanne Flatauer (New York: Stein & Day, 1979), 165.

p.208 *lose the war:* Wisnia, interview with Toltz, April 7, 2011.

p.209 *work at the Sauna:* Wisnia, interview with Zarlin.

p.209 *write out his song:* "David Wisnia Songs Written in Auschwitz (Oswiecim)," USHMM, https://collections.ushmm.org/search/catalog/irn500168#?rsc=146653&cv=0&c=0&m=0&s=0&xywh=-1245%2C-1%2C6255%2C5209, accessed February 17, 2023.

p.209 *described the transports:* Wisnia, interview with Toltz, April 7, 2011.

p.209 *"The Blessing of Hanukkah":* Wisnia, interview with Zarlin.

Chapter Eighteen: "Always Forward"

p.211 *frenzied Nazis:* Filip Müller, *Eyewitness Auschwitz: Three Years in the Gas Chambers,* ed. and trans. Susanne Flatauer (New York: Stein & Day, 1979), 165.

NOTES

p.211 *given orders to evacuate:* Yehuda Bauer, "The Death Marches January–May 1944," *Modern Judaism: A Journal of Jewish Ideas and Experience* 3, no. 1 (February 1983): 1–21.

p.211 *told to prepare:* Müller, *Eyewitness Auschwitz,* 165.

p.212 *hidden prisoners:* Erich Kulka, interview with Linda Kuzmack, 1990, USHMM.

p.212 *organized extra rations:* David Wisnia, interview with Brad Zarlin, USHMM.

p.212 *armed SS men:* Müller, *Eyewitness Auschwitz,* 165.

p.212 *toss them out of the way:* Anonymous eyewitness account, "The Terrors of the Evacuation of Auschwitz in January 1945," Wiener-HL, Index Number: P. III.h. No. 653, 1957.

p.212 *a tinge of hope:* David Wisnia, interview with Joseph Toltz (transcript), April 7, 2011, USHMM.

p.213 *urine to quench their thirst:* Alexander Ehrmann, interview with Sidney M. Bolkosky, May 13, 1983, USHMM.

p.213 *stopped to unload the dead:* Anonymous, "The Terrors of the Evacuation."

p.213 *Documents, death certificates, and files:* Danuta Czech, *Auschwitz Chronicle 1939-1945: From the Archives of The Auschwitz Memorial and The German Federal Archives,* (New York: Henry Holt and Company, 1990), 780.

p.213 *first list to coil into fire:* Anna Palarczyk, interview with Joan Ringelheim, 1996, USHMM

p.213 *behind a bookcase:* Helen Tichauer, interview with David Boder, "Voices of the Holocaust," Illinois Institute of Technology, September 23, 1946.

p.213 *she could help:* Konrad Kwiet, "Designing Survival," in *Approaching an Auschwitz Survivor,* ed. Jürgen Matthäus (Oxford: Oxford University Press, 2010), 22.

p.213 *three heavy packages:* Helen Tichauer, Transcript of the Preliminary Investigation, February 1, 1971, General Consulate of Germany, New York (trans. Anabel Aliaga-Buchenau).

p.214 *a block of gold:* Kwiet, "Designing Survival," 23.

p.214 *burn for five days:* Andrzej Strzelecki, "Evacuation, Liquidation and Liberation of the Camp," in Piper and Swiebocka, *Auschwitz: Nazi Death Camp,* 272.

p.214 *mustered up the strength:* Mala Kahn Schulesser, interview transcribed by Barbara Marshall, USHMM.

p.214 *remains of prisoners' files:* Czech, *Auschwitz Chronicle 1939-1945,* 785.

p.214 *Bonfires of burning barracks:* Strzelecki, "Evacuation, Liquidation and Liberation," photo insert.

p.214 *January 18, 1945:* Tichauer, Transcript of the Preliminary Investigation.

p.214 *in rows of five:* Ivonne Razon, interview, March 18, 1993, USHMM.

p.214 *and were electrocuted:* Jolana Hollander, interview with Barbara Barer, Evelyn Fielden, and Anne G. Saldinger, July 29, 1993, USHMM.

p.215 *blankets strewn across:* Hadassah Marcus, interview with David Boder, "Voices of the Holocaust," Illinois Institute of Technology, September 13, 1946.

p.215 *Where are we going?:* Hollander, interview with Barer et al., July 29, 1993.

p.215 *accused of sabotage:* Strzelecki, "Evacuation, Liquidation," 272.

p.215 *echoed around them:* Palarczyk, interview with Ringelheim, 1996.

p.215 *a bag of sugar:* Schulesser interview.

p.215 *blood-soaked mud:* Razon interview, March 18, 1993.

p.215 *back of her head:* Strzelecki, "Evacuation, Liquidation," 276.

p.215 *hope to carry on:* Alice Jakubovic, interview with Joan Ringelheim, August 27, 2002, USHMM.

p.215   *two or three:* Tichauer, Transcript of the Preliminary Investigation.

Chapter Nineteen: "You Are Free!"

p.219   *snapping like twigs:* Alice Jakubovic, interview with Joan Ringelheim, August 27, 2002, USHMM.

p.219   *relatively clean snow:* Hadassah Marcus, interview with David Boder, "Voices of the Holocaust," Illinois Institute of Technology, September 13, 1946.

p.219   *made it through Berlin:* Anna Palarczyk, interview with Joan Ringelheim, 1996, USHMM.

p.219   *evading fire:* Helen Tichauer, interview with David Boder, "Voices of the Holocaust," Illinois Institute of Technology, September 23, 1946.

p.219   *What a satisfying sight:* Susan Cernyak-Spatz, *Protective Custody Prisoner 34042* (Cortland, N.Y.: N and S Publishers, 2005).

p.220   *figured the Ravensbrück:* Tichauer, "Voices of the Holocaust."

p.220   *in a single room:* Nelly Bondy, interview with David Boder, "Voices of the Holocaust," Illinois Institute of Technology, August 22, 1946.

p.220   *disorder, and devastating famine:* Tichauer, "Voices of the Holocaust."

p.220   *Go back to Auschwitz:* Palarczyk, interview with Ringelheim, 1996.

p.220   *windows that could be opened:* Cernyak-Spatz, *Protective Custody Prisoner 34042.*

p.220   *a cauldron materialized:* Lina Stumachin, interview with David Boder, "Voices of the Holocaust," Illinois Institute of Technology, September 8, 1946.

p.220   *someone pushed her:* Helen Tichauer, Transcript of the Preliminary Investigation, February 1, 1971, General Consulate of Germany, New York (trans. Anabel Aliaga-Buchenau).

p.221   *"You are free!":* Andrzej Strzelecki, "Evacuation, Liquidation and Liberation of the Camp," in *Auschwitz: Nazi Death Camp,* ed. Franciszek Piper and Teresa Swiebocka, trans. Douglas Selvage (Oswiecim: Auschwitz-Birkenau State Museum, 2009), 280.

p.221   *fifteen thousand pounds:* "Liberation of Auschwitz: Film Footage," USHMM, https://encyclopedia.ushmm.org/content/en/gallery/liberation-of-auschwitz-film-footage, accessed January 30, 2023.

p.221   *six hundred charred corpses:* Mykola Karpenko, "Ukrainian Veteran Recalls Liberation of Auschwitz," Radio Free Europe, (RFE/RL's Ukrainian Service), https://www.rferl.org/a/ukraine-world-war-two-auschwitz-soviet-army/26816158.html, accessed February 17, 2023.

p.221   *around the gallows:* Richard Horowitz interview with Imperial War Records Museum, May 12, 1983, USHMM.

p.222   *years of searching:* Strzelecki, "Evacuation, Liquidation," 285.

p.222   *inmate helped her get up:* Helen Tichauer, unpublished interview with Michael Berkowitz, August 3, 2003.

p.222   *The women were told:* Palarczyk, interview with Ringelheim, 1996.

p.222   *three slices of dry bread:* Bondy, "Voices of the Holocaust."

p.222   *ate grass:* Tecia Grynberg, interview with Jill Margo, June 6, 1991, USHMM.

p.223   *subterranean ammunition factory:* "Paula Stern," in *The Union Kommando in Auschwitz: The Auschwitz Munition Factory Through the Eyes of Its Former Slave Laborers,* ed. and trans. Lore Shelley (Lanham, Md.: University Press of America, 1996), 101.

p.223   *making bullets:* Ruth Krautwirth Meyerowitz, interview with Linda G. Kuzmack, February 20, 1990, USHMM.

p.223   *worked in the kitchen:* Helen Tichauer, Transcript of the Preliminary Investigation, February 1, 1971, General Consulate of Germany, New York (trans. Anabel Aliaga-Buchenau).

p.223   *the Swedish Red Cross:* Sarah Helm, "The Swedish Schindler: How Count Bernadotte Saved Thousands of Jews from Death," *Newsweek,* May 14, 2015.

p.223   *Zippi looked on:* Tichauer Transcript of the Preliminary Investigation.

p.223   *inmates were wary:* Itka Zygmuntowicz, interview with Randy M. Goldman, May 30, 1996, USHMM.

p.223   *a Red Cross logo:* Cernyak-Spatz, *Protective Custody Prisoner 34042.*

p.223   *packages of food:* Meyerowitz, interview with Kuzmack, February 20, 1990.

p.224   *didn't get any of it:* Tichauer, Transcript of the Preliminary Investigation.

p.224   *allowed herself to believe:* Tichauer, "Voices of the Holocaust."

p.224   *The Führer is dead!:* Cernyak-Spatz, *Protective Custody Prisoner 34042.*

p.224   *a neighboring town:* Dora Freilich, interview with Helen Grassman, October 24, 1984, USHMM.

p.224   *even more sadistic:* Yehuda Bauer, "The Death Marches January–May 1944," *Modern Judaism: A Journal of Jewish Ideas and Experience* 3, no. 1 (February 1983): 1–21.

p.224   *boils and lice:* Freilich, interview with Grassman, October 24, 1984.

p.225   *tried to disappear:* Gabriela Truly interview with Edith Millman, May 27, 1990, USHMM.

p.225   *removed the stripes:* Tichauer, "Voices of the Holocaust."

p.225   *allowing her and Sara:* According to both Sara's and Zippi's testimonies, a third (unknown) woman escaped with them. It's unclear how long she remained with Zippi and Sara.

Chapter Twenty: White Star

p.227   *live without garments:* John Komski, interview with Sandra Bradley, January 30, 1992, USHMM.

p.227   *bit of food:* David Wisnia, interview with Brad Zarlin, USHMM.

p.227   *living skeletons:* Irving Schaffer, interview with Mira Hodos, October 19, 1993, USHMM.

p.227   *stench of the dead bodies:* Paul Schneiderman, "Departing Dachau: A Holocaust Survivor's Liberation Story," *Newsweek,* January 27, 2015.

p.228   *the squalor of Dachau:* David Wisnia, interview with Joseph Toltz (transcript), April 7, 2011, USHMM.

p.228   *no roll call:* Schneiderman, "Departing Dachau."

p.228   *sent to Mühldorf:* Wisnia, interview with Toltz, April 7, 2011.

p.228   *David said:* David Wisnia, taped interview with Robin Black, August 13, 2007.

p.230–231   *skulked through the fields:* Wisnia, interview with Zarlin.

p.231   *This is my fate:* Wisnia, taped interview with Robin Black, 2007.

p.231   *began to climb:* Unless otherwise noted, descriptions come from David Wisnia from two lengthy interviews conducted at his home in Levittown, Pa., on January 19, 2018, and June 24, 2019.

p.233   *a Gallup poll:* "Americans and the Holocaust," USHMM, https://exhibitions.ushmm.org/americans-and-the-holocaust/us-public-opinion-world-war-II-1939-1941, accessed April 10, 2023.

p.233   *explained to his mother:* "Louis Vecchi, Paratrooper, US Army 101st Airborne," YouTube, January 15, 2010, https://www.youtube.com/watch?v=dJZEFXSHX-0, accessed March 24, 2023.

NOTES

p.233   *a thirty-four-foot tower:* Leonard Rapport and Arthur Northwood Jr., *Rendezvous with Destiny: A History of the 101st Airborne Division* (Potomac, Md.: Pickle Partners Publishing, 2015).

p.233   *parachuting shows for Winston Churchill:* Fred A. Bahlau Collection (AFC/2001/001/74212), Veterans History Project, American Folklife Center, Library of Congress.

p.233   *missions and jumps:* Mark Bando, *101st Airborne, The Screaming Eagles in World War II* (Minneapolis: Zenith Press, 2007).

p.234   *thousands of troops:* Fred Bahlau, Veterans History Project.

p.234   *they couldn't tell:* "Louis Vecchi, Paratrooper, US Army 101st Airborne."

p.234   *jumped some twelve hundred feet:* Fred Bahlau, Veterans History Project.

p.234   *crawled over bridges:* Bando, *101st Airborne.*

p.234   *American newspapers:* "The Battle in Normandy," *New York Times,* June 8, 1944.

p.234   *more than sixty-five hundred:* "Fact Sheet: Normandy Landings," White House Office of the Press Secretary, June 6, 2014, https://obamawhitehouse.archives.gov/the-press-office/2014/06/06/fact-sheet-normandy-landings, accessed February 17, 2023.

p.234   *41 percent:* RJ Reinhart, "Gallup Vault: Americans' Sentiments Toward D-Day," Gallup, June 5, 2019, https://news.gallup.com/vault/258068/gallup-vault-americans-surprising-sentiments-toward-day.aspx, accessed April 10, 2023.

p.235   *stories of concentration camps:* Stephen E. Ambrose, *Band of Brothers: E Company, 506th Regiment, 101st Airborne from Normandy to Hitler's Eagle's Nest* (New York: Simon & Schuster, 2001), 250.

p.235   *much too slowly:* Fred Bahlau, Veterans History Project.

p.235   *furloughed in Paris:* "Louis Vecchi, Paratrooper, US Army 101st Airborne."

p.235   *slept on the open ground:* Bando, *101st Airborne.*

p.235   *boots in blankets:* Fred Bahlau, Veterans History Project.

p.236   *they could've ever prepared:* Jason Dawsey, Ph.D., Research Historian, Institute for the Study of War and Democracy, National World War II Museum, interview with author.

p.236   *where they asphyxiate people:* Wisnia, interview with Toltz, April 7, 2011.

p.236   *clothing he'd smuggled:* Wisnia, interview with Black, June 28, 2007.

p.236   *the soldiers had made a decision:* It's unclear exactly where or when David's path intersected with Company H. David arrived in Dachau on January 28, 1945, and left for Mühldorf, fewer than sixty-two miles away, on February 21. Military archives indicate that the 101st troops were sent to Starnberg around the end of April. This was likely the week that David spent with the German family. Military Morning Reports, daily records that highlight changes in personnel status, unit locations, and often mention significant events that occur within the troop unit, show no record of David's encounter with Company H (I reviewed February 1 to June 15, 1945). According to an April 6, 2023, email from Holly Rivet, an archives specialist at the National Archives, since the army didn't need to account for David, it's doubtful he would have been mentioned in the Morning Reports. She added that while it wasn't common practice for a unit to "adopt" a civilian, it wasn't unheard of and "was indeed casual."

p.237   *On April 29, 1945:* "Liberation of Dachau," USHMM, https://encyclopedia.ushmm.org/content/en/timeline-event/holocaust/1942-1945/liberation-of-dachau, accessed April 20, 2023.

p.237 *thirty-two thousand inmates:* "Dachau Captured by Americans Who Kill Guards, Liberate 32,000," Associated Press, May 1, 1945.

p.237 *"they began to kiss us":* Sidney A. Olson, "Dachau," *Time*, May 7, 1945.

p.237 *said Joseph Pulitzer:* "US Editors Back, Urge Harsh Peace," *New York Times*, May 9, 1945.

p.238 *to assemble in Starnberg:* Wisnia, interview with Black, August 13, 2007.

Chapter Twenty-One: "Are We Free?"

p.239 *Zippi offered him:* Helen Tichauer, interview with Peter Hellman, May 3, 2004.

p.240 *needed to locate him:* Helen Tichauer, interview with David Boder, "Voices of the Holocaust," Illinois Institute of Technology, September 23, 1946.

p.000 *needed to locate him:* Sara Radomski, interview with Bard Zarlin, 2007, USHMM.

p.240 *flung white sheets:* Charles Lindbergh, *The Wartime Journals of Charles A. Lindbergh* (New York: Harcourt, 1970), 947–48.

p.240 *breakdowns, and overcrowding:* Yehuda Bauer, *Flight and Rescue: Brichah* (New York: Random House, 1970), 5.

p.240–241 *sexual violence and rape:* Atina Grossmann, *Jews, Germans, and Allies: Close Encounters in Occupied Germany* (Princeton, N.J.: Princeton University Press, 2007), 49.

p.241 *where they'd be safer:* Radomski, interview with Zarlin.

p.241 *Soviet army vehicle:* Tichauer, "Voices of the Holocaust."

p.242 *took a cattle train:* Helen Tichauer, unpublished interview with Jürgen Matthäus, March 5, 2011.

p.242 *reported the New York Times:* W. H. Lawrence, "Lublin Poles Hold Front at Warsaw," *New York Times*, January 15, 1945.

p.242 *bombed-out metropolis:* "WWII: Warsaw Liberated—1945; Today in History; 17 Jan 18," British Movietone, January 17, 2018, YouTube, https://www.youtube.com/watch?v=qabP8-px-zE, accessed February 14, 2023.

p.242 *hoping to find anyone:* "Jews in Poland Ask for Aid from United States and Palestine; Many Hope to Emigrate," Jewish Telegraphic Agency, May 23,1945.

p.242 *soup kitchens around town:* Linda Levi, Assistant EVP, Director of Global Archives, AJDCA, email to author, February 3, 2021.

p.242 *streetlights remained:* "Zofia Chometowska," Un-Posed, https://un-posed.com/pioneers/zofia-chometowska, accessed February 1, 2023.

p.243 *a grand piano:* Henryk Lagodski, "Polish Witness to the Holocaust Project," interview by Patrycja Bukalska, USHMM, May 6, 2010.

p.243 *found his wife:* Romana Koplewicz, interview with Gail Schwartz, October 8, 1993, USHMM.

p.243 *waiting before an older sister:* Doris Greenberg, interview with Melissa Block, November 22, 1988, USHMM.

Chapter Twenty-Two: Little Davey

p.244 *wanted to know:* David Wisnia, taped interview with Robin Black, August 13, 2007.

p.245 *Back in the fold:* Unless otherwise noted, descriptions come from David Wisnia from two lengthy interviews conducted with the author at his home in Levittown, Pa., on January 19, 2018, and June 24, 2019.

p.246 *to Berchtesgaden:* Leonard Rapport and Arthur Northwood Jr., *Rendezvous with Destiny: A History of the 101st Airborne Division* (Potomac, Md.: Pickle Partners Publishing, 2015).

p.247 *littered the roads:* Rapport and Northwood Jr., *Rendezvous with Destiny.*

p.247 *abandoned German helmets:* Fred A. Bahlau Collection (AFC/2001/001/74212), Veterans History Project, American Folklife Center, Library of Congress.

p.247 *nearly twenty million:* Atina Grossmann, *Jews, Germans, and Allies: Close Encounters in Occupied Germany* (Princeton, N.J.: Princeton University Press, 2007), 131.

p.247 *He could kill somebody:* Wisnia, interview with Black, August 13, 2007.

p.247 *draw up surrender terms:* Rapport and Northwood Jr., *Rendezvous with Destiny.*

p.248 *Hermann Göring:* "Goering Yields to Seventh Army," *New York Times,* May 5, 1945.

Chapter Twenty-Three: "How Are You Still Alive?"

p.251 *flag of the Czech Red Cross:* Helen Tichauer, unpublished interview with Jürgen Matthäus, March 5, 2011.

p.251 *Some travelers:* Lotte Weiss, interview with Jason Bruce Spinak, VHA/USC-Shoah, March 1, 1995.

p.251 *another love lost:* Helen Tichauer, interview with David Boder "Voices of the Holocaust," Illinois Institute of Technology, September 23, 1946.

p.252 *a ghost town:* Victor Ungar, interview with Sandy Jacobson, VHA/USC-Shoah, February 15, 1995.

p.252 *saw a stranger:* Edith Lowy, interview with Nonie Akman, VHA/USC-Shoah, October 18, 1996.

p.252 *didn't want to give up:* Keith Lowe, *Savage Continent: Europe in the Aftermath of World War II* (New York: St. Martin's, 2012), 197.

p.252 *Freshly liberated:* Edith Lowy, 1996.

p.252 *all-too-common conversation:* Linda Breder interview with Judith Helm, July 17, 1990, USHMM.

p.253 *early, for good behavior:* Samuel Spitzer's account is derived from Samuel Spitzer, interview with D. I. Ritch, March 7, 1996, VHA/USC-Shoah.

p.253 *Slovak National Council:* Stanislav J. Kirschbaum, "Federalism in Slovak Communist Parties," *Canadian Slavonic Papers / Revue Canadienne des Slavistes* 19, no. 4 (December 1977): 444–67.

p.254 *1st Czechoslovak Army Corps:* Ibid. For a deeper understanding of the political forces at play and negotiations between the Slovaks and Czechoslovaks, see also J. R., "Czechoslovakia During the War: I—The Policy of the Government in London," *Bulletin of International News,* 21, no. 22 (October 28, 1944): 897–906.

p.255 *some twenty thousand Slovak fighters:* "Slovak National Uprising 1944," Museum of Slovak National Uprising, Ministry of Foreign and European Affairs of the Slovak Republic.

p.257 *Sam remembered:* Quoted material comes directly from Spitzer's interview with Ritch, 1996.

p.257 *Palestine that was fighting:* "Synopsis of Palmach History," Palmach Museum, https://palmach.org.il/en/history/about/, accessed February 17, 2023.

p.259 *tried to return home:* Lowe, *Savage Continent,* 206.

p.259 *the Brichah:* Yehuda Bauer, *Flight and Rescue: Brichah* (New York: Random House, 1970), 107.

p.259 *would escort refugees:* Atina Grossmann, *Jews, Germans, and Allies: Close Encounters in Occupied Germany* (Princeton, N.J.: Princeton University Press, 2007), 121.

p.259   *agreed not to stay:* Bauer, *Flight and Rescue,* 183.

p.259   *She escorted them:* Helen Tichauer, unpublished interview with Michael Berkowitz, August 3, 2003.

p.260   *Sara made the journey:* Helen Tichauer, interview with Jürgen Matthäus, February 26, 2011.

p.260   *How are you still alive?:* Sara Lewin Radomski, interview with Brad Zarlin, 2007, USHMM.

p.261   *hundreds of survivors were arriving:* Tichauer, interview with Berkowitz, August 3, 2003.

Chapter Twenty-Four: An Example for the Rest of the World

p.262   *175-pound soldier:* David Wisnia, World War II Draft Registration Card, National Archives and Records Administration, February 8, 1946. According to NARA archivist Holly Rivet, it was common for men between the age of 18 and 40 to register for a draft card as part of their US citizenship application process. In his case, David began his application process shortly after arriving in New York.

p.262   *I was just working:* this passage description comes from David Wisnia's taped interview with Robin Black, August 13, 2007.

p.262   *designed and developed:* "German Walther P38 Pistol," National Museum of American History Behring Center, https://americanhistory.si.edu/collections /search/object/nmah_415180, accessed February 17, 2023.

p.262   *He shot the man:* David Wisnia interview with the author on January 19, 2018.

p.263   *Only the subways:* Katie Louchheim, "The DP Summer," *Virginia Quarterly Review* 61, no. 4 (1985): 691–707.

p.264   *American troops:* Leonard Rapport and Arthur Northwood Jr., *Rendezvous with Destiny: A History of the 101st Airborne Division* (Potomac, Md.: Pickle Partners Publishing, 2015).

p.264   *a Pocket Guide to Paris:* "Pocket Guide to Paris and the Cities of Northern France," United States Army Service Forces Information and Education Division, 1944.

p.264   *"GIs in Paris usually flock":* "European Vacationland," *Stars and Stripes,* July 22, 1945.

p.265   *his American friends:* Wisnia. interview with Black, August 13, 2007.

p.265   *celebrated Bastille Day:* "Paris to dance in streets again on Bastille Day," *The New York Times,* June 26, 1945.

p.265   *evacuated from the Louvre:* "Reunion at the Louvre," *New York Times,* July 29, 1945.

p.265   *tried to convince him:* Wisnia, interview with Black, August 13, 2007.

p.265   *managing a gift warehouse:* David Wisnia, interview with Brad Zarlin, 2006, USHMM.

p.265   *Postwar Paris was short:* David A. Gordon, "Hunger in the Spring Air," *Stars and Stripes,* June 23, 1945.

p.266   *the Attorney General and the FBI:* "Clark Pledges to Search Out War Profiteers," *Stars and Stripes,* July 9, 1945.

p.266   *American and British zones alone:* Atina Grossmann, *Jews, Germans, and Allies: Close Encounters in Occupied Germany* (Princeton, N.J.: Princeton University Press, 2007), 131–132.

p.266   *Americans did not want:* In August 1946, a Gallup poll asked Americans whether they'd support President Harry Truman's plan to ask Congress to allow more

Jewish and other European refugees to come to the U.S. to live than were allowed under the current law. Seventy-two percent of respondents disapproved.

p.266　*"alleviating human misery"*: Harry S. Truman, "Statement and Directive by the President on Immigration to the United States of Certain Displaced Persons and Refugees in Europe," The American Presidency Project, https://www.presidency .ucsb.edu/documents/statement-and-directive-the-president-immigration-the -united-states-certain-displaced, accessed April 28, 2023.

p.268　*Americans had committed:* Grossman, *Jews, Germans, and Allies,* 142.

p.268　*find ways to adopt orphans:* Keren Blankfeld, "Bela: The Forgotten War Orphan," *New York Times,* December 7, 2017.

p.268　*bar mitzvahs and weddings:* Grossman, *Jews, Germans, and Allies,* 144.

Chapter Twenty-Five: "The Loneliness of Survival"

p.273　*Zippi prided herself:* Helen Tichauer, interview with Jürgen Matthäus, March 12, 2020.

p.274　*dark eyes and curly hair:* Gad Beck and Frank Heibert, *An Underground Life: Memoirs of a Gay Jew in Nazi Berlin,* trans. Allison Brown (Madison: University of Wisconsin Press, 1999), 50.

p.274　*"peculiar" and "moody":* Helen Tichauer, interview with Joan Ringelheim, 2000, USHMM.

p.274　*liaised with the American military:* Atina Grossmann, interview with author, 2019.

p.274　*was a Berliner:* Inconsistencies abound when it comes to Erwin's beginnings. Some documents state he was born in 1918; others say 1920. Auschwitz Registration Records and various German documents state Erwin was born in Budapest. However, DP Registration Papers and census forms state that he was born in Berlin. I've opted to use the birthdate and birthplace listed on his New York University c.v.

p.274　*tinkering with clocks:* Issachar Gilad, "Editorial: Professor Erwin R. Tichauer 1918–1996," *International Journal of Industrial Ergonomics* 23: 251–53.

p.274　*Berlin law professor:* Michael Berkowitz, *The Crime of My Very Existence* (Berkeley: University of California Press, 2007), 216.

p.274–275　*military training:* Michael Berkowitz, interview with author, February 19, 2021.

p.275　*scrutinizing animals' movements:* Gilad, "Editorial: Professor Erwin R. Tichauer."

p.275　*He amused himself:* "Building a Better Mousetrap," *Time,* May 2, 1969, 46.

p.275　*or surgery:* Beck and Heibert, *An Underground Life,* 50.

p.275　*University of Königsberg:* International Labour Organization, P-File no.: 7884, International Labour Office Records and Archives Management Services, email to author February 26, 2021. For the most part, however, these activities were closed to Jews during these prewar years. Adding to the contradictions in Erwin's biography, Zippi said that Erwin was unable to pursue an education or career in Germany after his high school degree. (See Epilogue, in *Skull and Zebra Suits: A Berin Jew in Auschwitz,* ed. Jürgen Matthäus, trans. Anabel Aliaga-Buchenau (Berlin: Metropol, 2000.)

p.275　*work at a German carton factory:* Beck and Heibert, *An Underground Life,* 50-51.

p.275　*detonated a homemade bomb:* Ibid., 65.

p.275　*Erwin was arrested:* Matthäus, "Epilogue," in *Skull and Zebra.*

p.275　*The Gestapo yanked:* "The Rosenstrasse Demonstration, 1943," Holocaust Encyclopdia, USHMM, https://encyclopedia.ushmm.org/content/en/article/the-rosen strasse-demonstration-1943, accessed July 17, 2023

p.275　*among those who knew him:* Erna Elerat interview, March 28, 1993, USHMM.

p.276   *donned the red triangle:* Erwin Tichauer, Auschwitz Registration documents, The Arolsen Archives, formerly the International Tracing Service archive (ITS), located in Bad Arolsen, Germany.

p.276   *assigned to a subcamp, Jawischowitz:* Matthäus, "Epilogue," *Skull and Zebra Suits.*

p.276   *death march to Dachau:* Documents filed in the Arolsen Archives, formerly the International Tracing Service archive (ITS), located in Bad Arolsen, Germany, June 23, 1954.

p.276   *a spy for the MI5:* Konrad Kwiet, interview with author, 2020.

p.276   *US Army's Counterintelligence Corps:* Elerat interview, 1993.

p.276   *military unit that liberated him:* "Erwin Tichauer," Intergovernmental Committee on Refugees, Reference no. 863, Arolsen Archives, formerly the International Tracing Service archive (ITS), located in Bad Arolsen, Germany.

p.276   *a breakthrough moment:* "9th Armored Division," United States Military History, US Army, https://history.army.mil/html/forcestruc/cbtchron/cc/009ad.htm, accessed February 17, 2023.

p.276   *Zippi later said:* Berkowitz, *Crime of My Very Existence,* 217.

p.277   *Third US Army:* International Labour Organization, P-File no.: 7884.

p.277   *Inter-governmental Committee on Refugees:* "Foreign Relations of the United States Diplomatic Papers, 1938, General, Volume I," Office of the Historian, Department of State, https://history.state.gov/historicaldocuments/frus1938v01/comp7, accessed April 20, 2023.

p.277   *Harrison described refugees:* Earl G. Harrison, "The Harrison Report," Eisenhower Presidential Library, July 1945.

p.277   *an ideal candidate:* Helen Tichauer, unpublished interview with Michael Berkowitz, August 3, 2003.

p.277   *honor court tribunals:* Photograph No. 10130A, "Jewish DP lawyers (in the white shirts) serve as judges in a trial involving a fellow DP, who is accused of having sold his identification card to a former Nazi," USHMM.

p.277   *everyday crimes:* Berkowitz, *Crime of My Very Existence,* 216-217.

p.277   *American diplomat Katie Louchheim:* Katie Louchheim, "The DP Summer," *Virginia Quarterly Review* 61, no. 4 (1985): 691–707.

p.278   *hope of a new beginning:* Bernard Dichek, "Why a Year after the Holocaust, My Parents Are Happy in DP Camp Photos," *Times of Israel,* January 27, 2021, https://www.timesofisrael.com/why-a-year-after-the-holocaust-my-parents-are-happy-in-dp-camp-photos/, accessed February 17, 2023.

p.279   *After touring Feldafing:* Berkowitz, *Crime of My Very Existence,* 216, 88.

p.279   *two men had known:* Ibid., 217. Beyond Zippi's retelling of the incident, however, no corroboration has been found regarding the men's friendship.

p.280   *Erwin had every intention:* Tichauer, interview with Berkowitz, August 3, 2003.

p.281   *had news of David:* Helen Tichauer, unpublished interview with Jürgen Matthäus, 2011.

p.282   *not to marry:* Atina Grossmann, "Living On," in *Approaching an Auschwitz Survivor,* ed. Jürgen Matthäus (Oxford: Oxford University Press, 2010), 85.

p.282   *married in Tutzing:* Tichauer Marriage Certificate, March 15, 1946, Arolsen Archives, formerly the International Tracing Service archive (ITS), located in Bad Arolsen, Germany.

p.282   *had been requisitioned:* Grossmann, "Living On," 86-87.

p.282   *"escape the loneliness":* Ibid., 78.

p.282   *babies at record numbers:* Ibid., 184.

p.283   *remove broken bones:* Krankheitsgeschichte, UNRRA Hospital, 1947, Arolsen Archives, formerly the International Tracing Service archive (ITS), located in Bad Arolsen, Germany..

p.283   *decided it was time:* Tichauer, unpublished interview with Berkowitz, August 3, 2003.

Chapter Twenty-Six: "That's an American"

p.286   *he would be on his way:* David Wisnia, interview with Brad Zarlin, 2006, USHMM.

p.286   *boarded the SS Monarch of the Seas:* Manifest of Alien Passengers, U.S. Department of Labor, National Archives and Records Administration, February 20, 1946.

p.287   *accumulated some $5,000:* Wisnia, interview with Zarlin.

p.290   *drove his black Chevy:* Ibid.

p.290   *Hope would say later:* Ann Schmidt, "'I Lived by the Minute, Not Even by the Week': The Incredible Story of an Auschwitz Survivor Who Lived Thanks to His Singing Talent—Which He Still Proudly Shows Off 75 Years Later," *The Daily Mail,* October 18, 2017.

p.290   *used the money:* Wisnia, interview with Zarlin.

p.290   *Jewish soul music:* Debra Rubin, "Cantor's Journey from Auschwitz to Bima," *New Jersey Jewish News,* June 3, 2013.

p.291   *naturalized in 1951:* David Wisnia Certificate of Naturalization, April 26, 1951, National Archives and Records Administration at Philadelphia. In April 1946 David registered for military service in the U.S. According to Holly Rivet, an archivist at the National Archives, this was part of the citizenship application process for men among his age group.

p.291   *wedding in Munich:* Sara Radomski, interview with Brad Zarlin, USHMM.

Chapter Twenty-Seven: "Just the Ticket"

p.294   *not interested:* Helen Tichauer, interview with Jürgen Matthäus, February 26, 2011.

p.294   *partner and collaborator:* Based on conversations with Jürgen Matthäus, Konrad Kwiet, Wendy Lower, Michael Berkowitz, Atina Grossmann, Joan Ringelheim, and Peter Hellman.

p.294   *Erwin worked for:* Erwin Tichauer, curriculum vitae, New York University Special Collections Archives.

p.295   *welcomed more Holocaust survivors:* Konrad Kwiet, interview with author, 2020.

p.295   *equipment company in Brisbane:* Pope, Mayne & Southern, Who's Who Bio, https://trove.nla.gov.au/newspaper/article/49673416, accessed February 17, 2023.

p.296   *would haunt her:* Wendy Lower, interview with author, June 9, 2020.

p.296   *survived the war:* Hana Nichtberurgerova, email to author, June 25, 2020.

p.297   *never feel safe in Europe:* Samuel Spitzer, interview with D. I. Ritch, March 7, 1996, VHA/USC-Shoah.

p.297   *International Labour Organization:* International Labour Organization, P-File no.: 7884, International Labour Office Records and Archives Management Services, email to author February 26, 2021..

p.297 *designed cans:* Atina Grossmann, "Living On," in *Approaching an Auschwitz Survivor,* ed. Jürgen Matthäus (Oxford: Oxford University Press, 2010), 93.

p.298 *Erwin to join the faculty:* Issachar Gilad, "Editorial: Professor Erwin R. Tichauer 1918–1996," *International Journal of Industrial Ergonomics* 23: 251–53.

Chapter Twenty-Eight: "Ask Me Anything"

p.300 *Zippi never showed:* Unless otherwise noted, descriptions come from David Wisnia from two lengthy interviews conducted with the author at his home in Levittown, Pa., on January 19, 2018, and June 24, 2019.

p.300 *he couldn't help but look:* Ibid.

p.300 *Sauna had collapsed:* "Visitor Numbers," Auschwitz–Birkenau Memorial and Museum, https://www.auschwitz.org/en/museum/history-of-the-memorial/the -first-years-of-the-memorial/visitor-numbers/, accessed April 20, 2023.

p.300 *readers had no interest:* from Helen Tichauer's personal estate, USHMM, letter from Manfred George to Erwin, January 9, 1951.

p.301 *three million Jews:* "The JUST Act Report: Poland," U.S. Department of State, https://www.state.gov/reports/just-act-report-to-congress/poland/, accessed April 28, 2023.

p.306 *felt sheepish:* Peter Hellman, various interviews with author, 2020–2022.

p.306 *becoming more fragile:* Wendy Lower, interview with author, June 9, 2020.

p.307 *Petra said:* Petra Nichtburgerova, interview with author, July 16, 2020.

p.307 *Thanks to Zippi:* Hana Nichtburgerova, interview with author, June 26, 2020.

p.309 *he'd have to wait:* Helen Tichauer, unpublished interview with Jürgen Matthäus, March 5, 2011.

Chapter Twenty-Nine: *Isn't Life Strange*

p.310 *Five years later:* David and Avi Wisnia, interviews with author, 2019.

Epilogue

p.315 *historian's historian:* Atina Grossmann, interview with author, 2019.

p.316 *never attended:* Veronica McKay, interview with author, July 3, 2019.

p.316 *Ferd's death in 2013:* Ferd Wilczek, obituary, https://lincolnfuneralhome.org /obituaries/obit_view.php?id=522, accessed February 17, 2023.

p.317 *became Zippi's lifeline:* Grossmann, interview with author, 2019.

p.318 *Zippi obsessed:* Wendy Lower, interview with author, June 9, 2020.

p.319 *"has so many qualifications":* "Erwin Tichauer," *Safety & Rescue,* August 1973, 1.

p.320 *Central Tracing Agency Bureau:* letter from B. Sambonoff, Chief Representative of Central Tracing Bureau, U.S. Army, Arolsen Archives, formerly the International Tracing Service archive (ITS), located in Bad Arolsen, Germany, File No. 130.211/12/13, September 2, 1947.

p.320 *singing for each:* Lisa Jacobson, interview with author, October 5, 2020.

p.320 *Roza Robota Gates at the Sir Moses Montefiore Jewish Home:* Rosa Robota Gate, Sam Spitzer radio interview with Rachael Kohn, Australian Broadcasting Corporation, October 12, 2008, https://www.abc.net.au/radionational/programs /archived/ark/rosa-robota-gate/3189334, accessed February 17, 2023.

p.321   *Carl Clauberg:* Clauberg was arrested in 1955 but died in August 1957, shortly before his trial should have started.

p.321   *The conversation:* Susan Cernyak-Spatz and Joel Shatzky, "Record-Keeping for the Nazis—and Saving Lives," *Jewish Currents,* May 1, 2011.

p.321   *Katya died in 1995:* Helen Tichauer, interview with Joan Ringelheim, USHMM, 2000.

p.321   *at least sixteen hundred women:* Cernyak-Spatz and Shatzky, "Record-Keeping."

ILLUSTRATION CREDITS

Page	Image Credits
xii	Zippi and Erwin Tichauer in the snow. *United States Holocaust Memorial Museum Collection, Gift of the Estate of Helen Tichauer. Previously published in* Approaching an Auschwitz Survivor: Holocaust Testimony and Its Transformations *(ed. JM), Oxford UP 2009.*
17	Zippi in Bratislava, 1938. *United States Holocaust Memorial Museum Collection, Gift of the Estate of Helen Tichauer. Previously published in* Approaching an Auschwitz Survivor: Holocaust Testimony and Its Transformations *(ed. JM), Oxford UP 2009.*
23	Warsaw's Great Synagogue. *Portrait of "View of the Great Synagogue on Tlomackie Street in Warsaw, destroyed by the Germans in May 1943." United States Holocaust Memorial Museum Photo Archives #07069. Courtesy of Jerzy Ficowski. Copyright of United States Holocaust Memorial Museum.*
25	David Wisnia at his bar mitzvah. *Courtesy of the David Wisnia Literary Trust*
31	Zippi as photographed by Tibor Justh. *Courtesy of Michael Berkowitz*
31	Tibor as photographed by Zippi. *Courtesy of Frank Dabba Smith*
42	The Warsaw Ghetto, 1941. *Portrait of "Ghetto residents make purchases from street vendors in the Warsaw ghetto." United States Holocaust Memorial Museum Photo Archives #15993.*

ILLUSTRATION CREDITS

Courtesy of Rafael Scharf. Copyright of United States Holocaust Memorial Museum.

46   Sam Spitzer's mugshot.
Image taken from the interview of Samuel Spitzer provided by the USC Shoah Foundation – The Institute for Visual History and Education

77   Jewish women marching towards their barracks.
United States Holocaust Memorial Museum, courtesy of Yad Vashem

90   Auschwitz prisoners undergo selection.
United States Holocaust Memorial Museum, courtesy of Yad Vashem

91   A Jewish woman and her children walking towards a gas chamber after selection.
United States Holocaust Memorial Museum, courtesy of Yad Vashem

109   Prisoners outside the *Canada* warehouse in Auschwitz.
United States Holocaust Memorial Museum, courtesy of Yad Vashem

110   An aerial reconnaissance photo of Auschwitz II–Birkenau.
United States Holocaust Memorial Museum, courtesy of National Archives and Records Administration, College Park

119   SS officer Gerhard Palitzsch.
The Archive of The State Museum Auschwitz-Birkenau in Oświęcim

119   The Black Wall, Auschwitz.
Portrait of "View of the Black Wall in Auschwitz I." Courtesy of National Archives and Records Administration, College Park, MD.

173   Mala Zimetbaum.
The Archive of The State Museum Auschwitz-Birkenau in Oświęcim

195   Edek Galiński.
The Archive of The State Museum Auschwitz-Birkenau in Oświęcim

245   David in his U.S. Army uniform.
Courtesy of the David Wisnia Literary Trust

256   Sam Spitzer's identification papers.
Image taken from the interview of Samuel Spitzer provided by the USC Shoah Foundation – The Institute for Visual History and Education. http://sfi.usc.edu/

258   Zippi after liberation, 1945.
United States Holocaust Memorial Museum Collection, Gift of the Estate of Helen Tichauer. Previously published in Approaching an Auschwitz Survivor: Holocaust Testimony and Its Transformations *(ed. JM), Oxford UP 2009.*

ILLUSTRATION CREDITS

278   Zippi at her chicken coop, 1946.
United States Holocaust Memorial Museum Collection, Gift of the Estate of Helen Tichauer. Previously published in Approaching an Auschwitz Survivor: Holocaust Testimony and Its Transformations *(ed. JM), Oxford UP 2009.*

279   Zippi and Erwin in Feldafing, 1946.
United States Holocaust Memorial Museum Collection, Gift of the Estate of Helen Tichauer. Previously published in Approaching an Auschwitz Survivor: Holocaust Testimony and Its Transformations *(ed. JM), Oxford UP 2009.*

280   Erwin and General Dwight Eisenhower in Feldafing, 1945.
United States Holocaust Memorial Museum Collection, Gift of the Estate of Helen Tichauer. Previously published in Approaching an Auschwitz Survivor: Holocaust Testimony and Its Transformations *(ed. JM), Oxford UP 2009.*

284   Zippi after the war.
United States Holocaust Memorial Museum Collection, Gift of the Estate of Helen Tichauer. Previously published in Approaching an Auschwitz Survivor: Holocaust Testimony and Its Transformations *(ed. JM), Oxford UP 2009.*

309   David in Levittown, Pennsylvania.
Danna Singer/The New York Times/Redux

INDEX

INDEX

INDEX

INDEX

INDEX